COMMON PHANTOMS

SPIRITUAL PHENOMENA

TANYA MARIE LUHRMANN and ANN TAVES, Series Editors

Common Phantoms

An American History of Psychic Science

. . .

ALICIA PUGLIONESI

Stanford University Press • Stanford, California

STANFORD UNIVERSITY PRESS
Stanford, California

Printed in the United States of America on acid-free, archival-quality paper

Library of Congress Cataloging-in-Publication Data
Names: Puglionesi, Alicia, author.
Title: Common phantoms : an American history of psychic science /
    Alicia Puglionesi.
Other titles: Spiritual phenomena.
Description: Stanford : Stanford University Press, 2020. | Series: Spiritual
    phenomena | Includes bibliographical references and index.
Identifiers: LCCN 2019051022 (print) | LCCN 2019051023 (ebook) |
    ISBN 9781503608375 (cloth) | ISBN 9781503612778 (paperback) |
    ISBN 9781503612785 (ebook)
Subjects: LCSH: American Society for Psychical Research—History. |
    Parapsychology—Research—United States—History—19th century. |
    Parapsychology—Research—United States—History—20th century. |
    Parapsychology and science—United States—History—19th century. |
    Parapsychology and science—United States—History—20th century.
Classification: LCC BF1028.5.U6 P84 2020 (print) | LCC BF1028.5.U6 (ebook) |
    DDC 130.973—dc23
LC record available at https://lccn.loc.gov/2019051022
LC ebook record available at https://lccn.loc.gov/2019051023

Cover design by Kevin Barrett Kane

Typeset by Kevin Barrett Kane in 10/15 ITC New Baskerville

CONTENTS

FIGURES

ACKNOWLEDGMENTS

This book was written with people not named in its pages. Their presence is integral to the work, and I thank them for being around in body and spirit—I don't work well alone. My gratitude for the support of friends, family, and colleagues exceeds the available formulas, which I nevertheless recite here.

I received a lot of sympathetic advice. Mary Fissell never appeared fazed by the strangeness of this undertaking, helping me to realize a project which I could only dimly envision. Daniel Todes was a tremendous spiritual resource, often locating my meaning more clearly than I could myself. The Institute for the History of Medicine at Johns Hopkins, its faculty, staff, and students, created a space for wide-ranging intellectual exploration in which freedom was balanced by rigorous and meaningful criticism.

I am grateful to Ronald Walters, Rebecca Lemov, and Ruth Leys for providing feedback on the early manuscript. Conversations with Katja Guenther, Alison Winter, Andreas Sommer, Katy Price, Adrian Holme, Mikita Brottman, and many others clarified and enriched my thinking. Emily-Jane Cohen was incredibly generous in guiding this project during her time at Stanford University Press, and Faith Wilson Stein and Kate Wahl enabled its completion. Tanya Luhrmann and Ann Taves, co-editors of the Spiritual Phenomena series, lent their support and insight, and I was honored by the opportunity to discuss my research as part of Tanya's Cultures, Minds, and Medicines workshop at Stanford.

The archive that shaped this book belongs to the American Society for Psychical Research (ASPR). The society's president, Patrice Keane, granted me access to their material, went out of her way to provide staff and resources during my visits, and shared invaluable information about the society's history. Gabrielle Dean, curator of Literary Rare Books & Manuscripts at the Sheridan Libraries of Johns Hopkins, offered an invigorating perspective on the project; I also owe thanks to the Chesney Medical Archives, especially Nancy McCall and Marjorie Kehoe, the American Philosophical Society, the Rubenstein Rare Book & Manuscript Library at Duke University, the Library of Congress, and the Smithsonian Institution Archives.

My years of research and writing were supported by a number of grants and fellowships to which I owe my material survival: the History of Medicine Collections Travel Grant, David M. Rubenstein Rare Book & Manuscript Library, Duke University; the Sheridan Libraries' Special Collections Research Center Graduate Student Summer Fellowship in 19th, 20th, and 21st-Century Studies; and the American Council of Learned Societies Mellon Dissertation Completion Fellowship. A postdoctoral fellowship at the Consortium for the History of Science, Technology, and Medicine supported rewriting of the manuscript with valuable input from fellows including Sarah Basham, Rosanna Dent, Lawrence Kessler, Joseph Martin, Michelle Smiley, and the consortium's wonderful director and guiding spirit, Babak Ashrafi.

Christine Ruggere, curator of the Institute of the History of Medicine's collections, provided the letter of reference that I initially slipped under the barred front door of the ASPR's headquarters on West 73rd Street; without that letter this project could never have begun. This was not Christine's first correspondence with the society; she joined its ranks briefly as a teenager. Her ongoing encouragement has been invaluable, as has the aid of assistant librarian Eliza Hill.

To a great extent this book emerged from the mental atmosphere of Baltimore, a city which makes many things possible; here I learned to balance critical thought with radical openness. I owe my friends thanks not just for their kind tolerance of me but also for making weird and challenging art, for living curious and committed lives. My parents, Lois and Peter, have always supported me in my efforts to build a life that's interesting and true, and I can only offer my profoundest love in return. I've never felt very far from their influence.

This book is dedicated to the memory of Henrika Kuklick, a savagely intelligent, incisive, and riotous mentor. When Riki said that this project might be "too weird," I knew I had to see it through. She was the first person to tell me, as an undergraduate, that this was work I could do and how to go about doing it.

COMMON PHANTOMS

AT HOME, WITH GHOSTS

There's no need to introduce you to what you already know.

We all have strange experiences, some stranger than others. People who think of themselves as basically rational might decline to call that noise in the attic a ghost or to celebrate a narrow escape from danger as a miracle. At the same time, the mechanisms of the physical world can fail to account for things seen, heard, and felt—things that take on the power of revelation in the course of individual lives and collective histories. This book maps the unstable terrain where assumptions clash with direct experience. It's a space defined by absence: the absence of logical explanation, of the fixed laws and evidence that are supposed to govern modern life. It also encompasses the people we love who are gone— beyond reach, yet always present.

"The hour was high noon, and the sun was shining cheerfully. While busily smoking a cigar, and writing out my orders, I suddenly became conscious that someone was sitting on my left, with one arm resting on the table." This is how a man from Boston, with the initials F. G., remembered the day in 1876 when he saw his dead sister. Prior to her appearance, he was having a very successful business trip in St. Josephs, Missouri. "Naturally I was startled and dumbfounded, almost doubting my senses; but the cigar in my mouth, and pen in hand, with the ink still moist on my letter, I satisfied myself I had not been dreaming and was wide awake."[1]

Often, what pulls us into this confounding space is something intimately familiar, indeed central to who we think we are. The feeling of relation is instantaneous, natural—F. G. "sprang forward in delight" at the sight of his sister—yet disrupted by the knowledge that this particular relation is not possible. Some people search for a portal to this realm, but the majority wind up there by accident. For a lawyer from St. Paul, Minnesota, whose friends called him a "successful man of affairs and not at all a dreamer," seeing a ghost also threw his sense of sanity into question.[2] A young woman in New York, disturbed by a series of premonitions, wrote that "I should be glad to prove I am not psychic."[3] They feared exile from the shared reality of a secular, scientific age. Seeing things that weren't there banished them to a corner of the map where superstition and madness reigned.

Others, however, use their strange experiences to argue for an expanded definition of reality. "This power I possess may be wave thought produced by the magnetism of the world passing through space," wrote a psychic medium from Illinois.[4] An oil company agent in California confidently explained, "I have seen so many instances where the existence of this power has been demonstrated . . . that I have accepted it as a fact in the same way that I have accepted the X-Rays, Wireless Telegraphy, etc."[5] Nineteenth-century Americans saw the horizons of the known universe expanding before their eyes.

Making sense of experience can be deeply personal work, but in thousands of cases like these, individuals looked to an emerging science, called psychical research, to figure out what happened to them. If the name sounds unfamiliar, that's because psychical research no longer exists for practical purposes. It coalesced in the late nineteenth century, at a moment when scientists began seeking objective explanations for a set of experiences that included trance, hypnotism, clairvoyance, dissociation—all involving some perception, thought, or action that appeared to enter the subject's consciousness from elsewhere but had no external, material correlate.[6] Since they were the subject matter of psychical research, we might simply term these psychical experiences, but I will also describe them in a broader historical context as liminal states and contested experiences. Witnesses described them as occurring in a liminal space between sleeping and waking, madness and sanity, self and other. Historian Marlene Tromp describes them as altered states, for their power to reconfigure individuals, communities, and ideas of where the nation begins and ends.[7] Indeed, popular writers of the time fixed on the metaphor of "borderlands" for all things psychical, turning an elusive fringe into a sensational center.

Further, from the seventeenth century onward, Anglo-American observers sought to make a distinction between experiences that were religious and those that were psychological in nature. As Ann Taves points out, this contestation mapped onto social divides, with the established Protestant elite attempting to discredit and control unruly religious enthusiasm by explaining it with the science of mental disorder.[8] A third view emerged in this period that characterized psychical experiences as neither revelations from God nor pathological delusions, but rather as natural capacities of the human brain. Followers of Franz Anton Mesmer proclaimed, in the late eighteenth and early nineteenth centuries, that they could harness this natural capacity to heal the sick through magnetic influence. Yet the boundaries between religious, natural, and pathological interpretations were never solid.

In many ways, ensuing debates around these experiences centered on the question of what is normal and natural—and therefore possible in the material universe—versus what is divine or disordered. Natural mental functions like perception and memory could be explained without at all diminishing their concrete reality. Most scientists maintained a general commitment to Christian values which placed divine experiences safely above explanation, though the criteria for "true religion" were disputed and evolving. Finally, pathological experiences fell below the threshold of respectful engagement; to explain them was to explain them away and label their subjects as fundamentally mistaken about reality. Of course, these categories are human creations, and debating them was also a process of purifying a heterogeneous field of experience to make the world more legible and controllable for those who had power or sought to secure it. This book focuses on people who troubled the purity of the posited categories.

Contested experiences proliferated, and their social valence shifted, in the mid-nineteenth century with the spread of Spiritualism, a popular religious movement that originated in upstate New York and quickly swept the U.S. and Europe with dramatic demonstrations of trance mediumship. Spiritualists saw themselves as mediating between religious and pathological interpretations of liminal states, asserting that they communicated with the dead through a natural process, a yet-to-be-discovered scientific law. They appealed this claim to academic authorities, many of whom felt compelled by the overwhelming popularity of the movement to investigate for themselves. Whereas Spiritualists considered their theory that the dead speak to be proven by firsthand experience, wary investigators termed this the "spirit hypothesis," one among many possible explanations. Though not sold on spirits, liberal-leaning Protestants and those drifting away from the church were inclined to experiment with a "both/and" option that allowed for communion with some kind of transcendent universal force to occur through physical pathways.[9] With the discipline of psychology in its infancy, a wide variety of investigators weighed in, and those who were drawn more deeply into the realm of séances and telepathy called this field of investigation psychical research.

The psychical researcher was a peculiar kind of authority: not a psychiatrist or a theologian, but an expert in the collection and classification of experiences; versed in detecting superstition and deceit, yet interested in a middle way between these possibilities. No special training certified psychical researchers to counsel the distressed or to experiment on the curious. No diagnosis or therapy came out of a consultation. Psychical research, in fact, had no conclusive answers for any of its participants, yet they eagerly wrote letters, filled out questionnaires, attended lectures, and read every shred of literature on the subject. Ordinary people contributed their raw experiences in the hope of building up a new field of scientific knowledge where none had existed.

A Regular System for the Highly Irregular

"We number at present only twenty," the letter writer explained, "but all of them are persons of intellect and trained observers, and especially interested in this kind of study." William James read this missive in 1890, a year after securing an endowed chair in psychology at Harvard and a month before he would ship the manuscript for his *Principles of Psychology* to the New York offices of publisher Henry Holt. James was a rising academic star at the forefront of his field. His correspondent, Herbert L. Spence, who led a circle of psychical investigators in Cincinnati, was not. Little remains of Spence's life, mostly nominal mentions in the records of a local literary club. Yet Spence reached out to James as a colleague in psychical research—albeit a senior colleague who was integral in establishing the American Society for Psychical Research (ASPR), the first national organization devoted to spearheading work on the topic.

Spence's group of twenty Ohioans convened once a week to conduct experiments just like those that James performed with and on his Harvard graduate students. Though James is remembered for establishing the first academic psychology laboratory in the United States, he never made much use of the chronometers and resonators there. He preferred less structured tests of telepathy and clairvoyance, sittings with mediums, and collecting case reports—the kind of thing that Spence and his friends could do at home. Indeed, groups like Spence's met across the United States and Europe throughout the 1880s and 90s and well into the twentieth century. Similar groups are at work today. Most of them gathered in private homes and parlors, and even those based in universities rarely had the formal support of a psychology department.

What should we call these participants in psychical research? For the most part they were not professional scientists or psychologists—although some groups started with local professors of psychology, and many participants worked in other branches of the sciences. They might be called amateurs; even William James deemed himself "a dabbler and amateur" in psychical research compared to the more experienced British leaders in the field.[10] But no academic degree existed to make such formal distinctions; James deferred to his self-taught British colleagues because of their practical success in documenting cases. Psychical researchers might be called hobbyists, since many participated out of casual interest, enjoying the sociability and amusement of their gatherings. However, they viewed this activity as something more than a diversion. They understood it as part of a larger, knowledge-generating project, requiring special skills of observation and critical thought. Scientific rigor and experimental control were their gold standards, though they debated what exactly such ideals meant in practice. In this book I will often call them investigators—defining them by their activity rather than a fixed identity or formal role.

Spence wrote to William James with specific questions about how to do psychical research, hoping to improve the quality of his group's work. Only later did he suggest that the Cincinnati investigators might want to join the ASPR and contribute to a national project. Spence did not view a formal institution run by academics as inherently superior to the first-hand experience available in his own parlor. When he asked James if he could "fall into regular, systematic work" with the ASPR, he wanted reassurance that the ASPR would help his group measure up to the scientific ideals which they had already adopted for themselves.[11]

From 1885 onward, scores of other psychical investigators would contact the ASPR on similar terms. After a few years, James admitted that this onslaught of correspondence had become "almost intolerable," occupying more of his scarce time than he'd ever expected.[12] He sometimes spoke condescendingly of informal investigators, bemoaning their stream of "anecdotes and other disjointed details." His attempts to structure knowledge-making around some differential of expertise were in tension with the desire of the society's membership to participate not as data sources, but as peers.[13] In the heterodox world of psychical research, the preeminent expert could call himself an amateur while still looking down his nose at people who'd seen more phenomena than he had. Meanwhile, truly self-taught amateurs, moved by the conviction of firsthand experience, could declare themselves experts. Such an unstable assemblage seemed destined to fly apart.

I located the mortal remains of American psychical research on the third floor of an Upper West Side brownstone in New York City: bundles of letters, yellowed newspaper clippings, surveys, and circulars lining the walls of crypt-like storage rooms. This was my reward for a gamble of a research trip: after many unanswered phone calls, voicemail messages, and emails to the ASPR, I simply took a bus to New York and sat vigil on the building's steps, in front of the locked iron gate, slipping a letter of support from my librarian through the bars. A morning and afternoon passed. For good luck, I paged through James's *The Varieties of Religious Experience* in the shade.

Varieties posits that human encounters with the divine or absolute have an essential core which manifests differently to individuals in different cultural contexts; many people today are happy to interpret the paranormal, spirit voices, and clairvoyance in this way, granting to experiencers the subjective reality of their inner worlds. This approach makes no claim on the public, empirical reality sanctioned by science—and was profoundly shaped by the historical, political, and ideological projects that carved out separate spheres for faith and reason.[14] Psychical research, however, did make a claim on public reality, by interpreting the experiences it collected first as natural and only second as potentially spiritual. Moreover, the process and methods of psychical research suggested, often inadvertently, the argument of more recent scholars that what we call experience is a crystallization of shared histories.[15] The letters I was seeking at the ASPR are part of the crystalline structure—histories-relations-experience—that I imagined encrusting 73rd Street, New York City, permeating every surface of the world, obliterating boundaries between inside and outside. This vision did not remove the obstacle of the iron gate.

My patient meditation was punctuated by rounds of obnoxious bell-ringing, which finally got me through the gates and into the marble lobby decorated with elaborate "gift drawings" created by Shaker visionaries in the 1840s. The fact that these drawings, acquired by the ASPR in 1917, got lost in the archives for nearly thirty years attests to the skeletal staffing and lack of funds that made the building so difficult to access. The society's longtime president, Patrice Keane, explained to me this situation and the concerns about unscrupulous media coverage that led her to carefully screen research requests. Though I expressed no opinion, sympathetic or skeptical, on the reality of psychic phenomena, our conversation must have satisfied her that I did not work for a cable TV ghost-hunting show.

In compliance with the schedule of a part-time volunteer archivist, I ascended to the second-floor library each day. With its floor-to-ceiling bookshelves, oriental rug, and antique furniture, it could be the dignified clubhouse of any literary or professional society, though there is a sensory deprivation chamber upstairs. Ghosts didn't emerge from the woodwork—the brownstone was purchased in 1966, before which the society moved offices several times. Instead, a subtle disorientation crept over me hour by hour as I rummaged through bankers' boxes full of crumbling letters. Many people had strange experiences to report and urgently wanted to be believed. Did I believe them? The only proof lay in the chaotic bundles of documents that James once hoped would yield "a mass of facts concrete enough to found a decent theory upon."[16]

James and other ASPR leaders sometimes referred to their membership as foot soldiers. This might sound like an elitist division of labor where those lower down the ladder did the grunt work, while experts in their tower performed the calculations and synthesis. However, as we've seen, James did not worship scientific expertise and did not claim to be an authority. He argued that no one could anticipate the outcome of their massive undertaking at such an early stage—that everyone, himself included, had to behave as a foot soldier and collect, collect, collect, until more was known. They collected premonitions of death, clairvoyant visions of French pastry, lost keepsakes, boiler explosions, and silly doodles transmitted from mind to mind. Many participants viewed psychical research as a democratic science to which they contributed and in which they had a say, leading them to defy James's prohibition on theorizing and to question the hierarchical management of this particular scientific society.

I use the term *democratic* not normatively but to evoke the contradictions of this ideal in the American context where exclusion and inequality are its shadows. The notion of a unique impulse towards democratic self-determination infuses many accounts of American science and religion, yet, as legal scholar Aziz Rana observes, such freedom has been premised on capitalist-imperial exploitation since the nation's founding. At first glance this may seem like a political backdrop far removed from the concerns of psychical research, but it shaped the possibilities of public scientific inquiry in two major ways: first, the problem of power relations in a participatory community that nonetheless required expertise and compliance in order to produce knowledge as a commodity; and second, the spectral presence of those Americans denied full citizenship, whose experiences were appropriated in various ways without their participation or consent, and who constituted their own knowledge communities outside of white middle- and upper-class discourse.[17]

These tensions appear to the historian in retrospect but were also very much present to those attempting the work of psychical research. In the first decade of the twentieth century, William James became increasingly concerned that the hegemonic forces of capitalism and imperialism were overrunning America's liberal ideal of individual political participation.[18] While he then argued that small groups of individuals should always be the locus of social agency, his earlier efforts to organize the ASPR in the 1880s and 90s laid bare his personal difficulties with supporting that agency when it emanated from people who did not share his intellectual orientation. Decades later, a new generation of ASPR leaders would clash over the same issue, the "too liberal democracy" that drew the society away from rigorous methods and towards popular enthusiasm for the spirit hypothesis.[19] The question of how to coordinate small, organic groups with formal, expert leadership towards disciplinarily productive ends—and indeed, whether they could produce anything legible as knowledge at all—was one that James and his successors did not resolve. They conjured a fleeting and unstable republic of experience which many participants looked to the ASPR to define, represent, and govern.

The second tension emerged from the first: a significant portion of the population was denied a voice in this nascent republic. Psychical research sought to map the transcendent core of human experience, but representing was also a process of sorting by class, gender, and race. The voices in the psychical archive come from disparate corners of American life—engineers, poets, insurance salesmen, housewives, professors, con men—and for this reason, I sometimes call them "ordinary" to differentiate them from the "great men" who often drive historical narratives. However, most of these voices belong to people of European descent; people of color are depicted as shadows, vanishing Indians, and servants. The ASPR for the most part presumed a universalized white mind.

Ideas appropriated from enslaved people and Indians shaped the white-led Spiritualist movement, but the movement so effectively spectralized people of color that they could rarely gain access to its central discourse. There were many nonwhite engagements with

Spiritualism—figures like reformer Pascal Beverly Randolph, historian and abolitionist William Cooper Nell, and leaders of the Ghost Dance religion on the Great Plains. Such individuals and groups interpreted psychical phenomena through their own history, research, and political struggles—practicing what Britt Rusert terms "fugitive science."[20] The ASPR's universalizing impulse reflected their political need to generalize the Protestant, middle-class, Euro-American standpoint and place other autonomous ways of knowing within a framework that they could comprehend and control. This impulse also screened them from the hybridity inherent in their own eclectic practices, which nevertheless manifests in their archive as a preoccupation with boundaries and identification. They built elaborate criteria for determining who was speaking.

For the most part, the active voices in the ASPR belonged to the white, Protestant middle and upper classes, people with access to books and periodicals and time to participate in a democratic project that they intuitively recognized was designed for them. This exogenous self-selection process was clearly shaped by social inequalities.[21] Yet the society also imposed internal selection processes, which applied ideals of scientific rationality that sometimes excluded even educated white men accustomed to having their word taken on faith—while including others who were not so accustomed. Specifically, it accepted and evaluated women's testimony of their own experiences and events they'd witnessed. This is not to say that the ASPR's uneven protocols created a scientific meritocracy, but participants were attracted by this promise: that the quality of their observations, not their social status, mattered. Women and men took pains to craft themselves as virtuous observers and subjected themselves to the indignity of cross-examination, because they believed that they were contributing to a scientific enterprise and respected science as an arbiter of truth. When the ASPR failed to meet participants' criteria for rigor and impartiality, the ensuing conflicts suggest how the expectation of individual and small-group autonomy threatened the cohesion of psychical research as a science.

In many ways this book follows the ASPR's blueprint in order to show how it worked and how it failed. Like the ASPR officials whose files I sifted through, I faced tensions and frustrations: Whose accounts could I trust? What was the context of these experiences, whose narrators left so little else behind? I wanted to tell the story of psychical research in America through the eyes of participants, yet their words are filtered through authoritative discourses and record-keeping systems, and so many people are simply left out. History is often the story of those who govern. But in psychical research of all places, other kinds of narrative are surely possible. Everyone involved was in some way marginal, struggling for recognition, clinging to legitimacy. Their experiences drew them into a murky boundary zone where the categories of self and other, internal and external, were called into question. Rather than a top-down or bottom-up narrative, I wound up with a roughly horizontal tangle.

Yet when I looked at the shambolic, roughly horizontal knowledge-making of the ASPR, I saw something more vital than today's dominant approach to science communication, where researchers dispense press releases to journalists, who derive clickbait headlines for a passive audience. Unnervingly, I suspected that fringe challenges to scientific authority, such as the crusade to link childhood vaccines with autism, are rooted in an impulse similar to the one that fueled psychical research: the power of anecdotes and firsthand testimony, plus a dearth of scientific answers for a mystery that deeply impacts people's lives. More benignly, the popularity of parapsychology, UFOlogy, and ghost hunting attest to this dynamic. The knowledge that people prize most highly emerges from their own direct experience or from the accounts of others whom they perceive as like them. Only a hundred years ago, a more reciprocal relationship between experts and the public meant that people had compelling alternatives to the trap of suspicion and conspiracy—though again, that reciprocity was bounded by race, class, and education.

Questions of how to inform or edify the nonspecialist public plague present-day scientists—part of the lingering fallout of the science wars of the 1990s and of politicized debates over how science should guide social policy. In these rhetorical clashes, the objective knowledge claims of researchers and the experiential knowledge claims of laypeople work at cross-purposes rather than generating shared understanding.[22] Although the production of scientific knowledge by trained experts is desirable for many reasons, the investment of laypeople in generating knowledge has benefits as well. Production and generation are differently structured activities, with subtly divergent norms and practices. Psychical research failed, as a scientific enterprise, to produce, but it aroused in many participants a passion for rigorous observation and critical thinking. It gave them a forum for ideas and inquiries, a sense of belonging to a meaningful collective endeavor, and linked them with experts who took their contributions seriously. The possibilities that they generated circulated through the media, scientific institutions, education, politics, and art. In telepathic communication, channeling, and clairvoyance, some saw the workings of a natural law that justified the social relations of their era, while others saw psychic forces as a radical challenge to the boundaries of self and social order. I explore what happened to this configuration of knowledge: Was the ASPR's blueprint too messy to stand alongside increasingly rarified sciences? Or were nonscientists, even the white, middle-class public of psychical research, ultimately unable to fit themselves into the disciplined routines of subjectivity it demanded?

The Web of Spiritualism, Psychical Research, and Psychology

An offshoot of the British Society for Psychical Research (SPR), the ASPR was founded in 1885 with an agenda imported from its parent organization. Psychical research, as defined by the SPR, was "an organized and systematic attempt to investigate that large group of debatable phenomena designated by such terms as 'mesmeric,' 'psychical,' and 'spiritualistic' . . . without prejudice or prepossession of any kind, and in the same spirit of exact and unimpassioned inquiry which has enabled science to solve so many problems."[23] Although the ASPR represented the first such "organized and systematic" endeavor in the United States, Americans were no strangers to amazing powers of mind.

Thanks to the massive popularity of Spiritualism in the second half of the nineteenth century—and to animal magnetism before that— most people had some familiarity with trances, clairvoyants, and spirit communication. The Spiritualists' gospel challenged skeptics to witness and judge for themselves; the empiricist mantra that "seeing is believing" formed the experiential bedrock of a nineteenth-century religious sensibility shaped simultaneously by evangelism and secularization.[24]

Psychical research offered to do what Spiritualists said they wanted to do: to test mediums under rigorous, controlled conditions, sorting out fraud from genuine phenomena. Believers, skeptics, and everyone in between looked to the rising authority of experimental science to produce authoritative answers, though their notions of what was "scientific" often conflicted.[25]

Precisely because they had so much difficulty controlling the definition of science as applied to séances, most American psychologists worked frantically to divorce their nascent discipline from psychical research in the early twentieth century. Their efforts shaped how the history of the mind sciences was written. The conventional narrative begins in the German laboratories of Wilhelm Wundt and crosses the Atlantic with his students, who established pioneering psychology departments around the United States.[26] This narrative enshrines a mechanistic approach to quantifying sensory and motor responses—caricatured in the zealous behaviorism of John B. Watson and B. F. Skinner, and extending through recent developments in brain imaging that promise, once again, to reduce the mind to its wiring. However, the singular search for mechanisms is not what drove psychology during its fitful maturation. It emerged from a stew of experimentation, pedagogy, philosophy, psychical research, mental hygiene, psychometrics, and psychoanalysis.

Origin stories that hew to a narrow definition of science serve a purpose, making professionalization seem inevitable and warding off perceived threats to researchers' funding and legitimacy. Many ideas that would become central to psychology and psychoanalysis have roots in late-nineteenth-century psychical research. It's not a dark secret; historians since the 1970s have poked and prodded at the occult interests of luminaries such as William James and Sigmund Freud, recovering neglected aspects of their thought once seen as foolhardy diversions from their truly valuable work.[27] In exposing these repressed influences, historians effected a "re-enchantment" of the mind sciences—or rather, as Jason Josephson-Storm argues, they revealed that enchantment never really went away.[28]

With the occult concerns of leading intellectuals on display, it's also time to take seriously the scientific concerns and resources of ordinary

people as they confronted the same mysterious phenomena. Fascination with powers of mind and occult forces fed on new media technologies—telegraph, telephone, sound recording, and photography—that
transformed global communications over the course of the century.[29]
As communication across time and space was decoupled from geographical proximity, a "thought substance" that directly linked human
minds became more plausible, suggested by the "subtle fluids"—electricity, magnetism, and ether—in vogue during the 1830s and 40s.[30]
Electricity and magnetism kept a hold on the popular and scientific
imaginations through the 1850s and 60s, entering the vocabulary of
Spiritualists, mental healers, and scientists in the United States who
often spoke of that unifying something which allowed mind to act on
matter as "psychic force."[31]

   The very notion of an individual "self" also transformed during the
nineteenth century. A succession of phenomena from mesmerism to
trance mediumship to hypnotism and dissociation called into question
the unity of the mind. If a mesmerist could control subjects through
magnetic influence, the mind must be permeable; if an alternate personality could write letters while the main consciousness slept, the mind
must be multiple; and all of it might reduce to blind automatism rather
than divine purpose. While Spiritualists embraced these phenomena as
signs from heaven, leaders of traditional faiths worked hard to protect
their more conservative ideas of divine communion. As Ann Taves documents, mainline Protestants often regarded "fits, trances, and visions"
as mental weakness or pathology, mobilizing scientific explanations to
discredit them while preserving the integrity of experiences sanctioned
by church authority—generally defined by willpower, self-control, and
conscious introspection. Christopher G. White further elaborates on this
trend of "neuromuscular Christianity" by which Protestants sought insights from physiology and neurology to hold the self together in the
face of modern threats.[32] Both Taves and White emphasize how religious
thinkers engaged deeply with the emerging science of psychology, which
itself was led by Protestants concerned with preserving public morals
from base materialism. Yet it remains that the resort of the faithful to
psychology, and the efforts of psychologists to delineate healthy modes of

faith, was a response to new instabilities in the basic notion of self. These were gambits to maintain control over a shifting terrain, undertaken because something very real was at risk.

Liminal states also created anxieties for the medical and legal systems, where standards for sanity and madness, guilt and innocence were called into question.[33] Neurologists attempted to seize control of trance and related phenomena by classifying them as nervous disorders—but the same neurologists warned that nervous disorders were becoming a modern epidemic. Leading physicians George Miller Beard and Silas Weir Mitchell, like their peers in the Protestant clergy, preached willpower as the necessary preventative.[34] Novelists were less bullish about the individual's ability to fend off the strange, seething mental forces around and within. Anyone could become entranced, perhaps even against their will, like the protagonist of George du Maurier's *Trilby*, and made to do another's bidding. Robert Louis Stevenson's *Dr. Jekyll and Mr. Hyde* staged the inevitable return of that which was repressed under Beard's rigorous willpower regimen. Wilkie Collins, Marie Corelli, Henry James, and Oscar Wilde all experimented with psychological automatism in their narratives, and modernists like W. B. Yeats and T. S. Eliot would incorporate it into their literary practices—appropriating the nineteenth century's popular and feminized spirit-writing for the masculine poetic avant garde. Public fascination with liminal experiences prodded medical men and moral philosophers in their quest for intellectual mastery over these phenomena.[35]

Many who experimented directly with trance and dissociation found neurological and moral explanations unsatisfactory, and sought a psychological explanation rooted not in disordered nerves but rather in the heretofore unfathomed depths of consciousness. Pierre Janet and Alfred Binet in France, William James and Morton Prince in the U.S., and Edmund Gurney and Frederic Myers in England advanced related theories of the subconscious or subliminal self—theories which were also arguments for establishing a distinctive scientific field of psychical research. To varying degrees, they asserted that the "normal" experience of cohesive consciousness represents only a small portion of the countless memories, impulses, and perceptions that churn below the threshold of awareness. For Janet and his Salpêtrière school, intrusions of the subconscious led to hysteria. But for Myers and James, the fact that the mind contains multiple streams of consciousness which at times rise to the surface was not something to be feared. They sought to orient psychical research towards the study of liminal experiences in mentally healthy individuals, underscoring that these were not exclusively pathological phenomena; rather, the plurality of the mind was a simple fact of human psychology. Adapting the mediating logic used by Spiritualists, Myers and James suggested that the subconscious could be an experimentally verified mechanism for communion with whatever lay beyond material reality.[36]

Freud's well-known theory of the unconscious modified these earlier notions of the subconscious or subliminal self; the three terms *unconscious*, *subconscious*, and *subliminal* had distinct meanings for different theorists at different times. I will often use *unconscious* in a general way, as did many of this story's actors, to speak of those mental realms inaccessible to conscious reflection which manifest in liminal states—whether their explanation lies in neurological wiring or in dynamics of the psyche. The many competing theories developed from the 1850s onward to account for the mysterious forces within us are sometimes eclipsed by Freud, whose schema of sexual desire and repression infused the art, literature, and social anxieties of the early twentieth century. But the fragmentation of the subject revealed by the study of liminal experiences became a cultural and social preoccupation much earlier. A discourse of anxiety tends to suffuse histories of this fin du siècle "discovery of the unconscious," in which the subversive practices of mesmerists and mediums inspired heroic efforts at scientific and moral control on the part of traditional institutions—and for this reason, psychical research figures as a minor caveat to this narrative of scientific debunking. But just as psychical research represented a theoretical middle path between religious supernaturalism and materialist pathologizing, in practice it offered an alternative to anxiety for the middle class of people who were not, after all, so invested in the authority of the churches or that of the laboratory. That alternative was inquiry; participants in psychical research responded to modernity's unstable self by pursuing firsthand exploration and self-discovery. A deep fear of dissolution, a sense of peering over the precipice of madness, appears in some of their letters just as it appears in the poems of Eliot and the tales of H. P. Lovecraft. But they act on a counterbalancing curiosity about what could be, a desire to recover meaning at the limits of the mind.

Another reason that psychical research was long excluded from the history of the mind sciences is that it had less in common with laboratory psychology than it did with observational field sciences like meteorology and astronomy. The ASPR built on the tradition of networked knowledge-making that those disciplines established in the nineteenth century; it mobilized a similar demographic—and indeed, many of the same individuals—for the purpose of large-scale data collection. By 1900, scientists began to regard collecting data through correspondence networks as a dated approach compared to the control and precision attainable in laboratories, which yielded dramatic discoveries in fields from microbiology to physics. In practice, observational and experimental methods almost always blend together, but the rapid advances associated with laboratories drew psychologists into that space, where they embraced a rhetoric of active intervention very different from the responsive, incremental work that happened in the field.

The dominance of the laboratory was not instant or uncontested. Across the sciences, researchers debated whether it was best to study spontaneously occurring natural phenomena or their artificial surrogates—for instance, biologists questioned whether laboratory conditions could truly replicate the evolutionary milieu of complex ecosystems. However, fundamental points about the limits of the laboratory receded into the background as more careers and institutions became invested in its ascent. The image of pristine control in the biosciences remains so dominant that only recently has the importance of context reasserted itself; concepts such as environmental determinants of health, epigenetics, and the microbiome reveal the field creeping back into the lab, trailing all its messy historical contingencies. Scientists in the nineteenth century saw the wind blowing in the opposite direction, though, and rushed to embrace the laboratory image of modernity, even in disciplines formerly devoted to spontaneous, context-bound events.

In the midst of this shift, James's vision for psychical research and for psychology represented an old-fashioned way of doing science. Waiting for data to accumulate, building a massive network to capture spontaneous phenomena over many decades—these were not efficient, aggressive means for extracting knowledge from the world. James knew this all too well, and his defense of psychical research was also a defense of observational methods throughout the sciences, a philosophical argument for context and complexity. He happily endorsed laboratory methods to the full extent of their usefulness—it was James who brought the first psychological laboratory to America. Yet he rejected the totalizing urge that arose from yoking the study of the mind to reductive experimental scenarios. A two-way relationship between experimental and observational methods, between control and complexity, was possible and, in his view, necessary. When he saw psychology succumbing to reductionism, he poured more energy into asserting the situated, field-based agenda of psychical research as a project open to the plurality of human experiences. James's scientific ideals dovetailed with his ideals for a pluralistic American society, where differences among observers and between citizens allowed for a richer articulation of reality. James Rodger Fleming writes of American meteorology that "the expansion of volunteer observational systems in America was aided by a common language, polity, and sense of democratic values," and James looked to these values, however exclusionary we now understand them to be, as a foundation for psychical research.[37]

Ghosts in the Archive Machine

The ASPR was supposed to be a public archive of psychical experiences, an extended recording device for the nation's liminal states. Its scientific mission consisted of collecting, storing, sorting, and analyzing data until such a time as it had "a mass of facts concrete enough to found a decent theory upon." James warned not to expect rapid progress; finding the answers they sought could take "half-centuries or whole centuries," therefore the society's "first duty is simply to exist from year to year and perform this recording function well."[38] It is ironic, though a natural result of the society's chronic dysfunction, that archives became their albatross. Reports flowed in but time and patience to sort them were in short supply. Money ran out and secretarial labor became a precious commodity. Crammed file cabinets became pawns in internecine disputes, and the dead appeared through mediums to argue over paperwork. The archive was simultaneously precious and disastrous, very much as I first encountered it in the summer of 2012.

The ASPR's archives are closely tied to its fitful institutional history. Inspired by an 1884 visit from Sir William Barrett of the British SPR, a group of American academics convened to form their own society the following year, electing astronomer Simon Newcomb as president. Almost from the start it struggled to produce publishable research, in part due to methodological disputes within the ranks, but mostly because it lacked time and money to support serious study. William James, integral to the founding and early operations and a vocal public supporter throughout his life, was also representative of this problem; ASPR business often came after more pressing professional matters. In 1888, the society imported British investigator Richard Hodgson to serve as full-time secretary, a role he undertook with great zeal until 1905. Though Hodgson nearly single-handedly kept the society's mission alive, it was forced to merge with the British SPR for financial support and became the "American branch" during this period.

Upon Hodgson's death, a philosophy professor named James Hervey Hyslop, who had just retired from his Columbia University post due to ill health, put in motion a bold scheme to re-form an independent ASPR. The American branch was dissolved and its remains absorbed into the new American Institute for Scientific Research. Hyslop, a prickly personality who repelled even William James from sitting on the revived ASPR's board, presided until his death in 1920. At that point Harvard psychology professor William McDougall was elected president, but those in the society who supported the spirit hypothesis staged an insurrection against his plans to create a scientific review board, and from 1923 to 1941 the ASPR was controlled by professed Spiritualists who emphasized sensational mediumistic phenomena with popular appeal. They invested their credibility in a years-long defense of a medium named Mina Crandon, known as "Margery," whose phenomena were repeatedly proved to be fraudulent. McDougall and other refugees, including Hyslop's former research officer Walter Franklin Prince, regrouped to form the Boston Society for Psychical Research, which claimed the mantle of scientific investigation until another coup placed neurologist George H. Hyslop (James Hyslop's son) and Columbia psychologist Gardner Murphy at the ASPR's helm in 1941.

Also during these years, quantitative telepathy research conducted under McDougall and Joseph Banks Rhine at Duke University initiated the transformation of psychical research into parapsychology. While many of the nineteenth-century practices discussed in this book continue into the present among amateur groups, Rhine's coining of *extrasensory perception* and his hard-won academic laboratory marked a new strategy of professionalization that psychical researchers-cum-parapsychologists hoped would position them among the leading sciences of the twentieth century.[39] This by-no-means-comprehensive overview introduces some of the characters who will appear in these pages, though I will only engage in institutional history to help contextualize the thematic stories of each chapter.

The ASPR's archiving system changed over the years depending on who kept the files; one person's precious data became another's maddening clutter. Only two people could navigate the ASPR's early files: its secretary, Richard Hodgson, and his assistant, Lucy Edmunds. They developed an idiosyncratic system "built up from our needs," as Edmunds explained. She added that it soon "became unwieldy." News clippings, testimonials, and follow-up letters accumulated in various stages of verification, so that the process of transforming a report into a usable case was inscribed in the cluttered topography of their tiny office at 5 Boyleston Street in Boston. Evidence is a material thing, and the work of science often comes down to organizing information. Participants eagerly attended séances and conducted telepathy tests, but the society could never find money for the unglamorous office labor needed to preserve and make sense of that data. Hodgson couldn't afford carbon copies, so original documents sometimes vanished when he sent them out for verification. Edmunds routinely went without her paycheck. Bulging boxes threatened to topple off shelves and bury the pair in an avalanche of ghost stories.

No one in the society complained about the disarray of the office—James was glad to leave logistics in the hands of someone like Hodgson, who showed great enthusiasm for corresponding with the public. Indeed, Hodgson was beloved for his good humor and equipoise towards all who took an interest in psychical research. Even Edmunds, initially business-like and detached, grew deeply committed to Hodgson and his work. In an era when formal and informal sexism barred most women from high-level careers in science, secretaries were often integral to the intellectual output of their male employers. As we've seen, managing data is not a passive or automated activity; it entails a chain of decisions, often tacit but requiring expertise and judgment. At one point, Edmunds tried to implement the Library Bureau's system of vertical filing; she found it "of no use . . . in work of this kind," asserting her expertise in tending to the unique needs of the collection.[40]

When Hodgson dropped dead unexpectedly in the middle of a tennis match in 1905, leaving no will, Edmunds may have wished for guidance from beyond the grave to decide the fate of their chaotic archive. Factions of the ASPR and its parent society in England went to war over the documents, especially séance records that contained valuable but very personal information. Edmunds became a pawn in these transatlantic machinations: J. G. Piddington of the British SPR demanded the records directly form Edmunds, cutting out the American Society's leadership; when William James got wind of Piddington's power play, he "wired Miss E. not to send 'em."[41] Meanwhile, Edmunds had to tie up Hodgson's correspondence and continue the daily work of the office. She wanted to transfer the archive to James Hyslop, the only person with a clear plan to continue the ASPR's work. When crates of bundled letters and clippings started arriving at his New York address, however, Hyslop began to second-guess the coveted prize.

Unable to make heads or tails of the files, he complained that Edmunds had saddled him with useless detritus. Edmunds replied, defensively, that "everything may seem to be unsorted . . . but as they were in the office, each thing had its place and was quickly found."[42] As a parting shot, she added, "You do not seem to either understand or appreciate why I have sent you the catalog or the careful notes. . . . I made a mistake in sending you anything." Once again, salvaging the society's core data became a matter of secretarial labor. Gertrude Tubby, the ASPR's secretary under Hyslop from 1907 to 1920, adopted Edmunds's organizational schema and added still more case files, finding no time for a large-scale reordering. She passed the entire ragtag archive along to the society's next secretary, William Prince, who sorted the sprawling files into four categories: mediumship, phenomena, correspondence, and history. This material was refiled in 1970 and again by historian James Matlock in 1986. Matlock refined Prince's categories to develop the Psychical Phenomena Files, the current organization of the ASPR's holdings, arrayed from Apparitions and Automatisms to Spirit Photography and Telepathy.

Numerous other archives contribute to a fuller picture of psychical research in America, as does coverage in contemporaneous newspapers and periodicals. Essential source material comes from Duke University's Parapsychology Laboratory, the University of Pennsylvania's Seybert Commission for the Investigation of Modern Spiritualism, the Library of Congress Manuscript Division, and the American Philosophical Society's collections. Psychical research generated enormous and enduring interest among journalists, critics, and the public; thus, the press often served as its instrument, both an information source and a mode of dissemination.

The Plan of This Book

Beginning this story when the ASPR formed, in 1884, would isolate it from the broad, interconnected forces that flowed through it: an overwhelming popular interest in liminal states, psychic force, and mental permeability; the persistence of American Spiritualism; and the development of psychology as a scientific discipline claiming objective knowledge of the mind. Each chapter follows these twined threads into a different setting, exploring particular metaphorical and methodological resonances. I pursue sympathetic connections, looking historically at mediumship while also accepting its usefulness for any writer or reader who hopes to engage with the past.

The first chapter anchors psychical research in the context of other nineteenth-century amateur observational sciences, with a focus on meteorology as a metaphor used by many psychical researchers to capture the complexity and elusiveness of the human mind as an object of investigation. Meteorology also served as a functional model of how to organize a scientific discipline dependent on public participation, through the distribution of networked observers across the continent.

Psychical researchers amassed countless reports of dreams, premonitions, and coincidences. The second chapter examines changing modes of dream interpretation during the nineteenth century in their popular and scientific dimensions. Dreams were a crucial shared object of inquiry in psychology and psychical research; they exemplified the challenges of capturing fleeting mental phenomena and authenticating their contents. At the same time, their very universality made dreams an entry point for curious laypeople who sought a scientific explanation for their experiences. Taking engineer and psychical researcher Coleman Sellers as a case study, this chapter focuses on the tension between meaning and mechanism in theories of dreaming, revealing what was at stake in social and scientific understandings of the unconscious mind.

Returning from the unruly dreamworld to the ostensibly controlled setting of parlors and laboratories, the third chapter traces the use of drawings as scientific evidence in the study of the mind. Beginning with the child study movement of the 1870s, psychologists began to conceive of drawings as stable, portable traces of otherwise subjective mental processes. This evidentiary status of drawings was extended to the telepathic drawings of psychical researchers, and the chapter centers on the case of George Albert Smith and Douglas Blackburn. This case, despite its eventual debunking, helped to establish drawing as direct line to the mind's hidden interior, which still persists in the behavioral sciences.

The fourth chapter focuses on the psychical research career of Mary Craig Sinclair and her husband, Upton, as it illuminates the possibilities and limitations for female investigators seeking citizenship in the republic of experience. The validity of Mary Craig's research was premised, in complex ways, on her ability to passively channel male desires while carefully containing her own feelings to frame herself as an objective observer.

The final chapter tackles the question of whether psychical researchers were "crazy" or, more specifically, if some suffered from psychiatric disorders that caused their strange experiences. Retrospectively diagnosing mental illness could easily reinforce a reductive pathological explanation for psychical phenomena. However, the rise of this pathologizing impulse—the tendency to dismiss unwelcome perspectives as "crazy"—was itself a large factor in the marginalization of psychical research and parapsychology. This chapter tracks discussion within the community of psychical researchers about how to navigate the borderlands of sanity, where some of their best evidence lay. Though investigators felt unfairly stigmatized by the materialist stance of clinical psychiatrists, they also recognized the authority of psychiatry and sought to harness it for their own discipline-building projects, namely, the establishment of a clinic dedicated to experimental treatments of mental illness.

Interspersed between the five chapters are a series of interludes which offer space for meditation on my own experience as a researcher and writer in relation to specific cases from the archive. This approach is provisional, intended to evoke the episodic nature of psychical research itself. Consumed by barometric pressure, burial mounds, and a tantalizing cream puff, I allowed myself to become a medium for the concerns of psychical researchers which reached deep into the society and politics of their times, and ours.

Many psychical researchers did want to prove the immortality of the soul, but this very desire—to have objective material proof of what was previously demonstrated through Scripture—reflected a discourse that had long been hybridized. Their (often liberal or heterodox) understanding of religion encouraged investigation of the natural world and the human mind. It was at the mind's limits where they expected to find a mechanism, process, or clue that pointed beyond, establishing a seamless unity of religion and science. Of course, many Americans believed that this was already accomplished through Spiritualism, Christian Science, and other new religions of the fin du siècle. Psychical researchers distinguished themselves from these groups by attempting to limit and decompose their inquiries in ways that were more closely aligned with the professionalizing sciences of the period. Most importantly, they did not want to create a parascience discourse that was, like the new religions, validated by a metaphysical leap which they criticized as grounded in dogma. Indeed, opposition to dogma was a refrain repeated by everyone from William James to Mary Craig Sinclair, and it targeted the dogmas of religion and of science. A stance of openness was, they argued, more scientific than the skeptical assumptions of many psychologists.

Maintaining this space of possibility around contested experiences became increasingly untenable in the pages of scientific journals and within the walls of academic institutions, though polls consistently show that Americans at large still take precisely this view of the paranormal, that there is "something to it" which they can't presume to explain.[43] Over the course of the twentieth century, experiences categorized as mystical or religious became the purview of anthropology, religious studies, and theology, which treat them as subjective internal states. Psychical researchers wanted to understand the objective basis of their experiences, which they often asserted belonged to the mundane material realm rather than the exalted plane of prophecy and revelation. Meanwhile, experiences categorized as psychopathological are explained in clinical and increasingly in neuromolecular terms by psychologists and psychiatrists. But psychical researchers strongly rejected the notion that liminal states were merely disease processes or coping mechanisms; these states suggested the capacity of the normal mind to reach beyond the recognized boundaries of the real. This book's centrifugal structure aims to illuminate the unstable space of possibility held open by psychical researchers' explorations, rather than following a single arc towards the field's failure. Although the souls of our dead may be dispersed, unreachable, their traces circulate through systems that the nineteenth century built: continental air masses, telecommunications, photomechanical copies, and the vast interior of the self that is also a meeting place for our common phantoms.

CHAPTER 1

THE WEATHER MAP AT
THE BOTTOM OF THE MIND

I n 1873, Thomas Davison Crothers, a young doctor in Albany, New York, published a set of clinical cases in which a "sudden disturbance of the atmosphere of mind" caused his patients to get sicker. These disturbances did not emanate from within; rather, they traveled from far-off fires, disasters, or riots. When the worldly trouble ended, the patients improved. This strange phenomenon, he argued, was produced by "waves of mental influence, drifting over the half-susceptible brains" of the sick, whose weakened state made them unusually sensitive to psychic weather. He asserted frankly that "such an atmosphere exists; the indications of its presence are as real and manifest as that of the air about us." Distressingly, this meant that no seaside retreat or mountain sanitarium was safe from the ills of society. On the positive side, it suggested a new methodology for studying the human mind, modeled on the science of "the air about us"—meteorology.[1]

While Crothers never joined the American Society for Psychical Research, he was one of many whose work wove around the ASPR's for decades, from his early interest in the mental atmosphere, which predated the society's founding, to his later study of psychical phenomena in substance users. He remained convinced that thought could travel from mind to mind and that thought-transmission followed laws "infinitely more complex" than the facile idea of spirits whispering from the afterlife. Writing in support of the ASPR's research methods, Crothers used another analogy to the field sciences: "As in observations of the heavens, both the observer, the means of observation, and the phenomena studied, all need verifying, and correction by others."[2] References to meteorology and astronomy bookend Crothers's thinking on psychical research, and in this he was hardly alone.

The ASPR looked to the iconic field sciences of the nineteenth century for both methods and metaphors, organizational strategies and epistemological foundations. Indeed, it's difficult to pinpoint where tools blend into practices which shade into theories, and this chapter considers the influence of meteorology and astronomy on psychical research across each of these modes. All three sciences faced a similar challenge: how to identify and fix fleeting phenomena encountered only in their indirect emanations. Weather, nebulae, and spirits took shape through networks of scientific observers: signals sent and received; careful recording of dates, times, and locations; the good faith and steady eyes of trustworthy witnesses. As Crothers pointed out, this process acknowledged and was designed to correct for the personal equation, a certain degree of inevitable perceptual variability among observers. By self-consciously adopting meteorology and astronomy as models, ASPR leaders not only asserted the feasibility of capturing the invisible, they also sought to counter the materialist orthodoxy of the lab. William James, especially, saw individual mental events as inextricable from the context in which they occurred—a context impossible to reproduce under artificially controlled conditions. It was no more realistic to study the mind in a laboratory than to study a tornado in a test tube.

Catching the Unseen

Astronomy and meteorology shaped the very notion of science in the nineteenth century, reaching into industry, agriculture, politics, and trade in ways that impressed ordinary people with the benefits of increasing mastery over nature. They pioneered techniques of large-scale observation and recording, which both enabled and made visible the expanding reach of American empire. Mostly white, mostly male Americans—the same Americans entitled to political participation—participated in this effort, which resembled what is today called citizen science: initiatives in which laypeople follow a set of protocols to collect data or specimens for the use of scientists. The citizen in twenty-first-century citizen science, often a concerned advocate for the environment or public health, is positioned differently than the citizen of nineteenth-century science to whom I refer in this book. This nineteenth-century citizen was more exclusively defined, subject to intimate scrutiny and discipline, and yet closer in social and intellectual space to the scientists with whom he or she worked (who may not have had formal training in science at all). This citizen saw unpaid scientific work as part of their investment in an ordered society and a modernized nation.[3]

Predicting the weather and improving navigation were part of domesticating a landscape perceived as hostile to white settlers, and were connected with other forms of scientific mapping and control applied to indigenous peoples, as well as to unstable elements inside settler society.[4] Large-scale observational techniques changed the style of scientific work from a studied narration of individual experiences to an objective, mechanical practice of registering information.[5] Assured that their data were uniform, researchers could apply new statistical methods to derive general laws. Psychical researchers argued that their field was on precisely the same trajectory: from an idiosyncratic hobby to a rigorous science with strategic value for managing the nation's sometimes chaotic mental atmosphere.

Decades before Freud planted his flag in the supposed terra incognita of the unconscious, psychical researchers developed their own notion of mental forces operating beyond the level of ordinary awareness, according to obscure laws that science had only begun to probe.[6] Rather than digging in the depths of the individual psyche, where Freud unearthed the primal neuroses of bourgeois family relations, psychical research tracked mental forces across the boundaries of the self. In doing so, it tapped into diffuse nineteenth-century conversations about what many termed the "mental atmosphere." The concept of atmosphere extended from the gaseous layer enveloping the earth to hypotheticals like an "electrical atmosphere" and "magnetic atmosphere"; all denoted invisible forces circulating within a closed system. The mental atmosphere was the realm of mysterious phenomena like premonition, clairvoyance, and telepathy. It also gave a name to growing anxiety around social contagions—mob behavior and subversive elements within the body politic. These fears grew especially fevered in the United States as the tumult of the Civil War flowed into an era of urbanization, expansionism, and market instability.[7]

"The weather—does it sympathize with these times?" asked Walt Whitman, one of many Americans who kept a detailed weather diary and perceived in it interconnected social and meteorological forces.[8] The barometer was especially useful in making sense of such invisible, large-scale fluctuations and thus provided a ready-to-hand analogy for how the mind involuntarily registers collective experience. For better or worse, individuals were permeable to national weather that did not respect the boundaries of class, race, or distance.

This figuration of humans as weather apparatuses brings to mind literary critic Terry Castle, whose book *The Female Thermometer* tells the remarkable story of how weather instruments decorating genteel eighteenth-century parlors contributed to the development of the modern psychological subject.[9] As people got used to watching thermometers fluctuate, this became a popular metaphor for volatile emotions and for the bourgeois practice of monitoring one's interior states. She points out that technologies, especially everyday ones, shape how people talk and think about their feelings—hot and cold became synonyms for passion and indifference. However, psychical researchers and medical writers like Crothers used the mental atmosphere in a more literal sense. Rather than a metaphor for the individual psyche as an isolated microcosm, it evoked a macroscopic collective experience.

National-level meteorological networks helped to shape this macrocosmic perspective by binding science with citizenship, putting instruments in people's hands, and producing synoptic weather maps. Beginning in the 1830s, the Franklin Institute and then the Smithsonian Institution distributed free or discounted thermometers and barometers to volunteer observers, along with instructions and standardized data forms. Measuring the temperature was intuitive enough, but participants received extra instruction on the barometer that highlighted its sensitivity to the movement of distant air masses.[10] Becoming a Smithsonian correspondent connected small-town and rural Americans with a continent-wide project—their data would literally transcend the earthbound observer to be synthesized in the God's-eye view of the weather map.

Participants received these maps in the mail so that they could see the product of their labor.

The barometer's sensitivity and its ability to commune with far-off forces became a matter of great interest, and weather enthusiasts could obtain highly refined instruments like those advertised by the American Aelloscope Company. The company boasted that "a storm a thousand miles off makes [the barometer] tremble. And when all other indicators give promise of an undisturbed sky . . . the Aelloscope will speak distinctly and correctly of changes marching on their way."[11] Differing levels of sensitivity also characterized the human barometers that so intrigued Thomas Crothers. In his treatise on the health effects of the mental atmosphere, he explained that people who were subject to premonitions and prophecies had a "keen susceptibility [to] the direction and force of the cerebral powers" circulating among human minds.[12] Such sensitivity could be useful—for instance, to gain the upper hand in a business meeting or to find a missing relative—but his patients had become hypersensitized, like the overrefined Aelloscope, trembling in the grasp of distant emotional tempests.

If the barometer registered the motion of distant air masses, the human barometer registered collective emotional experience, sometimes of a traumatic nature. Crothers told of Civil War officers who sensed the approach of the enemy side due to the "disturbed mental atmosphere" of fearful, angry soldiers on the march. The same principle applied to one of Crothers's patients, a "lawyer of note" taking the rest cure in a country retreat. This lawyer, after making a near-recovery, became "violently agitated" one afternoon. Crothers deduced that his fit was brought on by a political convention in the distant city where the lawyer had been nominated to run for Congress. The "intense excitement" of the convention-goers as they cast their ballots produced a "sudden disturbance of the atmosphere of mind"—demonstrating, literally, the unconscious reach of the democratic mob. Crothers included "political gathering" along with fires and riots in the litany of urban disasters that caused mass "excitement," "passion," and "agitation."[13] Individuals within these crowds were also functioning barometrically, sensing and amplifying each other's responses to the situation.

Crothers's mental atmosphere was not far from the mainstream of nineteenth-century medical thinking; it built on the long discourse about weather and human health rooted in Hippocratic theory. Indeed, it was the Army Medical Department that spearheaded the first effort at nationwide meteorological observation in the U.S., hoping to improve the health of soldiers. Recognizing that weather impacted the mind as well as the body, some psychical researchers tried to correlate atmospheric fluctuations directly with mental activity. Ernest Hollenbeck, an avid amateur scientist whom we'll meet later in this chapter, used his personal set of weather instruments to test the effect of air pressure on telepathy, finding that "low barometer conditions depress the psychical power."[14] Walt Whitman entertained the reverse notion, that human events of great magnitude could bring down the fury of storms; amid the upheaval of war, "all the meteorological influences . . . run riot."[15] Crothers, as well as most psychical researchers, understood the relationship a bit more metaphorically, but not by many degrees.

The idea of a mental atmosphere emerged alongside the discipline of meteorology, and both reflected new techniques for synthesizing national identity from the disparate experiences of observers on the ground. Premonition, hypnotic suggestion, and clairvoyance revealed involuntary forces connecting Americans across lines of gender, race, and class, which would become fodder for sociologists and psychologists of group behavior.[16] William McDougall, who led the ASPR in the 1920s, is better remembered as a founder of social psychology, a field preoccupied with such phenomena as the contagion of the crowd and, later, mass hysteria. Given the permeability of the mental atmosphere to unwholesome influence, McDougall saw eugenic population control as the only way to render America "safe for democracy."[17] Conversely, harnessing the mental atmosphere for purposes of solidarity could lead to a utopia of perfect understanding—at least this was the hopeful position of some ASPR correspondents, including socialist writer Upton Sinclair and his wife, Mary Craig Sinclair.[18] The widespread appeal of meteorological thinking as a vehicle for social and psychological concerns helps to explain why the ASPR looked to meteorology as a model on technological, organizational, and theoretical levels.

The story of how nineteenth-century meteorology and other observational sciences became scientific, and how psychical researchers hoped to become scientific too, interweaves with the trend of professionalization in American society after the Civil War.[19] Professionalization meant that authority shifted away from amateur communities and into the hands of trained, salaried experts, employed by universities or governments and organized into specialized subfields. This transition was not sudden, uniform, or clear-cut, and the endpoint of excluding amateurs from meaningful scientific work was not a given—many hybrid arrangements emerged. While meteorology thrived in a moment when amateur scientific networks were highly esteemed, it was also organized around official centers of calculation—the Smithsonian and the Weather Bureau—which had funding to synthesize data and present it to the public in an authoritative form.

Only at the turn of the twentieth century did the sciences swing heavily towards a professionalization that cut out amateurs, and this unlucky timing meant that the networks built by psychical researchers would face a struggle for academic recognition.[20] In the moment of the ASPR's founding, however, creating an organization led by respected intellectuals and supplied with data through a network of amateur observers seemed like the most strategic and scientifically fruitful approach. In 1884, William James and his colleagues had good reason to believe that the interest and motivation for such a project as theirs was already in the air; eager participants were just waiting for something to bring them together. Meteorology's network offered a proven template.

The recruiting pool for amateur science organizations consisted mainly of members of the literate middle and upper classes eager to do their part in the march of scientific progress. Their zeal reflected a received commitment to Enlightenment reason as a founding principle of the nation. Thomas Jefferson, statesman and scientist, proclaimed the inherent ability of all white, male, landowning citizens to determine the truth through rational induction from evidence; he specifically praised seventeenth-century British philosopher Francis Bacon, figurehead of the scientific method. Bacon became a guiding spirit for formally educated and self-taught Americans who embraced the truth of science over the received doctrines of traditional authorities.[21] In his American incarnation, Bacon stood for home-grown common sense rooted in direct experience. This empirical stance, promulgated through the popular press, dominated the thinking of everyone from health guru Sylvester Graham to showman P. T. Barnum, their mantras variations on "seeing is believing."[22] Given the proximity of Baconian common sense to the founding ideals of the United States, and the need for knowledge to master an uncharted natural world, participation in science was close to a civic duty.

This spirit was reflected in the Smithsonian Institution's motto, "Every man is a valuable member of society who by his observations, researches, and experiments procures knowledge for men."[23] Established in 1846, the Smithsonian developed the first nationwide networks of amateur observers in botany, meteorology, and other natural sciences. Spencer F. Baird, appointed as its first curator in 1850, was among the first generation of semiprofessional scientists in the U.S., yet he and most of his colleagues were self-taught, learning through participation in amateur groups. Baird, in turn, built the Smithsonian's collection by cultivating a vast network of amateurs plugged in to a central hub in Washington. For thirty-seven years, he corresponded at length with farmers, clerks, students, blacksmiths—anyone who would send him specimens or data. In return, they received advice, tools, and collegial support, and the Smithsonian became the leading edge of nation-building through knowledge-making.[24] Ironically, psychical researchers did not embrace comparisons with Baird's Smithsonian network, which had passed its heyday by the 1880s. Their explicit rejection of this link to natural history indicates how seriously they took the task of positioning themselves among advantageous influences. They sought more modern exemplars in meteorology and astronomy—which shared the distinctive problem of studying ephemeral signs rather than fixed specimens—without acknowledging that these fields built upon Baird's approach to marshalling volunteers and organizing knowledge. Indeed, Baird's template was the key to making invisible phenomena visible.

The study of invisible forces was undeniably a task of a different order from collecting insects or birds and became a signature quest of the nineteenth century. Despite widespread veneration of Francis Bacon, it was a dissonant time for the project of enlightenment.[25] The very scientific discoveries that crowned an age of progress also illustrated its limits: it became clear that the "imponderable fluids"—electricity, magnetism, heat, and light—were not accounted for in Newtonian physics, and many believed that they were facets of a single universal fluid that held the secrets of life itself. Direct measurement of such forces was impossible, but physicists developed increasingly complex devices for registering and quantifying their activity. Historian John Tresch characterizes these as "romantic machines" for their capacity to "feel around in the invisible."[26]

The almost mystical reach of magnetism and electricity was easily extended to mental forces—indeed, discovering the fluid of thought would complete the Romantic picture of a universe in which mind held final sway over matter.[27] The same Parisian intellectuals who hosted electrical demonstrations in their parlors in the 1810s and 20s also convened committees to look into animal magnetism.[28] This process of official scientific investigation into psychical phenomena would repeat throughout the century as new practices emerged. In the 1880s, the Seybert Commission for Investigating Modern Spiritualism enlisted leading American academics to the same end. Though no such investigation ever found the proof it sought, neither did they explain away the phenomena to the satisfaction of believers and witnesses. As William James opined in 1886, "So long as the physicists have to acknowledge action at a distance of gravity . . . it is certainly no dishonor to any intellect to accede to the possibility of the action at a distance of mind."[29] Conquering this frontier seemed like a matter of manifest destiny, but the tools to capture and quantify mental forces remained tantalizingly out of reach.

One prong of this effort involved building better machines. American chemist Robert Hare, inventor of the oxy-hydrogen blowpipe, developed a series of tools called spiritscopes to test for mediumistic powers. Hare is a perfect emblem for the tensions born of republican science: he left his university post in 1847 to pursue imponderable matter in the realms of Spiritualism, meteorology, and politics, where he asserted the need for a patrician social elite to control the tempestuous mob.[30] His popular spiritscopes influenced the elaborate devices of Englishmen William Crookes and William Fletcher Barrett in the 1870s, which took techniques from radiation physics and chemical spectroscopy and applied them to the human soul.[31] Despite ingenious engineering, laboratory tests only generated more controversy. Both scientists and believers often argued that the phenomena could not manifest properly under artificial conditions. Yet phenomena abounded in the field, from the wards of Charcot's Salpêtrière asylum to the table-tipping séances of the Fox sisters in upstate New York.

The second prong of capturing psychical forces required an organized ground game. From the 1840s onward, countless ordinary people wrote about psychical incidents and performances, sending anecdotes to newspapers and to scientists whom they hoped could shed light upon their experiences. Those interested in a rigorous study of psychical phenomena tended to characterize it as a field or observational science, requiring the accumulation of many carefully documented reports. Though they never abandoned faith in the power of the laboratory, they saw the field as the realm of immediate practical activity.

Field science came with its own challenges, however—namely, how to produce standardized data from subjective observers. When astronomers in the early nineteenth century realized that two viewers looking through identical telescopes often recorded a planet's transit at slightly different times, they brought to light a crisis affecting all the sciences. How could any observation be valid if everyone has a unique personal equation governing their perception and response time? Rather than abandoning the field, astronomers adopted an array of measures to mechanize and standardize their procedures. They emphasized willpower and discipline, often imposed by higher-level scientific workers on lower-level technicians.[32] By studying individual differences, they developed techniques to control for variability, calibrating bodies as one would calibrate instruments. This understanding of the body as an instrument resonated for psychical researchers, whose work depended upon sensitive human barometers.

Thus, the nineteenth century's faith in scientific progress crystallized around the germ of Romanticism: imponderable fluids, invisible forces, and idiosyncratic selves were expected to yield to routinized mechanical probing. Psychical research pushed that optimism to its limit by attempting to contain powers of mind within a system of observation.

Becoming Big Science

Astronomy and meteorology were the Big Science of the nineteenth century, seen as advancing the nation's strategic and symbolic goals.[33] At the same time, nonscientists participated in and proudly identified with their achievements. Because these disciplines held a prominent place in public discourse and also operated on the ground in far-flung communities, they became powerful standard-bearers for the scientific method. It was no coincidence that the newly formed ASPR recruited Simon Newcomb, an astronomer, mathematician, and outspoken proponent of rationalization in all areas of American life, to serve as its first president in 1885.[34] Though no prominent meteorologists were enlisted in the ASPR's leadership, that field was also a constant point of reference for a generation that came of age alongside the Weather Bureau.

Newcomb, the self-taught son of an itinerant schoolmaster, got his start working as a human calculator for the Nautical Almanac Office. There, he synthesized telescope observations into navigational charts for commercial shipping and naval defense. A task that would have bored most people inspired Newcomb to reexamine widely accepted astronomical constants, which he discovered were based on flawed data. He soon became the director of the Almanac Office and one of America's most renowned scientists. In his role as a systematizer of mass observational data, he epitomized the ASPR's aspirations. He and his colleagues in astronomical observatories around the country also understood how to build what we might now call "relevance": astronomers made themselves useful to colleges, industry, the military, and their local communities, fostering an appreciation of basic science. Part of their evangelism was self-serving, to secure federal funds and to enlist amateurs as unpaid data collectors.[35] Yet they also presented astronomy as a self-improving discipline that forged better citizens and better democracy.[36] Indeed, this was Newcomb's particular hobbyhorse, and his broad agenda of scientific social reform is what led him to take the helm of a society devoted to supernatural phenomena.[37] Before accepting the ASPR presidency, he penned columns in *Science* magazine decrying the methods of the British Society for Psychical Research; he aimed to bring reason to bear on the subject and call out Spiritualist exploitation of a gullible public.

Drawing parallels with the theories and methods of astronomy was also useful in protecting the phenomena of psychical research from debunkers. As William James explained, the elusiveness of certain psychical events mirrored that of astronomical events: "extremely feeble" telepathic signals were lost in the noise of daily life "just as the feeble sensations from the stars are obliterated by sunlight." He warned that "a man conscious only during the day would not discover the stars."[38] This comparison at once normalized the unusual settings of psychical research—darkened rooms at odd hours—and elevated its personnel alongside astronomers whose labor reveals what is hidden from ordinary sight. Richard Hodgson echoed this point, writing that "it might be easier to duplicate the fall of a meteorite" in the laboratory than to reproduce psychical phenomena there.[39] Ironically, Hodgson addressed these words to Simon Newcomb; the astronomer had become increasingly skeptical of psychic mediums who refused to work under controlled conditions. Hodgson urged him to recall the value of watching and waiting for spontaneous events.[40]

Beyond such analogies, there were concrete hopes for psychical insight from the emerging field of astrophysics, which promised to discover physical causes for mysterious action at a distance. Newcomb expressed this sense of a boundless horizon in a 1903 column declaring that there are "other agencies whose exact nature is yet unknown to us" and which join together the universe in "a connected whole."[41] While Newcomb turned for spiritual fulfillment to the physics of fourth-dimensional space, nonastronomers were more likely to extend these speculations along psychical lines, envisioning a cosmic unity of mind and matter that individuals could channel. Their hopes were not unreasonable in the context of astronomy's recent achievements.

Meteorology was another pillar of the nineteenth-century narrative of ever-increasing scientific mastery. Like astronomy, it carved out a professional role for experts while nurturing its amateurs to produce more and better data. Its model of citizen science was hierarchical but highly collegial, motivated by shared curiosity and enthusiasm. Like astronomers, meteorologists hoped to play an important civic role as ambassadors of the scientific method. As "Storm King" James P. Espy pointed out, astronomers all look at the same stars, while meteorologists capture local phenomena that represent a small piece of a much larger, and constantly changing, picture; this distinction helps to explain why meteorology would have a more specific influence on psychical research than astronomy did. Moreover, long-standing interest in the mental atmosphere had already popularized the analogy that psychical researchers sought to harness.

Historian James Rodger Fleming divides the history of American meteorology into three stages: a pre-1800 stage, characterized by networks of interested individuals keeping weather diaries; the development of organized "systems of observation" between 1800 and 1870; and the post-1870 dominance of formal, government-run meteorological institutions.[42] This progression, which meteorologists and the public celebrated as part of science's forward march, was exactly what psychical researchers desired; the formation of the ASPR represented their advance into the second stage—becoming a "system of observation"—and they borrowed methods directly from the weather-watchers of previous decades.

Meteorology's largest amateur system of observation came together in 1848 under the leadership of the Smithsonian's Joseph Henry, who planned the distribution of instruments and the collection of data at regional hubs. Though always short on money and supplies, the Smithsonian intended for observers to use standardized tools all produced by the same Baltimore manufacturer. Princeton geologist Arnold Guyot spent his summers traveling from Maine to Georgia, inspecting weather stations and calibrating their instruments. As the Smithsonian's network grew into what Henry termed a "great meteorological crusade," reaching out through newspapers, local clubs, and telegraph offices, it implemented standardized reporting forms and new techniques. It harnessed the energies of about 600 volunteers, who provided not only daily measurements but also detailed descriptions of rare phenomena. Significantly, the Smithsonian built on and consolidated previous efforts by the American Philosophical Society, the Franklin Institute, state governments, and colleges around the country; as observers saw the power of their regional reports, they realized the need for a centralized national project.

The dedication of the nineteenth-century weather enthusiast cannot be underestimated. Americans lived and died by the weather, experienced it as a truly awesome force dictating their earthly fortunes, and in this light it's no surprise that many laypeople devoted near-obsessive energies to tracking and studying it. The realization that everyone labored under the weather's whims, and that citizens could share their knowledge across great distances to anticipate what was coming, fueled an ethos of scientific solidarity that went far beyond curiosity or edification.[43] The reports of psychical researchers carried the same communal urgency. Feeling dangerously exposed to vast and unknown forces, witnesses hastened to fit singular, dramatic, and sometimes shattering incidents into a larger map of human experience.

The Smithsonian invested significant resources into training observers to produce better data, but not without considering other options. While it dispatched professional expeditions to study paleontology, archaeology, and geology, the weather did not sit still waiting for scientists to arrive. Moreover, there was little hope of reproducing meteorological phenomena in the controlled setting of the laboratory. Though simple demonstrations had been tried in the 1830s and 40s, actual events were too large and complex to model. Critics easily poked holes in indoor experiments by pointing to all the variables—terrain, pressure gradients, electric charge—not represented.[44]

Despite their rejection of laboratory experiment, meteorologists did benefit from the increasingly refined instruments developed for physics and chemistry labs, and psychical research followed their lead. The invention of self-registering instruments—barometers that inscribed their own fluctuations on a continuous chart—facilitated a new rhetoric of objectivity for those who could afford such labor-saving devices. While hundreds of observers received free instruments from the Smithsonian, for a higher price they could obtain the latest self-recording versions, such as the barometer in Figure 1, which freed them from thrice-daily manual readings. The ASPR similarly recommended a self-recording model of the "Combined Die-Thrower and Tally Keeper" (Figure 2) to use in home experiments, "lessen[ing] the labor . . . and insuring an absolutely correct record."[45] The value of

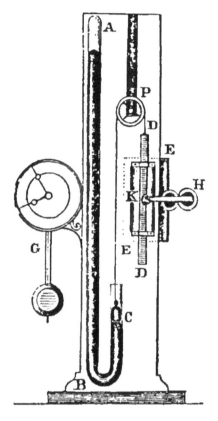

FIGURE 1. The self-registering barometer, recommended for meteorological observers. Elias Loomis, *A Treatise on Meteorology* (New York: Harper & Brothers, 1868), 17.

these laboratory-approved devices lay not just in convenience, but in their mechanical fidelity.

However, the most important meteorological tool for producing regular observations and collating large quantities of data were the paper instruments of forms and tables like the one shown in Figure 3.[46] The Smithsonian project hinged on the circulation of blank forms from Washington, D.C., to volunteer observers around the country via an ever-improving mail system.[47] Forms imposed some degree of control for variations in the experience and skill level of observers. These were particular problems for psychical researchers, who desperately needed hard data but were swamped by highly irregular anecdotal reports. They too

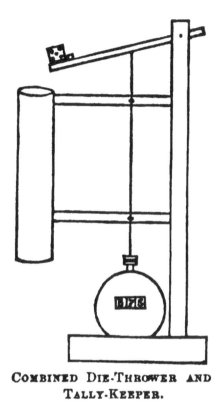

**COMBINED DIE-THROWER AND
TALLY-KEEPER.**

FIGURE 2. The self-registering dice roller, recommended for telepathic experimenters. *PASPR* 1 (1885), 13.

developed an arsenal of forms and recording tables and circulated them in popular science publications aimed at the same readers that meteorologists recruited.

In an 1896 address before the British Society for Psychical Research, William James sketched his own analogy between observing the mind and observing the weather: "We must accustom ourselves more and more to playing the role of a meteorological bureau, be satisfied for many a year to go without definitive conclusions, confident that if we only keep alive and heap up data, the natural types (if there are any) will surely crystallize out."[48] This was the faith of a man who had seen amateurs' data solve the mysteries of storms and atmospheric circulation. Indeed, though its

	Day.
	Hour.
	Temperature of Air.
	Temperature of Wet-bulb.
	Dew point.
	Course of Wind.
	Lower strata of Clouds.
	Mddle strata of Clouds.
	Upper strata of Clouds.
	Strength of Wind.
	Weather.
	Beginning of Rain.
	End of Rain.
	Barometer.
	OBSERVATIONS.

FIGURE 3. A standardized weather reporting form distributed by the Joint Committee on Meteorology of the American Philosophical Society and Franklin Institute. *Hazard's Register of Pennsylvania* (December 1834): 393.

methods were old, meteorology was still quite visibly on the ascent when James made these remarks. In 1870, the federal government folded the Smithsonian's project into the War Department; this service became the Weather Bureau in 1891, a moment of great pride for American science boosters who had long argued for more resources and professional infrastructure. The Weather Bureau showed how an amateur science could prove its worth and gain both popular and governmental support.

Building a System of Psychical Observation

Given the participatory zeal of the American public for recording barometric pressure, the founders of the ASPR were optimistic about building a nationwide system for collecting psychical events. The first meetings of the society, convened in the chambers of Boston's Academy of Arts and Sciences, produced a series of circulars to recruit "competent persons who might be willing to engage in such labor."[49] They envisioned a largely self-directed and autonomous workforce, asking respondents to indicate what subjects they wanted to study and "how many hours a week you might possibly give."[50] Nearly every man present at these early meetings had a background in the natural or experimental sciences, and they expected this new organization to function much as their familiar scientific networks did: by gathering facts, from both experts and nonexperts, into a center of calculation where leaders would compile, analyze, and derive conclusions.

Administering this system required topical and geographical divisions. The initial plan of the society included branches in New York and Philadelphia, and proposed six committees to address different areas of inquiry: hypnotism, thought-transference, apparitions, physical phenomena, Reichenbach's phenomenon, and a committee for reviewing current literature. The staffing of these committees was left up to society members. "It is earnestly hoped that volunteers will be forthcoming," wrote William James and Henry Bowditch. "Without such volunteers, it is to be feared that the American Society for Psychical Research may fail to justify its foundation."[51] Fear of failure would remain a constant theme for an organization whose legitimacy was contingent on proving the existence of the very phenomena it was established to study. No meteorologist had ever been asked to prove that it rains.

The initial response to this plea was healthy, if less than overwhelming. At the highest levels of the ASPR, James's elite colleagues such as Bowditch and Newcomb provided symbolic legitimacy. The real task before them, however, involved collecting and verifying firsthand accounts of psychical phenomena from across the nation. From among the middling ranks of university professors and medical men there emerged a group with consistent interest in psychical research who, though rarely at leisure to produce original work, served as important regional nodes in the network through which facts were gathered and vetted. One of these participants, Dr. Weston D. Bayley of Pennsylvania, provides a glimpse into the day-to-day production of psychical knowledge as part of the intellectual life of upper-middle-class, educated male professionals and their families.

Dr. Weston D. Bayley would eventually become an important figure in the ASPR, serving as a trustee of the society from 1920 to 1922. His interest in psychical research began much earlier; he first reached out to ASPR secretary Richard Hodgson in the 1890s. During this early period, Bayley served as a representative and investigator for the ASPR in Pennsylvania, sending frequent newspaper clippings, references, and reports. He did not, however, conduct his own investigations or publish any findings in the society's first two decades, despite the urgent need for new work. Bayley's role in the ASPR illustrates how a common set of social practices and Baconian sensibilities unified different areas of scientific knowledge production in this period. His understanding of science as a system of observation came not from meteorology or another field science, but rather from homeopathic medicine, which functioned in remarkably similar ways.

Bayley graduated from the homeopathic Hahnemann Medical College in 1888. The medicine of his day was characterized by power struggles among competing sects: allopathic physicians (today's mainstream medicine), homeopaths, osteopaths, and various others, each with their own theory about the causes and cures of disease. Despite efforts by mainstream doctors to ban homeopathy, Hahnemann Medical College was widely respected for placing science above sectarian dogma. During Bayley's time as a student, the college was ahead of many allopathic peers in cutting-edge clinical training. Embracing new methods from France and Germany, the school built sophisticated histology, pathology, and bacteriology labs; students learned that the modern scientific method was consistent with the experimental approach taken by homeopathy's founder, Samuel Hahnemann.[52]

The values that emerged from the intersection of Baconian empiricism and homeopathy, particularly the homeopathic principle of "proving," would profoundly shape Bayley's study of mental phenomena.[53] Hahnemann, the Leipzig physician who developed homeopathy in response to violent eighteenth-century therapies such as bloodletting and purging, built up his healing system by exhaustively testing countless medicines on himself, his family, colleagues, and students—a process he termed "proving." Proving resembled other inductive natural sciences in that it collated many observations of the particular in order to produce knowledge of the general. In the 1810s, Hahnemann formed the Union for Proving Remedies, devoted to the "holy purpose of seeking new and indispensable discoveries for the welfare of suffering humanity."[54] Those of his colleagues interested in "giving [their] time, even sacrificing [their] health" were invited to conduct systematic self-observation as they consumed various drugs. They were held to a rigorous dosage schedule, kept obsessive records of their bodily states, and submitted to regular interviews with Hahnemann, who vouched for their "absolute honesty of purpose."[55] Self-observation, he argued, produced not only better remedies, but also better physicians and scientists: "The best opportunity for exercising our sense of observation and to perfect it, is by proving medicines ourselves."[56]

Hahnemann's followers brought his philosophy to the United States in the 1830s and 40s. Among them was Constantine Hering, a German physician who founded the Hahnemann Medical College in the auspicious year of 1848, while the Smithsonian launched its weather project, the residents of Rochester made contact with the spirit world, and Europe erupted in revolutions.[57] Each of these developments emerged in its own way from improved communication technology producing or revealing new kinds of phenomena, seemingly crystallizing them out of the mental atmosphere. Hering made use of the United States' postal system to organize an American Provers' Union whose data flowed to his office in Philadelphia. Participants would develop "skill in self-observation . . . in distinguishing the minutest details of all the phenomena, objective and subjective . . . with a continually increasing certainty."[58] This focus on honing observational skill through introspective awareness placed homeopathic doctors in close and unexpected company with Smithsonian meteorologists and psychical researchers. All sought disciplined use of human and mechanical instruments "to see what others do not observe."[59]

The American Provers' Union represents another strand of a nineteenth-century epistemological web set up to capture subjective experience. Psychical researchers like Weston D. Bayley often joined a variety of such projects that used a common method of systematic but individualized observation. We can better understand Bayley's attraction to psychical research when we position him in the intellectual lineage of homeopathy, but a similar argument could be made for psychical researchers trained in any other observational science, whether heterodox or mainstream, amateur or professional.

In the early years of his medical practice, we find Bayley vigorously devoted to the advancement of his profession. He took on leadership roles in scientific societies—most charmingly, he served as secretary of the "Saturday Night Club for Microscopists."[60] He traveled around Pennsylvania, New Jersey, and Delaware presenting research to local homeopathic societies.[61] Obligatory reports on diuretics, however, did not prevent him from delving into psychical matters. At the 1897 meeting of Pennsylvania homeopaths, "much interest was awakened by a brilliantly successful hypnotic demonstration [of] mental phenomena by Weston D. Bayley, M.D., of Philadelphia."[62] Though Bayley's personal papers are lost, we know that he dedicated substantial correspondence to psychical phenomena—writing to friends, neighbors, and people he read about in the newspaper to collect their testimony on events they'd witnessed. He then passed his leads to Richard Hodgson, who endeavored, mostly without success, to follow up.

Hodgson's side of their correspondence survives; it begins in November of 1898, when he replied to Bayley's inquiry about a medium performing in the Philadelphia area as "Mrs. Ross." "There can be no doubt that she is a complete fraud," Hodgson wrote.[63] He received countless one-off queries about the veracity of this or that medium; because mediums were often itinerant, these letters would issue from one town after another following the performer's trail. But Bayley's interest was not limited to Mrs. Ross. The following spring, Bayley reported to Hodgson on three more mediums, along with a case of a premonition of death.[64] He included articles clipped from local newspapers, valuable information which would not otherwise have reached Hodgson in New York. His work was not limited to passing along news reports; he provided instructions for an "ingenious invention" to catch cheating mediums, which he designed and tested in a séance. "I am delighted . . . very glad indeed to have your record," Hodgson replied. Recognizing Bayley as a potentially valuable researcher, he began an effort to recruit him, inquiring "how far you might be inclined in case of such experiments to make a formal record with the view of publication." He suggested, repeatedly, that he "should be glad to have a formal report."

Although a formal report never materialized, Hodgson and Bayley became fast friends through their informal exchanges on the latest psychical happenings. Bayley continued to send newspaper clippings and anecdotal accounts to Hodgson, who continued to request more substantial investigations. "I am entertained by the summary of your experiences," Hodgson wrote in 1901. "Why couldn't you write an article about them for *Journal* or *Proceedings*?"[65] Nearly every letter from Hodgson contains such a plea; the answer seems always to have been a polite deferral.

Although Bayley was unable to provide Hodgson with the kind of scientific reports that the society so badly needed, he was hardly dead weight. In addition to conducting sporadic investigations, he also recruited badly needed new members. He referred at least four people for membership between 1900 and 1902 and vetted two others who made inquiries with Hodgson. If those members failed to pay their dues or behaved badly, it was Bayley who checked up on them.[66] When the society issued circulars and questionnaires to the public, Bayley received bundles to distribute among respectable Philadelphia families.[67] Bayley and Hodgson were soon exchanging theoretical fancies and vacationing together in neighboring cabins in the Maine woods. Neither could have anticipated that these would be Hodgson's last years; Bayley later described him as "athletic and dynamic," to all appearances in the prime of his life.[68]

Between 1898 and 1905, the ASPR was one among many of Bayley's commitments as a gentleman of science. He seemed more interested in the sociable aspects of the work than in producing the kind of documented results that Hodgson so desired. It is also noteworthy that his wife, Emily Bayley, appears in the rolls of the ASPR (at that time, technically the American Branch of the British SPR) in 1899, a year before Bayley himself joined. The interest of women in séances and trance mediums often influenced their husbands to seriously consider such phenomena, whether to affirm or disprove them, as Chapter 4 argues in greater depth.[69] Emily's membership could also have familiarized Bayley with the society's materials and convinced him of its respectability; simply getting the *Proceedings* of the ASPR into the hands of the curious was a powerful tool for the society. A scientific journal signified the professional values that set the ASPR above Spiritualists and showmen. Although Bayley was finally persuaded to put his name on the society's rolls, he mainly worked behind the scenes until Hodgson died. If the death of a loved one finally shifted his engagement with the spirit world into a more earnest register, he was certainly not alone among psychical researchers.

Friendship aside, Bayley did have a clear intellectual basis for moving between homeopathy, neurology, and psychical research. In 1903, he published an essay in Hahnemann's monthly newsletter urging a critical reexamination of the entire modern pharmacopeia in light of recent discoveries about the power of mental suggestion, the "potent influence" of mind upon body demonstrated in hypnosis and "alternating personality."[70] He went so far as to warn homeopaths that even the proving process could be thrown off by the personal equations of both patient and doctor. Like astronomers, homeopaths had to mold themselves into better, more disciplined instruments. Fifteen years later, Bayley would assert in the pages of the ASPR's *Proceedings* that "the chief material for the edifice of Psychical Research is the careful, accurate, detailed, scientific record of cases, to be used as material for classification, comparison, and interpretation."[71] In a sense, the ASPR was a type of provers' union, amassing the experiences of many percipients to seek underlying laws. Investigators wrangled with individual variability, the slipperiness of language, the inadequacy of self-report, and the indeterminacy of the phenomena themselves. Against this tide of uncertainty they built up a bulwark of cases.

Bayley was in many ways a representative turn-of-the-century physician, absorbed in advancing his profession and championing the scientific method as a universal balm for modern society. His early involvement with psychical research follows the pattern of scientists like Newcomb, who sought to extend the methodology of their own disciplines to the study of mind. Whether due to his choice of medical schools, his professional priorities, or his personal limitations, however, Bayley did not rise to Newcomb's elite status. For years he worked the middle ranks of the ASPR, where he brought new cases before the society, provided recruits, references, and local knowledge, and connected the "army of observers" to the society's leadership.

Knowledge at Ground Level: Local Societies

The ASPR's hierarchical structure was hardly the only model for psychical research in the United States. Widespread interest in Spiritualism, and long-standing popular devotion to the epistemology associated with Francis Bacon, led people across the country to form groups that applied the standards of the latter to the phenomena of the former. The injunction to test out and experience for oneself was built into the Spiritualist and mind-cure movements.[72] Participation in clubs and societies provided entertainment and gave expression to intellectual curiosity, especially for the growing number of Americans living far from East Coast urban centers.[73] Although we would class most of these small, local scientific societies as amateur in that they had no institutional affiliation or professional standing, their activities were widely respected.[74]

Respect for amateur groups also reflected the horizontal, networked structure of the country's emerging systems of scientific knowledge production. As discussed earlier in this chapter, trustworthy local observers were indispensable in the pursuit of Big Science's goals. Twentieth-century amateur science took on the stigma of the dilettante, the garage-putterer, and the hobbyist; it was a leisure pursuit because it duplicated labor already performed at a higher level by career researchers in universities and corporations—though in the twenty-first century, the ideology of "disruptive innovation" has led to an embrace of outsiders whose lack of expertise helps attract venture capital.[75] Still, doubting the authority of professional scientists carries undertones of paranoia; the most vigorous amateur research occurs in areas, like UFOlogy and cryptozoology, driven by conspiracy theories. Such amateurs are an irritant to the astrophysicist and the evolutionary biologist, who would prefer that the public tune in at the end of the research process as consumers of information or users of technology.[76]

Americans in the nineteenth and early twentieth centuries brought a different set of values to amateur science. When a phenomenon interested them, they could discuss it with neighbors and start a group to study it for themselves—as many did in fields from botany to psychical research. The ASPR, like the Smithsonian meteorological project, was attempting to unify a piecemeal observational system that included regional, state, and local groups. In practice, however, cooperation was not as self-evidently beneficial for psychical researchers as it was for weather watchers. Local groups declined to limit their investigations to the tedious mechanical tasks requested by the ASPR, and once the curiosity of participants was satisfied, they had difficulty continuing their work. In these local groups the inherent tensions between Baconianism, oriented towards individual experience, and observational science, dependent on large-scale standardized data collection, emerge most clearly.

The Davison Society for Psychical Research was formed in Davison, Michigan, in July of 1887. By October, the society had disbanded, each of its six members called elsewhere on business or personal matters. Ernest Hollenbeck, a retired schoolteacher and farmer, was the leader of the group, which included the Reverend Harold Bryant, Mrs. Bryant, their ten-year-old son Harry, and Merritt Custer Hutchins, the town's dentist. They met in the evenings in the Bryants' parlor. During four months of activity, the group specialized in the quantitative random-guessing experiments that the ASPR so desperately needed; the society had been soliciting this data in newspapers and magazines since 1885. One such advertisement inspired Hollenbeck to send his first letter to Richard Hodgson. "We have an informal society arranged to experimentation," he explained on August 2, enclosing with his letter the group's meeting minutes.[77]

Hollenbeck's minutes reveal careful attention to the standards of scientific experimentation. An agent and a percipient were chosen for each test, and the same test was performed repeatedly with different combinations of agents and percipients.[78] Tests involved random guessing—the agent opened to an arbitrary page in a book or drew a card from a deck of colors, numbers, or shapes and attempted to transmit this knowledge to the mind of the percipient. Hollenbeck sought to control for personal equations through careful record-keeping and cross-referencing of results (see Figure 4). "There seems to be a marked difference" in the thought-transference abilities of different subjects, he wrote. "Hutchins does better on numbers, Mrs. Bryant on color and form."[79] Further, he noted that "special bonds of sympathy exist between individuals." The Reverend Bryant and young Harry had remarkable success in guessing each other's thoughts, a phenomenon examined more closely in the Intimacy interlude following Chapter 3.[80]

The way he organized these experiments suggests that Hollenbeck was a careful reader of the psychical literature. Obtaining good information was challenging, however, as there were many texts and limited funds. "Which parts of Exp. Proceed. would you recommend us to get first as a guide to experimentation?" he asked Hodgson in his first letter, adding that "any suggestions from you in regard to methods will be well received."[81] Like many correspondents, Hollenbeck placed great value on the ASPR's publications and wanted to maximize the useful knowledge gained from purchasing the *Proceedings*; other writers found the journal in a library or begged for free copies, which were not forthcoming from the cash-strapped organization.

Hodgson praised Hollenbeck's pilot experiments and urged him to continue the group's work. Hollenbeck, however, had already moved off

BLANK A.

EXPERIMENTS ON THOUGHT-TRANSFERENCE.

GUESSING THE COLOR OF CARDS.

Agent's Name and Address ....

....

Percipient's Name and Address ....

....

PLACE,

Date.	RIGHT.			WRONG.			Total Answers.	Agent knowing Card. Yes or No.
	Red.	Black.	Totals.	Red.	Black.	Totals.		

FIGURE 4. A standardized form for recording telepathic card-guessing experiments. Blank A, Circular 4, *PASPR* 1 (1885): 14.

in a theoretical direction. In his next letters, he explained his theory about barometric pressure and thought-transference—a literal intrusion of the mental atmosphere which Hodgson did not welcome. From Hollenbeck's perspective, the theory was a perfectly good one based on empirical data from his career as a schoolteacher: "I observed things carefully," he explained, "as bearing on my professional success."[82] In this case, he noted that changes in his students' behavior correlated with the classroom's barometer (the presence of this instrument also tells us that Hollenbeck took readings at work and perhaps taught about the science of weather). The students misbehaved when the pressure dropped, suggesting a larger "relation of meteorology to morals."[83] This line of thinking clearly informed his telepathy experiments, in which he tried to find personal and environmental variables that explained changes in telepathic reception. Hodgson saw such ideas as an unfortunate distraction from reporting statistical data.

Not satisfied with his anecdotal observations, Hollenbeck proposed a large-scale experiment on public schoolchildren using the methods of psychologist G. Stanley Hall, whose work Hollenbeck, as an "enthusiast in education," would have encountered in pedagogy journals.[84] Hollenbeck went so far as to specify that his study should take place "in four Boston schools," an interesting detail since he had only lived and worked in small-town Michigan. He may have been following Hall's example, but this also suggests his hope that the ASPR, with its strong Boston presence, would actually implement his plan to measure the effect of barometric pressure on the "moral conditions of pupils."[85]

If the ASPR had been a fully horizontal or a fully democratic organization, Hollenbeck's proposal would have just as strong a claim on its resources as the many others it received; participants were very interested in the mental atmosphere. However, the society had clearly outlined a research agenda more compatible with current academic psychology, and Hodgson struggled to keep his correspondents focused on that agenda. The ASPR lacked funding and personnel to launch additional projects, no matter how complementary they might be. It needed foot soldiers, competent people like Hollenbeck, to generate data by guessing numbers, shapes, and colors. However, people with the enthusiasm to organize their friends and neighbors into scientific societies were rarely content to serve as mere observing and recording machines. They were motivated by a curiosity and desire for meaning that made psychical researchers very difficult to regiment.

Another problem for the ASPR was the transience of groups like the Davison Society. By October of 1887, all the members of Hollenbeck's circle had left central Michigan. Hollenbeck wrote that he hoped to "renew our work when opportunity presents," but this would be his last letter to Hodgson regarding their circle.[86] Hollenbeck only joined the ASPR briefly, in 1888, and published a report in the *Proceedings* about an experience of dream telepathy.[87] He disappeared from the rolls within a year, perhaps deciding to spend his money on other scientific journals. Psychical research was one of many outlets for Hollenbeck's ample intellectual curiosity. His letters reveal wide-ranging interests, from fruit preserving to Greek poetry to bird-watching. He subscribed to an assortment of technical and scientific periodicals and plunged into the community of inquiry that these publications brought to his door. Hollenbeck was prepared to observe any interesting phenomenon that presented itself, be it passenger pigeons or telepathic dreams. Everyday life was a field for scientific observation.

Hollenbeck and the Davison Society for Psychical Research were no anomaly. Similar groups thrived in an American landscape of subscription books, periodicals, and lecture tours catering to science enthusiasts.[88] They belonged to a community of inquiry, and of inquisitiveness, that valued careful observation, respectability, and common sense. In this book's Introduction, we met Herbert L. Spence of Cincinnati, Ohio, who wrote to William James seeking guidance for his own club of psychical investigators.[89] Spence did not, however, see the ASPR as an obviously superior venue for such research. "If we join the American branch," he asked warily, "can we here fall into regular systematic work?"[90] Spence was well aware of the irregularities that plagued psychical research at all levels and needed assurances that his scientific values would be upheld.

James forwarded Spence's letter to Richard Hodgson, who satisfied Spence's concerns about the rigor of the ASPR's work. "For some years," Spence enthused, "I have failed to find such a source of information as your Society now offers."[91] To Hodgson's dismay, he seemed to view the ASPR not as the destination for data generated in his research, but rather as a model of how to produce better data for his own club. This attitude, common to many local groups, led to the frequent disappointment of ASPR leaders hoping for energetic foot soldiers. "Send them circulars!" James urged Hodgson upon receiving Spence's first letter. "I have written to him urging investigation for the sake of publication. Do thou likewise!"[92] No such publication would result from Spence's work; if his club pursued psychical investigation, they felt no need to register their experiences in the would-be center of calculation.

This pattern repeated with various other local groups. Wealthy knitting-machine manufacturer John Edward Woodhead, who established the Western Society for Psychical Research in Chicago the same year that the ASPR was founded in Boston, wrote to Richard Hodgson in a somewhat defensive tone. "I have collected quite an array of coincidences," he declared, but he did "not wish to furnish my evidence to any Society or individual for publication, I think I ought to reserve that privilege for myself." Woodhead supposed the two societies in competition, although there's no evidence that Hodgson asked for his data. Remarkably, despite refusing in advance to cooperate with the ASPR, Woodhead sought Hodgson's expert advice on how to assure "vigilance and judgment in collecting the evidence."[93]

As their correspondence proceeded, Woodhead warmed to the idea of working together to standardize psychical research. Finally, he sent Hodgson his strongest cases to authenticate "as you may deem best, and then send me a report of the result of your investigation."[94] This conversion is a testament to Hodgson's personal magnetism. Within a few months, he'd persuaded a rival organization that pooling their cases was essential for the success of their shared endeavor: "Your committee are at liberty to use any report I may make," Woodhead granted, even allowing, in the name of science, that the ASPR could "criticize [the reports], as they chose."[95] At least one prospective foot soldier had embraced the need for an objective, centralized "bureau for apparitions."

Although younger and less authoritative than Woodhead, Solomon Quint of Brooklyn wrote the ASPR to air his club's concerns. He and his colleagues were upset by James Hyslop's public statements deriding a popular medium named Joseph Mercedes. "We are a number of college graduates and have ever since our leaving college belonged to a society for psychical research," he explained, foregrounding the education and experience of his group. He excoriated Hyslop for presuming to dismiss "a subject that is still such a mystery."[96] The ASPR aspired to be the national face of psychical research and used its authority to debunk fraudulent mediums like Mercedes, but it faced perhaps greater difficulty disciplining constituents like Quint. Hodgson successfully persuaded Woodhead to join the program as a data collector, but Quint saw this demand as hypocritical, since the ASPR had drawn a conclusion about the medium Mercedes before all the facts were in. In a democratic science, Quint argued, there should be no exceptions to the laws of inductive reasoning, and his group would henceforward spurn any connection with the ASPR.

Observing Individuals

The majority of reports sent to the ASPR were not from members of organized groups who sought out psychical phenomena in a controlled way. Rather, they came from individuals who had seen things they could not explain, individuals like New Jersey circuit court judge Frank T. Lloyd, who confessed, "I have always been disinclined to give credence to such incidents . . . but this occurrence has impressed me."[97] Often, these people were referred to the ASPR by friends or had spotted an advertisement in the newspaper. Flora Ticknor found a "post-note" for the ASPR in her high school psychology textbook—William James's *Psychology*—and wrote the author hoping that he could "solve the mystery" of a telepathic coincidence.[98] A report required no sustained commitment—only a passing interest. Because they described events that had already occurred, there was no preemptive opportunity for the ASPR to shape reporters into skilled observers. Proper record-keeping procedures were rarely observed in spontaneous occurrences, and witnesses struggled to recall details after the fact.

Given these difficulties with using anecdotal reports as evidence, one might wonder why the ASPR devoted scarce resources to soliciting and verifying them. On one hand, this commitment reflected their under-standing of psychical research as a field science pursuing rare, unpredict-able phenomena. On the other hand, they used such correspondence to train observers to follow the scientific method in the future. Over the course of countless exchanges, we see Hodgson, James, Hyslop, and Walter Franklin Prince trying to inculcate habits of critical analysis and generally to craft a public that was sober and savvy about psychical phenomena.

Efforts along these lines were not often successful. Individuals re-pelled by the ASPR's insistence on scientific protocols sought out Spiri-tualists, Theosophists, and other groups that embraced the sensational. "The whole civilized world increasingly becomes the scene of a confused welter of amateur investigation," William McDougall complained in 1927.[99] Enforcing the values of academic science on amateur partici-pants who came to the table with a variety of motivations was a challenge that also affected meteorology and astronomy in the late nineteenth cen-tury. These disciplines show that different strategies were available for managing scientific societies in flux, but the comparison also highlights the unique constraints of organized psychical research.

In the early years of the society, many letters arrived addressed to its most well-known figure, William James. Quickly overwhelmed by this on-slaught, James forwarded the letters to Richard Hodgson, who effectively ran the society from 1886 until his death in 1905.[100] James Hyslop and Walter Prince managed the bulk of correspondence after reestablishing the ASPR in 1906. Between Hodgson, Hyslop, and Prince, we see a range of styles for attempting to discipline and direct the energies of new re-cruits. I discuss them in order of critical severity, rather than chrono-logically, beginning with the generous Hodgson, then the sterner Prince, and finally Hyslop, who generally acted the curmudgeon.

During almost two decades as ASPR secretary, Hodgson fostered the enthusiasm, if not the productivity, of correspondents with an air of ge-nial encouragement, as we saw with Bayley the homeopath and Woodson the Chicago industrialist. Hodgson relied on the tools of gentlemanly science—testimonials from witnesses, inquiries about the character and education of the individuals involved—and his correspondents often answered with more goodwill than accuracy. Mary Paddock Reese, of Mound City, Kansas, communicated with Hodgson for four years, sending copies of articles that she wrote for popular magazines. When he asked for experimental results, she replied that she would "furnish anything interesting" and stopped writing shortly thereafter.[101] William Romaine Newbold, a philosopher at the University of Pennsylvania, concluded that his own report was "in no sense evidential and wouldn't do for print."[102] In his correspondence with the public, Hodgson simply urged better record-keeping, tactfully withholding his opinion about the evidence on the table. His criticism appears only in margin notes used within the ASPR office to indicate the value of reports: "Conditions of expt. not very clearly described"; "no corroborative evidence given"; "experiments not systematic"; "unsupported and too laconic assertion."[103] Despite dealing with many thousands of reports that failed to meet scientific standards, Hodgson found value in the narratives as a corpus of experience that supported his own personal beliefs. He seemed to draw energy from the act of correspondence itself and continued his work in excellent spirits until his untimely death.

Walter Prince was the most insistent of the ASPR's leaders on the need for large-scale collection of data from the public.[104] However, his desire for scientific rigor led him to take a prescriptive and occasionally admonitory tone, in contrast with Hodgson's collegiality. Some correspondents were amenable to Prince's demands; Anna Berger, of Bridgeport, Connecticut, gamely answered an extensive list of questions that he posed about her treasured collection of spirit photographs, only to receive the disappointing reply that the photographer "was having a little fun with you."[105] Many less committed correspondents lost interest in the face of burdensome demands for details and witnesses; they'd hoped for expert validation of their experiences and instead received a curt interrogation.

Others took umbrage at criticism that they perceived, not incorrectly, as a slight to their mental capacities. "I ran across something which looked like telepathy last week," wrote Prince's friend Samuel Copp Worthen, describing a psychic stage show in which the performer located objects hidden by audience members.[106] Prince replied by chastising Worthen for his "very meager description," but excused his friend on the grounds that "it would be a difficult matter for one who is an amateur in these things, even though he is a most intelligent lawyer, to note and report any sufficient account which to a person of long experience in this particular line would be eloquent of the method used."[107] That is to say, Worthen wasn't quick enough to catch the performer's sleight of hand.

Worthen, a prominent New York attorney, was not pleased with the intimation of base amateurism: "No; I did not suppose I had given you sufficient data," he huffed. "I did not undertake to approach the matter as a careful or close observer . . . I did not imagine that I was conducting an experiment of any kind." He was merely curious, he wrote, as to whether Prince knew of the performer's methods. "I don't think I shall take up your line of research," Worthen concluded.[108] Although Worthen took it personally, the "very meager description" was a refrain of Prince's; he repeatedly chastised correspondents for neglecting to record important information.

James Hyslop's correspondence style resembled Prince's, with the distinction that Hyslop, who served as ASPR president from 1906 until 1920, was less tactful about criticizing his would-be scientific foot soldiers. For example, G. H. Hinrichs, of Davenport, Iowa, wrote to the ASPR in 1909 reporting a telepathic experience: his friend had a vision of a picture at the same moment that Hinrichs was painting it. Hyslop dismissed Hinrichs's story as unsubstantiated; in his next letter, Hinrichs was "riled" that Hyslop ignored his offer to "gather for you such data as you might want" in regard to the incident. "If you are waiting for the colleges to move the world, you will have to wait a long while," Hinrichs admonished, alluding to the fact that psychical research depended upon independent researchers like himself. Hinrichs had belonged to the Davenport Academy of Natural Sciences since 1883, serving on the academy's finance committee and donating specimens from his travels.[109] "This is a case where an ounce of personal experience is worth more than a ton of evidence given by others, be it ever so scientific."[110] William James could have uttered these very words about the value of first-hand experience, and Hyslop, in the abstract, could have agreed; but in practice, Hyslop's response to a poorly documented report was to chastise and alienate the reporter.

Hyslop declined many opportunities for the cultivation of amateur observers. In 1918, he rejected the membership application of a self-described "sixteen-year-old boy psychologist" from San Diego on the grounds that the teenager could not afford to pay dues. J. R. Ashton's letter shows a precocious appreciation of the ASPR's scientific goals: "I have always tried to analyze and get to the bottom as scientifically as possible," Ashton wrote, explaining that he had mastered sleight of hand so that he could better expose fraudulent psychic mediums. "I read the Journal at the public library, and may subscribe to it as I like the cautious and careful investigations of your organization." When he admitted, however, that he had no money, Hyslop replied, "I do not know of any way that membership may be obtained except through payment of fees." To seal the rejection, Hyslop accused him of being a childish wonder-seeker—whereas a scientific society is "occupied solely with the collection and recording of certified facts."[111]

Given the hundreds of letters that they received each month, it seems plausible that Hyslop and Prince simply could not equal Hodgson's enthusiasm in dealing with the public. Hyslop was known among colleagues for his gruff disposition, while Prince, though quite personable, saw himself as a torchbearer of the scientific method and refused to compromise by entertaining enthusiasts and Spiritualists.[112] Their role as ambivalent gatekeepers was not unique. Meteorologists and astronomers dealt with the same issue—amateurs accustomed to the appreciative reception of their work had to be disciplined more strictly as standards of evidence became more precise.

Psychical experiences were inextricably attached to their witnesses. In turn, those witnesses were attached to identities, social roles, beliefs, and histories. As long as amateurs could use psychical research as a staging ground for the interests that motivated them, they would not stop writing letters, and as long as expert psychical researchers could not detach phenomena from subjective experience, they would continue to plead for more details, better record-keeping, and character testimonials. During the time that they were bound together by a shared process of inquiry, they managed their differences and functioned as a scientific community. The ASPR's disintegration—or in the assessment of some, its failure to launch—corresponded with challenges facing similar communities devoted to meteorology and astronomy around the turn of the century.

The network of weather observers first mobilized in the late 1830s continued to form the backbone of meteorology into the 1870s, when the federal government took charge of the system.[113] This development met with little opposition from amateur observers, as it furthered the shared goal of obtaining more and better data. Even with a new generation of trained professional meteorologists on staff, the Weather Bureau continued to rely in part on amateurs to take readings; in 1890, under pressure from states to provide better local information, it established the Cooperative Observer Program, which formally integrated volunteer observers into the Bureau. Their productive working relationship was based on a shared understanding of weather as integral to human welfare and commerce.[114]

The ASPR's leaders at first sought a similar congenial relationship with amateurs, a mutually accepted hierarchy in which data collectors in the field served the needs of experts in a center of calculation, while still enjoying their encounters with interesting phenomena. However, amateur psychical researchers had a very limited interest in standardizing their observations. They understood and extolled this principle in theory, but it seldom motivated them in practice. Enforcing such a hierarchy from the top required some claim to superior expertise—yet, as the disgruntled G. H. Hinrichs pointed out, universities did not accept the basic premise of psychical research, there were no departments to grant degrees, and the authority of the ASPR's leaders was easily challenged. Moreover, the society's paper instruments, though designed with clear guidelines, still allowed and in fact required subjective storytelling. Psychical researchers could not hope to simply factor out the personal equation as some meteorologists and astronomers claimed to have done with the advent of self-registering precision instruments. Looking more closely at debates within these disciplines, we see that the personal equation never truly went away but was enclosed in the black box of objectivity and professionalization—a box which the ASPR could not nail shut.

It now appears that the discipline of psychology made a strategic choice by rejecting the field and the "mental atmosphere," instead turning inward to the laboratory and the individual. However, the need to choose one or the other course was itself a construction of psychology's professionalizers, men like Hugo Münsterberg and Joseph Jastrow, who felt their ascent in the academy threatened by amateur participation and sensational phenomena. The personal equation was simply removed from public view in laboratories devoted to psychophysics and behaviorism, heading off the public contention over the nature of experience that dragged psychical research to the fringes.

William James, of course, believed that human experience was psychology's central concern. He resisted the mechanistic models of mind that would dominate his discipline in the twentieth century, and for that reason, was remembered by philosophers and forgotten, for decades, by psychologists.[115] It is an atmospheric notion of mind, as a system of pressures and currents sometimes erupting into storms, that weaves through his work. His weather metaphors evoke meteorology's success in capturing an elusive phenomenon; they also gesture toward the possibility of uniting amateur and professional, lab and field.

In *Pragmatism*, James compared the Weather Bureau's systematization of meteorological data with the mental process of stringing together "the everlasting weather of our perceptions" into a coherent conscious experience.

> The word weather is a good one to use here. In Boston, for example, the weather has almost no routine. Weather experience as it thus comes to Boston, is discontinuous and chaotic . . . it may change three times a day. But the Washington weather-bureau intellectualizes this disorder by making each successive bit of Boston weather episodic. It refers it to its place and moment in a continental cyclone, on the history of which the local changes everywhere are strung as beads are strung upon a cord.[116]

The "discontinuous and chaotic" nature of our sensorium and the mind's amazing ability to produce a unified experience of self are central concepts in James's philosophy. At the same time, this metaphor highlights the practical work that psychical research could do to translate its field reports into a unified scientific vision of mental phenomena as a "continental cyclone" governed by higher laws not apparent to observers on the ground. Just as the Weather Bureau "intellectualizes this disorder" of Boston's chaotic climate, James hoped to generate a synoptic map of the mental atmosphere that revealed the continuity of seemingly disparate experiences.

Despite his commitment to this project—for which he risked career and reputation—the chaos of correspondence constantly undermined James's efforts. He admitted that the piles of narratives he received were "a weariness, and I must confess . . . almost intolerable to me." He again dreamed of "a central bureau in the charge of proved experts, towards which all threads converge, thereby providing for a maximum of facts."[117] We don't know what James's synoptic map of the mind would have looked like, or what it could have revealed, because this process inevitably stalled without institutional resources and clerical labor. What we do have are the voices of psychical researchers at all levels—national leaders, regional representatives, and ordinary foot soldiers—and a rich record of their working relationships. Their difficulty staying within the lines of standardized tables and forms allows us to see not just data, but also the work of crafting oneself into a scientific observer, and to feel the limitations of parsing experience in this way. As much as they felt themselves part of a mental atmosphere, and despite the scientific and social urgency of mapping it, they often refused to relinquish authority over their experiences—which is to say, in the spirit of American Baconianism, they reserved the right to draw their own conclusions.

TEDIUM

By 1892, the ASPR had tallied 6,311 responses to the Census of Hallucinations that William James launched in the United States three years previously. Fortunately for James, 5,459 people answered no to the question, "Have you ever, when believing yourself to be completely awake, had the vivid impression of seeing or being touched by a living being . . . or of hearing a voice . . . not due to any external cause?" It was the remaining 852 cases that would bog him down for years in what he called a "terribly slouchy piece of work": trying to coax names, dates, corroborating testimony, or any response at all from the yeses. Never a data hound, he admitted to letting the correspondence "get into arrears," while the correspondents themselves "obstinately refused to reply in a great many cases."[1] Ultimately, the ASPR's secretary, Richard Hodgson, and assistant secretary, Lucy Edmunds, salvaged the American census enough to compose a brief final report. Despite the astonishing narratives buried among the census returns, despite the potential for proof of communication between minds or the survival of the soul after death, making good stories into good science was mind-numbing work. It required a plodding determination that James, to his embarrassment, could not muster. Still, he did his best to inspire that commitment in others, hoping to find personalities more suited to tedium—those who could reap the rewards that he sincerely believed it would yield.

The moralization of attention is familiar to us in the twenty-first century, as people struggle against or give way to the endless distraction of the internet and smart devices. The ability to leap from one hyperlinked fact to another, to glide across the surface of things, has shaped our thinking in subtle ways—experts warn that we consume more information and understand less. That warning can carry a moral charge, pushing guilt and anxiety on technology users for their sins of impatience, their addiction to novel stimuli. When I need to answer a question, I often catch myself thinking in search engine keywords. Is knowledge what appears on a screen when I enter the right combination of terms?

Our attenuated time frame of thought affects how researchers work and how the public experiences research: powerful algorithms do tedious things for us, and we publicize the results using powerful algorithms. This approach is very beneficial to the careers of those who use it, rapidly churning out information that no one will ever pause to understand. In science, as in everyday life, moral arguments come into play: while technology generates immediate economic value, critics assert the moral value of slowness. True scientific inquiry attends to the epistemological basis of knowledge, takes care to correct error, and identifies the need for new paradigms. Perhaps the ideal scientist is one who combs all the data herself, as James tried and failed to do with his Census of Hallucinations. At the same time, actual scientists in real research settings have long been insulated from the laborious process of data accumulation and sorting by secretaries, calculators, and technicians. Digital computers easily replaced human calculators, and today's entrepreneurs intend to automate other low-status technical jobs in the name of efficiency. Under inspection, tedium has very strange properties. It's both a prime scientific virtue and an unpleasant necessity outsourced to workers whose attention is less valuable. Psychical research forces us to confront the double life of tedium because its tasks never resolved into high and low, scientist and technician; the kind of knowledge needed to generate its basic data was self-knowledge, which proved impossible to standardize and scale up.

The heroism of tedium is not a uniquely modern sentiment. It conjures older scenes, of desert hermits and manuscript-copying monks, a disciplined devotion to something beyond the self, something so vast that it can only be glimpsed through the labor of many human lifetimes. For early modern natural philosophers, the effort to know and praise God was synonymous with the effort to know and praise nature. A sanctity inherent to this economically nonproductive labor carried through to the nineteenth century and shines like a gold-leafed halo around the stately mien of Charles Darwin, the secular saint of modern science— Darwin, who famously spent twenty years accumulating evidence for his theory of evolution. Writers celebrating his epoch-making achievement cast him as something of a hermit in the desert whose prayer was data. The tragic turn in this analogy is that Darwin, a man of deep religious faith, would be accused of killing God and undermining the sanctity of creation. However, few promoters of evolutionary theory in the nineteenth century espoused atheism, and in the disputes between liberal and conservative Christians that followed *On the Origin of Species*, Darwin's liberal defenders continued to associate his solitary labors with practices of spiritual devotion, even penance. Darwin regretted certain youthful publications that partook in "the sin of speculation" and dedicated his subsequent career to a rigorous and austere pursuit of data.[2] There were other examples of widely admired "slow science" before and after, but Darwin became its figurehead, unbowed by worldly temptations.

Saintly tedium was certainly not the only scientific ideal. Thomas Edison represents its inverse, the frantic speed and excitement of ever-accelerating progress, the immense wealth to be gained through the merger of genius and enterprise. Promoters of this ideal were unabashed about the selfish ends of science. "There is not an element in nature, or a known property of matter," proclaimed the South Carolina orator Charles Fraser, "that has not been rendered subservient to [man's] comfort."[3] Such grandiose claims, however, did not speak to the growing ranks of academic scientists. Though eager to gain authority and respect, they feared yoking basic science to profitable applications. Most research, they knew, produced nothing tangible; increased mastery yielded increasingly obscure and useless knowledge. When attempting to shape their own narrative, they would choose tedium over speed, the saint over the dynamo. An emerging science would do well to decline the rhetoric of acceleration and depict itself as slow and boring but virtuous and respectable.

Psychical research in the 1880s was struggling to escape it association with tawdry séances where mediums vomited gauze and played levitating trumpets. For psychical researchers, boredom and the mundane became talismans of belonging to proper science. Inherently unorthodox in theory, they strove for orthodoxy in their methods and rhetoric, emulating Darwin, but also disciplines like astronomy, physics, and meteorology that had successfully professionalized over the previous fifty years. While press coverage of psychical phenomena gladly wallowed in the sensational ("Ghost stories tested—Weird tales investigated") the ASPR tried to disseminate normalizing narratives of tedium. "There will be no room for curiosity seekers or triflers," one journalist warned of a New York ASPR meeting; a Philadelphia reporter noted that investigators "fully recognize the exceptional difficulties," yet "they hope that by patient and systematic effort some results of permanent value may be attained."[4] This was the gospel of St. Darwin, and, in addition to psychical researchers, it won some unexpected adherents.

Elizabeth Stuart Phelps was the author of *The Gates Ajar*, a blockbuster novel that introduced millions of Americans to Spiritualism in the 1860s. *Gates* established a new popular vision of the afterlife: its protagonists rejoined family, friends, and even pets in an idyllic domestic sphere where the dead baked pies and pruned roses. Though this vision seems treacly today, Phelps's sentimental heaven offered a liberating alternative to fire-and-brimstone revivalism that emphasized the agonies of hell. Moreover, Phelps based her account on what many believed was objective evidence: the revelations of mediums who received direct communication from the spirit world. Spiritualists saw themselves as champions of scientific empiricism, insisting that knowledge would emerge from the collection of verified firsthand experiences. They invited academic study of spirit communication and cheered on scientific progress—at least until the late 1880s and 90s, when continued rebuffs from psychical researchers and psychologists finally led to an unamicable parting of ways. In 1885, though, with organized psychical research just beginning, Phelps saw the ASPR as an ally in her cause. She reported on the society's formation in an article for the popular *North American Review* that underscored the scientific virtue of tedium: "Here we have to deal with an inchoate accumulation of mind-facts or soul-facts . . . land-slides of material . . . [Researchers] must condescend—to the infinite drudgery of discovery."[5]

James's agony over the Census of Hallucinations had its counterpart in the parlors of ASPR members who generated their own "land-slides" of data. The Committee on Thought Transference distributed instructions for experiments that used playing cards, numbers, colors, and dice to test for telepathy. An "agent" would draw a playing card or roll the dice and concentrate on the result, while the "percipient" attempted to receive this message from the agent without any communication through the "known avenues of sense."[6] Ten-year-old Harry Bryant, of Davison, Michigan, showed a knack for this telepathic guessing game when his parents brought him to a meeting of their psychical research circle. Enduring the repetition proved a greater challenge because "he was impatient to be away at play."[7] The instructions called for one hundred guesses per series. Researchers believed that attention was a crucial variable in telepathy, so when Harry flubbed, his parents blamed his distractedness. "After the failures his father remonstrated sharply," the secretary noted, "after which the answers came promptly and correct." Experimenter fatigue was a notorious impediment to collecting quantitative data.

For a ten-year-old, guessing cards was a tedious chore; for adults who enjoyed sophisticated intellectual pursuits, James acknowledged that it might feel like drudge work that fell below their station, "repellent and undignified."[8] Members of the Committee on Thought Transference pressured their family, friends, and neighbors into generating the results discussed at their June 1885 meeting. Unfortunately, this cosmopolitan crowd of professors and businessmen produced "an insufficient number of trials" to draw statistically sound conclusions. Boston offered a cornucopia of lectures, concerts, and parties; like Harry Bryant, these potential experimenters were "impatient to be away at play."

One solution to attention deficit lay in America's sleepy hinterland, where city dwellers imagined that people had nothing better to do than sit around trying to read each other's minds. ASPR president Simon Newcomb quipped that "west of the Mississippi River there are probably several hundred thousand persons whose chief amusement is the playing of a game of cards," and thus it wouldn't be hard to switch them from gin rummy to telepathy.[9] Newcomb's rather insulting view of small-town life overlooked the reality that people in the west, like the

Bryants in Michigan, were eager for connections with centers of learning in the east; they subscribed to scientific news and participated in amateur societies. The country's founders staked the success of participatory democracy on just such an enlightened populace, but the ASPR found self-directed learners unsuited to their needs. Despite Newcomb's fantasy that the Midwest was full of dull, unquestioning card-guessers, a small-town pastor could be just as distractible as a Boston socialite.

Newcomb flippantly presumed that a group of people different from himself in location and social status had a lower bar for what constituted a fulfilling experience. William James, on the other hand, was one of the most prominent scientific writers to empathize with the human need for meaning in an increasingly trivial and materialistic world.[10] Many expressions of this need arrived directly in James's mailbox, and as a public philosopher he guided people towards the pursuit of meaning in everyday life. Yet he, too, got snagged on what he called the "accidental fences" of language, class, education, and self-presentation that separate us.[11] In psychical research, the problem of tedium wasn't limited to telepathic card-guessing. People, not cards, were the real data, and certain kinds of people appeared unworthy of sustained attention.

These accidental fences become part of the archive, determining how people's intimate, profound experiences are stored, accessed, and valued by history. I wish that, as a researcher, I could approach the ASPR's bales of yellowing letters with unguarded openness. But I feel the same recoil that James described. First: what a tedious task lies before me—everything is out of order, none of the names mean anything, terrible penmanship is the rule—my day will be an aimless drift through the flotsam of the unremembered dead. And second, the unbidden thought: Who are these people, and why should I believe them? I fix on meaningless clues to make assumptions about whether a letter is worth deciphering. I know these assumptions are unfair; I attribute my skepticism to the overwhelming scale of the task. A traveling salesman writes from Duluth on hotel stationery, his ornate script looks disingenuous. Another letter is scrawled illegibly across fifteen newsprint rectangles, whose intended order I spend half an hour reconstructing. Could I narrow my search criteria to screen some of this out? If I did, I'd never know what I was missing.

Unlike James, I have no scientific ambitions. Yet the virtue of tediousness is very much at the heart of historical work as well: unearthing new evidence, combing through it, building a case. Initially, I suggested that my project would include the coding and quantitative analysis of the ASPR archives. I stated my intention to sort these hundreds of letters according to the location, gender, occupation, and experience of their authors. This is embarrassing to admit, because it wouldn't be very hard; it simply, in the end, did not interest me. There is much that could be made visible with these methods, much that I can't see from within the forest of documents. I inhabited the tedium of reading strangers' intimate experiences as a sort of devotional practice. The accidental fences broke down, the reflex to judge, dismiss, or recoil faded away. I felt that I had glimpsed something true and much larger than myself, but this is not an objectively verifiable claim. Looking at it now, I realize that I was caught up in the same current of experience that pulled psychical researchers away from ever finishing their work. There is something to the fear of contamination that made reputable scientists edge away from this field. One takes on an anecdotal hyperspecificity and a metaphysical vagueness. Though it's possible I was like that already.

The ASPR recognized these tendencies and tried both psychological and technical tricks to channel participants into quantitatively productive labor. Elizabeth Phelps's ode to drudgery made "tedious and repellent" work romantic by infusing it with a deep spiritual purpose, part of a distant revelation that the individual investigator might not live to see. James similarly praised the nobility of "patient study," evoking Darwin and Pasteur to galvanize amateur participants for long evenings of card-guessing which he himself found "almost intolerable."[12] Preprinted forms and the automatic dice-roller smoothed over logistical annoyances. ASPR leaders recognized, from their own experience, that monotony had a real impact on data quality, even when participants endured it willingly. The repetitive motion of rolling a die allows the mind to wander. Try it; after twenty rolls, numbers become meaningless.

People who began the ASPR's tasks in good faith soon discovered obstacles to diligent experimentation. Correspondents would begin enthusiastically enough; "I shall be glad to be made of use!" exclaimed W.

Lambert, of Chicago.[13] Vida D. Scudder assumed that "psychical experiments are pouring in . . . and that you are formulating hosts of interesting conclusions," but her own aborted effort was more the norm. After a promising initial round, she "tried to organize some more experiments, but . . . found it impossible, since no one seemed to be in the right mood."[14] Time was short, conditions were bad, confederates withdrew.

As William James pointed out, the need to work for a living stood in the way of saintly devotion to psychical research for most middle-class American participants, in contrast to their English counterparts who funded scientific pursuits with hereditary wealth.[15] The desert hermit takes a vow of poverty, the monk lives on churchgoers' tithes, and Darwin's father purchased the famous Down House for him. Tedium was a luxury that Americans in their economic rat race could not afford. The ASPR received regular inquiries about academic programs that might support full-time psychical research, of which there were none. James Wiswell Mudge, a Harvard Law School graduate, asked where he could receive "a thorough training in psychology" to advance the science of psychical research. "I am not a person of independent wealth, unfortunately, and have to earn my own living," he wrote, explaining that he had hoped to return to Harvard for a psychology degree but found it unaffordable.[16]

Within academic disciplines, configurations of power, expertise, and authority determine who plays what role in the process of knowledge-making. Amateur psychical researchers had no reason to limit themselves to the mundane role that the ASPR envisioned for them. No one paid them to endure the tedious rigors of normal science; in that regard, it was only fair that they wore their emotional, philosophical, and social motivations on their sleeves. Although they valued the quantitative paradigm that called for mechanized, depersonalized labor, they, like Melville's Bartleby, simply preferred not to. Their correspondence quickly veered into the topics of wireless telegraphy, demonic possession, or the role of atmospheric pressure in human behavior, while the promised experiments never materialized. Here was another boundary problem: when it came to the human mind as an object of study, the "collection and recording of certified facts" constantly overflowed into meaning, narrative, and experience.[17]

Elizabeth Stuart Phelps, attempting to rouse psychical researchers to Darwin's "superhuman patience of observation and recording," posed the question, "Why, then, should not a man keep tally of the relative number of times that a blindfold subject will select the right card from a pack?"[18] Certainly, this practice reflected the tedious virtue of normal science. However, many amateurs answered that a man should not keep such a tally because it was very boring. Like E. E. Adele of Groveport, Ohio, they were most intrigued by psychical occurrences stemming from "healthy, joyous, natural" activities, where "there seemed to be no effort made."[19] The kind of reward they expected from their research differed in kind from Darwin's "masterpiece of relentless logic." It came in fleeting experience: "The agent feeling a sensation of transmitted power quite indescribable; the percipient responding instantly with the correct number, and with an intense mental certainty that it was correct."[20] Ernest Hollenbeck, of the Davison circle of psychical researchers, recorded this vivid telepathic moment a few months before the group parted ways forever and left its investigation unfinished.

CHAPTER 2

MACHINES THAT
DREAM TOGETHER

"I work all the time, even while sleeping—
even in my dreams!"[1]

I n the predawn of July 21, 1865, a young man in Cambridge, Massachusetts, woke from a deep sleep with strange words on his lips. "What they
dare to dream of dare to die for," he recalled saying to himself, before slipping back into unconsciousness, wondering dimly "whether [the words]
really expressed a lofty thought, or were merely lofty in sound."[2] Later that
day, the man was surprised to hear the line delivered from a podium by
the eminent poet James Russell Lowell, at a Harvard commemoration ceremony for students killed in the Civil War. Lowell's version replaced "dare
to die for" with "dare to do," a discrepancy which left the man, who gave
his name as Mr. W., pondering "whether I liked his sentiment or mine the
most." Decades after the coincidence, Mr. W. still recalled it vividly enough
to submit his account to Harvard psychologist William James, "hoping that
these reminiscences may be amusing to your society"—that is, the ASPR.
The correspondent's effort in submitting a report after a lapse of more
than thirty years perhaps belies his self-deprecating tone.

Whatever amusement Mr. W. felt was clearly mixed with a real conviction that he had received the line during a liminal state of consciousness, possibly as a telepathic impression direct from Lowell's mind. If
this was Mr. W.'s understanding, it would be consistent with a myth of artistic inspiration which later grew up around Lowell's performance that
day. The poet claimed that he was stricken with writer's block until the
night before the ceremony, when "[the Ode] was written with vehement
speed . . . it all came with a rush, literally making me lean and so nervous

that I was weeks in getting over it."[3] He reported writing most of the piece between 10 p.m. and 4 a.m.[4] Literary scholars treat this origin story with a bit of skepticism, suggesting that it is a "psychologically realistic, but historically unreliable" piece of self-mythologizing on Lowell's part. It's difficult to say whether Mr. W.'s retrospective account, submitted in 1889, was influenced by Lowell's story, which made the rounds in literary circles for years before appearing in print in his 1893 collected letters. Mr. W. implies that he was in sympathy with Lowell's sudden inspiration, reflecting a widespread understanding that intense psychic impressions were transmissible to the unguarded mind during sleep. Even the mismatch between "die for" and "do" could be explained; Lowell admitted to editing the line to fit his rhyme scheme.

Based on personal details provided in his letter, we can identify Mr. W. as Charles Pickard Ware, a former English professor known for publishing a collection of American slave songs in the 1870s.[5] Harvard philosopher Josiah Royce, presenting the incident in the *Proceedings of the American Society for Psychical Research*, deemed it a case of "pseudo-presentiment," a false memory constructed by Ware in the heightened state of emotional arousal that accompanied Lowell's delivery of the "Commemoration Ode."[6] "Of course," Royce explained, "if pseudo-presentiments exist, they may easily be created or reinforced by dreams."[7] Royce used Ware's case to demonstrate a continuum of susceptible mental states ranging from the temporary unreason of sleep, to the elation of poetry, to full-fledged insanity.

How could Ware's story serve as evidence both for and against mental permeability? He and Royce interpreted the familiar trope of inspiration arriving in sleep through different explanatory frameworks. Ware implied that ideas could travel between minds, sleeping minds were susceptible, and novel or important ideas moved with special force. Royce took the position increasingly shared by scientific psychologists in the nineteenth century, namely that inspiration was an arbitrary side effect of subliminal mental processes. These competing models of the unconscious mind had serious implications for the waking world of politics and commerce. Already, powerful ideas were crisscrossing the nation through new communication channels like the telegraph. What if ideas could spread of their own accord, along mysterious wavelengths that eluded human control? This would badly undermine the notion of intellectual property, not to mention the marketplace of ideas where rational consumers deliberate over political issues. Radical utopians saw a path to progress and uplift, while conservatives saw a volatile threat to the social order. Though some dismissed thought-transference as preposterous, the strength of the anecdotal tradition around such events led serious psychologists and philosophers to speculate on their meaning.

When Josiah Royce reached out to confirm the story of the "Ode," James Russell Lowell responded that "had I known of [Ware's] talent, I might have saved myself a very killing piece of work." The joke was that private inspiration is not transferable; his poem belonged to him. "Did I steal it?" Lowell asked patronizingly. "It might be well to set a literary detective on my trail."[8] If Lowell insisted too much on this point, he had a reason for feeling uneasy. The tumult of the Civil War, still vivid in the national consciousness, suggested that the stirrings of individual hearts were in fact highly contagious. The line at the center of this small controversy, "and what they dare to dream of, dare to die for," refers to the dream that led Harvard's undergraduates into battle for the Union cause—a collective vision of a country united in justice. This dream became a "killing piece of work" for hundreds of thousands less fortunate than Lowell, including three of his beloved nephews whose loss he bitterly mourned.[9]

Rendering dreams into reality was a concrete activity for many nineteenth-century Americans. Lowell, along with Whitman and their literary peers, certainly believed in spreading the dream of freedom through verse. Lowell clearly felt that this metaphorical dream was carried on the wing of artistic genius. Actual nocturnal dreams, according to Royce, lacked a scientifically recognized mode of action. However, the many ordinary Americans who recorded their dreams during the Civil War were not so wedded to hard distinctions between metaphor and action, art and life.

Dreamlands of the Past

The phenomena of psychical research blurred the boundaries of sleeping and waking, conscious and unconscious, public and private selves. Thus, dreams are an entry point into the variety of liminal experiences that researchers collected and organized, yet which continually slipped the bounds of taxonomic description. Leading psychologists explained dreams as meaningless "unconscious cerebration." Yet these deeply personal experiences had the power to link individuals, families, and society at large through a real, as well as symbolic, mental currency. The incident of Lowell's "Commemoration Ode" illustrates how dreams also threatened the integrity of the rational individual upon which the American social and economic order was premised. Authorship and ownership, privacy and reason, all appeared permeable to psychic forces.

The public registered and reported a kind of "dream-work" distinct from the later Freudian sense of that term, which has come to dominate modern conceptions of dreams as an outlet for repressed desires. Before Freud, dreams "worked" in the narrative context of people's lives.[10] They reinforced relationships and gave hints about the future; sometimes they revealed solutions to problems. As the nineteenth century progressed, a growing swath of the literate middle and upper-middle classes read popular accounts of current psychological science, leading them to understand dreaming as a physiological activity of the brain—often described with an industrial vocabulary that figured the mind as a piece of automated machinery.[11]

Some psychologists reconciled the meaningful and useful properties of dreams with mechanistic explanations by combining these forms of dream-work into a process that they termed unconscious cerebration. Coleman Sellers, a Philadelphia inventor and frequent ASPR correspondent, credited his many engineering breakthroughs to unconscious cerebration. The term, however, allowed for ambiguity as to where the boundaries of the mind fell—was unconscious cerebration restricted to the individual, or was it part of a larger psychic economy? Sellers walked the line on this question, asserting his disenchanted materialism while relishing stories about dreams, destiny, and transpersonal communion.

By the 1920s, the notion of unconscious cerebration would seem antiquated compared to edgier Freudian dream analysis. With his scandalous insistence on the power of repressed desires, Freud resolved the boundary problem that dogged previous explanations of dreaming. His was an entirely self-contained unconscious; at least in its early and most widely adopted form, psychoanalysis tunneled deep within the individual. The Freudian unconscious ran on a symbolic rather than literal currency, positing that teeth, strawberries, or syringes stood for unspeakable repressed desires. Psychical research provides a view of pre-Freudian understandings of dream-work, unconscious cerebration, and the shared psychic economy that were, and remain, lodged deeply in many areas of American cultural and social life. For psychical researchers, the ubiquitous experience of dreaming was an entry point to the stranger and more elusive phenomena of telepathy, clairvoyance, and premonition. They were among the first to attempt systematic and large-scale study of dreams, but the reports they collected, supposed to represent private mental events, were also generated by and participating in the long history of narrative dream interpretation.

To dream of bees "is a very lucky dream, it forebodes great success by your own industry," says *The New and Complete Fortune Teller*.[12] The *New Dream Book* adds an important clarification: "To dream of bees is good and bad; good if they sting not."[13] Around 1800, a common way of understanding dreams was through oneirocriticism, the practice of decoding a dream's meaning based on symbols passed along through oral or written traditions, including a vast corpus of popular dream books. In this tradition, a mix of historical authorities from Aristotle to the Persian poet Hafez were joined by more contemporary figures like Mrs. Blair, who offered *Dreams and Dreaming Philosophically and Scripturally Considered* in 1843. Such books sold in volume and morphed through frequent reprints, filling a demand by the increasingly literate public for cheap, accessible, and useful literature.

Their vivid illustrations offer a more specific clue to these books' intended audience: the frontispiece of *The Dreamer's Oracle* shows a young woman sprawled in an elegant bed, with her vision of a future husband floating in a cloud.[14] Some historians see dream books as a genre targeted at women, who turned to prognostication because they had so little control over their own fates.[15] Indeed, many dream books emphasized courtship, marriage, and childbearing. At the same time, nineteenth-century physicians associated dreams with femininity because they saw the dream state as one of mental passivity and weakness. Many doctors regarded dreaming as a mild form of hysteria or insanity brought on by the surrender of reason during sleep, and the post-Enlightenment medicalization of dreams occurred alongside the rise of hysteria as a psychiatric diagnosis.[16] In addition to gender, oneiromancy was linked to the low class status of readers who purchased cheap dream books. The better-educated looked down upon them as superstitious and gullible, exploited by fortune-telling charlatans.

However, more recent studies shed new light on the social and cultural status of dreams in the nineteenth century, suggesting a widespread interest that cuts across lines of gender, class, and race, though expressions of this interest took different forms in different social contexts.[17] Indeed, dreams were central to the middle-class sentimental culture of the period, connected with ideals of domesticity, family, and sympathy that stabilized the social order amid the upheavals of industrial capitalism. Belief in dreams as direct prophecy became suspect, but people continued to understand them as meaningful experiences, informed by long-standing religious traditions.[18] Dreams were clearly on the minds of the educated, middle-class readers who reported them to newspapers and periodicals, in addition to sharing them in private correspondence. Philosophers and physicians felt increasingly frustrated by their inability to explain dreaming as a natural phenomenon using the tools of science. Their efforts to do so would act as a countervailing current, isolating dreams from communities and rendering them strange.

By mid-century, growing interest in the science of psychology produced a new language which spoke of dreams as a result of mechanical operations of the body and brain.[19] In the 1820s and 30s, popularly accessible works such as those by Robert Macnish, Walter Cooper Dendy, and John Addington Symonds aimed to demystify dreams for the public by presenting them as hybrid medical-moral phenomena.[20] These experts encouraged attention to nocturnal visions because they could be symptoms of poor self-governance—overindulgence in food, drink, or passions "of a grosser character."[21] In reducing mental experience to an accumulated chain of sensory impressions, they built on the associationist theories that dominated British psychology from the 1750s onward. A dream of cascading water when the dreamer needed to urinate, or of a sun-scorched desert when their throat was dry, demonstrated the laws of mental association. However, scientific authors seemed satisfied to use the vernacular and mystical dream literature that they so despised as evidence for their own arguments, citing a miscellany of anecdotes drawn from hearsay, the popular press, the Bible, and folklore—they loved reports from sailors, who were notoriously superstitious. Science remained bound to the everyday vernacular of dreams through these recycled citations. Many psychologists reframed these stories as instances of mechanically generated illusion, but rivals within psychology cited the same canon of evidence to argue that the soul is independent from the brain's biologically determined hardware. These fissures within science over the nature of the unconscious mind showed how little certainty had been gained as the nineteenth century drew to a close.

British and American psychical researchers entered the fray in the 1880s, declaring their intent to gather comprehensive data and from this data to build up universal laws. Given that the most respected scientists of the day chose to analyze literary accounts of dreaming like Coleridge's *Kubla Khan* and De Quincey's *Confessions of an English Opium Eater*, no one knew what might emerge from a broad survey of actual experiences. Though the public eagerly supplied accounts of dreams, coincidences, and premonitions to the popular press, obtaining hard data—exact, unambiguous, standardized pieces of information—proved a thankless task. Once psychical researchers were up to their shoulders in the actual phenomena, they had to reckon with the fact that dreams came tangled in significance and meaning, as well as the mundane challenges of paperwork and verification.

Psychical researchers also brought a new explanatory tool to the table: thought-transference, or telepathy. They proposed that the power of mind-to-mind communication displayed by telepaths might lie dormant in the general population and manifest during sleep. This would explain dream messages, coincidences, and seeming prophecies—they came from the minds of others, remotely and unknowingly in rapport with the sleeper and sharing their inner thoughts. The telepathic hypothesis did not exclude those that preceded it. Proponents mixed in elements of physiological and evolutionary explanations, boosting the scientific plausibility of their claim. At the same time, they openly entertained possibilities of spiritual and interpersonal significance that resonated with the public while raising eyebrows among scientists.

Again, new speculations challenged and merged into older ones without creeping any closer to a definitive explanation of dreaming. A traveler on his way to New York's Grand Central Depot in 1876 might have stopped to browse a book stall that displayed Philip A. Emery's *The Rational Dream Book* alongside the latest issue of *Cornhill Magazine* with an article by Sully on the "laws of dream-fancy."[22] After an uneasy night of tossing and turning in a hotel bed, the traveler could have bought both publications and boarded his train optimistic about decoding his nightmares. The two authors boldly promised to bring scientific order to our traveler's dream life but diverged completely on the method—the former employing oneirocriticism, the latter ascribing dreams to indigestion. The reader would arrive at his destination no more certain of the facts than when he began.

Sigmund Freud portrayed himself as a scientific renegade cutting through this thicket of dream theories. In his introduction to *The Interpretation of Dreams* (1899), he disparaged the past century's work without acknowledging the many threads from which he borrowed. His skill in building an intellectual and institutional legacy won him a spot in the pantheon of psychology, despite criticism that psychoanalysis was a cult rather than a science. If we set aside his revolutionary framing and return Freud to the context of his field in 1900, the idea that dreams were a form of unconscious wish fulfillment was not entirely novel.[23] The history of dream science abounds in such stagecraft, where bold claims mask the persistence of old ideas and the absence of objective criteria. Indeed, how could one view objectively a phenomenon inaccessible to all but the person experiencing it, yet familiar to all from their nightly slumber? Freud's method of mining deep within the individual's psyche cut off a possibility of great interest to many Americans: the possibility that dreams were not individual and isolated, but shared.

Psychical research developed a new way of looking at dreams, and their meanings, through the practices of recording, reporting, and collecting that it cultivated. At a pivotal moment when the psychology of dreaming was about to turn inward, psychical research briefly gestured outward towards the expanding horizons of American mental life. It shared Freud's preoccupation with family affairs, but envisioned family as a radiant force that domesticated alien and alienating spaces, whether a Civil War battlefield or a crowded New York streetcar. Further, it had a quite un-Freudian conception of dream-work that figured the unconscious as a sturdy engine of capitalism rather than a reservoir and censor of illicit desire. Between the decline of oneirocriticism and the rise of psychoanalytic interpretation, psychical research provided a respectable outlet for a near-universal curiosity. People who followed their curiosity to the point of sending in dream reports inadvertently archived an intimate network of human relations: the ordinary affections, longings, and fears that held together their sleeping and waking selves, as well as their families and communities. These dream narratives contain the imprint of the teeming cities, lightning-quick technologies, medical breakthroughs, and supernatural possibilities of their time. Psychical research specialized in the clairvoyant or telepathic properties of dreams, but in order to evaluate these properties it had to weigh in on the normal and pathological processes of body and mind that create dreams, firmly embedding itself in the larger conversation around dreaming in America in the second half of the nineteenth century.

An Engineer's Dreams

Coleman Sellers II was a man of eclectic interests. Born into an illustrious Philadelphia family in 1827, he became a prominent engineer, inventor, and civic leader. Today, it might seem odd for a such distinguished personage to expose his dreams to public scrutiny—but again, this shows how deeply we've imbibed Freud's hypothesis that all dreams enact repressed desires. Sellers ascribed to a different, completely mundane philosophy of dreaming, and as a scientist, he believed in sharing his evidence. Yet this mechanically minded engineer often lingered on the borders of what could be explained by science. From his great-grandfather's prophecies to his own numerous inventions, a series of significant dreams wove together Sellers's life story in a way that clearly intrigued him.

Sellers used the genre of autobiography to present his evidence but also to present himself as a credible authority. He identified foremost as an engineer, a profession beloved by nineteenth-century Americans as the epitome of practical common sense and efficiency. Thus, he made a refreshing guide through the murky waters of psychology, espousing the mechanistic view that dreams resulted from the brain's activity while cut off from sensory input during sleep. This unconscious activity was arbitrary, Sellers assured, but its content came from the conscious mind's daytime occupations. Coleman Sellers, being an inventor, dreamed of patents.

His practical dreams reveal how people imagined and experienced the unconscious embedded in larger concerns about productivity, invention, and labor, a sort of spiritual-industrial complex. The massive growth of American industry, with its volatile boom-and-bust cycles, permeated the awareness of ordinary citizens. Cheery up-by-the-bootstraps biographies of robber barons like Andrew Carnegie and Cornelius Vanderbilt had a rather dire undercurrent: those who did not strive would not survive. Horatio Alger's fictional street urchin Ragged Dick "knew that he had only himself to depend upon," and his scrappy rise to fame and fortune quickly came to epitomize the archetype of the self-made man.[24] Thomas Edison represented this gospel of success in the realm of science: an inexhaustible American genius, at work in his laboratory through the watches of the night, racing against the competition to forge his ideas into profit.

Edison's alchemical power to transmute personal ingenuity into capital elevated the inventor to the status of a mythic figure, looming large in the nineteenth-century popular imagination. At times a dreamer, at times a ruthless pragmatist, he leapt from the pages of newspapers, magazines, and dime novels, a heroic Edison avatar eternally shouting "Eureka!" through a cloud of smoke.[25] For a nation that worshiped progress but dreaded falling behind in the race for success, the mysterious inner workings of the inventor's mind were a source of much anxiety. How could it be optimized? What if it dried up? It's no surprise, then, that the scientific study of dreams and dreaming held great interest for sober industrial capitalists like Coleman Sellers.

Though the ASPR never claimed to take a representative statistical sample, it amassed a great number of dreams and coincidences which Josiah Royce, Harvard philosopher and chair of the Committee on Phantasms and Presentiments, described as "documents illustrating the psychology of the American people."[26] The national psyche, he admitted, was generally mundane, occupied with small-time business, domestic trifles, missed trains, and childhood memories, but Royce took a particular interest in the mind of "the fantastic man, of the dreamer, of the man who lives a perfectly sane life in all but one or two realms."[27] He hoped to find, in that dreamer, a variable that might link psychic sensitivity to creative genius. Indeed, his "fantastic man" evoked contemporaneous accounts of inventors such as Humphry Davy, "pursued at night by horrible images," or James Watt, who suffered fits of madness. Popular biographies of these men suggested that their brilliance emerged from volatile combinations of mental traits.[28] For Royce, this raised the question: Did borderline psychopathologies underlie both eccentric genius and psychic mediumship, or were mediums and geniuses in communion with some force beyond themselves?

Coleman Sellers decried both pathological and supernatural explanations for reasons not entirely impersonal. The "languid, depressed, and fanciful" Watt invented the steam engine and is still celebrated as a herald of modernity; Coleman Sellers, a specimen of sturdy American common sense, invented a system for standardized screws and is hardly remembered at all.[29] Nevertheless, in his day Sellers was a prominent public representative of science. Deliberately opposed to Romantic notions of mad genius, he answered Royce's thirst for the fantastic with a resolute insistence that invention came from routine mental processes. In this regard he was in sympathy with psychical researchers who aimed to desensationalize abnormal experiences by placing them on a continuum with normal ones and highlighting their shared mechanisms. At the same time, the narratives Sellers served up as evidence convey an uncanny tension between mechanism and meaning that he never resolved, a sense that our knowledge of even the most familiar things is incomplete. He concluded that we need only know enough to make the contraption run.

Sellers began his correspondence with the ASPR in the 1880s, towards the end of a highly productive career. He reported on a peculiar aspect of his working process: many of his best ideas came to him in dreams or similar states of mental automatism. "This has happened so often that I am no longer surprised at it," he wrote.[30] Well-versed in the latest psychology, Sellers happily attributed his flashes of insight to random unconscious processes without motivation, direction, or meaning. In one anecdote, he described working on a customized part for a planing machine. He thought of a design, explained it to his draftsman, and went home. That night, on the brink of sleep, he was suddenly "impressed with the notion that the idea was not original, but had been patented," meaning that he had no right to use it in his planing machine. The next morning he explained this to the draftsman, who "looked surprised . . . and went to the patent-drawing drawer and showed me my patent for the invention, taken out some years before." His nocturnal impression warned Sellers of a grave danger: stealing an idea, and thus violating the code by which inventors made their living. The punch line, that Sellers stole his own invention, closes what historian Zorina Khan terms the "virtuous circle of democracy and technology" on the level of the individual psyche. Ideas are private property, and they even recognize their masters.[31]

Sellers did not see an incongruity between his practical calling and his voyages on the tides of the unconscious. "I have so much confidence in this kind of mind-work," he wrote, "that I am used to trusting to it many times when I want to reach any desired conclusion regarding invention."[32] What scientific literature of the period termed "unconscious cerebration"—the unceasing, subliminal activity of the mind at rest—Sellers believed was the key to his productivity.[33] He claimed to embrace its arbitrariness, relinquishing conscious control in a manner we might today associate with Eastern-inspired meditation techniques deployed by corporations to improve workplace productivity.[34] Rather than threatening the cohesion of the ego, as in Freud's analysis, Sellers's unconscious was remarkably consistent with the goals of his conscious self; as we shall see, it helped to constitute his larger social and historical identity. That submerged mysterious realm was thoroughly and recognizably the property of Coleman Sellers.

Sellers held thirty patents under his own name, and his firm contributed to almost a hundred more.[35] Though he never produced a blockbuster technology like the steam engine, Sellers was an inventor's inventor: he rationalized the very process of invention by collecting masses of data on efficiency, productivity, and industrial logistics. Based on this data, he found small but cumulatively significant solutions to problems that no one knew existed.[36] As in psychical research, information management was pivotal to identifying invisible phenomena at work in complex systems. His cousin and former apprentice John Sellers Bancroft described their shop's drawing room as a "bureau of record" where patents, plans, and blueprints were analyzed to generate parameters for further inventions. Maintaining such a bureau was no easy task—applications to the United States Patent Office had rocketed from 785 in 1840 to more than 21,000 in 1875.[37] Patent Office clerks complained bitterly of administrative challenges—understaffing, disorderly files—that also afflicted psychical research.[38]

Despite the starkly rational nature of Sellers's work, a narrative of predestination weaves through his life story. Unlike the ragtag boy-inventors of dime novels, Coleman Sellers was not quite an up-by-the-bootstraps case. His family traced its lineage to Samuel Sellers, a gentleman from Derbyshire and among the first to obtain a land grant in Pennsylvania in 1682.[39] Crucially, Samuel embarked on this venture because of a dream in which he purchased land from a "very singular person" in America. He sailed to Philadelphia, identified the man from his dream as William Penn, and hastily bought the destined acres. At least, so went the family lore. The fact that the Sellerses belonged to the Religious Society of Friends would have inclined the family to take such a vision seriously as a message from God. Historian Carla Gerona has traced a Quaker tradition of recording, sharing, and interpreting dreams, which she calls "Quaker dreamwork," through the seventeenth and eighteenth centuries. In the uncharted American colonies, dreams sometimes became maps that "helped Quakers get to where they were going," as was clearly the case for Samuel Sellers.[40]

The family thrived in Pennsylvania; Coleman's grandfather and father built a fiefdom of light industry (wire weaving, paper molds, wool carding) in Upper Darby. Sellers recounted a fateful moment in the progress of their enterprise: "My father invented a machine to lay paper moulds . . . the machine did not work well and [he was] bothered over the failure . . . One night my father dreamed that an old man came to him and said, 'If you want that machine to work you must turn it upside down.' " Coleman's father immediately jumped in a carriage and raced to the office, where his own father was waiting for him, having woken from an identical dream.[41] Once again, an older generation of Quakers trusted their night visions as a guide. Father and son dreaming the same dream at the same time carried spiritual undertones, while the object of their fancy—a paper mold—brings the story into an economic context.

Of course, there's more to making it in America than a timely mechanical fix. The Sellers family became well connected in Philadelphia society, prominent in local government as well as scholarly and civic groups like the American Philosophical Society, the Franklin Institute, and the SPCA.[42] Coleman Sellers Sr. built a thriving business, but his three sons all proved better engineers than capitalists. When Coleman Sr. died unexpectedly, the mills fell to his elder sons George Escol and Charles. (George Escol's unusual middle name was revealed to his father in a dream about the biblical river of Eschol.)[43] The brothers' inexperience collided with a financial panic in 1837; their assets evaporated, Sellers & Sons folded, and George and Charles migrated west for a fresh start in Ohio. Their younger sibling, Coleman II, dropped out of school to join his brothers at a rolling mill in Cincinnati. There, he learned draftsmanship and mechanical engineering on the job and through exhaustive reading.[44] The young Coleman also attended séances with Margaret Fox Kane, the founder of the modern Spiritualist movement, beginning a lifelong interest in investigating the supernatural.[45]

Sellers didn't want very much besides a machine shop, a drafting table, and a steady supply of engineering problems to solve. Once the financial storm of the early 1840s passed, he returned to Philadelphia to work as draftsman for a cousin's firm. He would remain there for thirty years, and his most productive decades were filled with dreams, spontaneous insights, and other forms of unconscious cerebration. The William

Penn story, the anecdote of the paper molds, and the vision of the river Eschol make the men of the Sellers family out to be felicitous dreamers—they elevate the symbolic justification of the dream over the hard work, savvy investment, and cutthroat dealing that got the Sellerses their land and money (they rebuilt their fortunes in part by laying railroads with slave labor in the 1840s). This connects Sellers to the long tradition of American expansionist and evangelical dreaming ranging from Joseph Smith Jr.'s vision of a Mormon utopia in the west to prospector D. M. Cook's "interior promptings" that unfailingly led him to a vein of gold.[46] Traditions of Quaker dreamwork as mode of communal introspection, and of oneiromancy as a tool for coping with life's unknowns, mingled with and were often eclipsed by this teleological function of dreams in the later nineteenth century—an emergent "American dream" that ascribed a higher purpose to the pursuit of power and profit.[47] Tension between the capricious amorality of capitalism and the need for meaning in national identity echoes in rival conceptions of the unconscious as blind mechanism or as purposive medium. Sellers displayed a kind of double consciousness towards these questions, brandishing the rhetoric of disenchantment while also using dreams to affirm the rightness of the burgeoning industrial order he represented.

Dreaming in Public

We know about Sellers' practical dreams because he reported them to the ASPR in a series of letters in 1888, responding to a public call for "cases [of] remarkable experience, such as an exceptionally vivid and disturbing dream or strong waking impression."[48] His correspondence wound up in the hands of Josiah Royce, chair of the Committee on Phantasms and Presentiments. Royce presented his committee's findings in the March, 1889 number of the *Proceedings* with a careful methodological justification. American scientists had criticized the British SPR for soliciting "ghosts, dreams, and vain imaginations" from a superstitious public, but Royce asserted his ability to extract good data from such personal narratives: he disregarded correspondents' interpretation of events in search of "the characteristics that are common to many of their separate stories." Looking down from above at a mass of stories revealed "the unconscious testimony, so to speak, of all the many persons."[49] Royce didn't blame his correspondents for lacking the scientist's aerial perspective; he spoke sympathetically of their capitulation to psychological error.[50]

In this preamble Royce neatly combined two currents in nineteenth-century science. First he cited the tradition of amateur natural history, with its faith in the ability of disciplined nonprofessionals to serve as trustworthy witnesses. Yet he broke with the gentlemanly code of this community when he subjected his witnesses to clinical objectification, deeming them unable to correctly account for their own experiences. Though not a physician himself, Royce easily slid into the power relations that had come to characterize elite medicine over the preceding century, when doctors began observing disease across large numbers of patients, attending to patterns of pathological signs.[51] Royce was certainly reading the contemporaneous work of Charcot and Janet on hysterical patients in Paris's Salpêtrière asylum.

Applying the clinical gaze to people who wanted to participate as equals in an amateur community might seem like a bait-and-switch; mediums complained of this whenever they subjected themselves to scientific examination. The ASPR still used class, education, and social standing to substantiate testimony, but it was easy to back away from the old system of trust when the subject matter aroused so much passionate conviction—sometimes compared to fits of hysteria—among otherwise respectable individuals. Royce, obscuring the move with friendly jocularity, peeled back his correspondents' self-report in search of an underlying mechanism like a medical student slicing open a cadaver.

Coleman Sellers was one of many correspondents who confounded this effort by wrapping his data inextricably in his own psychological interpretation. Royce complained of "popular prejudices and superstitions," but just as often, dream narratives came with popular psychology already built in. Further, participants mobilized their specialized knowledge about everything from engineering to teaching to gambling to corroborate their analyses, very much expecting researchers to respect their expertise. Leaders of psychical research who worked to strip down and standardize evidence brushed past the richness of interpretation already present in their mountains of letters.

Sellers had a substantial claim to interpretive authority over his psychical experiences. He made a hobby of exposing Spiritualist frauds, and in the early 1880s was drafted to serve on the Seybert Commission for Investigating Modern Spiritualism, a distinguished group of Philadelphia professors and scientists tasked with reaching a final verdict on the authenticity of spirit mediums. (After issuing a negative report that drew the ire of powerful Spiritualist organizations, the committee quietly dissolved.) In addition to field investigation, Sellers kept abreast of the psychological literature, reading popular texts like Oliver Wendell Holmes's "Mechanism in Thought and Morals" and James E. Garretson's *Nineteenth-Century Sense*, which discussed the latest theories of unconscious cerebration in depth.[52] Holmes explained dreaming using industrial metaphors that may have resonated with Sellers: the sleeping mind is "the underground workshop of thought"; "the industries of all the factories and trading establishments in the world are mere indolence and awkwardness and unproductiveness compared to the miraculous activities" of which it is capable.[53] That Sellers literally dreamed of engineering problems is unusual, but the association of mind and factory was a common one, reflecting how economies and built environments structure our imagination of human interiority.

Other ASPR correspondents drew their psychological language from periodicals and fiction, which canonized certain tactics of narrative realism that recur in many private accounts of dreaming. Popular magazines like *Harper's* and *The Atlantic Monthly* ran stories on dream interpretation which presented the scientific view of dreams as extensions of waking activities. At the same time, they showcased prophetic dreams like that of an Ohio farmer who saved a passenger train from careening over a collapsed bridge, presented in a neutral reportorial style.[54] In literature, Charles Dickens, Samuel Taylor Coleridge, Wilkie Collins, and other celebrated writers used current psychology to make the fictional dreams of their characters seem realistic. Of course, literary dreams were crafted as a means to a narrative end, but the pretense of scientific description helped to conceal the author's hand.[55] Psychologists' fondness for citing these literary accounts was a perturbingly circular acknowledgment that all dream reports are to some degree fictions.

Most early- to mid-nineteenth-century dream narratives, in fiction and in science, depicted somewhat logical and linear sequences of events. Scientific writers acknowledged that dreams could be strange, incoherent, and unwholesome, but they adroitly shifted their focus to the subset of dreams that related to actual things, events, and people. This tendency speaks to how received literary forms shape our recollection of dreams and foreshadows how the quest for more accurate dream descriptions led away from realism. The satirist Ambrose Bierce shared some of his unusual dreams in an 1887 newspaper essay that began by pointing to the inadequacy of existing forms: "Who can so relate a dream that it shall seem one? No poet has so light a touch."[56] Bierce's description of psychic events defied the conventions of nineteenth-century literary realism which, Bierce argued, was not realistic at all. In his dream, a horse spoke indecipherable words, and a ring of bleeding corpses fed a river of blood.

He created an atmosphere of heightened symbolism and emotion, without the neatness of retroactive sense-making—a quality that his writing shares with forerunners of modernism Edgar Allan Poe and Charles Baudelaire. The surrealist movements that followed in the twentieth century would thrive on the dissonant terrain of the unconscious. Bierce, however, was an American reporter, not a French poet, and his musings on dreams brought him around to business matters. "By taming our dreams," he suggested, impoverished writers could "double our working hours and our most fruitful labor will be done in sleep."[57] The idea of wringing economic value from sleep would seem a satire on Americans' compulsive (and compulsory) productivity, except that we've heard the same idea presented seriously by Coleman Sellers under the banner of unconscious cerebration.

Confronting the strangeness of dreams became a wellspring for art and psychoanalysis around the turn of the twentieth century. Much as Bierce predicted, artists also harnessed the dream's uncanny productivity for new mass media entertainments. On September 10, 1904, readers of the *New York Evening Telegram* got their first taste of a soon-to-be classic comic strip gag. The scene begins in the windswept Arctic, where a solitary explorer longs for a last cigarette before he freezes to death. Miraculously, another man appears over the horizon with rolling paper. A third man arrives with tobacco, and they rejoice until they realize that they have no matches. Just in time, a fourth man staggers across the icy wastes proffering his last match. As they light it, the wind blows it out, leaving them to "lay down and die in agony." Then, as all seems lost, the last panel cuts to a man in bed at home. It was only a nightmare; his hair still standing on end, he lights a cigarette. This was Winsor McCay's *Dream of the Rarebit Fiend*, where the bizarre dreams of ordinary people were, in Bierce's words, "caught and fixed and made to serve."[58] In this case, they served the booming newspaper industry's demand for an unending stream of illustrated content.

The *Fiend*, as well as McCay's better-remembered *Little Nemo in Slumberland*, both use the waking-from-a-nightmare device in a way that reflects the associationism of psychologists like Walter Cooper Dendy and Alexander Bain: a bodily sensation or desire seems to drive the dream narrative.[59] The *Fiend* took as a premise the common wisdom, reinforced by popular psychology, that eating cheese before bed causes nightmares; Welsh rarebit, an open-faced cheese sandwich served in late-night dining establishments, was often blamed in the final panel.[60] While McCay took this scientific theory as a starting point, he often appeared to question its limits, dropping clues that the reductionist explanation was a screen for deeper and darker psychic significance.

Figure 5 shows how McCay often used last-minute perspective shifts to confound readers' expectations, jolting us from the masculine city streets to the feminine space of the bedroom. The recurring trope of the anxious mother or wife reflected real dangers lurking outside the home, where women had no power to protect their loved ones.[61] The same newspapers that ran the *Fiend* carried graphic descriptions of train wrecks, fires, and freak accidents to people's breakfast tables; McCay merely "caught and fixed" what sometimes seemed like the waking nightmare of modern life. The explosiveness and radical changes of scale that mark his style reflect his concerns about new technology and urban alienation. Like Bierce, who toyed with the pose of scientific objectivity, McCay insisted that "I merely tell the story, like any other newspaper gatherer or reporter."[62] He adopted, and stood by, the premise that the *Fiend* was based on real dreams submitted to him by the public, evoking the ASPR's Census of Hallucinations from a decade earlier.

FIGURE 5. A rarebit nightmare in which a hapless pedestrian is mauled by a succession of vehicles on a busy city street. Winsor McCay, "Dream of the Rarebit Fiend," October 26, 1904.

In the early months of his strip, claiming that he'd run out of material, McCay "inserted a note inviting the public to send their dreams" and supposedly received "thousands of good ideas."[63] His putative correspondence follows the pattern of psychical research: letters traveled from the hinterlands of the United States to a center of calculation in a major East Coast city for expert processing. The final product purported (whether seriously or in jest) to be an objective representation of psychological universals. "I am an illustrator," McCay quipped, again using the newspaper profession to ground his objectivity. "One newspaper artist is sent to a big fire, another to a banquet . . . I am assigned to illustrate the rarebit dream of some poor unfortunate in Hoboken, N.J."[64] Always a consummate showman, McCay played this scientific posture for laughs—but comics historian Ulrich Merkel found that McCay did, indeed, receive correspondence from the public, and he credited specific individuals in some of his strips. Much like the ASPR, McCay toyed with the idea that his collection of dreams provided a glimpse into the national psyche, and he offered his strip as a site for public dreaming.[65] "I try to put the facts just as I receive them," he declared, and they were "illustrated and published for the public good," aligning himself playfully with the scientific mission of the ASPR.[66]

The real joke of the *Rarebit Fiend* is the idea that we could blame cheese for America's nightmares—every strip offers both this reductionist punch line and a glimpse into the terror, stress, and isolation of modern life. Cumulatively, McCay's comics insinuate that something more fundamental than the nation's digestion had gone awry in the onslaught of industrial capitalism. McCay came to embody his own joke, representing himself as a mechanical man whose interiority was tragically foreshortened in the struggle for survival. As a boy he had dreamed of becoming a great painter. The *Rarebit Fiend* began when "I woke up about ten years ago from [this] dream," he explained.[67] Instead of composing priceless masterpieces, McCay hustled for a living as a quick-draw illustrator; his productivity was frenetic and mechanical, careening at a pace that many considered inhuman. At one point he wrote to his art director at the *New York Herald* asking for a raise: "You know what to do to a thrashing machine to make it run better? Grease it."[68]

Unlike Coleman Sellers, whose individualized, productive dreams remained connected to a familial tradition and a sense of national destiny, McCay's chaotic and kaleidoscopic visions depicted the permeation of capitalism into the American unconscious as a centrifugal force that stripped away identity and meaning. The *Rarebit Fiend* conveyed a shared public experience of noise, speed, peril, and social change that could only be communicated through fantastical distortions of an already uncertain reality. Correspondents to the ASPR tried to negotiate the discrepancies between Sellers's teleological assurance and McCay's frenetic contingency as they recounted their own dreams, which often staged the obliteration of the individual in the maw of machines.

The Fatal Boiler: A Taxonomy of Nineteenth-Century Dreams

In his *Principles of Psychology*, William James tackled the problem of how to talk about dreams using his philosophy of pragmatism as a guide. Psychologists, he said, can only study those aspects of experience that we can communicate and which are anchored in mutually agreed-upon realities of mind and world.[69] By a strictly materialistic standard, we have no definite evidence of dreams at all—they leave no mark on external reality. However, the same problem goes for most of our experiences: we can't prove that we feel love or envy; emotions don't turn a dial, though the quest to locate them continues apace in today's neuroimaging.

As a frequent guest at Boston's séance tables, James was intimately familiar with the fallibility of memory and the false conviction that comes with articulating an incident to others.[70] These were fundamental challenges for psychical research, but dreams provided an illustration of why elusive experiences are nonetheless worth trying to understand. They were a platform for researchers to work out what we can communicate about the unconscious and how to correlate internal experience to a shared world.

Anyone who has tried to talk about a dream will recognize the implicit craft of stringing together disjointed, barely remembered images and feelings into some kind of speakable story. We retroactively apply logic and chronology, but even so, most dream reports are much less engaging to listeners than to the teller. The ASPR also found rambling, nonsensical dreams unattractive. Sane people rarely sent them in, and few were published in the society's *Proceedings*. That people perceived incoherent dreams as lacking scientific value is illustrated in a dispatch from C.H.H., an engineer and surveyor, who describes two dreams that he had about a missing gold ring.

The first was "a hazy sort of dream about the ring, but nothing definite"; he declined to elaborate on its content. The second dream, however, was "very impressive . . . a good, square, honest and useful dream" in which the exact location of the ring was vividly revealed.[71] C.H.H.'s distinction between a "hazy dream" and a "useful dream" imposes a standard of productivity based on positive correspondence with some thing or event in the outside world. He saw no use in wandering through the haze of atmosphere and affect—such dreams were perhaps even dishonest, shirking their duty. Productive dreams satisfied James's stipulation that, for an inner experience to become an object of knowledge, it must "exist outside as well as inside the mind in question."[72] Unfortunately for C.H.H., his unconscious proved less industrious than that of Coleman Sellers. He concluded his letter by noting that "I have endeavored to work this dream business up to a practical use in the years gone by; but it has been a total failure, so far."[73]

Even dreams with a strong work ethic can't record themselves. Producing good dream reports required reliable bedfellows, or at least tolerant friends and family to hear the story as soon as possible after waking. The ASPR tried to publicize protocols for disciplined witnessing and record-keeping so that dreamers would write down their experiences before engaging in confounding activities like reading the morning newspaper. When W. S. of Boston was startled from sleep by a nightmare about a friend's death, his wife commanded "that I should get up at once, write down my dream, with the date and hour, which I did." ASPR investigators were grateful whenever someone like Mrs. W. S. had her scientific wits about her in the middle of the night. Josiah Royce pointed out the exemplary "kindness and forethought of our correspondent in making an exact note of his dream at once," though he declined to credit the wife's insistence.[74] Royce took the case as an opportunity to "beg all our friends and correspondents to make instant note of their dreams . . . with mention of day, hour, and precise content."[75]

The society's correspondents actively modified their behavior and that of their bedfellows in order to become better observers. The surprising ability of a scientific society to mold people's intimate lives in this way is further illustrated in an account from R.B.C. of Evanston, Illinois, who woke his wife one night with a prophetic dream of their son's injury. Capturing this piece of evidence inspired him with a new sense of scientific discipline: "I don't remember if I was in habit of repeating my dreams to her before this incident, but have since."[76] Mrs. L. Z. recalled sleeping in the same bed with her mother as a child of ten and waking from a dream in which she swallowed a pin. The mother had had the same dream, and both reported immediately to the father when he entered the room in the morning.[77] Imposing discipline on the age-old act of sharing one's dreams required significant reach on the part of psychical research: it relied on access to kitchens and bedrooms, spouses and children. Many other scientific practices transpired in domestic settings, but the capture of dreams was among the most intimate.

How people understand dreams in a given time and place tells us much about their waking universe; the popular discourse of dreaming in mid-nineteenth-century America contains literal gold mines, as well as buried treasure, divine revelations, medical cures, and psychic communion with the living and the dead.[78] Psychical researchers sifted through such stories with the aim of classifying mental experience, paring away their content to isolate cognitive processes. Sifting these psychical anecdotes in a different way, I wanted to know what types of work these dreams performed for their dreamers. In the ASPR's archives, three loose subgenres illustrate the ways in which dreams emerged from and responded to a world of industry and commerce that, in turn, made the large-scale collection of dreams possible and worthwhile.

The first subgenre of dream reports are those in which a dream points the way to a concrete object. For instance, a "mania of money-digging" struck rural New England and New York during the early decades of the nineteenth century. Men had dreams that revealed the specific location of pirate's gold and rallied their neighbors to find and excavate these sites.[79] Historian Alan Taylor has collected more than forty such reports, concluding that "the rural Yankee's subconscious was peculiarly concerned with finding money."[80] This period's understanding of what dreams were good for was not, however, limited to lucre; consider Joseph Smith Jr. whose dream led him to a golden tablet containing the Book of Mormon, another sort of buried treasure. On a humbler plane, the ASPR received frequent reports of lost objects recovered when the dreamer was guided to their location, sometimes by a deceased loved one. C.H.H.'s missing ring, for instance, was a treasured memento from his sister. Objects hidden in the mind corresponded to objects hidden in the ground in a manner both concrete and symbolic. Because these spontaneous dreams revealed wealth that would require untold amounts of labor to produce through traditional means, they underscored the mind's ability to create seemingly disproportionate value—literally spinning dreams into gold.

Just as the dreams of rural farmers bespoke a fantasy of access to the great wealth amassed, seemingly overnight, by industrial barons, the dreams of urban dwellers helped assign sense and meaning to capitalism's arbitrary risks. This second subgenre of dream reports deals with risks encountered in city and commercial life, especially when traveling: railroads, trolley cars, coaches, and steamboats were moving at unprecedented speeds and causing unprecedented mortality.[81] Newspapers covered vehicular disaster with a certain macabre relish. A fascination with accidents pervaded American culture; McCay's *Rarebit Fiend* rarely passed a week without a spectacular crash.[82] Historian Wolfgang Schivelbusch calls the danger of acceleration an "ever-present subliminal fear" for nineteenth-century travelers. The perceived threat of sudden death on the road gave rise to a great many dreams that seemed to predict vehicular accidents.[83]

"I dreamed I was at a railway-station . . . and I knew there was to be a collision," wrote a woman who gave her name as Mrs. C. "I heard a terrific bang and woke with the shock of it."[84] The following evening, Mrs. C. learned of a crash at the same station she'd seen in the dream. Mary H. Watkins, of Detroit, "had an intensely vivid dream of the drowning of someone dear to me, and awoke in tears . . . That afternoon, on my return from school, I was told that my brother had been drowned that morning by the burning of the steamer 'Sea Bird' on Lake Michigan."[85]

She believed that her close connection with her brother allowed him to communicate with her during his last moments. Josiah Royce cited Watkins's story as a case of pseudopresentiment, but he wasn't the first person to give her a psychological explanation. At the time of the disaster, when Watkins turned to her church for support, the rector "was desirous of finding a cause for my sleeping vision, and thought that it probably lay in the association of ideas"—as a learned man, the rector was up-to-date on associationist psychology. After grilling her about the dream, "he was unable to find anything in support of his theory." The reverend was just as eager as Royce to find a cognitive explanation, perhaps hoping to discourage popular belief in dream-prophecy that conflicted with his church's doctrines. Though, as Pamela Klassen demonstrates, mainstream Protestants certainly engaged in an array of experimental spiritual practices, church authorities often looked upon these practices with suspicion.[86]

Sometimes the unconscious could actually intervene in the onward rush of vehicular events: Dr. E. W. Keith, of Chicago, awoke one morning and raced, unsummoned, to the scene of a carriage accident just in time to save the life of a bleeding victim.[87] Future ASPR president James Hervey Hyslop, while a professor at Columbia University, spotted a friend crossing the street but got a "sudden impulse" not to call out a greeting. In the next instant the friend leaped from the path of a speeding carriage, which he would not have seen if Hyslop had distracted him.[88] This could be the setup for yet another *Rarebit Fiend* about a decapitated pedestrian, but rather than a nightmare of helplessness in the face of modernity, Hyslop saw a productive unconscious at work for the public benefit.

Whether on a train, a boat, or even walking down a city street, nineteenth-century travel fatalities often shared the same culprit: the boiler, the part of a steam engine where water is heated into high-pressure steam. Boiler explosions, caused by shoddy construction or improper use, were ubiquitous thanks to the hasty uptake of James Watt's invention and the absence of safety regulations. They struck at random, and no one was safe; in 1890, the boiler of a pumping engine for a Philadelphia hotel exploded and a passing pedestrian "was thrown almost fifty feet" to his death.[89] In 1883, the *New York Herald* would headline one such occurrence simply, "The Fatal Boiler Again."[90] The need to standardize and inspect these devices might seem a likely cause for a reform-minded engineer like Coleman Sellers. Indeed, Sellers took an activist stance on regulating boilers, despairing that "steam boilers have been made to serve the purpose of death traps."[91] English psychologist Havelock Ellis used these industrial explosions as a metaphor for, of all things, the shock of waking up from sleep—reiterating the gag of the *Rarebit Fiend*.[92]

Skeptics reasoned that apparent disaster prophecies were the result of statistical illiteracy: people dreamed of disaster all the time, but only remembered or recorded these dreams when they happened to correspond with real events, and this produced a skewed sample.[93] However, psychologists, psychical research societies, magazines, and newspapers continued to collect and publish accident dreams without subjecting them to statistical scrutiny, in part because they helped make sense of a new kind of senselessness in human affairs. At least, in the moment a loved one was snatched away, you might receive some affirmation of a bond that transcended the physical world. Such visions also offered an inverted (perhaps remote) semblance of the "good death." Most nineteenth-century Americans hoped to die at home, in their beds, with family nearby—not in a crowded railway car full of strangers. Failing that, they could hope to make psychic contact with their loved ones in a last moment of comfort.[94]

The most common subgenre of psychical anecdote, however, occupies a domestic middle ground between wilderness revelation and industrial annihilation. The ASPR amassed countless mundane stories of coincidences, presentiments, and telepathic missives, often associated with liminal states of consciousness. Apparent foreknowledge of an unexpected guest or a letter from a long-lost relative, especially when such instances recurred, provoked wonder in a world that seemed increasingly vast and anonymous. In an 1891 essay in *Harper's*, American humorist Mark Twain announced his discovery of a new phenomenon, "mental telegraphy," that connected people's thoughts at a distance, "exactly as if you two were harnessed together like the Siamese twins."[95] The public might have interpreted this as a joke, but Twain was serious. An avid collector of anecdotes, he'd tracked the phenomenon for over a decade.

Twain was spurred to publish his musings by the work of the psychical research societies, which he said gave scientific backing to his theory.

Though the ASPR's leadership at times attempted to argue probability and statistics to overzealous correspondents, they also found their own firsthand experiences quite compelling. In contrast to Twain's persuasive tone, their anecdotes attempted to model detached self-observation and neutrality towards the phenomenon. For instance, in 1894, James Hyslop reported that he heard his doorbell ring and felt a sudden certainty that it was "Mr. W., a friend from Indianapolis . . . and sure enough, it was he." He acknowledged the wonder and curiosity of this experience, reserving for the end the "interesting fact" that Mr. W.'s visit to New York was reported in that week's papers, which Hyslop had glanced over that morning. Rather than another case of telepathic premonition, Hyslop illustrated a common source of error: unconscious or forgotten information that created the sensation of "knowing in advance."[96] Hyslop's account of how he reached a naturalistic explanation provided the public with new tools for interpreting such apparent incidents of telepathy or premonition.

This question of how to differentiate unconscious knowledge or mere coincidence from supernormal communication was the subject of much debate. Philosopher Charles Sanders Peirce and psychologist Charles Sedgwick Minot argued that the simple operations of chance were sufficient to explain all the results obtained thus far by psychical researchers. Those like Hyslop and Sellers who sought a reasonable middle ground would argue that there was nothing "mere" about coincidences, but that they revealed complex unconscious processes which observers should learn to scrutinize. Twain, like many psychical researchers and members of the public, was a partisan for telepathy. Recourse to coincidence "is a cheap and convenient way of disposing of a grave and very puzzling mystery," he quipped.[97]

Not only was Twain convinced by his experiences of mental telegraphy, he envisioned a future when "communication of mind with mind may be brought under command and reduced to certainty and system," putting Western Union out of business.[98] He was not the only American eagerly awaiting such a development, as the incoming mail of the ASPR attests. "I am inclined to believe in telepathy, and there is certainly wireless telegraphy. Under certain right conditions, why may we not communicate through the air?" asked Orlando C. Blackmer, of Oak Park, Illinois.[99] Walter Franklin Prince, during his tenure as the ASPR's research officer, complained that "there are far more paranoiacs whose delusions revolve around wireless telegraphy . . . than whose delusions center in spiritualism," underscoring the attraction of technology for those seeking to reconcile abnormal experiences with scientific reality.[100] One ASPR correspondent, a medical student, claimed to anticipate when the telephone would ring and who was calling, while countless others amused themselves with telegraph and telephone synchronicity in the course of their everyday affairs.[101] Alfred Church Lane, a former student of William James who made a career in geology, wrote to his old professor that he "certainly should like to be freed from the bondage of the telephone" and was undertaking experiments towards that end in his leisure time.[102]

Twain extrapolated the potential impact of mental telegraphy on America's technology-driven economy—a realm that he knew something about, after losing half a million dollars investing in failed inventions. Chroniclers of nineteenth-century scientific progress noted that often a major invention or discovery was made simultaneously by two individuals in different places—popular examples included the steam engine, the telegraph, evolution, and spectrum analysis. Some explained it as the "spirit of the age," but Twain saw mental telegraphy at work: "Is it not possible that inventors are constantly and unwittingly stealing each other's ideas?"[103] Twain had experienced this in his own literary career when, as he "lay in bed idly musing," a "red-hot new idea" for a book dropped into his mind. However, he soon received an outline of that very book written by a friend, and he concluded that "his" idea was a telepathic emanation from the true author.[104] Lesser-known correspondents to the ASPR reported similar experiences: a San Quentin prison chaplain anticipated a newspaper story because "my mind was en-wrapped" with the mind of the story's author, producing a "sympathetic relation" that allowed the thought to travel.[105] The same notion was at play when Charles Pickard Ware claimed to anticipate Lowell's "Commemoration Ode": a work of art ultimately intended for public consumption might become public too

soon, escaping the author's mind and dashing along the psychic telegraph wire of its own accord. The implications of this theory for patent
law and authorial attribution were decidedly nightmarish.

Twain complained that "this age does seem to have exhausted invention," and certainly its inventions had exhausted his finances. Thus, his
proposal for an invention to end invention, "something which conveys our
thoughts through the air from brain to brain," has the ring of revenge
about it.[106] No one could claim priority, take out a patent, or court inves-
tors in a world where discoveries were instantaneously and subliminally
shared. His vision of knowledge radiating freely across the boundaries that
demarcate individuals, corporations, and nations would spell the end of
capitalism and the bootstrapping American Dream. However far-fetched
Twain's scenario, communion during liminal states seemed to enthrall the
public with the possibility that thoughts were not private property.

In the 1850s, Coleman Sellers awoke in the middle of the night,
seized with the certainty that he had violated U.S. patent law. In the
1780s, Sellers's father and grandfather rose from slumber and dashed
to their shop to build a paper mold that would make their fortune
and speed printed publications throughout the newly formed United
States. In the 1630s, Samuel Sellers dreamed of a colonial land agent,
crossed the Atlantic, and bought into the American Dream at its mythical
wellspring.

All of this, Coleman Sellers cautioned in his correspondence with the
ASPR, was the product of individual minds acting automatically and at random, doing what brains do when left to their own devices. Dreams and revelations have no external source; their surprising contents merely reflect
the fact that "our minds receive impressions in the most heedless manner," so that we are always seeing things without consciously noticing them.
Indeed, it is the quality of solitary, unceasing work which seems to have
stirred Sellers's admiration of the human brain. "Our brain works after we
have striven to give it rest," he observed, and frequently it wrenched his
tired body from sleep with an urgent missive from the interior.[107]

The unconscious seemed like an ideal worker in that it never slum-
bered. Unfortunately, it was unpredictable. It could take days or weeks
to cough up the solution to a difficult problem. Sellers had confidence

and was "used to trusting to it," but certainly this was no model for the increasingly rationalized and automated world of industry—a world that Sellers's innovations had helped create.[108] Many of the problems that Sellers's unconscious mind set itself to solving were problems of doing more, faster, with less human labor; at the same time, he described his unconscious as a sort of high-quality artisan: "Sometimes the mind, if not forced, will do work more rapidly for the want of attention." By the 1880s such a notion was antiquated for the vast majority of American workers, who labored by the clock.[109]

The Freudian concept of dream-work belongs to a long history of labor in, by, and around dreams. Oneiromancy and oneirocriticism assumed that dreams are fundamentally meaningful and contain useful information about the future encoded in symbols of divine or mystical origin. Judeo-Christian dream visions held high social and political value in the seventeenth- and eighteenth-century Atlantic world, but clerical officials often tried to control their interpretation, externalizing the work of censorship.[110] Criticisms of oneiromancy in the early American colonies centered around fears that dreams were either idle fancies—the result of moral and mental sloth—or, relatedly, the work of the devil.[111] It became the task of nineteenth-century psychology to explain the "natural" purpose of dreaming, first by elucidating its mechanisms and later by placing it within the evolutionary context of a brain optimized for the struggle to survive. Writers like George Henry Lewes described mental functions in terms of their historical utility, and for him dreams were an inefficient vestige of man's primitive social contests. To others, like Francis Power Cobbe, who examined the internal economy of the psyche, dreams seemed to conduct a useful business by preserving memories and explanatory myths. These forms of dream-work reflected forces acting on the entire species, rather than within the individual mind.

Both Twain and Sellers saw universal unconscious forces, arbitrary and transpersonal, lurking behind the myth of the American inventor as solitary genius. In addition to demystifying invention as a mental process, Sellers rationalized it as an engineering process in his firm. Invention was changing in the 1880s and would change even more dramatically in the century to come. One might compare Twain's vision of mental telegraphy with the close collaborative ethos of the research team established by corporations like Bell Telephone and General Electric in the 1920s, as they attempted to institutionalize the mysterious psychic processes that had won them initial market success.

Dreams did not cease to be of interest in psychology and popular culture, but their usefulness shifted away from the shared material reality of invention and industry to the internal psychic economy. Their significance in the twentieth century will always be tied up with Freud, lending them an air of the taboo notably absent in the dreams of Coleman Sellers. The idea of the unconscious as a practical tool for solving concrete problems—or for transcending the limits of human communication—was not an attractive one to twentieth-century American psychology, which was busy inventing itself as an experimental discipline. What remains of turn-of-the-century psychical research is an immense quantity of evidence that speaks to the material relationship between Americans and their dreams.

Though nose-deep in dream narratives and anecdotes, psychical researchers seldom theorized. Sellers felt that he had grasped the mechanisms of unconscious cerebration only enough to use it for his own ends—he offered no advice for young would-be inventors as to how they might harness this industrious, unsleeping resource. Twain's semiserious proposal that the unconscious be capitalized (with the possible side effect of destroying capital) was not quite ready for prime time, but many researchers speculated that some such use was indeed on the horizon, if only science would take seriously the mysteries of dreams.[112] Josiah Royce echoed this hope in his reflection on "the fantastic man," about whom "we know in a scientific way far too little."[113] Royce was willing to put in the hard labor of extracting the data, but few professional psychologists wanted to continue his work in the coming decades.

Royce's call was taken up with the greatest intensity not by the scientific men and institutions of the early twentieth century, but by movements like symbolism, surrealism, occultism, psychoanalysis, and parapsychology, which also claimed some basis in scientific practices. All were active sites for the amateur study of dreams, but they declined to separate psychology from a broad concern with history, society, and personal fulfillment. Across the United States, readers of Freud sought out psychoanalysts or, failing that, took on their own Freudian interpretations with the aid of popular magazines like *Ladies' Home Journal* and *McClure's*. Such practices continued the use of narrative and anecdote that formed the basis of nineteenth-century dream theorizing.[114] And they continued to explore the uses of dreams, what work they perform, and how they shape and respond to ordinary life.

Psychical research, the vestiges of which re-formed under the banner of parapsychology in the 1940s and 50s, would also pursue "that fantastic man, the dreamer," across the terrain of everyday life but remained committed to the paradigm of dreams as meaningful communications pegged to external reality. The Freudian apparatus of latent content, censorship, and manifest content was not necessary, in the view of parapsychologists, to explain how dreams shunted information within the individual psyche and along networks of relations. Invention served as a powerful symbol for the efficacy of this process: inventions were real things, with real economic value, that crystallized from the obscure work of the unconscious. William James lamented that the only way for a psychologist to study dreaming objectively was if dreams could materially intervene in the world. Many Americans understood them exactly in this way, as sites of production: dreams built the machines that built modern America, and modernization transformed Americans' experience of dreams through new idioms of communication and utility. Histories that trace an evolution from religious to mechanistic to psychoanalytic modes of dream interpretation must also account for the ongoing usefulness of dreams in the context of everyday life.

Further, the recording and collection of dreams reveal turn-of-the-century American attitudes towards science and self-observation. The expansionist visions of the Sellers family, McCay's dreamscapes of urban peril, and Twain's patent-foiling mental telegraph all belong to an extended archive created under amateur scientific auspices, an accumulation of evidence that contributors hoped would reveal larger truths. The multiplicity of archival sites, ranging from the ASPR to popular magazines to newspaper comics, attests to the perceived urgency of documenting Americans' collective dream-work.

In the profusion of dream reports, critics of this genre saw popular indulgence in superstition and magical thinking. However, reading such anecdotes within a circuit of meaning that linked mental and material production quickly takes us, with Walter Benjamin, "beyond the pleasures of the anecdotal landscape into the barrenness of a battlefield."[115] This was the battlefield of clashes between labor and management in streamlined factories, between the Edison myth and the realities of market volatility, and between domestic intimacy and the impersonal risks of urban life. A generation scarred by the upheaval of the Civil War sought to reconcile these violent contrasts; in philosophy, James, Peirce, and John Dewey presented pragmatism as a way to ground a stable collective reality. The ASPR's dream archives suggest that Americans were already doing this work while they slept, "linking things satisfactorily . . . saving labor."[116] The dyspeptic visions of modernity that plagued Winsor McCay's rarebit eaters would not melt into air.

CONTACT

T he Miamisburg mound is a sixty-five-foot-tall cone of earth built by indigenous people of the Ohio River Valley about two thousand years ago. When I visited on a scorching day in June, the park around it was full of picnicking families. I climbed a flight of stairs to a platform at the mound's pinnacle, where I found a young man sitting cross-legged in the sun, his bare torso tattooed with spiritual symbols from various traditions. New Age flute music played at top volume from his smartphone speaker. Though Miamisburg is one of the largest, thousands of mounds once dotted the landscape from present-day Wisconsin to Florida, varying in form and function; some were still in use as burial sites in the eighteenth century. In addition to the historical information on the park's placards, there are many alternative theories about the mounds positing that someone besides Native American ancestors—perhaps Vikings, perhaps UFOs—constructed these monuments. So I asked the man what he thought: Who built the mound we stood on, and what did it mean?

He explained that the mound, for him, was a focal point of cosmic energy. Along with the pyramids and other ancient monuments, it was built to bring humanity into contact with this force that transcends time and space. He visited the mound often; the idea that we can access ancient wisdom helped him find meaning in his own life. When I pressed him on the mound's origins, he replied, "That's lost history."

One hundred twenty-five years earlier, in 1892, a woman who identified herself as Mrs. S. E. Herschel took a tour of the famous Miamisburg mound and had a peculiar experience. While standing at the apex, Herschel fell to her hands and knees, seized by a vision that transported her many centuries into the past. There, she witnessed Indians at work on the foundation of the Miamisburg mound. She observed the construction scene in some detail. "They commenced by pointing trees together like a wigwam and laid the first earth upon these trees." The mound was "to a great height hollow" and, she reported, functioned as a burial site.[1]

Mrs. Herschel's psychic revelation may seem a less reliable source on the mound's origins than an archaeological dig, but by the 1890s archaeologists had laid waste to hundreds of mounds in the Ohio Valley, with many amateurs and even some professionals concluding that Indians were incapable of such works. They attributed the mounds, instead, to hypothetical "lost races," Eurasian groups including Welsh, Vikings, and Phoenicians, which they saw as their predecessors in bringing civilization to the New World.[2] Both Mrs. Herschel and these amateur archaeologists sought connection with a North American past by projecting themselves backward into it. Yet Mrs. Herschel, in an altered state most often associated with Spiritualist mediums, reached a more accurate conclusion than that of would-be scientists. As I tried to make sense of her letter to the ASPR, I found two strands of American colonialism tied together in a perplexing knot: first, the legacy of mediums speaking for "vanished" Indians and second, the attempt to erase Indian antiquity with the myth of a lost race.

White mediums possessed by Indian spirits were a common spectacle in séances for most of the nineteenth century, just as the systematic dispossession and murder of Indians was a commonplace on the nation's westward-marching frontier. Indian spirits seldom expressed anger about the genocide, preferring to convey messages of hope for the realization of America's destiny—a destiny which, by their own account, did not include them. While the Spiritualist movement borrowed notions of communication with the dead from Native American and African religions, these influences were supplanted by a Eurocentric cosmology that cast Indians as blithe and dutiful trail guides to the white afterlife.[3] This character, the "Indian control," inhabited the lowest sphere of the spirit world and therefore served as the point of first contact for mediums, re-enacting Squanto's mythical service to the Mayflower Pilgrims.[4]

Indian controls had fanciful names like Waunie and Prairie Flower, a seventeen-year-old woman said to guide "a great many different mediums in a great many parts of the United States."[5] Legendary figures like Pocahontas and Samoset, as well as Black Hawk and other more recent Indian leaders, appeared in séances to affirm the narrative of the "vanishing Indian"—that North America's indigenous peoples would inevitably fade away in the face of modernity, bequeathing to whites their land, rugged strength, and simple nobility.[6] Black Hawk and his spirit peers were part of a pop culture fad for Indian iconography; popular theater, especially, provided a stock of Indian archetypes, dialects, and costumes that mediums drew upon to "play Indian."[7] By the century's close, neither mediums nor their audiences, especially in Eastern cities, were likely to have spoken with a living Native American.

They would, however, read about Indians in the newspaper, which kept the latest frontier massacres and treaties in public view. Despite what looks today like heartless appropriation, many Spiritualists saw themselves as advocates for the Indian cause, in line with their progressive stance on abolition and women's rights. At the time, white advocacy for Indians meant opposing genocide in favor of forced cultural assimilation—yet even this was a risky stance in the decades after the Civil War, when the press caricatured Plains tribes especially as diabolic enemies of civilization. Spiritualists sometimes allowed their Indian controls to contest such slander, mourning the theft of their land and the murder of their people. Less political strains of Spiritualism also had a stake in stopping the genocide, as they believed that mediumship depended on Indian spirit guides who might abandon them if sufficiently angered by U.S. policies.

All of these contradictions converged in a Spiritualist camp meeting outside Chicago in the summer of 1895, five years after the massacre of Sioux at Wounded Knee brought decades of Indian wars to a shameful dénouement.[8] The weeklong meeting featured a day devoted to Indian channeling and pseudo-Indian rituals: "the Indian council in the morning, the sun dance in the afternoon, and the campfire pow-wow at sunset."[9] While Spiritualists may have felt galvanized to voice Indian grievances in the wake of Wounded Knee, newspaper reporters were merciless in making fun of them. To be clear, journalists had no objection to the cultural appropriation on display, but rather heaped disdain upon white people who would associate themselves in any way with savages. The *Chicago Daily Tribune*'s reporter equated Indians with "dirt, illiteracy, and general cussedness."[10] He described a scene of heathen frenzy in which mediums "flourished imaginary tomahawks . . . howling, yelling, shrieking, and expressing an insatiable desire for the front locks of the whites."[11] These white Spiritualists, through Indian controls, called for their own scalping as vengeance—in the fervor of playacting, they voiced their complicity in colonial crimes.

Spiritualist regret for these crimes was often sentimental and trite. They took for granted that Indians were doomed, ghostly protagonists of a failed struggle who could only hope to serve as a resource for future struggles over gender, race, and citizenship. The *Tribune* reporter encountered recent immigrants at the camp meeting who seemed attuned to the hypocrisy of white American nativism. A German medium stated that the Indian "certainly had a good right to speak out in this old hunting ground of his forefathers."[12] The medium, too, asserted her "right to speak out" based on universal spiritual truths rather than racial and gender hierarchies. Indians authenticated these truths but were artfully ghosted from the Spiritualist vision of the future.

Shakespeare scholar Horace Howard Furness, who sat through countless séances as chair of the Seybert Commission for the Investigation of Modern Spiritualism in the 1880s, wryly noted "the attractive charms which the [medium's] Cabinet seems to possess for the aboriginal Indian."[13] He then marked the glaring absence of another racial group from the spirit world: "It is strange [that] departed black men . . . have hitherto developed no such materializing proclivities."[14] This discrepancy underscores the mythical function of Indian ghosts, compared with the very real prospect of African American enfranchisement after the Civil War. Had Furness's commission extended its study to the Black Spiritualist churches of New Orleans, they would have encountered the shades of Toussaint L'Ouverture, United States Colored Troops veterans, and tortured slaves who were far less forgiving of white sins than was the cheerful Prairie Flower.[15]

Mrs. Herschel's prehistoric vision on the Miamisburg mound was starkly different from "Indian day" at the Spiritualist camp meeting in many ways. She did not pretend to embody Indianness, to dance or take on voices that were not hers to channel, and thereby claim a meaningful relationship to the land. Rather, her point of contact with the Indian past was sight—she simply observed a scene from an earlier time, with scientific attention to detail, as though peering through a window. The spontaneous opening of this window to Mrs. Herschel was a subtler proof of her worthiness as a medium and an American. Indeed, it rivaled the claim of other white Americans who had long labored to *uncover* the meaning of the mounds: amateur antiquarians, and increasingly, professional archaeologists.

The fact that mounds were built by the ancestors of modern Indians was a commonsense conclusion drawn by the first white settlers. Yet early observers began to sow the seeds of doubt by insinuating that Indians lacked the tools, industry, and manpower for such monuments, and thus some larger mystery must be afoot. Careful excavators, from Thomas Jefferson to the Smithsonian's Cyrus Thomas, confirmed that they were Indian constructions filled with Indian artifacts and Indian remains.[16] Others, however, cultivated the mystery, and popular literature on the "lost race" of mound builders flourished throughout the nineteenth century.

Most of it fell into the category of florid armchair speculation, which fully grasped and exploited white America's deep-seated desire to colonize the past. Smithsonian archaeologist Gerald Fowke accused lost race theorists of stoking "a feverish excitement" not unlike the frenzy of the Spiritualist séance. He urged that "the work must finally be done by someone who has not derived all his information at secondhand or from his inner consciousness."[17] According to Fowke, the new, scientific discipline of archaeology should have quickly resolved the issue. And yet, for many decades, it could not. The implications of granting Indians a history beyond the "primitive" cycle of hunting and gathering were too great.

Mrs. Herschel's vision certainly unfolded on the stage of her "inner consciousness." She seems to fit Fowke's profile of the lost race believer with "a vivid imagination . . . acting upon an untrained mind or a soul filled with emotions."[18] Yet she described a specific and plausible scene of indigenous people constructing the Miamisburg mound. She sent her experience to the ASPR inviting them to verify, to the best of their ability, whether her clairvoyant observations squared with the archaeological evidence. Was it really possible to gain knowledge of the ancient past through revelation?

Richard Hodgson received Mrs. Herschel's letter on April 1, 1892, and wrote directly to the archaeological authorities. Was the mound, in fact, built on a timber frame and hollow inside? An 1869 exploration party, which included then-Ohio-governor Rutherford B. Hayes, had conducted the only excavation at Miamisburg. Hayes replied to Hodgson that he remembered no hollow cavern in the mound.[19] Hayes passed Hodgson's query to his friend Manning Ferguson Force, an antiquarian who supplied a lengthy treatise on the "race of the Mound Builders."[20] Neither of these authorities could verify the presence of a hollow chamber. How had this detail become fixed in Mrs. Herschel's mind's eye?

J. G. Owens of Harvard's Peabody Museum suspected that Mrs. Herschel got the content of her vision from reading about other mounds, such as the one at Grave Creek, whose burial chambers were widely publicized.[21] Archaeologist George Ephraim Squier published his firsthand account in the popular *Frank Leslie's Weekly*, describing the mound's interior as "a kind of vault made of rough timber"—exactly the notion that Mrs. Herschel borrowed. Yet even Squier, the levelheaded professional, declared that no ancestors of modern Indians could possess the "skill in design and execution" needed to build a seventy-foot-tall mound.[22] Again, Herschel's account doesn't square with widespread popular narratives upon which she supposedly drew. To learn about the argument for Indian mound builders, Herschel would have had to read beyond the headlines, seeking out journals and books and deciding which authors she trusted. Or perhaps she felt a spiritual certainty that made expert knowledge irrelevant.

"I am always open to suggestions, visions, information, etc. concerning America in pre-Columbian times," wrote dean of American archaeology Warren K. Moorehead, then curator of the Ohio Historical and Archaeological Society. He explained to Hodgson that Mrs. Herschel's was far from the only prophecy he'd received; in his long career of mound excavations, "many persons tried in a general way to tell what the mounds would contain." These visions were inevitably too vague to aid in excavation and too vague to be substantiated by its results. In the end, "the practical archaeologist was the only person who 'saw' the contents." Moorehead upheld the primacy of the scientific method: "The shovel and pick are the only true agents." Unfortunately, the scientific method could shed no light on the interior structure of the Miamisburg mound. "The mound at Miamisburg has never been thoroughly explored," Moorehead confessed. "No report was [published], no scientist did the work."[23] The haphazard 1869 dig has been the only major excavation of the mound to this day. Looking through local newspaper reports from 1869, I found some stating that Hayes and his crew did in fact discover a hollow chamber built from logs, about forty feet down.

Baking in the clear hot air at the mound's peak, I certainly wondered what it meant for the people who lay within, how they saw their valley and their world. Maybe it's just my dislike of flute music, but I also felt rather alone atop this ancient monument, talking to the tattooed man about ley lines. Whatever the mound meant, my presence there meant nothing—a chance consequence of that two-faced idea of America as a place where everyone can have a voice, the promise that drew my family in flight from persecution and poverty. They had no nostalgia, they never forgave the Old World for trying to kill them, and they didn't ask about the killing that happened here to make their prosperity possible. Those dark contingent threads seem utterly remote from the immaculate sunshine of the Ohio Valley. I can understand how, wanting it all to mean something, one would attempt to make contact with a vanished past or an unreachable other. We all want to feel connected to a home.

Mrs. Herschel's experience seems more than a case of vivid imagination. Or perhaps less—perhaps it's much simpler. Despite the lack of scientific study and documentation at this particular site, Mrs. Herschel applied a commonsense rubric: the continent was inhabited by Indians for thousands of years, and they built the Miamisburg mound. It's not lost history, it was simply never ours. Whatever we might believe about energy, time, and psychic communion, no one is entitled to contact that destroys.

.

CHAPTER 3

DRAWINGS FROM
THE OTHER SIDE

T he preceding chapters have emphasized the vast scope of psychical research in the nineteenth- and early twentieth-century United
States. Viewed from above, its subject matter was an immense, circulating
system of human experience; viewed from the ground, it dissolved into
an unruly army of observers chasing after what William James called "wild
facts." By submitting to the judgment of a scientific society, ASPR participants hoped that their isolated experiences could help illuminate the
truth of the greater whole. Psychical research was deeply entwined, in this
regard, with other nineteenth-century field sciences that presented scientific inquiry as an element of good citizenship. These sciences cultivated
curiosity and critical thought, and saw themselves as enacting a democratic project where individuals contributed to a mutually formed account
of reality. Today, we might also see in meteorology, astronomy, and their
kin a nationalist logic of securing mastery over the American landscape
and its human terrain. In the twenty-first century many Americans still
struggle for a voice in the nation's dominant account of reality, which
makes any celebration of narrow nineteenth-century scientific communities ring hollow. Yet there is something in psychical research, engaged as it
was in reconciling the singularity of experience with communal life, that
offers generative ways of thinking through its own blind spots.

The final chapters of this book turn from a large-scale natural-histori-
cal conception of the mind to the more intimate practices through which
investigators explored their individual perceptions and possibilities. They
move through interior spaces of home, office, and clinic, to the ultimate
interior, the psyche, and perhaps back out again. Psychical researchers'

simultaneous hope for and fear of mental permeability scraped against psychology's description of minds as closed, private spaces, analogous to the locked room of a Sherlock Holmes mystery—and just as fundamentally Victorian and middle class. In Conan Doyle's stories, as in Freud's psychoanalysis, the locked room is the scene of criminal acts and criminal desires. The crime is associated with invasion by alien races and classes, but often traces back to a dark secret within the victimized family itself. Though this scandalous diagnosis certainly intrigued readers, they did not uniformly accept it as the key to interpreting their own experiences of the subliminal self. The locked room was one available metaphor that could model varying degrees and kinds of permeability. The fervor with which Americans and Europeans of this period took up experiments in intersubjectivity reflects a desire to keep the door ajar. As Jason Josephson-Storm argues, this desire only appears to emanate from an occult fringe due to the retrospective historical narrative of disenchantment.[1] Both laypeople and scientists contributed to the séances, telepathic missives, and other strange forms of intimacy that deeply inflected the epistemological foundation of the modern mind sciences.

Though participants in psychical research challenged the notion that only pathological conditions led to cracks in the locked room of the unconscious mind, the metaphor certainly shaped their ideas and methods. They recognized that a great deal of our mental activity, from sensory processing to hunches or intuitions, is not directly accessible by conscious reflection. Reaching this shrouded interior posed a challenge for the entire project of the mind sciences, and psychical researchers paid close attention to the strategies developed by psychologists and neurologists. Psychophysics relied on precise measurements of stimulus thresholds and response times, while neurologists like Charcot and Janet placed their subjects in trance states, in each case hoping to bypass the conscious subject and get an objective read on the underlying cognitive architecture and its subliminal contents.

This chapter proposes that psychical researchers did not merely imitate such strategies, but helped to articulate new experimental practices for accessing the unconscious mind at a critical moment in the formalization of both laboratory and clinical psychology. I focus on the development of drawing tasks—any experimental procedure in which a subject is asked to draw, whether spontaneously or from memory. These tasks emerged from multiple sources, but they crystallized as a scientific tool thanks to the practices of psychical researchers in the late nineteenth century, who used drawing to test the permeability of the mind's locked room—often by placing their test subjects in actual locked rooms and asking them to reproduce an image drawn by a distant telepathic agent.[2] Drawing gradually gained acceptance in mainstream psychology as a reliable way to reach the mind via the hand while bypassing the conscious subject. The widespread use of drawing in both neuropsychology and psychotherapy takes on a new significance when we understand its roots in psychical research: an experiment meant to join two minds in communion became a routine tool for examining solitary brains.

Hand-to-Mind Science

The three faces in Figures 6, 7, and 8 represent three stages in which drawing became naturalized as a technology of direct inscription, able to record hidden mental processes. Each image appeared in a scientific publication as objective evidence of what a subject was thinking and how they were thinking it. Scientists claimed that they could read the mechanisms, structures, and content of thoughts in these drawings, without needing to ask the subject what he or she meant. Though some researchers doubted that the brain expressed itself through the pen in this way, the simplicity and apparent directness of drawing held an irresistible appeal. It allowed psychology to bypass what James called "the misleading influence of speech," producing objective evidence that could secure the discipline's scientific bona fides.[3]

Figure 6, from the child study movement of the late nineteenth century, was meant to show that a child's skill at representational drawing correlates with her overall cognitive development. Figure 7, produced by psychical researchers, shows the telepathic transmission of a picture from one mind to another. Figure 8, produced in a twentieth-century clinical test, shows how a neurological injury causes specific deficits in the patient's ability to represent a human face. Taken together, these images encapsulate an assumed relationship between

FIGURE 6. A child's response when prompted to draw a human face. Herman T. Lukens, "A Study of Children's Drawings in the Early Years," *Pedagogical Seminary*, 4:1 (1896): 109.

FIGURE 7. George Albert Smith's drawing of a face, received telepathically from his partner Douglas Blackburn. Edmund Gurney et. al., "Third Report on Thought Transference," *PSPR* 1 (1883): 205.

drawing and thinking that's become ubiquitous in the mind sciences. Many tangled pathways mediate these two functions, but researchers often collapsed this complexity because the method produced such striking visual results. A logic of direct access emerged, minimizing subjective factors like history, personality, voice, and experience in the move towards the standardized subject of laboratory psychology. For psychical researchers, drawing tests were part of the larger effort to become scientific by collecting standardized, reproducible evidence from the public, which included the reporting forms discussed in Chapter 1. Like self-registering instruments in meteorology, drawing became a tool that inscribed fleeting mental activity as a material trace. However, in contrast to tedious random guessing, drawing allowed experimenters to communicate meaningful semiotic content. Even the most rudimentary shapes and figures engaged participants in an interpretive process guided by their prior knowledge and theories. Though sifting

FIGURE 8. Face drawn by a forty-five-year-old woman who has suffered a stroke. Theodore Herman Weisenburg and Katharine E. McBride, *Aphasia: A Clinical and Psychological Study* (New York: The Commonwealth Fund, 1935), 402–3.

through these homegrown theories was a headache for the ASPR secretary, the intellectual interest of drawing tests—underpinned by the sheer desire to communicate—produced better results.

Random guessing and drawing enjoyed equal popularity, and were often used interchangeably, among psychical researchers in the 1880s and 90s, but disagreements arose over which method promised irrefutable proof of telepathy. Critics of random guessing identified two major problems: First, guessing tests presumed that telepathic signals functioned independently from the content they carried, while many people felt that telepathy depended on emotional intensity for its strength. Second, researchers realized that the standard probabilities of choosing from a card deck actually made fraud easier. They hoped that more complex telepathic transmissions would be impossible to fake. Departing from randomized guessing tasks meant leaving behind the realm of Simon Newcomb's statistical tables, but for those concerned more with the nature of thought than with statistics, it held great allure. Though William James agreed with Newcomb that quantitative experimentation was psychology's ticket into the scientific mainstream, he never stopped bemoaning the paucity of "these new prism, pendulum, and chronograph-philosophers."[4] In psychical research, he saw a possible alternative configuration that allowed experiments with meaning and consciousness itself.

For the ASPR's participants, telepathic drawings were simply more interesting and thus better for morale. Beginners complained of frustration and boredom with the endless repetition of card guessing and generally gave up before producing enough data. James advised one aspiring investigator that cards were "fearfully dull work, and might be exchanged for words or diagrams if the statistics were favorable"—that is, if the medium showed promise in rudimentary tasks, they should advance to richer material as soon as possible.[5] Other psychical investigators felt that "free-drawing" tasks should be the first method for finding "sensitives," people with particular aptitude for receiving telepathic messages.[6] "Words or diagrams" introduced weighty interpretive questions, allowing participants to apply their intellects, rather than slavishly generating data for analysis by the experts.

Automatic writing and drawing produced spontaneously by trance mediums was always an object of fascination for Spiritualists and psychical researchers—dramatically scrawled reams of script fill countless folders in the ASPR's archives, while William James's papers at Harvard contain a single automatic writing specimen which his son preserved as "an example of many, many documents that have been destroyed."[7] Seeing the words of the dead filtered through the medium's bodily struggle to maintain a channel to the other world was deeply compelling and provided a visual anchor for Spiritualist practice. But for most psychical researchers the existence of otherworldly spirits was not a foregone conclusion, and telepathy among the living seemed the more likely explanation. Parsimoniously bypassing dead relatives, they decomposed thought into an information flow that might travel from mind to mind and exit through the hand. Evidence of image transmission was a cornerstone of the case for telepathy which persuaded many leaders in the SPR and

ASPR in the 1880s. It also aligned psychical research with other sciences of the period that began using hand-drawn images to study the mind.

The establishment of drawing as an experimental method proceeded in three broad phases. Initially, in the 1870s, drawing emerged as a technique of direct inscription in which the hand mechanically externalized mental contents, which were then compared and classified. As researchers in different areas of the mind sciences amassed large image collections, they began to read images figuratively for emotional and biographical content, which led to a divergent interpretive tradition in parapsychology, psychoanalysis, and art therapy. Finally, in the wake of scandals that discredited telepathic drawing experiments, neuropsychologists quietly reappropriated drawing as a purely mechanical heuristic to study the brain's visual and motor processing systems. Stripping images of individual history and meaning solidified their value as objective evidence, but it also meant that psychical researchers' interpretive arguments for telepathic communication were no longer valid in professional science. This change in the status of images—from symbols of mental content to traces of cognitive process—accompanied a shift towards the psychological conception of the brain as a closed system.

Drawing in an experimental setting seems a straightforward process— a subject puts pencil to paper and an investigator studies the resulting image. Yet the experiment involves a feat of logical alchemy, collapsing the distinction between the object under observation (the brain) and the mechanism of observation and recording (also the brain, as it translates from sensory input to motor output). The psychological subject becomes a hybrid object-instrument for inscribing thought. Historians Lorraine Daston and Peter Galison describe the scientific ideal of objectivity as "blind sight, seeing without inference, interpretation, or intelligence," and indeed this was the goal of many drawing experiments.[8] Daston and Galison underscore the impossibility of blind sight; both scientists and subjects constantly reason about what is happening as it happens. Yet throughout its career as an experimental technique, drawing has been connected with certain kinds of subjects who were regarded as reduced in some way to the pure mechanisms of thought. We must attend carefully to this assumed difference in cognitive status between researcher

and subject, at times more or less pronounced. Some psychical researchers making this assumption fell into error when their subjects outwitted
them, while others took on the subject's perspective to achieve insight
into their own personal equations.

The Mind of the Child, in Pictures

Drawing as a tool for the investigation of thought blossomed around the
turn of the twentieth century, appearing almost simultaneously in disparate fields. Because the boundaries between philosophy, psychology,
neurology, and psychiatry were still permeable, it circulated among them
easily.[9] In each of these areas, researchers hoped to discover mental laws
by asking subjects to draw; many of them believed that drawings gave better, more direct evidence than verbal responses. Child study, a precursor
to child psychology that crested between 1870 and 1900, is an example
of success in this endeavor—its proponents set widely adopted norms for
child development that used drawing as a rubric. Psychical researchers
were paying attention and mobilized many of the same rhetorics and
methodologies in their efforts to prove telepathy. The story of how drawing tasks emerged in child study flows directly into their function for
psychical research.

The process by which drawings that were "bad," inaccurate, or ugly
became highly valued by science is especially remarkable given the social
functions of art in this period. The ability to make accurate and pleasing representational sketches was a sign of privilege in early nineteenth-
century Europe and America. It belonged to the set of genteel skills
cultivated in elite schools, along with dancing, declining Latin nouns,
and playing the piano—an edifying pastime that advertised one's status.[10]
Naturally, the middle classes followed suit, and drawing entered public
school curricula. At the same time, technical drawing increasingly had
applications in industrial trades that made it an important part of compulsory education for the lower classes.[11]

Because of this multipronged demand for drawing education, specialized instructors and textbooks became indispensable. Art teachers
waged impassioned pedagogical battles over the proper way to teach
perspective and shading. This meant that children were producing large

numbers of drawings at young ages under close supervision—whereas in the past, adults would not have paid much attention to children's idle scribbles. By the 1870s, researchers took an interest in those earliest drawings made before formal training began. Rather than rote techniques, these images seemed to offer a glimpse into the organic contents of the mind as it developed, revealing how children learn to think and perceive. Pioneers of the new child study movement set out to capture and analyze this data, conveniently available within the nation's growing public school system. They argued that written tests were not adequate for studying such young children, since children might know things that they lacked the vocabulary to describe. Only drawing could bypass the language problem and, so researchers claimed, access the actual content of the minds of children.[12]

G. Stanley Hall, a student of William James and the first American to receive a PhD in psychology, was in large part responsible for bringing child study to the United States from Germany. The earlier development of compulsory public education in Prussia had produced a vigorous pedagogy literature by the 1870s, concerned with measuring and standardizing student progress. Inspired by these studies, Hall undertook a more open-ended "inventory of the child mind" in 1880, in which he asked hundreds of Boston schoolchildren to simply list things that they knew: animals, places, tools, and so forth. Most of the prompts were verbal, but Hall expressed reservations about this method, noting that children's vocabulary lagged behind their functional understanding.[13] He thus included drawing tasks in the inventory, claiming that "drawings reveal the child's psychic life in an extraordinary way and show its motor development [and] the directions of its interests."[14] Hall's main interest lay with the collective "child" or the "child mind" as a universal abstraction whose patterns and developmental rules would emerge from his agglomeration of statistics.

Although Hall soon moved on from child study to other endeavors— he established the *American Journal of Psychology* and shaped the American social sciences as the first president of Clark University—his ideas about the importance of early childhood proved quite influential as they moved from academia to popular discourse. The child became the focus of widespread public anxiety over how to produce better citizens in the midst of rapid social and economic change. Rising immigration rates and stark poverty in cities forced the question of whether children were blank slates, highly adaptable to American life, or if their fates lay in their bloodlines. The new field of child study promised to answer these questions, generally taking the progressive stance that government intervention could mold an industrious citizenry. On the front lines, schoolteachers and mothers became active participants in collecting data and developing the science. They formed "Hall clubs," an amateur network which gathered to discuss and contribute to *Pedagogical Seminary*, the child study journal that Hall started in 1891.

As the field became more specialized, *Pedagogical Seminary* published analyses of children's drawings from psychologists and educators. Among the more prolific was the German-trained Herman T. Lukens, who held a fellowship under Hall at Clark University from 1894–1895 and returned as a docent in pedagogy from 1899–1900.[15] Lukens collected 3,400 drawings from children between two and sixteen years of age, publishing his findings in 1896. Such vast accumulations became a fad in child study for the same reasons that psychical researchers collected anecdotes of clairvoyant dreams: modern, inductive scientific reasoning needed a foundation in facts. Some child study projects netted many thousands of drawings and requested still more samples from the journal's readers, with the promise that treasured artworks would be duplicated and returned.[16] The materiality and reproducibility of these drawings was crucial to their evidentiary status. Unlike other traces of the child mind translated from words or behaviors into tables and charts, drawings could be printed as illustrations in professional journals, honing a visual rhetoric of directness and transparency. Lukens presented series of drawings done by the same children over the course of many years, to illustrate linear development from scribbles to "the complete clarification of the mental image" as a recognizable picture.[17]

Because Lukens assumed that the children he studied were naïve subjects, incapable of willful misrepresentation, he presented drawings as an unmediated glimpse into their minds, pictures of the world as the child understood it.[18] A certain level of expertise, however, was required

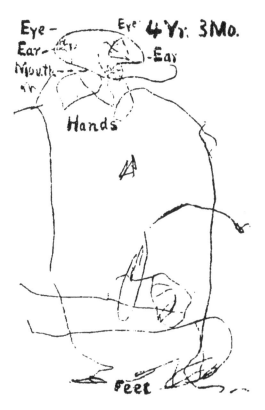

FIGURE 9. Drawing by Lillian L. at four years, three months old. Lukens, "A Study of Children's Drawings in the Early Years," *Pedagogical Seminary* 4:1 (1896): 102.

to interpret these glimpses, and we see Lukens ordering messy phenomena with a developmental logic. "The tangle of lines over the legs is not in any case to be interpreted as shading," he asserted of the child's drawing in Figure 9.[19] Though such an interpretation by the viewer seems unlikely, he still went out of his way to refute a possible deviation from his developmental chronology; four-year-olds were too primitive to use shading techniques. He also provided reassurances about his control over the research setting. Although the collection of drawings did not take place in a psychological laboratory, and parents or teachers were often present, Lukens maintained the objectivity of the process: "Her mother meanwhile looked on in silence, giving no suggestions"—an impartial experiment.[20]

While asserting that drawing correlated with mental development, Lukens could not ignore the possibility of a disjoint between mind and hand. What if young children had refined mental imagery and simply lacked motor skills? He tried to handicap for dexterity, allowing that the very youngest simply could not control a pencil. The drawings of Lillian L. at age two "show the utter lack of any apparent connection between a mental picture in consciousness and the movements made by the hand and fingers in attempting to draw it."[21] Once Lillian L.'s ability had improved to the point where she could capture basic contours, however, Lukens returned to linking cognition and representation: more accurate sketching "corresponds to a clarification of the mental image in the child's mind."[22] A discrimination made by the researcher, between motor capacity and "true" perception, thus became a step in the mental development of the child.

Like Hall, Lukens used children's drawings to argue for a recapitulation theory of human mental development: both men saw "striking analogies in the pictorial evolution of man between the child and the race."[23] Dominant social theories of the day, inspired by Charles Darwin's notorious popularizer, Herbert Spencer, held that ontogeny recapitulates phylogeny —that is, individual development from infant to adult follows the same pattern as racial development from "primitive" to "civilized." This notion, ubiquitous among social reformers, infantilized non-European races, justifying colonial exploitation as the white man's burden. As a strange corollary, recapitulation also equated white children with "savages." Art historians took up this concept, comparing images produced by ancient and non-European cultures with those collected in Western child study.

Lukens, however, sought to nuance this sort of "conventional and generic" gloss on children's drawings. In his work we see a step away from Hall's statistical abstractions about developmental stages and towards more personalized interpretation. Although he would not go so far as Freud or later promoters of art therapy, Lukens serves as a sort of bridge between Hall's survey method, modeled on big natural history projects like meteorology and astronomy, and the psychoanalytic method, which saw drawings as an outlet for the unconscious. For Lukens, drawing provided access to the individual's true inner life. Indeed, it was a better tool than speech for getting at the unique thinking of each child, since "words are often repeated meaninglessly," while drawings were "form synonyms for thoughts."[24]

While the amateur networks of child study gave way to laboratory-centered developmental psychology in the early twentieth century, the use of drawings to assess children's cognitive ability became formalized in much the way that Hall had envisioned. By the 1910s, drawing tasks as a measure of development were standard, with evaluations designed by Frederic L. Burke, James Mark Baldwin, James Sully, William Stern, and many others.[25] In 1926, the psychologist Florence Goodenough introduced the "Draw-a-Man" test, establishing a widely adopted rubric for correlating drawings with intelligence as measured by the Stanford-Binet Intelligence Scale.[26] Also in the 1920s, Jean Piaget developed his influential four-stage theory of artistic development in children, which reiterated the progression from scribbles to "visual realism"—the faithful rendering of three-dimensional space as a marker of cognitive sophistication.[27]

As a framework developed within professional psychology for cognitive evaluation using drawing tests, amateur investigators (namely, mothers and primary school teachers) stayed engaged with the field.[28] Amid the burgeoning technocratic expertise of the Progressive Era, mothers were encouraged to actively collect and evaluate evidence of their children's development; women's magazines, newspapers, and the popular press promoted drawing as an easily tracked indicator.[29] Indeed, the domestic setting and intimate context of these amateur studies resemble psychical research in the same period. As the following sections show, psychical investigators also used drawings to access mental contents and also moved away from collaboration with academic scientists as they pursued their own goals. In both cases, drawing tests allowed participants to produce and interpret evidence with value for their lives and relationships.

This gives us one history of how drawing became a tool for psychological insight around the turn of the twentieth century. Child study understood drawings as revealing the workings of the mind with little interference from language; however, drawings also required expert interpretation to take on psychological meaning. Most significantly for the episodes that follow, we see two divergent views of the relationship between mind and image. Hall's concept of the child mind was an objective, taxonomic one, and thus drawings fit into normalized developmental stages—"psychic levels" rather than individual psyches. This view gained currency as psychology fought to become a respected scientific profession in the early twentieth century. Practical applications like psychometry and intelligence testing were valued as routes to legitimacy and funding.[30] Such tests would have a long and frustratingly persistent hold, sorting and ranking Americans in schools, the military, and the corporate world to this day.

On the other hand, those who leaned towards interpretation believed that, as Lukens suggested, "children's drawings give us one of the surest ways with which to reach the contents of their minds"; the meaning of images lay in the subjectivity of their makers.[31] This inclination to interpret rather than taxonomize, and to read drawings as expressions of complex subjectivity, saw its realization in Freud's Wolf Man drawings, the art therapy of Margaret Naumburg, and the child psychoanalysis pioneered by Anna Freud and Melanie Klein. Whether interpretive or evaluative, "reading" drawings often became the work of female practitioners in the emerging area of applied psychology.

At the same time that child study took up drawings as psychological data, they became central to another fledgling field devoted to the investigation of the human mind. This field, psychical research, developed a similar experimental methodology in which the subject became an object-instrument. This hybrid subject-object-instrument produced images which, investigators believed, would prove the existence of a surprising new kind of mental activity.

Picturing Telepathy

The second portion of this chapter takes us from the drawings of children to those of grown men who studied telepathy.[32] Just as drawings could reveal an individual's thoughts, they could also demonstrate the transfer of thought between two minds. Psychical researchers employed many of the same techniques used by child study to render drawings into evidence. Their methods, publications, and rhetorical maneuvers helped to frame drawings as objective thought-pictures. Even critics aiming to debunk telepathy used drawing to prove their nonsupernatural explanations of the phenomenon. Skeptics such as the astronomer William Henry Pickering argued that the human brain has a repertoire of basic visual forms, and some appear with greater statistical frequency than others. Indeed, he attempted to chart the distribution of unconscious imagery by collecting representative drawings from the population, just as Hall's child study experts had done.

What, exactly, did psychical researchers mean by *telepathy*? Interest in mind-reading and thought-transference surged in Anglo-American culture of the 1870s, in an environment suffused with Spiritualist séances, mesmeric stage performances, and other supernormal manifestations— the environment that spurred the formation of the SPR and ASPR.[33] Within the psychical research community, the term *telepathy* was coined to describe a secular, rational alternative to the spirit hypothesis (which asserted that mediums' clairvoyant knowledge came from disembodied souls in the afterlife). If mediums inadvertently got their information from reading the minds of the living, at least researchers could avoid the metaphysics of immortality. Telepathy gained increasing acceptance as a scientific phenomenon in the 1880s, such that even Spiritualists wove it into their explanation, suggesting that spirit communication was essentially telepathy with the dead.

The idea of mind-to-mind communication was so compelling in part because of new discoveries in physics. Advocates compared it to the transmission of light, magnetism, and electricity, as described in the Introduction. If scientific instruments could measure and quantify such intangibles, it seemed plausible that human thought, too, might have its own yet-to-be-discovered wavelength and might travel from mind to mind like a telegraph message.[34] In an age when communication technology had broken down the barriers of time and distance, and scientists were working towards wireless telegraph and radio, such expectations were hardly far-fetched. Indeed, respectable men of science advertised their grand ambitions about mastering the invisible world. British engineer Cromwell Fleetwood Varley played a key role in laying the first transatlantic telegraph cable and embraced the "spirit telegraph" as a technology within reach of enterprising electricians. He also studied cathode rays, arguing that these strange electrical emanations were made of particles, not waves—and that they supported the material reality of spirits and thought-transference. Physicist and outspoken Spiritualist Oliver Lodge performed the first public demonstration of wireless telegraphy at a meeting of the British Association for the Advancement of Science in 1894, proving that ideas, encoded in electrical impulses, could leap across empty space.[35]

In this moment of speculative possibility, psychical researchers applied scientific methods to determine whether "impressions from the minds of those about us [can reach] our own minds by channels distinct from those of the senses"—a widely adopted definition of the phenomenon which they first termed *thought-transference* and in 1882 gave the more impressive name *telepathy*.[36] Although they aimed for controlled laboratory-style experimentation, researchers had to compromise with mediums who claimed that their powers appeared only under certain conditions—in a locked cabinet or a darkened parlor. Thus, the methods of psychical researchers were shaped by the colorful stage acts of thought readers, which involved locating hidden objects, reading concealed messages, and guessing randomly chosen numbers. Such activities were also the basis of common parlor games that led some ordinary people to identify themselves as possessing supernormal mental powers. These games and performances, along with new communication technologies discussed above, shaped cultural expectations about how powers of mind could be demonstrated.

The popular standard of Baconian science—empirical proof by witnessing—shaped mediumistic performance from the very beginning of Spiritualism. Spiritualists staged "demonstrations" for audiences of rational observers to draw their own conclusions; they performed in "halls of science" and advertised "scientific lectures."[37] Thus, when academics agreed to engage with mediums in testing psychical claims, they encountered a funhouse-mirror version of their own methods. Experimental principles like control, replication, and witnessing became stumbling blocks; some researchers assumed a shared vocabulary and failed to grasp when their subjects were using very different logics under the same name. Naturally, when they realized that mediums did not share their definition of experimental control, scientists decried Spiritualism as a fraud. Although psychical researchers worked to expose performers' tricks, ferreting out codes or muscle reading, their purpose in stripping away these explanations was to uncover evidence of a genuine mental force as yet undocumented by science. They seized upon drawing, a technology of direct inscription, to bypass the methodological and epistemological conflict that marked their relations with their subjects.

The British SPR conducted the first formal telepathy experiments on the daughters of a Buxton clergyman. The five girls successfully guessed cards, numbers, and names selected secretly by investigators. Because they were young, female, and from a respectable family, the Creery girls were assumed to be incapable of the deception to which they would later confess—which the SPR maintained did not discredit the results. A second set of foundational experiments involved the duo of George Albert Smith and Douglas Blackburn. Their well-documented success in visual thought-transference became a pillar of the SPR's argument for telepathy. Smith and Blackburn were adult men who performed on stage for profit, which made them more suspect than the Creery sisters—thus, they needed to produce more interesting phenomena, and the SPR had to develop more rigorous methods to prevent fraud. When Americans read the results, they were not impressed by this effort. Members of the ASPR accused their British counterparts of lax experimental control. Yet, amid the acrimony, they accepted the basic premise that drawing experiments were the logical way to prove or disprove telepathy.

In August of 1882, Douglas Blackburn, a newspaper editor in the resort town of Brighton, wrote to the Spiritualist periodical *Light* claiming that a young man named George Albert Smith could read his thoughts "with an accuracy that approaches the miraculous."[38] Smith, only eighteen years old at the time, had recently begun performing as a stage medium in Brighton. He and Blackburn collaborated to promote his act, with Blackburn serving as a confederate onstage at the same time that he published glowing reviews in his newspaper.[39] Their ambitions extended beyond the entertainment of Brighton tourists. With the earnest investigations of "credulous spiritualists" constantly in the news, Smith and

Blackburn schemed to show the public "how easy a matter it was to 'take in' scientific observers."[40] At least, this is how a jaded Blackburn described their intentions in a confession published decades later. It's impossible to say whether they really aimed to ensnare the SPR from the outset or simply took the opportunities that emerged as their deception escalated. What we know for sure is that Smith's confident, persuasive manner held up under the most intimate scrutiny, where most other mediums fell victim to headaches or exhaustion and withdrew from the experiments.

The SPR's Committee on Thought-Transference, led by Edmund Gurney, Frederic Myers, and William Barrett, reached out to Blackburn after his letter in *Light*, proposing a series of tests to verify Smith's powers. They began in the autumn of 1882 with the bread-and-butter demonstrations of thought reading: guessing numbers, names, and colors chosen by the experimenters, shown to Blackburn, and transmitted from Blackburn to Smith. These transmissions occurred, the SPR promised, with "no sound or movement of the lips of any one"; Smith and Blackburn were, however, allowed to hold hands.[41] When the two men were placed in separate rooms their run of successes came to an abrupt halt, and Blackburn complained of neuralgia caused by the strain of concentration.[42] Gurney and his colleagues allowed them to resume holding hands, and they produced more successful thought-transferences—a classic example of how the experimenters' ideal of control clashed with mediums' demands to set their own conditions. Although the SPR investigators appreciated that hand-holding could be a means of sending a coded message, their subjects asserted that it was also the channel through which their extrasensory thought-transference worked. To accommodate the medium's needs, the investigators decided to change the content of the messages, rather than altering the experimental setup. They would come up with something that could never be boiled down to a code: "drawings or geometrical figures," Gurney explained, "inexpressible in descriptive words."[43] The activity of drawing thus became an instrument for fraud-proof thought-transference in the eyes of the SPR.

On the second day of experiments, Gurney, Myers, and Barrett "drew some image at random, the figure being of such a character that its shape could not easily be conveyed in words . . . in order to meet the

FIGURE 10. The committee's drawing of a handled bowl. Gurney et al., "Third Report on Thought-Transference," *PSPR* 1 (1883): 213.

assumption that some code—such as the Morse alphabet—was used by S. and B."[44] They showed this image to Blackburn (Figure 10), Blackburn grasped Smith's hands, and Smith sat down and reproduced the image on paper, sometimes while wearing a blindfold. Smith's drawings, "about as like the original as a child's blindfold drawing of a pig is like a pig," were nonetheless "recognizable as intended to represent the original figure."[45] The rough, unpolished appearance of these images (Figure 11), and the speed and confidence with which Smith produced them—his motions not entirely automatic, but not entirely under conscious control—supported the assumption that drawing was a direct relay between the mind's eye and the hand. The fact that witnesses could discern the underlying intention beneath Smith's scrawl suggested that he had received a holistic image or concept, perhaps blurred by the noise of the transmission. Implicit in this analysis was the idea that Smith's cognitive-motor processes were recorded as subtle clues within his pictures.

The SPR took the Smith drawings as authoritative evidence of direct communication between minds, asserting that "the burden of explaining

FIGURE 11.   George Albert Smith's attempt to reproduce the bowl telepathically. Gurney et al., "Third Report on Thought-Transference," *PSPR* 1 (1883); 213.

these results rests upon those who deny the possibility of thought-transference."[46] They made a point of reproducing the successful matches in their journal, the *Proceedings of the Society for Psychical Research*, with the assurance that "the whole series of figures are given in the accompanying plates, which are engraved from photographic reproductions, *on the wood blocks*, of the original drawings."[47] To explain their italics, it's important to note that wood-block engraving, the illustration technique that generated the vast quantity of images demanded by nineteenth-century mass print, had transformed in the second half of the century from an interpretive art to a facsimile process. An engraver in the 1840s would have drawn or traced a copy of Smith's figures onto the block, potentially smoothing over the rough, unsteady lines to distill a more pleasing image. By 1883 Smith's figures could be photographed, the film printed directly onto a wood block, and this photographic block carved by a technician trained in mechanical exactitude. Engraving became an extension of photography, which made it possible for thousands of people all over the world to examine the same piece of evidence.[48] It preserved the errors and idiosyncrasies of individual research subjects like Smith, believed to hold the key to intricate mental processes. As engravings went from stylized representations to exact copies, readers could use scientific journals like the SPR's *Proceedings* to analyze evidence in a new way.

The terms that Gurney, Myers, and Barrett used to discuss image-transference took the drawn image as a badly needed material fact. In the world of psychical investigation, speech was often suspect, the province of dubious stage mediums who dealt in sensational utterances from beyond the grave. Witnesses produced wildly divergent reports of what was said and heard in any given séance. Spirit photographs, though promising direct capture of reality, were increasingly disregarded by psychical researchers who informed themselves about the film developing process, with its many opportunities for fraud. Even the standardized targets—cards, colors, numbers—that more statistically inclined psychical investigators endorsed were too easily translated into a code. These targets also gave little insight into the precise nature of thought-transference—were thoughts transmitted in the form of words, images, or as pure concepts, what William Barrett termed *ideoscopy*? The material solidity of Smith's drawings inspired the SPR to move forward with these interesting questions, instead of dwelling on the possibility of fraud.

Ongoing debates over the mechanics of perception that began in Germany in the 1860s inspired the SPR experimenters to search for specific mental processes at work during Smith's telepathic communication. The fact that Myers, Gurney, and Barrett were familiar with the latest psychophysics is not surprising, given their eagerness to position psychical research as a laboratory discipline among the mind sciences.[49] Although they lacked specialized equipment, they designed simple telepathic scenarios that attempted to disentangle perception from cognition with techniques borrowed from the Wundtian laboratory. For instance, they used different colored targets with Smith and Blackburn to test whether the optical illusions created by opposing-color afterimages were communicated telepathically. Since color perception was itself a subject of controversy, Myers, Gurney, and Barrett were hinting at the utility of psychical phenomena for answering questions in mainstream psychology.[50]

Rather than merely appropriating psychology's methods in a quest for legitimacy, the SPR hoped to kindle a mutualistic relationship with the emerging discipline.

In the SPR's thirteenth trial with Smith and Blackburn, Smith failed to produce a good likeness (compare the target image, Figure 12, with Smith's first attempt, Figure 13). Trying to pinpoint the source of the error, investigators asked Blackburn, the agent, to redraw the original image that he had communicated to Smith. They discovered that Blackburn had misremembered the target image and passed on his mistake telepathically. For the previous two decades, physiologists had clashed over the question of whether visual perception was more dependent on processes within the eye or on "unconscious inferences" at higher levels of the brain.[51] The SPR suggested telepathy as a useful tool for accessing the mind as it pivoted between sensation and perception—the recipient, Smith, could act as a recording device for the agent's perceptual process. "The main errors of Mr. Smith's drawing existed already in Mr. Blackburn's recollection of the drawing," they reported, demonstrating that Smith received the inaccurate image from Blackburn's perceptual memory rather than as a pure sense impression.[52] When investigators showed Blackburn the target image again and repeated the experiment (again allowing him to grasp Smith's hands), they attributed Smith's accuracy to his partner's improved recall (Figure 14).[53]

These very specific uses of drawing captured the real-time function of two minds as they supposedly communicated a visual image. The SPR's Gurney, Myers, and Barrett weighed the possibility of fraud and ruled it prohibitively difficult due to the "inexpressible" nature of the images—like Hall and Lukens, they believed that drawings conveyed dense information that could not be efficiently put into words. They challenged skeptics to explain Smith's feat by subterfuge. "Let our readers, who may be familiar with the Morse or other code of signals, try in some such way to convey a description of one of our drawings, to friend who is blindfolded and has not seen the original."[54] This argument for noncodability was both commonsense—there were simply too many permutations—and based in the experimenters' impression that Smith received a complete visual idea from Blackburn rather than an assemblage

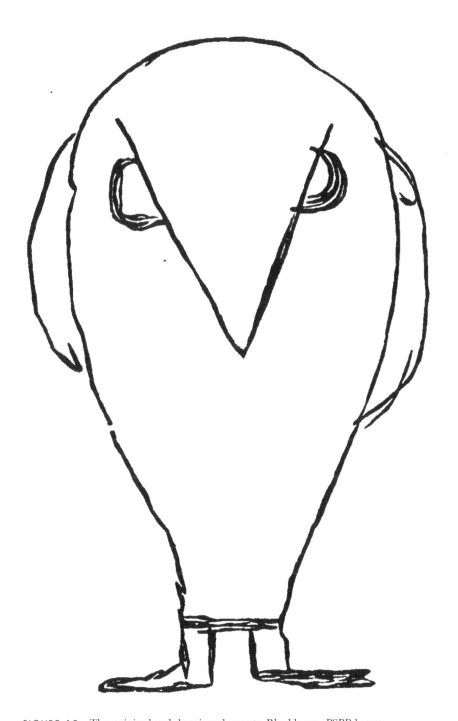

FIGURE 12. The original owl drawing shown to Blackburn. *PSPR* 1, 207.

FIGURE 13. Smith's first attempt at reproducing the drawing through thought-transference. *PSPR*, 1, 207.

of visual bits and pieces. Drawing was an invaluable instrument for the SPR because it seemed to capture the irreducible nature of thought in an objective format.

Descriptions of the Smith and Blackburn experiments arrived in the United States in the winter of 1882–83. American subscribers to the SPR's *Proceedings*, including William James, G. Stanley Hall, George S. Fullerton of the University of Pennsylvania, and Henry P. Bowditch of Harvard Medical School, would have seen the report, which received favorable notice in the scientific press as an "elaborate report on 'Thought Transference,' or mind-reading" which "eliminate[d] every possible element of charlatanism."[55] By the following year, with William James leading the charge for an American version of the SPR, the prospective leaders of this group revisited the British society's findings with a more critical eye.[56]

Although the American society represented itself, from the beginning, as a skeptical counterweight to the credulity of the British, their

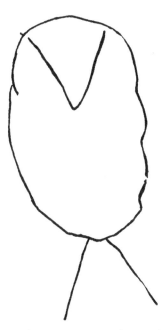

FIGURE 14. Smith's second attempt at reproducing the drawing, after Blackburn looked at the original again. *PSPR* 1, 207.

reviews of the Smith and Blackburn report did not challenge the use of drawing as an experimental method. In his first presidential address to the American society, in January of 1886, Simon Newcomb focused on the SPR's inconsistent protocols. Gurney freely admitted in his reports that Smith was sometimes blindfolded, sometimes not; sometimes Smith and Blackburn spoke to each other, sometimes silence was enforced. Conditions changed constantly as the experimenters thought of new scenarios they wanted to test. Whereas Gurney, Myers, and Barrett asserted that "our experiments derive much strength and coherence from their very multitude and variety," Newcomb regarded these conditions as unacceptably haphazard: without rigid controls, "we have no right to attribute the result to one cause [i.e., telepathy] rather than another."[57] This incompatibility between the rigid planning and record-keeping of the laboratory and the curiosity-driven exploration of the gentleman or amateur investigator would characterize the ASPR's relations with many of its own constituents, as well as with its British counterpart.

In Newcomb's estimation, the drawings represented the most stable, scientifically valid element of the entire undertaking. Even in less-than-ideal conditions, "drawings have a great advantage over verbal descriptions," Newcomb noted, "in that the record can be made the subject of future study."[58] The permanent, reproducible nature of images was an antidote to the anecdotal style that Newcomb and his colleagues found most galling in the SPR's work. The ASPR officially embraced drawing as a method in 1885, urging its members to attempt "the experiments which have attracted so much attention from the English society."[59] This meant an exciting expansion of their research program beyond the random-guessing experiments in the society's previous circulars. The society acknowledged the heightened appeal of personalized and infinitely variable drawing tasks: "As the experiment of free-drawing may prove more interesting to some persons, it is hoped that more elaborate figures may be tried, and the results forwarded."[60] Such figures were forwarded in quantity. As the society collected and transferred materials over the years, many drawings became detached from identifying context and were sorted into folders where they still testify to the common store of images and ideas shared by their anonymous artists.

William Henry Pickering, a Harvard astronomer and founding member of the ASPR, published the results of his own drawing experiment as a model in the 1885 *Proceedings*. Like the submissions of many ASPR participants, Pickering's drawings were made "on one or two evenings" as an amusement among friends, with a female acquaintance acting as "the sensitive, so called."[61] Like most psychical experiments, these were a parlor activity, but one with greater entertainment value and greater power as evidence than the tiresome and easily fudged guessing tasks.[62] The graphic summary of Pickering's experiment is particularly striking: all fifty-two pairs of drawings were reduced to thumbnail size and condensed into one page. This public presentation of a complete run of experiments asserted the scientific transparency of the ASPR in contradistinction to the SPR, which only printed examples of its successful results. The miniature images conserved valuable pages, but also created the effect of an unfolding conversation between two minds. A reader could trace Pickering's more and less convincing attempts at extrasensory communication, perhaps classify them, and judge whether any factor beyond mere coincidence was at work.

Such serial presentation became an important tool of visual rhetoric for nineteenth-century sciences ranging from physics to embryology, including Pickering's discipline of astronomy, where proponents of the nebular hypothesis in the 1830s arranged images of successively brighter nebulae in an order that showed condensation from diffuse clouds of matter to stars—boldly asserting that the earth's Sun, too, was a stage in this process rather than a divine creation.[63] The photographic motion studies of Eadweard Muybridge, and even the emergence of the comic strip in the mid-nineteenth century, also embody the visual logic of progression through sequential change. Amid this interest in directional transformation, series could also record seemingly random distributions of data which required more advanced mathematical analysis, furnished by the emerging field of statistics, to yield underlying laws. The way that Pickering framed his telepathic drawings, as an array without imposed order or progression, modeled the objectivity needed in the data collection stage of thought-transference investigations.

Pickering's playful, sometimes comical cascade of images might convince readers to try it themselves, if only as a curious diversion. Indeed, contributors like Vida D. Scudder, of Readville, Massachusetts, described her parlor experiments as "quite successful and entertaining."[64] She submitted to Hodgson "the records of a few picture-transference experiments, which we have amused ourselves by trying this summer." From the beginning, however, this amusement included keeping careful records; Scudder requested better instructions and diagrams from Hodgson and adopted the recording scheme that he recommended. Josiah Royce considered these results promising enough to mention them in his report in the *Proceedings*.[65] Scudder, meanwhile, proceeded to invite Hodgson to her house for dinner to direct the evening's experiments—an indication of how tightly experimental protocols intertwined with the social protocols of upper-middle-class society.[66]

Drawings and diagrams featured regularly in the first year of the ASPR's *Proceedings*, but for skeptics within the organization this visual evidence soon lost the luster of the early Smith and Blackburn successes—or rather, it was appropriated by a different camp within psychical research as proof against, rather than for, the reality of thought-transference. Gurney, Myers, and Barrett of the SPR interpreted resemblances between drawings as evidence of communication—demonstrating direct transmission of content between minds. When Simon Newcomb embraced drawings as evidence, however, he cited the possibility for *re*interpretation as their main advantage: they could be "made the subject of future study."[67] As the ASPR gathered drawings from its far-flung correspondents, some began to view the mass of responses as indicating unconscious habits or a collective community of thought rather than telepathy.

In the U.S., skeptics of thought-transference began to argue that apparent hits were most likely the result of "sustained attention of the mind to certain objects constantly encountered in a person's regular daily occupation."[68] Common objects were most likely to surface in drawing tasks, through no force more exceptional than probability. This probabilistic camp included Henry P. Bowditch, Samuel P. Langley, Charles S. Peirce, Charles S. Minot, and Edward C. Pickering. They worked in areas where the calculation of means, standard errors, and distributions were central to the production of scientific certainty, and initially joined the ASPR hoping to impose quantitative standards on psychical phenomena.

In order to evaluate the existing evidence for telepathy, which he found dubious, Charles S. Minot decided to quantify the general distribution of ideas in the American population. From this, he could calculate the baseline probability of any particular drawing being produced in a random test. Between 1887 and 1889, Minot, a Harvard professor of comparative anatomy and one of the ASPR's founders, used drawing tasks to survey the "community of thought" in a manner strongly reminiscent of Hall's inventory of the child mind.[69] In contrast to the circulars distributed by the ASPR's Committee on Thought-Transference, which detailed procedures for two-person thought-communication experiments, Minot's Committee on Experimental Psychology made a point of distributing hundreds of postcards requesting drawing samples from individuals "without receiving any suggestion from any other person." Rather than conceptualizing drawing as part of a horizontal communicative process, his mode of inquiry staged a vertical excavation into the mind's contents. Countering widespread popular anxiety in the 1880s and 90s around suggestion, invasion, and mental permeability, Minot's instructions also tacitly asserted that the mind is bounded such that one *can* introspect "without receiving any suggestion" of a subliminal nature.

In terms of the cognitive mechanics of drawing, Minot did not differ substantially from Gurney, Myers, or James, all advocates of thought-transference. He, too, believed that drawings externalized unconscious mental processes, coining the term *ejective* for these images which were "thrown out from the mind" through unbidden automatism.[70] Minot certainly did not militate against the kind of shared consciousness suggested by James and Gurney—in some ways he took a more radical stance on the interrelatedness of minds, asserting that individuality was largely an illusion: "Even in trifles we differ but little."[71] However, Minot believed that humans are "communists in thought" merely because our isolated minds draw their contents from a shared external world—the environment, rather than heredity or telepathy, stamped certain ideas in our heads. He used the results of the Committee on Experimental Psychology's circular, to which five hundred people responded with ten drawings each, to quantify an argument about the "laws of relative frequency of ideas" that he would reiterate in his later public criticisms of psychical research.[72] For Minot, supposed telepathic drawings were an illusion of probability rather than proof of supernormal communication.

Tables published with Minot's report tallied eighty-three types of figure furnished by his subjects—faces, moons, trees, ships, tools, cats, vases—in order of frequency. Minot pointed out differences between men and women, suggesting that gendered image preferences "may be seen as a natural consequence of our social condition."[73] Men drew objects related to business and worldly affairs, while women conjured items from the domestic sphere, flowers, hairpins, and so on. Given these patterns in mental imagery, he asserted, proponents of thought-transference were wrong to assume that the probability of two individuals thinking of the same image at the same time was infinitesimally small. Further, given a fixed canon of common images, the selection of one image using a code would be exceedingly simple—and Minot saw this as the likeliest explanation for George Albert Smith's telepathy. Like G. Stanley Hall,

Minot advocated charting the mind's contents through a systematic analysis of large quantities of drawings. To illustrate his article, he reproduced "the principal types of diagrams" arrayed in a grid; rather than comparing a matched series of drawings by an agent and percipient, as in thought-transference studies that illustrated communication between two particular minds, this typological format displayed the standard contents of the average human mind. Minot's probabilistic skepticism did not become the official position of the ASPR; indeed, supporters of the British society's research argued that the drawings used in successful person-to-person thought-transference were far more idiosyncratic and complex than the simple geometric shapes and icons that Minot elicited with his postcard. William James made this claim in his rebuttal to Minot, stating that "to most of [the Smith and Blackburn] evidence the existence of such a [picture] habit is wholly irrelevant."[74]

The idea of a developmentally acquired unconscious reservoir of ideas seemed to undermine the ASPR's model of thought-transference as a form of direct communication. Nor did it aid in the larger project of Myers, Gurney, and to a lesser extent, William James, who were coming to see telepathy as a manifestation of a more expansive subliminal self beneath the surface of ordinary awareness. Both Freud's id and Jung's collective unconscious emerged in relation to Myers's writing on this subject. Psychoanalysis would use drawing to dredge up the contents of these submerged realms for symbolic interpretation. In contrast, Minot suggested that shared ideas were largely mundane and learned through everyday activities; when they appeared in spontaneous drawings, their meaning was literal and material. We see the same literalism in G. Stanley Hall's studies of the child mind, which compared rates of learning in children from different geographical and economic circumstances assuming that their mental imagery directly reflected their attainment.[75] Like Hall, Minot sought to build a taxonomy of ideas from survey data. Though James boasted of and pleaded for just such an empirical foundation for psychical research, he ultimately mistrusted the shallowness of images without interpretations. He dismissed Minot's "postal cards with their diagrams" as an interesting footnote to the larger question. Drawing tests encapsulated a poorly understood cognitive transformation from sense data to concept to memory and eventually back into a visual image; with so many gaps in scientific understanding, James saw plenty of opportunities for minds to interact on a level that would elude Minot's literalism.[76]

Professional philosophers, physicists, and psychologists were not the only people with a stake in this core question of psychical research: Can individuals communicate without sensory mediation, through some radiant ether or submerged stratum of shared consciousness, or are we hopelessly isolated within our skulls? Scientists were also not the only people to employ drawing in the effort to distinguish between these explanations for apparent thought-transference. The ASPR's members and associates, who were called upon to generate large quantities of evidence, did not furnish it mutely. Importantly, the producers of drawings often presented their own theories about the nature of the mental forces that they observed.

The seeming transparency of drawings as evidence of mental processes meant that a layperson might analyze them without feeling at a disadvantage. By 1930, when the novelist Upton Sinclair published a book of his telepathic experiments entitled *Mental Radio*, the popularization of Freudian theory had opened up a wide range of new interpretive possibilities for mental imagery. Sinclair and his wife and co-experimenter, Mary Craig, positioned themselves as commonsense, rational investigators indifferent to the mysticism of psychoanalysis.[77] However, as I discuss in Chapter 4, the Sinclairs set their telepathic drawings within long passages of interpretive text describing the personal histories and daily routines that accumulated in their unconscious minds. In contrast to Coleman Sellers, who experienced his unconscious cerebration as arbitrary, Upton and Mary Craig Sinclair read meaning, history, and relationality into the images that surfaced during their mental dredging. They asserted that interpretation could fit within the bounds of rational empiricism and was, in fact, more scientific than refusing to interpret. This position reflected a complex interplay of new psychological trends. Behaviorism, Freudian analysis, and projective testing had fractured the field of psychology; some psychical researchers saw their future in the unconscious and dream telepathy while others maneuvered for a secure position in the university laboratory. The Sinclairs, as amateur psychical researchers, used drawing to elaborate an idiosyncratic fusion of the empirical and the interpretive which was increasingly difficult to sustain within the walls of the academy.

From Good Drawings by Bad Subjects to Bad Drawings by Good Subjects

The British Society for Psychical Research believed that they had arrived at a fraud-proof method with the use of drawings for thought-transference. These images also held great interest as direct inscriptions of mental processes—they had a persuasive appearance of automatism. Witnesses attested that George Albert Smith "showed no tentative, hesitating movements, as one waiting for signals, but worked deliberately and continuously, as if copying what was really in his own mind."[78] The SPR's Committee on Thought-Transference opined, "It is probably no exaggeration to say that several scores, if not hundreds, of precise signs would be required to convey an idea as exact as that conveyed in many of Mr. Smith's representations."[79]

The committee seemed unaware that techniques for translating drawings into code were widely accessible in cheap publications for amateur magicians. Indeed, the popular literature for aspiring thought readers provided ready-made systems for organizing and communicating hundreds of precise signs, using a memorized grid, with the appearance of effortlessness. Smith, Blackburn, and many others were familiar with such pamphlets, often attributed to famous stage performers such as W. Irving Bishop and Robert Houdin.[80] In his 1909 exposé of the SPR affair, Blackburn revealed the secret of his "masterpiece"—the experiment in which Smith reproduced a drawing while blindfolded and under a blanket. Apparently, Blackburn copied the drawing onto cigarette paper, hid it inside the metal eraser-holder of a pencil, and passed the pencil to Smith under the blanket, where Smith unfolded it in privacy, loosened the blindfold, and drew his own copy. The pencil-eraser trick was "well-known to stage mindreaders."[81]

For their less spectacular performances, Blackburn explained that he and Smith had used a numbered ten-by-ten grid to encode the SPR's images, communicating coordinates on the grid through hand squeezes, breathing, or tapping the carpet. This method yielded drawings with a global resemblance in form, although Smith often failed to recognize (or intentionally botched) the specific content of the original picture, turning a bunch of grapes into coins and a shoe into a horse's head. The errors in Smith's reproductions bolstered the SPR's belief that thought-transference operated in a nonverbal mode of pure mental forms.

The assumptions of Gurney, Myers, and Barrett about the nature of drawing were not essentially different from those of Herman T. Lukens and G. Stanley Hall in their study of children's pictures. The personnel of child study and psychical research overlapped in the small community of early twentieth-century psychology: Hall, one of William James's first doctoral students, joined the ASPR at its founding; James offered support for Hall's child study movement.[82] Both fields of inquiry relied on drawing as a straightforward instrument that accessed and recorded the contents of the mind. Both debated the extent to which psychological interpretation of drawings was appropriate to gain insight into complex mental and relational processes. And both fields attempted to remove subjectivity from their analyses by claiming a special status for the people they experimented on—asserting the naïveté of children and the automaticity of trance mediums. The reality that subjects were historical, complex, and potentially deceptive was an ever-present danger that researchers tried to keep at bay with methodology and rhetoric.

Superficially it would seem that Hall and Lukens succeeded while Gurney, Myers, and Barrett failed. Child study laid the groundwork for developmental psychology in many ways, including in the embrace of drawing tasks to measure children's cognitive abilities. Drawing was adopted as a reliable assay of subjects once referred to as "primitive"—children, as well as adults from non-Western cultures —codified in public school and military intelligence tests, and exported to ethnographic field sites around the world.[83] Drawings produced by normal Euro-American adults, however, were fraught with concerns about the unruliness of subjectivity—a significant obstacle in the search for empirical laws governing the mind.

Blackburn's 1909 exposé and his subsequent ridicule of the SPR in the press significantly deflated the society's case for telepathy in the twentieth century.[84] Skeptics came to expect that, like Smith and Blackburn and any number of supposed psychic mediums, adults brought hidden motives and resources to bear on drawing tasks. Understanding these motives would require more art than science and thus was not particularly useful in the goal of gaining scientific legitimacy for psychical research. Meanwhile, psychoanalysis threatened the integrity of drawing as a scientific instrument and undermined the evidentiary status of images by throwing open the gates of interpretation far wider than James had suggested. After these cataclysms, drawings could only count as evidence in the mainstream mind sciences if they came from a special kind of subject, a subject whose mind was easily reduced to basic cognitive functions.

This was the subject of clinical neuropsychology: a patient whose severe head injury rendered them an objective tool for troubleshooting the brain's processing pathways. The psychical study of communication between minds informed new methods for studying failures of communication within the individual brain, beginning in the late 1870s and continuing into the present day.[85] A set of characteristic drawing tasks emerged in the European and American neurological literature during this period, in part due to World War I, which produced a bumper crop of special subjects: gentleman officers whose skulls were pierced by shrapnel or bullets. They were both socially trustworthy and rendered naïve by their wounds. British neurologist Henry Head did his pioneering work on these patients; in his authoritative 1926 book on aphasia, he characterized four types of task for evaluating cognitive disability: drawing from a model, drawing from command (Head generally requested an elephant), drawing the ground plan of a familiar room, and drawing "anything that [comes] to mind."[86] Each of these tasks assumed a shared visual grammar: a normal subject understands the concepts of likeness, elephant, and aerial view. His work also presumed a shared social grammar of masculine self-making: his descriptions of their heroic efforts towards recovery show his deep empathy with his officer-patients and their fear of never reconnecting the broken pathways within themselves. Head printed their drawings as the only illustrations, aside from skull X-rays, in his two-volume tome. His explanatory captions follow the formula, "Attempt by [patient X] to draw [Y]." Sometimes, Head noted a "successful attempt," but most often, the failure of perception was manifest in the image and needed no textual explanation (Figure 15).

FIGURE 15. Patient No. 9's attempt to draw an elephant. From Henry Head, *Aphasia and Kindred Disorders of Speech* (Cambridge: Cambridge University Press: 1926), 131.

Head is a prominent example among many neurologists who adopted drawing tasks for the evaluation of patients suffering from a wide array of difficulties. This massive, mundane, and yet compelling visual corpus is a silent testimony to the struggle of countless individuals living with traumatic injuries that altered their basic experience of the world. Yet clinicians mainly used patients' attempts to represent three-dimensional space, assemble parts into wholes, or recall the forms of common objects to fit them into a typology of lesions, in the same way that developmental psychologists used the Draw-a-Man test to place children in an age-level IQ bracket. Indeed, Goodenough intended Draw-a-Man for nonliterate and non-English-speaking adults as well as for children, and it quickly crossed over into the clinic for patients with impaired speech.

Localizing a lesion based on clinical signs is difficult because injuries are rarely limited to a single area of the brain, and patients often suffer from a combination of agnosias, aphasias, and apraxias. However, drawing proved among the most useful tools for disaggregating these deficits in order to match them with corresponding brain regions. This systematic use of patient drawings in an experimental context to illuminate fundamental cognitive processes was not so distant from what the Society for Psychical Research envisioned in its experiments with Smith and Blackburn in the 1880s or from what G. Stanley Hall hoped to accomplish in child study. In each case, researchers posited the existence of a mental process that could only be demonstrated with evidence from the subject's internal visual world.

Many studies of scientific illustration and objectivity show how experts, whether scientists, technicians, or artists, are disciplined to act as "transparent" recording mediums for the phenomena they observe.[87] Their images are not up for personal psychological interpretation, although, of course, the producer's personal status is what gives the work its authority. On the other hand, psychoanalysis uses images to externalize symbolic clues about a patient's emotional life, interpreting them as part of diagnosis and therapy. This chapter has traced images of mental function and dysfunction that occupy a strange intermediate space. They were not professional scientific illustrations—they did not reproduce observed phenomena, but rather manifested hidden mental phenomena in visible form. Nor were they read for emotional content—rather, their scientific validity depended on excluding meaning, history, and individual voice. Researchers in vastly different contexts elicited these drawings aiming to make an objective study of subjectivity and to access the mind through the hand.

The intimacy of telepathic image transfers, as opposed to the stark isolation of damaged cerebral hemispheres in neuropsychology, foregrounds the metaphor of a shared psychic economy that structured the experiences of many psychical researchers. They were snagged on the line of demarcation between permeable and impermeable models of the mind. They alternated between convincing experiences of interconnectedness and moments of doubt, fear, and isolation. The obsession with capturing psychic intimacies on paper was a way of securing those moments and those beloved relationships. Perhaps this is what compelled so many people to try thought-transference on their families and friends. Beneath the rigor of experimental control, one senses in the lines the hope and tenderness of drawing together.

INTIMACY

Washington, DC, lawyer was sitting in his office one afternoon in 1924 when an idea suddenly leaped into his mind unbidden: "My poor wife is starving for a cream puff," he thought. That evening the lawyer described the strange occurrence to his wife, and she divulged that she had been standing in front of a bakery window, fighting the temptation to go inside and buy a cream puff at the moment of his insight.[1]

I, too, have become preoccupied with the cream puff, so frivolous that it must be a clue to something—Sherlock Holmes enjoins us to scrutinize another fluffy dessert, the trifle. Surely the wife's resistance to the cream puff exemplifies the rules of middle-class home economy which discipline even the smallest spontaneous desires. However repressed, these desires do not disappear. Rather, they travel along familiar paths. The cream puff illuminates how certain "natural" ties, in this case the bond of marriage, are supposed to act as conduits for psychic forces. We observe a kind of mutual attunement between husband and wife that defies language and distance. A common trope in Victorian literature, yet we still tell stories like this today: amusing trifles which nonetheless affirm a power in intimate relations that runs deeper than physical laws.[2]

I was overwhelmed by relations in the ASPR's archive: love, family, friendship, the bonds between parents and children, servants and masters, teachers and students. Intimate relationships served as a scaffolding upon which liminal experiences manifested, giving them concrete and meaningful form, almost foreshadowing the controlled environment of the laboratory. We absorb relational categories, and the narrative tools that extend, circumscribe, and modify them, through immersion in the

social, through institutions, culture, and media, until they become almost completely taken for granted. Yet relations, whether in the rigidity
of their order or the mystery of their disorder, can be quite perilous.

Most psychical researchers would probably say that their work embraced and enforced the kinds of relations they valued, what they regarded as natural familial bonds. Yet they constantly flirted with the dark
side of relationality: too much intimacy, the power of suggestion, invasion, a merging of self with dangerous others. In the 1894 novel *Trilby*, an
aspiring opera singer finally achieves fame under the control of foreign
hypnotist Svengali, who entrances and manipulates her like a puppet.
Countless novels returned to the predatory relation of hypnosis as a per-
verted mirror of love. This dark side of intimate relations also had female
perpetrators. The neurologist S. Weir Mitchell warned about the evils of
the female "octopus," the sick woman whose hysteria wraps its tentacles
around her hapless family. Yet the octopus merely exaggerates the ideal
of women as the family's emotional nerve center, just as Svengali exaggerates the ideal of male dominance and female passivity—exaggerates
not to question the ideal, but to protect it from corruption.

Defending ideals and policing boundaries was the work of private
as well as of public narratives. Reports of clairvoyance and telepathy in
the ASPR's archives most often concerned married couples and parents
and children. Many capture genuine, urgent love flashing between individuals in moments of terrible danger. Others evoke the tender rituals of daily life. It does not diminish their significance to observe that
between the lines of these reports lie marginalized and stigmatized intimacies against which normative categories defined themselves. Whether
one fell into the mainstream or the margins, the rules by which intimacy
was required or forbidden could do great violence. Yet, in a changing
and uncertain world, the ASPR's white, middle-class correspondents for
the most part identified with the rules as divine principles that secured
their social reality.

While traveling on business, a man named Owen from Louisville,
Kentucky, woke up one night with an overpowering impulse to phone
his wife.[3] She answered the phone to tell him that her beloved mother
had just died. Another business traveler, who signed as "W.B.C.", heard

his wife calling his name while he slept in a hotel room—meanwhile, at home, his wife was tending their dying child and called out to him in anguish.[4] Was capitalism tearing the American family apart as it forced men to traverse vast distances in pursuit of wealth? Not as long as these moments of communion held the family together, showing that love transcended distance and death. The wives whose disembodied voices carried the domestic sphere to innumerable lousy hotel rooms were seldom named in reports.

It's difficult to fathom today how deeply the notion of sympathy governed nineteenth-century relations, rendering selves permeable in ways both virtuous and risky. Broadly, sympathy connotes a mutual affective understanding between individuals—a sense of knowing and feeling together. Sympathy underpinned Darwin's reasoning about the evolution of morality in *The Descent of Man*, the shared emotion that made us human.[5] Nineteenth-century moral commentators such as Margaret Oliphant and Sarah Stickney Ellis promoted sympathy as the bedrock of a sound marriage and good parenting—but they cautioned that too much sympathy could lead to voluptuous affairs and degenerate children.[6] This strange feeling with the power to link individuals framed debates over familial, social, and political relations.[7] Can we truly know another person? Can we trust our fellow citizens? Sympathy was the answer to the limitations of the modern psychological self, isolated inside the skull and struggling to be known. It dramatically asserted that real connection was still possible.

Sympathy was also a core principle of Spiritualism. It allowed the medium to become attuned to the voices of the dead. For Spiritualists and many others, it named a real material force, similar to electricity and magnetism, that could be harnessed to better the lot of humanity. At least, bettering humanity was the promise. This force came with many unknowns: mediums fell under the control of Indians, criminals, and other dangerous types when they dabbled in trance communication. Participants in psychical research were often at pains to distance themselves from Spiritualism's transgressions across the borders of family, race, and class, and positioned themselves within narrower bounds of sympathy.

The married couple was the ideal unit of sympathetic communion. For the nineteenth-century middle class, love obscured economics as the basis of the marriage contract, and mutual attunement became a sort of domestic virtue, proof that the bond transcended worldly convenience.[8] This marriage of minds became literal in the acts of husband-and-wife psychic performers like Agnes and Julius Zancig, who advertised themselves as "Two Minds With But a Single Thought." An audience member handed an object to Julius, and Agnes named the object while blindfolded; Julius wrote a phrase and sealed it in an envelope, Agnes read it from the other side of the room, and so on, with the man sending and the woman receiving a signal. The Zancigs persuaded even the usually skeptical Henry James. He found it quite plausible based on his own ideas about intimacy; such wordless communication often appeared in his fiction, which was noted for its psychological realism.[9] Telepathic relations moved from home to stage to novel, and back to the home, where novels were both consumed and produced.

"You and I have not finished our work," the dead Violet Martin announced to her surviving partner, Edith Somerville, through a medium's hand in 1915. The two women had lived and worked together for twenty-seven years and remained in almost daily contact via automatic writing.[10] They produced eight more books in this way, published under their familiar pseudonym "Somerville and Ross." The popular Somerville and Ross novels were often pirated by imposters, who the true authors successfully sued—thus, Somerville understood the legal problems of using someone else's name without their consent. Martin, however, was not someone else. Their history of communion authorized Somerville to speak for and as her partner in a way that audiences could accept as genuine, or at least possible given the remarkable persistence of intimacy.

Somerville and Martin, two women who built a life and afterlife together, suggest how the laws of sympathetic communion could make certain queer relations acceptable in mainstream society. Yet Victorian reverence for the psychic bonds of marriage could not conceal the fact that telepathy also enabled other, more transgressive kinds of intimacy. As female typists, secretaries, telegraphers, and telephone operators entered the business world, they also entered into mundane intimacy with men outside of their family circles. The new relationship between female secretary and male employer mirrored the sacred spousal relationship in many ways: a shared routine and obligations, the duty of the woman to anticipate and serve the man's needs. Yet instead of family reproduction, it was sanctified by capitalist production, revealing that sympathy could in fact be bought and sold quite cheaply.

Women worked for less pay than men, and as a bonus, employers found female secretaries more sympathetic. This was how Theodora Bosanquet, a literary-minded suffragist, came to work for Henry James. Whether or not Bosanquet was psychic, she played a significant role in James's writing process—after burning through male secretaries who didn't understand him, he at last found "an intense aid" in Bosanquet, not to mention "a true economy."[11] The bicycle-riding, salon-hosting Bosanquet was far from a passive medium. She sought the job with James because she believed she could improve his writing, while also improving her own chances of publishing success. Only the first expectation panned out.

Seventeen years after James's death, her former employer appeared to Bosanquet in a séance and demanded that she resume her secretarial work, using automatic writing to channel his words from the spirit world.[12] "You remember my methods when I was dictating to you," he explained, which made her a more efficient medium.[13] Despite ongoing conflicts with spirit-James about her desire to write books under her own name, Bosanquet took down volumes of his communications. In life James dispensed scathing critiques of Spiritualists, depicting them as credulous hypocrites. Like many famous skeptics, he would suffer the indignity of repenting this opinion from beyond the grave. The secretarial bargain—perfect sympathy at rock-bottom prices—came with a dangerous caveat. Through the intimate process of dictation, the author's most prized resource, his voice, ceased to be entirely his own.

However, for those who believed in the spirit hypothesis while alive—and who saw death as an opportunity to test it—a sensitive secretary was an invaluable asset. Given a choice between psychic communication and the eternal silence of the grave, they saw no shame in mediumship's messy intimacies. ASPR president James Hyslop shared a number of telepathic experiences with his secretary, Gertrude Tubby, during their fourteen years in the office together, which gave him confidence in their rapport. Like Bosanquet, Tubby took the job to gain access to her employer's field—she wanted to conduct scientific investigations of psychical phenomena. Hyslop hired her in the same year that Henry James hired Bosanquet. Both men shared more daily intimacy with their secretaries than with any other woman—James conspicuously avoided marriage, while Hyslop was a widower. It was Tubby, then, who anticipated his small needs and yoked her personal fate to his professional fortunes.

After Hyslop died, it was Tubby who received hundreds of messages from him through various mediums around the world.[14] Weston Bayley, the homeopathic physician and sometime psychical researcher, found it quite natural that Hyslop would strive "to make himself manifest to the one person who was closest to him in his years of technical work."[15] Many colleagues accepted this reasoning, but like Bosanquet, Tubby was ever in danger of claiming intimacies inappropriate to her station.[16] In 1923, when a Spiritualist-led coup deposed the ASPR's scientific counsel, Tubby was demoted to a menial position as typist. She despaired that this drudgery kept her from scientific work—namely, channeling Hyslop, who held a low opinion of the new regime.[17] Old colleagues praised her loyalty to her dead employer, while the insurgent ASPR board condemned her as a selfish woman with a personal agenda. The behavior of channeling secretaries was often seen as emotionally disordered, either too selfish or too attached. It certainly threatened the orderly power relations that made marriage the ideal intimacy between men and women. A wife had no claim to compensation in this life or the next.

I think of these channeling secretaries whenever I write. In my fortunate life, I've rarely been denied a voice; women who make their way to certain niches in the twenty-first century world are invited to find their voices, to express their innermost selves. Yet I'm quite certain that nothing in my supposed interior is really my own. This is a curious sensation, as I spend most of my time stringing together thoughts which I represent as proprietary contributions—the singular, direct authorship that Bosanquet longed for. Certainly feminine sympathy as a logic for displacing women's ideas is still alive and well. In a meeting, the group will agree much faster if I speak as though my suggestion is actually that of a male participant. Enlisted from a young age in an elaborate performance dedicated to the illusion of male autonomy, I now regard the praise of singular voices with suspicion: none of us are as free as we suppose, never autonomous, never whole.

Cruel bargains were made to represent the rational public citizen as free from the web of relations, while in the sphere known as domestic, the spinning of webs continued apace. Web-spinning is the work that makes people—insistently, aggressively hidden from view and denied value so that we won't recognize its power. Given this history, it's reasonable to feel two things at once: the need to assert oneself and the knowledge of being spoken through, as each experienced moment is an inflection point between the time of the living and the time of the dead. I can understand how trances become useful in organizing, from within, a self that is both singular and plural. And I can understand how imposing a grid of normative relations serves, from without, to domesticate multiplicity, pruning unwanted branches to maximize its yield.

Sympathetic marriages have cream puffs, and loving mothers pick up their children's cries of distress from three thousand miles away. In 1906, Mrs. Joseph Slater of Boston saw an apparition of her son in mortal danger, at approximately the time that he was lying unconscious in the ruins of earthquake-devastated San Francisco.[18] It was not the national calamity that woke Mrs. Slater in the middle of the night, but the vibrating thread of maternal affection. Many correspondents to the ASPR did claim to be in sympathy with people who were strangers to them—both public figures and anonymous participants in major events. Letters from people who dreamed Abraham Lincoln's death on the night of the assassination were still landing on Hyslop's desk in 1911. Others described fleeting moments of communion on a sidewalk or streetcar. Psychical researchers found these less credible than reports about intimate relations and were more likely to use them as examples of fallacy or delusion. Yet we can also see them as a new way of imagining citizenship, a power of touching across difference, a latent solidarity.

The danger of telepathy was that one's secret interior became known to others; thus, psychical researchers gently constrained it within the private sphere, to wives and mothers who were already comfortably positioned as extensions of the male self. Though psychical research preferred to look away from the many inappropriate relations made possible by psychical phenomena, intimacy across boundaries was lodged in the heart of psychical research, in the office where Tubby and Hyslop exchanged wordless trivialities about the paper clip supply. Their orderly domestic tableau was the offspring of darkened séance rooms where anonymous hands groped under the table and dead strangers from parts unknown spoke through the lips of respectable young women.

Writing about the dead is also an intimacy, uninvited, unsanctioned. I wonder if this is a dangerous relation and for whom. I remind myself that, more than most archives, this one was meant for public scrutiny; correspondents willingly gave their experiences to science. The stories they offered have already been judged and used, sometimes harshly, while I am full of sympathy. I want to know a lot more than they put in their letters, and I'll go to great lengths to understand how they lived, what they believed, and where their dreams came from. Too much sympathy, we know, is dangerous, and the danger reaches beyond clouding the analytic lens. Now when I stand in front of a bakery window, I want a cream puff on behalf of the lawyer's wife whose name eludes me. I buy her a cream puff, she keeps her name. I wonder what else she wanted and if anyone knew.

CHAPTER 4

PSYCHIC DOMESTICITY

In 1927 Mary Craig Sinclair was having trouble keeping herself together. The Long Beach, California, home that she shared with her famous husband, Upton, belonged to stolid upper-middle-class America, but for Mary Craig, Long Beach was the end of the world, or the limit of the world. Nothing but a lonely stretch of sand stood between her front door and the "awe and wonder" of the Pacific Ocean.[1] Here the laws of nature and human capability would stretch and break.

Well into the third decade of a new century, Craig (as her friends and husband called her) still thought of herself, somewhat wryly, as a "Southern belle." Growing up in Reconstruction Georgia, Craig developed a sharp eye for the hypocrisies underpinning her family's anachronistic plantation life, threadbare after the devastation of the war but clinging to notions of honor and tradition with which they gilded the recollection of chattel slavery. Craig quickly grasped the arbitrariness of Southern manners—nothing but empty gestures and phrases elevated a bad person of good breeding over a good person of humble means. Yet she was a product of this culture, always attuned to social protocols and slights. After a dramatic broken engagement, a teenage Craig was bundled off to New York City for finishing school to save her family's reputation. She was well behaved, a paragon of grace and obedience, but she drifted restlessly towards the Lower East Side, where she mingled with the artists and writers of the fin-de-siècle Greenwich Village scene.

In 1913 she married the novelist Upton Sinclair. She had only known him for a year and mostly through letters in which he gave her writing advice. The wedding lifted her from the laconic, conservative eddies of her childhood into the dizzying rapids of progressive reform. Upton's endless crusades for political causes dragged the couple on a zigzag trail across the country. The circumstances of their marriage were not unusual for the literary scene of their time: Upton, recently divorced, had needed a secretary and household manager. It didn't hurt that Craig was a good writer. The book which he advised her on during their courtship was published under Upton's name to reviews declaring it his best work yet. She chose to devote herself to his causes and his career. They often wrote together but published under his name; many of his manuscripts are written or edited in her hand.[2]

A life of agitation for socialism and workers' rights took its toll. By 1927, Craig was forty-four years old and beginning to feel like "a nervous semi-invalid." Her husband was forty-eight, had run for Congress three times, and had recently been jailed for inciting a freedom-of-speech protest. Their relationship was loving—unlike that more famous literary Southern belle, Zelda Fitzgerald, Craig made no outward critique of the social conventions that bound her to a man for purposes of labor but not credit. The Sinclairs were older than Zelda and F. Scott Fitzgerald and of a more decorous disposition, but the situation in Long Beach was tempestuous in its own way. Craig was tired and unhappy. She actually sat down and tabulated the practical outcomes of their relentless reform work: "At the rate we were going, we would be old and gray before we could see much more than the beginning of the social changes for which we were striving," she despaired. "This was too slow!"[3] She complained of loneliness, stranded on an alien coast, with Upton holed up in his study chugging away mechanically at one project after another.

As her nervous affliction worsened Craig sought medical help, but "the best surgeons and medical men" assured her "that there was no organic trouble, and that it would be foolish to try to get relief from the psychiatrists. I had to 'take life easy' and stick it out . . . indefinitely!"[4] Finding this an unacceptable solution, Craig delved into the realm of alternative medicine known as mind cure. Blending mesmerism, therapeutic magnetism, and Mary Baker Eddy's Christian Science, mind-cure practitioners claimed that illness was in the mind and could be overcome via hypnosis or suggestion by a healer. The Sinclairs had dabbled in various health reform movements over the years—they first met at neur-asthenia guru John Harvey Kellogg's Battle Creek Sanitarium. But her reading of "Crile, Cannon, Janet, Richet, Bramwell, etc."—elite psychia-trists and physicians—led Craig to abandon fad diets and yogurt enemas for the utopian potential of psychic healing: "It meant a new philosophy, a new religion! And a relief from Socialism!"[5] It does not diminish the reality of Craig's malady to say that it was, at least in part, philosophical.

Based on her reading, Craig became convinced that the mind cure could work where mainstream medicine failed, though she hadn't yet ex-perienced it herself. But she worried that enthusiastic healers did not dis-tinguish "autosuggestion" (what we might call the placebo effect) from genuine supernormal mental power, and thus the basic nature of the phenomenon was still in question. To satisfy her critical curiosity, she had to experience its most dramatic manifestation firsthand. "I wanted some-one else to reach my subconscious mind with suggestions," she wrote, "to prove telepathy." Unfortunately, the licensed physicians of Southern California did not cooperate with her heterodox interests: "I could find no one to hypnotize me! The doctors laughed at me, and the psychia-trists out here seemed afraid to mention the word hypnotism."[6]

Just as Craig despaired of testing out her last hope for a cure, a new psychic medium arrived in California. His performances were sensa-tional—he walked on beds of nails, conversed with the spirit world, and allowed himself to be buried alive for hours at a time. He called himself Count Roman Ostoja, and claimed to be a Polish prince deposed dur-ing World War I and fallen on misfortune. Craig attended Ostoja's stage shows and hired him for private séances, glad of an opportunity to scru-tinize real-life psychical phenomena up close. She insisted, however, that Ostoja submit to tests of her own design; she knew that, much like the genteel Southern society of her youth, the world of stage mediumship was predicated on secrets and false appearances.

At first her driving concern was finding genuine relief from her own maladies. She reasoned that mind cure either triggered a psychoso-matic response, or it actually transmitted healing force from one mind to another. If it was merely autosuggestion, Craig feared that she was "too skeptical and sophisticated" to be deceived for long, and her illness would come back. But if the cure worked by direct communication between minds, "the implications were so immense": "It means that we must all become pacifists, optimists—else we are disarranging the universe with our thoughts!"[7] The risks of mental permeability occurred to her from the outset, but it would soon become a more concrete danger. As she engaged with the technical and metaphysical debates of psychical research, Craig's health problems receded into the background. "I became so interested in all these interesting things," she wrote, "I decided I did not want to be hypnotized because this might incapacitate me as a judge of [Ostoja's] work."[8]

What makes someone a competent judge of psychical phenomena? The question of judgment lies at the heart of the Sinclairs' psychical career. Mary Craig Sinclair, like many participants in psychical research, believed that the stakes in their project were higher than curing nerves or exposing charlatans. The possibility of grasping transcendent truths about the human mind motivated her to pursue a long and draining investigation that ultimately underscored, rather than resolved, her ambivalent status as a female scientific observer. She believed that Ostoja's powers, if proven, would have sweeping social effects, but she was caught in a double bind of verification. She could only believe in phenomena that she had experienced herself. At the same time, she was never quite satisfied with her ability to judge the truth of experience. She was far more attuned than most male psychical researchers to the shifting grounds of subjective conviction—what feels absolutely real one moment can crumble into illusion the next. As a woman, and especially a woman suffering from neurasthenia, she had taken to heart the mistrust directed at her by male doctors. To seek credibility in their world, she constantly had to acknowledge, in a rational, deliberative tone, the possibility that her experience was invalid.

Count Ostoja arrived in Long Beach in the spring of 1927, and by summer he was a daily guest in the Sinclair home, where Craig hoped to lure him away from seedy stage performances and towards the scientific work of proving telepathy. She plied him with an evangelist's zeal, "to save this medium for scientific purposes." By all appearances, Ostoja needed saving. Tall, gaunt, and pale, he cut a disquieting figure, especially in one of his deathlike trances.[9] Competition for audience dollars was fierce, and his feats of endurance were growing riskier—on one occasion he was found bleeding from the ears and mouth after spending hours buried in a sealed box.[10] Although Craig's nerves were precarious, she launched her investigation with vigor, winning Ostoja's trust and studying his behavior to see if he, in turn, could be trusted.

At first Upton saw Craig's interest in psychical research as a healthy intellectual exertion that distracted from her nervous symptoms. Over time, however, tolerance morphed into his characteristic utopian zeal: telepathy, he decided by the late 1920s, could bring about a better and more just world. Upton had collaborated closely with his wife for fifteen years; though he was one of the century's most strident ideologues, he valued her as a thinker and took her ideas seriously.[11] In close intellectual partnerships like that of the Sinclairs, women often originated or advanced a shared interest in psychical research; biographers have long debated the role of William James's wife, Alice Howe Gibbens James, in deepening his engagement with Spiritualist mediums.[12]

In July of 1927, Upton wrote to Walter Franklin Prince, then the president of the Boston Society for Psychical Research, requesting any information that his organization might have on Ostoja. The Sinclairs had read deeply enough into the psychical literature to discern that Prince's breakaway Boston Society, rather than the American Society under the spiritualist-inclined leadership of Frederick Edwards, held the scientific high ground in recent controversies. Prince had made a name for himself as a rigorous, conservative, and discerning judge of psychical phenomena.[13] This profile made him highly desirable. Upton sought him as an ally, but Craig saw him as something more: the definitive authority without whose judgment Ostoja's powers could never be satisfactorily confirmed.

The correspondence between Prince and the Sinclairs would continue for many years; at first it centered around Craig's efforts to bring Prince to California as an expert judge of Ostoja's phenomena. Upton proposed that his wife would be "a first-class assistant, or say, collaborator" for Prince's investigation, explaining that her intensive reading and scientific disposition fitted her to work alongside the foremost expert in the field. However, the trip out west was too expensive for any of them to afford (and one suspects, too much of an ordeal for the aging Prince). Their letters fluttered across an impossible American expanse, borne by Craig's desire for an external authority to validate her judgment. She never reached a conclusion, in part because she never had to—Upton, the "writing machine," plowed ahead with publishing their findings despite her desire for more experiments, more certainty, and most of all, the expert eye of Walter Prince to verify her results. She would always have Upton to declare "enough is enough" and lay down the facts as he saw them. She was left holding the imponderables.

The Ostoja Affair

The Sinclairs' psychical career proceeded in two stages. First came the formative episode with Ostoja, involving the group séances, corroborating testimony, and extensive correspondence that characterized the network of amateur psychical research in this period. In the wake of the Ostoja affair, they moved on to a markedly different mode of investigation. Retrenching to the home and to the dyad of the married couple, they conducted a long-running telepathy experiment with Craig as the receiver of Upton's often irreverent psychic messages. Serving as Upton's medium was, of course, part of Craig's ordinary domestic duties, so this configuration felt quite natural. It also represents a return to the normative gender dynamic that Craig's initial research with Ostoja had disrupted. Relations between a female investigator and a male medium proved too volatile to sustain. In her second attempt, she would gain stability but surrender autonomy by assuming the passive role of experimental instrument.

Craig was simultaneously enthusiastic and reserved about the early results of 1927. Some of her excitement stemmed from the remarkable phenomena that Ostoja produced, but much of her writing from these weeks described her zeal for the investigation itself and framed that zeal within the careful optimism of a scientist beginning a new experiment. "We naturally prefer to think that the medium is not capable of conscious cheating," she wrote to Walter Prince in an early letter, "but that is only a preference. We must not 'trust' it in making our investigations."[14]

The withholding of trust that she'd learned from her own physicians was a useful tool in dealing with mediums. Her repeated condemnations of the psychical researcher's fatal error—"believing what we want to believe"—positioned her as savvy, rigorous, and unsentimental.

This positioning mattered because without it Prince could dismiss her as a nervous woman, an unreliable and easily influenced observer. Among psychical researchers, "good health" functioned as a sort of code word for mental stability. They had to screen out reports from the mentally ill, which threatened to undermine their cause (as described in the final chapter of this book). Craig was not in good health. She barely left her house. In her letters she alluded to her changeable moods, her "over-emotionalism"—but these, she insisted, were part of the nervous illness, not part of her inherent makeup. Given that countless Americans suffered from neurasthenia in her time (perhaps comparable to the approximately 30 percent of the adult population suffering from clinical depression and anxiety today), doctors had begun to distinguish between the genuine self and the disease to preserve their patients' integrity. Patients, then, learned to view their own affliction with a sort of clinical detachment: becoming well meant becoming more objective, like their doctors. Craig took on the role of scientist as an antidote to her psychological turmoil. She described the discipline of experimentation as a step towards recovering her true, rational self.

At the same time, Craig's true self was also gendered female. She tried to turn what most male scientists viewed as a handicap into an asset. During her initial meetings with Ostoja, when she vetted his abilities in the privacy of the Sinclair library, she described using her "woman's wits" to find out "what his strange personality was."[15] This specific term, "woman's wits," appears repeatedly in *Mental Radio* to describe Craig's tactics with Ostoja. Because it appears first in a private letter from Craig to Walter Prince, it seems likely to have been Craig's formulation rather than one introduced by Upton.

Why bring the idea of woman's wits into an argument for taking a woman seriously as a scientific witness? It would seem counterproductive, after building up her credentials as a well-studied, "cold-blooded" investigator, to evoke such a homespun tradition. However, Craig's training as

a Southern lady had centered largely on the importance of pleasing and
flattering men in order to make one's way in the world.[16] Her application
of this principle to the amateur scientific network of psychical research
was in fact very apt. The conceptual framework of psychical research
hinged on the assumption that different relational roles structured the
kinds of psychical connection possible between individuals.

Women's service as mediums in various Euro-American contexts
drew upon assumptions about their passivity, sensitivity, and receptive-
ness that date back to Aristotle, but which reached new heights in Victorian sentimental culture.[17] Taken to extremes, these essential female
qualities were negative, causing the bad behavior of stage mediums,
hysterics, neurasthenics, and criminals. In moderation, however, they
epitomized ideal womanhood. Psychical researchers and psychiatrists
expended much ink on pathologizing women and undermining their
credibility, but they chose their targets with a complicated awareness of
social and cultural propriety—for instance, lower-class women like the
hysterics in the Paris asylum were easily objectified in clinical encounters with educated physicians like Jean-Martin Charcot. In a different
context, stereotyped expressions of femininity could actually validate a
woman's claims. For one thing, blithe compliance with gender norms
proved a woman's sanity. Further, "healthy, natural womanhood" included powers of love and intuition that were known to take on supernatural dimensions. There was a "healthy" inverse of the pathological
female mind which had all the same qualities, but controlled and directed them towards domestic fulfillment.

Craig had no children, although Upton had a son with his first wife.
She established her maternal credentials by caring for her husband,
protecting his "childlike faith in human nature" from the exigencies of
money and politics.[18] At times she played the mother hen, hounding him
to eat meals and put on socks, maintaining the conditions of life necessary for Upton to write. Of course, they were also romantic partners—biographers insinuate that Craig became Upton's mistress before he was
divorced from his first wife.[19] Craig was doubly well positioned to communicate telepathically with Upton: she slept with him and also tied his
shoes. But before realizing this possibility, she tried to read the mind of a

man who stubbornly defied the relational structures within which female telepathy could safely occur.

"Count Roman Mieszko Ostoja Maszerski, the eminent psychist of international reputation" was the sort of shadowy character common in the world of stage mediumship.[20] By his own account, he began his career in Europe after World War I, claiming to have fought variously for the armies of Poland, Russia, or Austria. Colorful stories circulated in the press involving his descent from Polish nobility and tragic misfortunes in love and politics. He surfaced in the United States in 1926 and showed his powers before men of science in Boston and New York, performing under the name Rom Romano or Eterno. His abilities included entering a state of catalepsy in which his stiffened body, laid flat and suspended between two chairs, could support hundred-pound weights or endure hours of containment in a sealed coffin. Psychical researchers considered him particularly interesting for his abilities of auto-hypnosis, while followers of the mind cure sought his services to relieve their nervous ailments.

For the purposes of this story I will call him Ostoja, as this is the name he assumed after fleeing New York. It's unclear why his fortunes soured there. The ASPR tested him and declared that he had "a high degree of auditory hyperaesthesia" but no supernatural powers, perhaps spoiling his sales pitch.[21] He surfaced in Miami in the spring of 1926, where he flattered locals by shedding his stage names and revealing himself as a scion of European nobility. He appeared in Pasadena and Los Angeles in early 1927, performing under the name Nostradamus. Having acquired the honorific "Doctor" somewhere in his travels, he was quickly embraced as an expert on matters psychical by the southern California press.

The boundaries between public performance and private séance were always quite flexible, in part because the precarious finances of mediums like Ostoja made them eager to take on any work they could get. The Sinclairs first encountered Ostoja at a Los Angeles theater, and they were not the only locals to enlist him for private demonstrations after his impressive shows. These demonstrations, to which prominent scientists and medical men were always invited, staged the spectacle of unexplainability. Often hosted by society women and featuring mediums from the unsavory margins, they represented a rather pointed challenge to the masculine rational order. Though the novelist Frank Norris portrayed the "lady presidents" who marshaled this parade of wonders as gullible, weak-minded busybodies, clubs and salons were one of the few spaces where women could pursue their interests and curiosities without male judgment as the ultimate arbiter of value.[22] Indeed, Judge Georgia Bullock, one of the nation's first female jurists, hosted a demonstration of Ostoja at her Los Angeles home in 1933, "where a dozen doctors and doubting Thomases were present."[23] The lady, in this exceptional case an actual judge, presided over a male jury and defendant.[24]

Soon after Craig's one-on-one tests with Ostoja in her parlor, she decided to stage a private séance to debut him before respectable Palo Alto society. In July she wrote to Sarah Bixby Smith, a feminist reformer and wife of the literary critic Paul Jordan Smith, requesting the use of their house for the event. They would submit Ostoja to the judgment of a social circle whose members felt assured of each other's education, intellect, and discrimination. The Smiths consented to host the séance, and in mid-July Ostoja sat among local physicians, scientists, and writers and channeled the spirits of their deceased relatives. The most valuable witness, and one whom the Sinclairs would cultivate to corroborate their case, was Dr. Melville Z. Ellis, a Long Beach osteopath who, Craig claimed in her letter to Prince, had once assisted the physicist Robert Millikan in his experiments with cosmic rays. Although he had never before taken an interest in psychical matters, Ellis applied himself with great seriousness to this new area: "I have assumed that I was invited to be present in order that I might observe and criticize the phenomena from a scientific viewpoint, rather than merely enjoy an evening's entertainment," he wrote to Upton, delivering his analysis and critique of the proceedings.[25] There was much to critique. As an osteopathic doctor, his philosophy tended towards the mechanistic; he was trained to trace all illnesses to an underlying misalignment of the body and thus was not inclined towards mind-cure notions.

The first sitting was, by all accounts, a success, but Ellis expressed reservations about Craig's behavior. He argued that her facial expressions and bodily carriage when Ostoja approached the correct answer to a question could be interpreted as cues. Ellis did not suspect actual cheating but rather cautioned against the appearance of "an unconscious confederate" in the room. She had the expression "'There, you see!' written on her countenance," he complained. "Her actions should surely not be permitted in case of a rigorous test." Ostoja had his eyes closed throughout the proceedings, and Ellis left convinced of his fine character and veracity—only the discipline of real scientific procedure was lacking. This discipline could be achieved, first, by reigning in Craig's feminine expressiveness. Beyond that, Ellis had a battery of suggestions for taking truly empirical measurements: "I would desire more careful control over various factors and more uniformity in the results."[26]

As a physician with some degree of laboratory experience, Ellis was both prepared to take psychical research seriously and able to grasp the monumental difficulty of conducting a controlled experiment on the mind of a human subject. The proper place for such an experiment was the laboratory, and he offered to apply himself to the task: "Perhaps by taking further thought a type of experiment can be devised that will not necessitate the construction of too elaborate an apparatus."[27] This, of course—the building of apparatuses and the recording of mechanical forces—was not what Craig had in mind when she invited doctors and scientists as witnesses. Rather, in keeping with the testimonial epistemology of psychical research, she wanted them to report what they had seen, banking on their good word as men of science.

Ellis was not particularly cooperative with this aim. He wrote a letter on his experience with Ostoja and sent it to Walter Prince, expressing reservations about the material reality of telepathy. He sent similar letters to Upton Sinclair, urging him to be cautious about staking his reputation on "such wisps of evidence as this."[28] With his characteristic lack of tact, Upton promptly shared Ellis's critical letter with Craig. Feeling betrayed, she dashed off a response the next day. She acknowledged that her behavior at the séance was not conducive to an objective investigation. But why had she acted so irrationally? "I am aware that I was not a well-poised observer at Mrs. Smith's—I did not want to go, as my health makes social affairs difficult . . . I do not want you to think I am at all times unfit as a witness."[29] Her errant nerves, rather than sloppy science, had led to her "over-emotionality." These she could overcome with greater effort at self-mastery.

A second séance at the Smiths' followed the next month, provoking another critical letter from Ellis to Upton, and again Craig replied in her own defense. An episode of nerves did not, she repeated, render her incapable of scientific observation. None of Ellis's doubt fell upon Ostoja, from whom he received "a favorable impression." The problem lay in Craig's approach, which Ellis saw as that of a flighty society woman playing transgressive parlor games. If certainty was desired, he wrote to Upton, they needed a male scientific investigator like Ellis, "willing to give a considerable portion of my time to aiding a promising investigation." Techniques could be developed, invisible forces registered on instruments, and the "repugnance that I feel towards unexplained things" could be dissipated through quantitative measures. As a working physician, however, Ellis admitted that he could not spearhead a whole new field of research: "I am not the person to direct such an undertaking."[30]

An economy of gender, judgment, and time underpins this nuanced exchange. Ellis felt that Craig was incapable as an investigator; her parlor, rife with agitating emotional ties, was not a properly controlled setting. The mystery belonged in a laboratory, the masculine space of authority where Ellis earned his credentials. Of course, Craig asked for his authority when she invited him to see Ostoja, but she didn't anticipate an attempted methodological coup. She intended to verify the performer's psychical phenomena through the collected testimony of qualified witnesses, standard procedure for amateur psychical research. Unfortunately, that procedure always left room for what Ellis so deeply disdained, "unknown forces . . . unexplained things." It's hard to say whether he was more distressed by fraud—hands touching under the séance table—or by the existence of forces with no natural explanation.

Although Ellis certainly could have bundled Ostoja into a laboratory and taken methodological control over the situation, he declined to do so. Like most American psychical investigators, he had to earn money and could not spare time from his medical practice. Moreover, not all doctors were as scientifically bulletproof as Craig supposed them to be. As an osteopath, Ellis had to navigate a politicized landscape in which mainstream, allopathic physicians tried to get alternative sects banned from practice.[31] He was actually arrested in 1920 for practicing without a license, under a newly passed California law designed to keep out "irregulars." However, many irregulars like Ellis passed the licensing exam, much to the chagrin of the MDs, and returned to work. Ellis would eventually sit on the Board of Chiropractic Examiners.

Craig prized Ellis's laboratory training; it didn't bother her at all that many conventional doctors dismissed osteopaths as quacks. Ellis, however, was well aware that a foray into psychical research, as anything more than a hobby or an evening's entertainment, could compromise him professionally. As a representative of a maligned medical sect, he had to tread carefully around the occult. Thus, he left the psychic stuff to women in their parlors, whose time had no money value. They could flirt with the unexplained or unexplainable without harming their reputations.

Criticism from her physician friend did not shut down Craig's investigation. Rather, she became determined to improve her procedures. Most mediums could not perform in a laboratory, and she believed that the domestic experiment, drawing together a network of experience, observation, and testimony, was the best way to probe Ostoja's fickle powers. She sent the entire Ellis correspondence to Walter Prince. In a note to Prince, she framed her exchange with Ellis as representative of the dismissive attitude of the scientific establishment towards psychical phenomena, but also of the obstacles facing an amateur female investigator: "The main reason I did not argue with him [Dr. Ellis] was because I know that men do not like it when 'the ladies' prove them mistaken." Sinclair never identified as a feminist, even during the peak of the women's suffrage movement, but her interest in psychical phenomena, mind cure, and eventually auto-experimentation was shaped by a pronounced awareness of the subject position of women in mainstream medical discourse. Neither her illness nor her quest to understand it made any sense in the somatic systems of "the best medical men," and though she sought them as witnesses, she rejected their terms.

In Prince, Craig found an ally in the cause of observational science, if not in the cause of women's intellectual parity. Upon receiving Ellis's skeptical reports, Prince declared: "I am not . . . in accord with Dr. Ellis in his statement that no science is worthy of the name until it has been put upon a quantitative basis."[32] Prince was committed to a model of psychical research driven by amateur observation, arguing that "we must . . . multiply the number of intelligent and reputable witnesses by teaching people how to observe and how to record."[33] Whether Ostoja's phenomena could hold up in a laboratory was immaterial to Prince; rather, he was concerned with ascertaining the character of the witnesses, and specifically, the reliability of Mary Craig Sinclair.

Of course, Prince had prior knowledge of Ostoja from his East Coast performances and was inclined to consider the case on the Polish count closed. His lukewarm interest in Ostoja is evident in his letters. From Prince's perspective, the goal of their correspondence was a gently edifying discourse about observation, method, and the practice of psychical research. Craig was far from unique; year after year, day in and day out, members of the public wrote to Prince describing extraordinary phenomena, and Prince wrote back to engage them on analysis and methods. The Ostoja case was an opportunity to identify and cultivate a critical observer, and Craig was promising material. In the course of her reading she absorbed the basic tenets of record-keeping and corroborating testimony from respectable witnesses. Her zealous enthusiasm seemed like the main unruly factor in the proceedings and clearly made Prince uncomfortable. He saw an unhealthy intensity of desire in her determination to unlock the secrets of the mind, and he worried that the revelation of Ostoja's disingenuousness would cause her to abandon psychical research, a familiar pattern among people taken in by a charismatic medium.[34]

Being fooled by Ostoja was not a concern of Craig's. She simultaneously acknowledged her enthusiasm and framed herself as a savvy, skeptical investigator, although not in the measured terms that Prince would have preferred. After the two séances at the Smiths', Craig found herself drained and nervous from social exertion. The goal of the proceeding at the Smiths' had been twofold: she wanted testimony from eminent scientists and respectable society people to send to Prince's Boston Society, but she also hoped to raise interest among her wealthy friends in funding a more extensive research project. Writing to Sarah Bixby Smith about the outcome of the séances, Craig perfunctorily thanked her host and then launched into a pitch for sponsorship: "Someone must endow him, of course"—someone like the wealthy Smiths, perhaps.[35] Ostoja had by then become a live-in guest of the Sinclairs so that Craig could work with him on a daily basis. His entry into the domestic space of the Sinclair home would trigger a shift in Craig's approach towards the study of telepathy.

In letters from this period, Craig began to assess Ostoja's character more critically. Where she originally viewed him as a childlike mystic innocent of worldly corruption, she quickly began to see him as a moody and unreliable adolescent. He could not keep appointments or take responsibility for his actions, which included associating with undesirable characters (Hollywood actresses, "a stout Jewish showman") and freely spending the Sinclair's money.[36] Craig, still sympathetic, pitied the helplessness and confusion with which he stumbled through the world. When he spent the funds that Craig gave "to keep him from starvation" on renting a venue for a stage show, Craig concluded that "there is simply no hope for such temperaments."[37]

At first Craig wanted Ostoja under her wing to observe and study his powers, but as she began to relate to him in a maternal way, describing him as helpless and erratic, his abilities became less exceptional. He was just another emotionally immature male who needed nurturing but couldn't accept it. "I've been every kind of mother—patient, friendly, severe and despairing! and have decided to see if he cannot learn by being left entirely to starve . . . I do not know what he wants—nor does he!"[38] At this point, in the spring of 1928, Craig's correspondence with Walter Prince dwindled to a halt. As Prince had expected, her disillusionment was severe: "I'm not in the fit mood at present to do anything but thank you for your cordial interest," she wrote, "and to hope that some day all this time we've spent in letters back and forth will bear some fruit."[39] He replied with words of consolation and encouragement, assuring her that it was "difficult to deal in a practical fashion" with mediums of Ostoja's type. Of course, he spoke from experience, having already investigated the count, but he made sure not to mention that he'd warned Craig from the beginning.[40]

As far as Prince was concerned, this was the end of the Ostoja affair. Like so many other amateur investigators, Craig had tired of the medium's game and lost interest. She stopped trying to extract a research fund from her wealthy acquaintances, and none of the Sinclair's correspondence after April mentions Ostoja's presence. His show-business friends offered opportunities more to his liking, and Ostoja performed profitable feats of daring in theaters up and down the West Coast. Investigators revealed that the supposed yogi was born in Cleveland. For Craig, however, the investigation of telepathy was just beginning in earnest.

Precisely because Ostoja had become a burden and a nuisance, Craig felt more convinced than ever of her capacities as a discerning judge. "I am no blind believer," she wrote in one of her last, careworn letters to Prince.[41] She continued to assert that Ostoja offered important insights into the human mind, but his complicated personality made him an impractical research subject. Just before he moved out of the Sinclair's house, Craig decided to take control of the situation by developing her own mental powers: she would extract from Ostoja the skills she needed, and by experiencing telepathy as a medium rather than a patient, she would prove to herself the reality of communication between minds.

Sadly, Ostoja's views on this project went unrecorded; he refused to teach Craig or share his secrets when pressed. Upton reported "regular evening arguments" between his wife and her recalcitrant live-in tutor. Craig came up with a plan. Although she had never before trusted Ostoja to hypnotize her, she invited him to attempt it and then "turned the tables," trying to overpower his will with her own.[42] Craig described the encounter triumphantly, claiming that she engaged Ostoja in a sort of psychic duel that gave her unfettered access to the contents of his mind. In a twenty-page document, she recorded her telepathic impressions of Ostoja's activities over the course of a single day, which Ostoja admitted were accurate. She used this insight with discretion, since her omniscient knowledge "was embarrassing to a young man who perhaps did not care to have his life so closely overseen."[43] In addition to penetrating his consciousness, Craig claimed to be able to influence Ostoja with her will; in keeping with her modest and purely experimental aims, Craig used her newly discovered powers to send Ostoja into the adjoining room to make a telephone call.[44] This stands in stark contrast to popular stories of cross-gender hypnotic control in newspapers and fiction of the time, where women were made to commit crimes or sexual indiscretions by malevolent, Svengali-like hypnotists. The reversal was complete: Ostoja, the would-be Oriental mystic, was domesticated.

The outcome of their psychic wrangling seems counterintuitive: Craig, the nervous woman, should surely have been susceptible to mental penetration by a professional hypnotist. In fact, her entire relationship with Ostoja should have played out quite differently according to the script of exotic villains and receptive females so popular at that time. Thinly veiled sexual motifs saturated Victorian and Edwardian genre fiction, from the Gothic romances of George du Maurier and Bram Stoker to the "shilling shockers" of Stuart Cumberland and Algernon Blackwood.[45] Fantastical literature mapped a social reality with which Craig was intimately familiar. She did not entirely reject it but negotiated an unusual sort of agency within it.

Turning the Tables: Gender and Powers of Mind

Foremost among the blockbuster novels of the late 1800s were du Maurier's *Trilby* (1894) and Stoker's *Dracula* (1897), both of which showed Western-European women penetrated and possessed by foreign men with mysterious powers. Of course, those powers were not sexual but psychic, and authors tactfully replaced bodily transgression with spiritual transgressions equally erotic and scandalizing. Hypnotic fictions were inspired by serious medical and scientific debates of the time, while they in turn inspired feverish reports of real-life cases in the popular press. The late-Victorian moral panic around hypnosis had settled into a commonplace trope by the 1920s, but it was no less frightening for its familiarity.[46]

Turn-of-the-century writers set the pattern for a gendered division of psychic powers based on imperiled female innocence. However, Mary Craig Sinclair's psychic experience was not unique in its disruption of the standard dime-novel script. We have to view the literary obsession with predatory hypnotists alongside the thriving contemporary literature of mind cure, Christian Science, and New Thought, which targeted the sick, and especially women, with a message of empowerment. These movements taught ordinary readers how to harness their powers of the mind, with titles like *Prosperity through Knowledge, Practical Methods for Self-Development,* and *Telepathy and the Subliminal Mind.*[47] Most aimed for better health or success in business, but many advocated causes like women's liberation and relief of poverty as part of a progressive psychic healing of humanity. The Sinclairs and other Americans who took psychical experimentation into their own hands were steeped in this literature. The frightening penetrations of Gothic romance were not the dominant lens through which they viewed powers of mind.

In the vast literary marketplace of psychic self-help, popular authors both stoked anxiety and promised control. They frightened readers with medical descriptions of nervous illness, hysteria, and multiple personality. These diseases revealed a submerged self, an unconscious that could act independently of the conscious subject. To govern the unruly subliminal self, they preached willful self-regulation. Only personal discipline could keep the unconscious in check. A strong enough will could even act upon the unconscious of other, weaker subjects. Depending on which advice book you picked up, you could read about how to manipulate business partners, beguile potential lovers, or win at cards. Powers of mind form an intersubjective nervous economy flowing through the nineteenth century from the followers of Franz Anton Mesmer to the hysterics in Charcot's Salpêtrière through the American rest cure and Christian Science.[48]

The neurologist and rest-cure pioneer Silas Weir Mitchell notoriously insisted that female mental illness stemmed from an excess of willpower: women who became ambitious and took on male activities exhausted their naturally weak nerves. Recovery required total, passive surrender to a dominating masculine will.[49] Mitchell was notorious for confining patients to bed for weeks at a time, where they were bathed and spoon-fed by nurses to avoid exerting any autonomy. Mitchell, of course, believed that his dominating will was benevolent rather than sinister—he was the doctor, after all. Though Mitchell had numerous critics, his theory of female nervous illness and its treatment was widely adopted; indeed, neurologists and psychiatrists had been using similar ideas before Mitchell codified them.

Without much evidence to support his therapy, Mitchell insisted somewhat desperately on the normative virtue of masculine medical science.[50] If a man with such unilateral control over a woman deviated from propriety, a predatory Svengali- or Dracula-type situation would surely result. Indeed, Mitchell clearly worried about this danger, whether the potential for violation lay deep within himself or in other doctors who might abuse his therapeutic protocols. In his side career as a rather heavy-handed novelist, Mitchell created the character of Victor St. Clair, a capricious poet who exercises a telepathic hold on his innocent friend Miss Maywood, damaging her health and sanity. Dr. North, the character who obviously stands in for Mitchell himself, claims to have some telepathic ability but refuses to cultivate it because mind powers are "full of pitfalls," even for self-possessed "men of intellect." In Mitchell's nervous economy, psychic regulation was the duty of men, but he saw this ideal as precarious, imperiled by the forces of the unconscious that churned below the surface.[51]

Other popular beliefs about powers of mind would turn the Victorian ideal of sympathetic, receptive womanhood to very different ends. Mary Baker Eddy, the founder of Christian Science, proposed an intersubjective nervous economy in which any person could cure illness simply by conveying the force of the divine spirit into the mind of the sufferer. Eddy maintained that disease, and indeed the entire material world, were false beliefs conquerable through mental force.[52] Further, she harnessed mind power to a feminized reading of Christian scripture that coalesced in mid-nineteenth-century America, portraying the divine as receptive, merciful, and maternal.[53] Despite the fact that her doctrine denied the existence of evil, Eddy lived in constant fear of psychic violation by male mesmerists, particularly her estranged mentors and students, which she termed "Malicious Animal Magnetism."

Historian Cynthia Schrager suggests that Eddy pinned anxieties about mind powers on these men as a strategy to promote her healing telepathy while attributing its misuse to already stigmatized figures such as itinerant mesmerists.[54] Eddy successfully argued from the position of virtuous but vulnerable femininity, convincing thousands of followers that she could heal them through the "Immaterial Mind." Christian Science was only one among many mind-cure sects with different dynamics of gender and power; beyond the potential for transgression, exploitation, and betrayal, they reached no consensus as to how mental healing ought to reshape the social order. Eddy, however, rose to the top as the controversial leader of a growing religious movement, and she represented dramatic female agency in the psychic realm.

Mary Craig Sinclair knew the gender politics of turn-of-the-century mind cure, health reform, and psychiatry all too well. As a young woman she accompanied her ailing mother to a variety of sanitariums, including Kellogg's mothership at Battle Creek. She later befriended Charlotte Perkins Gilman, whose book *The Yellow Wallpaper* now serves as a beginner's guide to the misogyny of Mitchell's rest cure. When she began to suffer from her own nervous illness, Craig delved once again into the world of heterodox medicine, keeping physicians and psychiatrists at a safe distance. Her extensive reading into the literature of mind cure and New Thought shaped her intellectual approach to psychical experimentation. In some ways she embraced Mary Baker Eddy's empowered version of sentimental femininity: doctors could not cure women because they denied the higher reality of the spirit in favor of "materia medica" that sedated and infantilized rather than cured.[55]

The ubiquitous and much debated philosophies of the mind-cure movement shaped how Americans practiced psychical research. Many, like Craig, arrived at psychical investigation by way of nervous illness, failed medical treatments, and initiation into the world of heterodox healing. Craig asserted her will and argued for the validity of the subjective experiences that constituted both nervous illness and psychical phenomena. However, she never rejected the gendering of nerves or mediumship as essentially feminine. Evoking Eddy's theories of female receptivity, Craig claimed that her gender enabled her to experience what the eminent scientists could not, an attitude also widely held by male psychical researchers. Likewise, with Ostoja, she constructed a narrative in which her feminine nature put her into a maternal relation with the "helpless" count and allowed her to infantilize him, gaining insight into (and even control over) his unconscious mind. What could easily have been a Gothic sexual seduction turned into a conquest of empiricism. In this process, however, Craig's femininity made her subject to the very scientific discourse in which she sought equal intellectual participation.

The "woman's wit" that Craig exercised on Ostoja was simultaneously romantic and maternal, consciously evoking the rituals of Southern courtship (coyness, flattery, white lies) that she continually returned to in her memoir as successful strategies for navigating a world of men. Ostoja represented the chauvinistic foil that Upton could certainly never be: "She thinks [Ostoja] does not want to allow any success to a woman," Upton wrote. "He is a 'continental male,' something she makes fierce feminist war upon."[56] By figuring herself as both mother and lover in a paradoxical courtship, Craig tried to orient her claim of psychic intimacy within stable relational categories, erasing its origins in the dubious public realm of stage telepathy.

Upton described the psychic relationship between Craig and Ostoja as one of "rapport," citing Pierre Janet's experiments with pathologically sensitive hysterics who could be made to experience the pain of their hypnotist.[57] Upton evoked Janet to give scientific credibility to hypnotism, but he passed over the strange scrambling of gender roles unfolding in his parlor—a hysterical woman subduing an equally hysterical man, with both of them claiming psychic powers over the other. Whether or not Ostoja believed that Craig had read his mind and influenced his actions, he found their mental intimacy jarring enough that he gave up free room and board in Long Beach, fleeing to Santa Barbara. Craig's unwelcome incursion into Ostoja's mind would be her last such endeavor. In Prince's assessment, Craig's desire for results was too strong for her to produce objective evidence. Granted, a Janet or a Mitchell could impress their will on female subjects and present the results with medical authority—but this was not an appropriate role for Craig. Instead, her receptive, sympathetic qualities would become the centerpiece of the second act of her psychical career.

Shedding the garb of the controlling mother/lover, Craig returned to her horizontal position on the couch in the drawing room, taking the role of passive recipient for a series of male telepathic agents. Of course, Craig was still the organizational force driving the experiments, obsessively recording her impressions and corroborating them with testimony and affidavits. She gained a level of control over her experimental scenarios that she could never achieve with another person as medium, but she won it by portraying herself as an instrument, rather than an agent, of telepathic communication.

Making *Mental Radio*

The most literal traces of nineteenth- and early twentieth-century psychical research are the thousands of drawings produced in thought-transference experiments, like those described in Chapter 3. Investigators developed countless variations to ensure against cheating and to facilitate better results. Positioning the agent and recipient in space was a delicate matter. They could stay in one room or be sent to opposite sides of the house, depending on the strength of the connection. Physical contact was rarely permitted after the debacle of the Smith and Blackburn fraud. These tests took place in studies, bedrooms, parlors, and libraries; the space of the home was central to their integrity. Many experimental records included a sketch of the home's floor plan; this series of sealed-off boxes mapped rules of individual privacy newly ascendant in middle- and upper-middle-class American life. From the public parlor to the "withdrawing room" to the bed chamber and the servant's staircase, domestic architecture mapped supposedly natural sympathies, and it shaped the kind of transgressions that were possible. Thought-transference experiments worked directly upon this map, upon the metaphor of mind as a closed room. They tested its contours, taking privacy as an objective condition yet fantasizing its violation. Perhaps, like a servant or lover, thought itself could move silently and freely through invisible fissures in the social order.

As nineteenth-century society reckoned with the secular proposition that individuals are nothing more than brains within bodies, it became ever more urgent to understand how we know each other. Without God as the basic guarantor of language and meaning, without a common origin and destination for all souls, genuine communication might not be possible in the way people had long assumed. These fears echoed in the spaces and rhythms of domestic life. Despite sharing a home and ancestry, members of a family were not limbs on a single body. They had hidden interiors that no one else could access.[58] A husband and wife could sit in separate studies, reading silently, books unknown to the other. Despite the efforts of scientists, the container of subjectivity was becoming increasingly opaque. For this reason, it was increasingly important for families to police and surveil what happened behind closed doors.[59]

Thus, telepathy represented a hope for wholesome intimacy as well as intimate surveillance. These were often one and the same thing in nineteenth-century advice literature. John Gunn's *New Domestic Physician* urged mothers to open the doors of their sons' bedrooms at unpredictable times to keep them from masturbation, a dreaded Victorian moral scourge. Fear of the "solitary vice" was informed by medical theories about semen and the loss of vital energy, but larger homes and shrinking families set the stage for the masturbation terror.[60] The far-seeing *New Domestic Physician* also instructed wives to sit with their husbands in the parlor after dinner, never leaving the men alone to smoke cigars and gamble.[61] Rather than a masculine force of technological penetration, Victorian virtue was a diffuse and all-pervading feminine ideal. Historian John Durham Peters points out that Christian theologians used angels, transparent beings who could see into the souls of men, to explain how perfect communication was possible.[62] It's no coincidence, then, that the Victorian "angel of the household" exerted her moral influence through psychic channels.

Many historians see the notion of telepathy as a response to new communication technologies and scientific discoveries. However, it is equally a product of changing domestic relations that drove a reactive embrace of "traditional" (though in many ways newly defined) gender roles. According to the popular advice literature, women were supposed to read minds and influence people—so it's not surprising that some identified these as moments of telepathy. Yet, as always, moralizers accused them of doing it wrong. Excessive sympathy given or received was the root cause of nervous illness. Moreover, the whole sympathetic psychic economy was ripe for abuse by mediums, mesmerists, and the occasional vampire.

The Ostoja affair featured all of these bogeymen. Craig could have told it as a Gothic nightmare tale with her as the victim; Upton could just as easily have made Craig the hysterical octopus, twining men in her needy grasp. But Upton and Craig sported a self-consciously modern outlook. In their published account, they wanted to separate the new science of telepathy from a dead century's moral panics. Making Ostoja into a light, comic anecdote defanged him, as it were, breezing past to the successful experiments that really mattered. Craig's private letters from 1927 and 1928 speak to a different and more intense experience, charged with eighty years of debate about gender, sympathy, and mediumship. This social context, which all proper science works so hard to obscure, shaped her understanding of the phenomena and guided her experimental choices. It explains why, if she wanted to produce good scientific evidence, Mary Craig Sinclair had to become a good wife and a good instrument.

Craig and Upton produced 290 sets of telepathic drawings between 1928 and 1929. They depict common household objects, current events, games, animals—the mundane visual effluvium of a human mind. Craig would recline on a couch in her study, while Upton sat in his study and drew. After Upton stared at the image for fifteen minutes, Craig would receive an impression, sit up, and sketch it out. Doors and hallway separated the two rooms. Upton evoked the integrity of domestic architecture: "When I go into my study . . . I certainly know that I am alone." Many of these images were reprinted in *Mental Radio*, framed by lengthy descriptions and analyses. Although Craig and Upton insisted that the numbers spoke for themselves—they claimed a success rate of 23 percent, far better than the infinitesimal odds of two different people producing identical drawings at random—the proof of thought-transference really lay in their interpretation. They often read commonality in images that look wholly dissimilar to the untrained eye. John Durham Peters comments that "[Upton's] zest to establish identity only reveals the intractability of difference."[63]

Take, for example, the narrative gymnastics that led from Upton's drawing of a football to Craig's drawing of a spotted cow (Figure 16). The text takes incongruous detours through visual resemblance (the stitching of the football's finger grips, the cow's bellyband), historical context (Upton was reading a book on the livestock industry), and biographical information (Craig's childhood experience with cattle restraints).[64] Unquantifiable variables across multiple axes, offered anecdotally, would spell doom for a psychology dissertation in 1929. For the Sinclairs, however, it was precisely the layering of visual, contextual, and biographical factors that made their account persuasive. Fortunately, these were also the standards of the community of psychical researchers represented by Walter Prince.

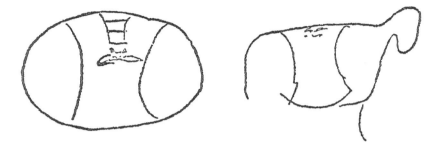

FIGURE 16. Upton Sinclair's drawing of a football and Mary Craig Sinclair's telepathic impression of the football as a cow. *Mental Radio* (New York: Albert & Charles Boni, 1930), 31.

After their correspondence about Ostoja dwindled to a halt, Prince heard nothing more from the Sinclairs until the publication of *Mental Radio* in 1930, which he learned of in the newspapers. He approached the book with some trepidation, admitting that he had "suspected, rightly or wrongly, that once or twice in the past [Upton] had failed to discover the devices of certain clever professionals."[65] Prince, however, found himself "interested beyond any expectation" in the Sinclairs' findings. He resoundingly agreed that they gave "evidence of telepathy, as good as any that could be imagined or desired."[66] With his characteristic diplomacy, he revised his opinion and incorporated Upton and Craig into the category of reliable witnesses.

Prince's support was not a simple matter of writing a jacket blurb or defending the Sinclairs in the press. Once he accepted them as reliable witnesses, he wanted to scrutinize their work firsthand. The Sinclairs had made an end-run around Prince and the BSPR network by consulting William McDougall, then the head of Duke University's psychology department, on drafts of their manuscript. McDougall visited them in California and wrote a friendly introduction for *Mental Radio*. In all likelihood they avoided Prince precisely because of Craig's awkward history with him, but the appearance of McDougall's name in the pages of *Mental Radio* was also an indicator of Prince's declining fortunes. McDougall represented the future of psychology as a science, anchored in the laboratory of a research university, while Prince held onto the gentlemanly tradition of the nineteenth century.

McDougall had seen the hopeless state of psychical research during his brief tenure at the ASPR and removed himself from the zone of spiritualist contamination, while Prince continued to fight for, and hold, his modest realm of scientific integrity within it.[67] What Prince did with *Mental Radio* was a triple assertion of his commitment to experiential knowledge: he reanalyzed and reinterpreted all of Craig and Upton's original drawings, he reproduced their experiments himself, and he urged all members of the public to do likewise. Although he respected McDougall's work and judgment, Prince's psychical research was rooted in a model of broad-based observation and knowledge-making rather than the opinions of professional psychologists.

All of this is to say that Prince took the Sinclairs' entire telepathy project and repurposed it as a case study for the *Bulletin of the Boston Society for Psychical Research*. Comparing Prince's journal article to the Sinclairs' text opens up the discursive play of observation, experience, and authority that is lost in assessments like that of John Durham Peters, who simply accuses the Sinclairs of reading too much into their images. I take their determined overreading of the telepathic drawings of 1928 and 1929 to reflect the epistemological standards and shared logics of an investigative community in flux. Establishing identity between a football and a cow became more than the pet project of ardent believers when it entered a network devoted to mapping the limits of communication.

Prince's article was a strange hybrid of book review, experimental report, and testimonial to the Sinclairs' integrity. He set out, first, to defend Upton and Craig as legitimate witnesses. He acknowledged that men of science might have misgivings because Upton was "a novelist" but argued that Upton's brand of fictionalized exposé required the same skill set as scientific research: "The fact that his novels also attempt to prove something, on the basis of studies made by him, is quite in his favor."[68] The grinding, didactic quality of his prose at least demonstrated that Upton Sinclair was not a man of florid imagination.

In asserting Craig's integrity, Prince disregarded the tactics that she tried to use on him and on readers of *Mental Radio*. Rather than portraying her as a sympathetic, maternal figure or a hard-boiled rationalist, Prince openly aired his concerns about the "intense . . . almost febrile" nature of her investigation. "There is something pathological" about her investment in proving telepathy which, he wrote, was "not an indication of perfect health."[69] Prince had the authority to make such diagnoses; he'd specialized in psychotherapeutics in his ministerial practice. Seeing this verdict in print would not merely be horrifying to Craig, whose conservative Southern upbringing rendered her allergic to public scrutiny, but might strike his readers as unnecessarily harsh. Against this instinct for propriety, Prince insisted that the public had to know "the make-up of the chief witnesses," as their personality and judgment were the bedrock for all subsequent claims. A major weakness common to psychical research and laboratory psychology, according to Prince, was that social and/or professional credentials were often mistaken for true objectivity. An accurate psychological profile was needed precisely to establish the *subjectivity* of the observer, which could never be eliminated and thus had to be registered as the "personal equation."[70] To this end, Prince actually included an excerpt from Craig's correspondence (which she had not intended for publication). Although Craig displayed many characteristics of the nervous, overemotional female, he concluded graciously that "the woman really thinks and reasons, which is more than many do."[71]

He proceeded to build up a logical argument for Craig's possession of reason: she was "not self-absorbed," nor naïve, nor credulous. Too much rationality, however, could enable women to manipulate.[72] Might she be canny enough to perpetrate fraud? Her writing sample also spoke against this: it displayed "a sincerity, earnestness and intensity of desire to know, which can hardly be counterfeited." Whereas Upton's public work as a novelist (much of it co-written with his wife) proved his scientific virtue, Prince had to publish Craig's private correspondence to preempt criticism. Only intimate exposure could demonstrate both her ability to reason and her inability to lie.

Essentially, Prince depicted Craig as a good-enough instrument for conducting experiments which were guaranteed by her husband and further verified by Prince—restoring the gendered hierarchy of judgment central to psychical research. The Sinclairs bypassed that hierarchy by self-publishing their book, so Prince had to reverse engineer it before he could accept their evidence. Craig's retreat to the couch was ultimately a successful strategy, insofar as it allowed Prince to place her in an appropriate relation with male authority. She finally had the approval of the prized expert. One wonders if she wanted it, at that point, and at the cost of such damning praise.

This approval was overwhelmingly thorough. After establishing the character of the experimenters, Prince proceeded step-by-step through his analysis of their results, highlighting the particular brilliance of certain interpretations such as the transformation of Upton's football into Craig's drawing of a cow. The weaving together of telepathically intuited ideas (the book about cattle that Upton was reading) with "subconscious mechanisms" (her childhood memories of a cow with a band that resembled the football's finger grip) was "most interesting." It suggested that mind reading went beyond the signal-and-response, telegraphic model of thought-transference that most experiments were designed to test. Instead, it might be more like what Craig experienced when she probed the private thoughts of Ostoja. The limited merging of consciousness posed no moral danger for a respectable married couple like the Sinclairs, though Prince had previously denied that it was possible between Craig and Ostoja.

Finally, Prince appended his own tests. To make a real statistical argument, he needed a baseline for the number of correct image-transmissions to be expected from a random sample of the population. As discussed in Chapter 3, Charles Sedgwick Minot had tried to establish this basic standard in the 1880s by collecting random sketches from the public on postcards. William James published an immediate rebuttal to Minot's study, in which he stated the obvious: the content of human consciousness varied across so many dimensions that it was impossible to say how many potential thoughts existed and how likely a person was to think them at any given time.[73] By 1930 such work had largely been abandoned. In the absence of any quantitative probability measures, the psychical research community had largely settled into a common-sense paradigm for judging the likelihood of matching images. In *Mental Radio*, Upton was speaking their language. "It is a matter to be judged by common sense . . . a million years would not be enough for such a set of coincidences. . . . No one can seriously claim that such a set of coincidences could happen by chance." It defied his imagination—and the limits of a particular period's imagination are often the contours of its common sense. He even asked "some mathematician friends to work out the probabilities," replicating Minot's statistical effort. Like James, however, Upton and the mathematicians concluded that "the problem was too complicated."[74]

This logic reduced probability to a commonsense judgment, an accepted standard among psychical researchers. Prince affirmed it in his analysis of *Mental Radio*. He performed a "counter-experiment"—using exact copies of the images in the Sinclairs' book—not to clear up his own doubts, but as a rhetorical gesture of due diligence. He addressed opponents for whom "the notion of the possibility of telepathy has long been obnoxious," condescending to persuade them with the tools of probability. To prove that "mere guessing" produced fewer matches than "genuine telepathy," he chose ten female percipients with no special "telepathic faculty." Acting as agent, he tried to send them images taken from *Mental Radio*. Because they did not produce a single match, "there was not the slightest reason to suppose that there was anything but chance in play." Zero matches proved that they were guessing at random, which proved that random guessing had minimal probability of producing a match. From this sample he concluded that the Sinclairs' results were "prodigiously beyond the reach of chance guessing."[75]

Prince found it "almost incredible that two human beings could come to so close an agreement" as Craig and Upton in their telepathic bond.[76] In light of Craig and Upton's intimate working relationship, this bond seems not-so-incredible; their eagerness to prove telepathy obscured the ordinary ways that people come to know each other's minds. Prince acknowledged that husbands and wives share "a community of thought and tendency to think about the same things," but he quickly minimized it as a "foolish" objection, arguing that mere familiarity could never produce such astounding matches.[77] Transcending interpersonal boundaries was the dream of telepathy, but the dream's charm lay in its mysterious mechanisms, whether atmospheric circuits or invisible wavelengths. Most psychical researchers believed that memory, personality, and relationships influenced telepathy, but these were the scaffolding, the experimental apparatus, upon which astonishing phenomena manifested. They did not articulate the ways in which relationships and social structures shaped phenomena because these invisible forces were taken for granted, understood as prior to the commencement of scientific inquiry.

There is an inherent persuasiveness of astonishment, the way that telepathy pulled communicants outside of themselves while still standing in their familiar world, like a brief parting of the veil around the closed mind. Prince's philosophy of psychical research was tied to these persuasive moments. Like previous ASPR leaders, he knew that they needed mountains of data from volunteers to make a convincing scientific case— but the real convincing would occur in the minds of those volunteers, disciplined into rigorous experimentation, as they encountered a force that defied their careful experimental controls. Prince declared Craig and Upton's work a model that should "urge readers to institute experiments of their own, and to give amateurs some directions as to procedure."[78]

Mental Radio is more or less an oddity today, a rather confounding effort from an author with an already tenuous position in the American literary canon. His legacy mostly rested on *The Jungle*'s shock value; Sinclair famously observed that he'd aimed for the nation's heart and hit its stomach with his meatpacking tragedy. As a popular work, *Mental Radio* also had little impact on the course of psychical research and parapsychology, which was already seeking refuge from the public in the laboratory. Yet it proved galvanizing for older researchers like Walter Prince and William McDougall, and for the ASPR's core constituency, all of whom held out hope that individual experiences could add up to something of scientific value.

The Sinclairs' book was a rallying point for beleaguered American psychical researchers because it revised nineteenth-century citizen science for a new generation, affirming that amateurs and professionals could participate in a shared conversation with cumulative impact. Prince declared, in endorsing their work, that "it is the duty of men of science to give whatever encouragement and sympathetic support may be possible to all amateurs who find themselves in a position to observe and carefully and honestly to study such phenomena."[79] In the same period, professional scientists in other areas, like botany and astronomy, withdrew their "sympathetic support" from amateurs and established internal disciplinary networks. With professional psychology largely focused on the laboratory, Craig and Upton's study centered on the home and on a married couple rather than a psychologist and his anonymous subjects. Yet Prince praised it as "among the very best hitherto reported" for capturing a phenomenon that could not exist under artificial conditions. *Mental Radio* dramatically staged the necessity of domestic knowledge production: real human minds and real human relations required a natural setting.[80]

Aside from giving a small boost to psychical research's legitimacy and methods, *Mental Radio* also reflects the confoundingly intersubjective nature of experience that would push psychical research further and further into the margins as the twentieth century wore on. The book's positive reception by a progressive, educated readership speaks to the "ever-not-quite-ness" of psychical research: ordinary people as well as many scientists accepted its questions as valid, they were intrigued and entertained by its findings, but nobody could figure out what to do with it. Craig worried that Upton's socialist utopia would never come to pass and pursued telepathy as a revolutionary medium. But the community of mind that she sought was hardly around the corner. From the perspective of today's science, it's simply impossible to design a falsifiable experiment for telepathy as defined by those who claim to experience it. Such an undertaking doesn't make sense in mind sciences that define consciousness as the activity of neurons inside brains inside skulls.[81] But the questions of psychical research only became incomprehensible gradually, as a universe of social and relational connections was pruned away to isolate a generic psychological subject.

At the end of her life, Mary Craig Sinclair reversed domestic and professional roles with her husband. Upton largely abandoned his writing and reform work. For almost a decade, all his energies went towards caring for Craig. Her nervous illness progressed into a serious heart ailment that required constant monitoring. Unable to type, she dictated her autobiography to him. Its final pages contain her musings about the purpose of their shared work and the mark they would leave on the world. Rather than triumph, she struck a note of regret. Although Upton was satisfied that, with the publication of *Mental Radio*, they had done their part to prove the truth of telepathy, Craig felt that "we have never gone as far as I want to in finding out what can be done." In all her years of supporting Upton, she confessed to and through her partner, "I never found time for my own crusade."[82]

This neglected crusade, rather than targeting the material conditions of life, encompassed the mind and its utopian possibilities. Influenced by Christian Science, New Thought, and later by the works of Carl Jung, in addition to her own experiences, Craig saw mental permeability as a fact that could transform human relations. While Upton labored in the realm of self-possessive individualism, trying fruitlessly to build a fellowship of man, Craig envisioned a far more radical fellowship in which the concerns of one were truly the concerns of all. The subordination of Craig's metaphysical concerns to Upton's materialist ones mirrors larger patterns in the sciences and in American culture in the first decades of the twentieth century. What happened to Craig is what happened to psychical research: there was simply not time for their questions in a world moving forward on a material basis. There was not time for sitting in parlors and opening oneself up to the subjectivity of others (with the exception of a new, shadowy figure, the psychoanalyst, who charged by the hour). Craig, moreover, was unable or unwilling to pursue psychical work without Upton. Looking back on their life together, she never implied that she had squandered her abilities or that her husband unfairly devalued her intellect. Rather, she feared that Upton had missed his opportunity for truly revolutionary work in the realm of psychology. "His mind, one of the best, might have been devoted to a study of the stuff of which it and all other minds are made."[83]

His mind was her mind, though. For decades they shared a mental and spiritual apparatus, writing with and through each other. The products of that apparatus had "Upton Sinclair" stamped on the cover, an arrangement which Craig seems to have sought from the beginning to protect her nerves and her modesty. Like many other writing partnerships, it became more than a convenient arrangement. It became a cognitive reality, a taken-for-granted mode of shared experience. Their intellectual work hinged on what they could see and do with the apparatus, as they pointed it at targets ranging from social ills to mental powers. Perhaps an instrument can't scrutinize itself—that's the basic dilemma of psychology, nestled behind many scrims of Cartesian assumptions. Perhaps it shouldn't. The Sinclairs' telepathic experiments reveal the social and psychological complexities of two people mutually producing each other precisely because they don't suspect that it's their relationship on the dissecting table. Yet, as Craig's story shows, opening up the apparatus is often the only way to find out what women contributed. More broadly, it reveals how the social and cultural world "outside" is inscribed on the lens we use to see it. The currents of sympathy flowed on a scaffold of relations made invisible by their ordinariness. Whatever apparatus we may peer through today, we can be sure that it shapes, and at times produces, phenomena both mundane and extraordinary.

LOSS

I 've been writing a book about a failed and forgotten science, poring over the testimony of people who saw and heard impossible things, for years now. I joke that it will make me crazy. People ask if I believe in ghosts, and I can tell if they're asking because they experience reality as haunted in some way, or because they think I've fixed on a wrong idea. Walking out of the icy ASPR library into the sunset-saturated clamor of evening on the Upper West Side, I feel like a shade among the living. I have my feet in other people's inner worlds, their yearnings and anxieties are mine. Traffic, bodegas, the cartoon animals on children's backpacks wash over me, meaning obscured by a curtain of sheer sensory noise. Unmoored, I take my cell phone out of my pocket and call whoever will answer. It's as simple as trading gossip with my high school best friend or an old roommate. Unbeknownst to them, they're talking me back into our common reality. But where am I when I'm drifting? What if no one answers the call? Over time, the people we love slip out of range.

I pick up work on a laptop in the backseat of a car northbound from Tampa to Baltimore. Behind me in the hatchback is a cardboard box of cremains. We are taking them to the Great Smokey Mountains, as per the request of the deceased. The ashes consist of a fine powder mingled with gravely chunks in a thick plastic bag. We are also transporting stacks of paintings created by my partner's father, Roger, who is in the cardboard box. Roger's paintings depict human-alligator men clutching hair dryers with their tails, a gigantic hammer and nails riding on a sailboat, and my favorite, *At Peace in the Great Void (With Chicken)* (Figure 17). The neon-laced acrylic surfaces seethe with creatures and words snaking around each other. A fruit pie sits by itself in a desert scattered with bones. The orange desert is rutted like the open-pit coal mines near Ferguson, Indiana, where Roger grew up.

He returned to Indiana at the lowest point in his life, divorced and in recovery. He took his two kids walking among the rubble of the coal pits, where Native American stone points poked out of the displaced earth. With most of an archaeology PhD under his belt, Roger picked up the artifacts and showed how they were made, what they were used for. Old tools brought to life by their fit in the hand. That's what my partner remembers about the walks they took during that time—not the despoiled present, but the way it allowed them to touch the past. Roger started painting decades later, in a sort of fantastical return to archaeology. We see many strata simultaneously; accidents churn up a history that belongs to someone else. It becomes lodged in our thinking. It remakes the world, or makes it possible to see the world through the eyes of a bear or a pair of scissors. But there's a magic trick each time: it's still unmistakably Roger. The paintings are a vivid, detailed map of a person. The ashes form an unmeaning constellation—or one we don't have the tools to make sense of—over the Tennessee River.

I know that both fear and love make us clutch the map. It's reasonable to be afraid of how much we have to lose. It's reasonable to ask if we really do lose it, or if there are alternative possibilities worth exploring. But I think I'm done for now. In transcribing the nineteenth century's fragile letters, in writing this book, I wasn't looking for an end to my personal fear. I was looking, I suspect, for the solidarity of the dead, which is different from a planchette moved by spirits. I feel closest to those who wondered, experimented, and then traveled on through the world not beholden to the desire for certainty. Who accepted that certainty is a feeling, not a logical proof, and wanting it stamped and ratified does a certain amount of violence to the very notion of spiritual truth. A double edge there, of course—the absence of certainty can also make loss unbearable.

It was hard for his friends to let William James go. "I always thought that [he] would continue forever," declared the irascible editor John Jay Chapman, "and I relied upon his sanctity as if it were sunlight."[1] James's

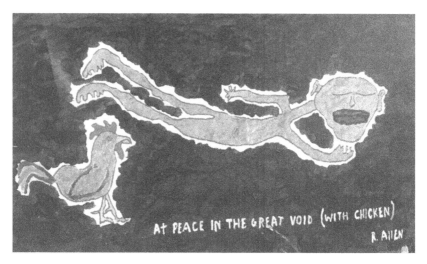

FIGURE 17. Roger Allen, *At Peace in the Great Void (With Chicken)*. Acrylic on wood, 2017. Photograph by Graham Coreil-Allen.

death in August of 1910 came on quickly, though he had long suffered from ill health. The fact that he was so often sick, and the causes of his illness so obscure, made even James doubt that his heart would finally fail. Perhaps he could still think his way out of it. If only he could overcome the growing anxiety that his major contributions to philosophy, 1907's *Pragmatism* and 1909's *A Pluralistic Universe*, were being misinterpreted and poorly received. His gasping for breath was "partly a spasmodic phenomenon," he insisted, something in the mind. Yet, as his brother and wife rushed him across the Atlantic after another failed Alpine rest cure, it became clear to all of them that it would be his last return to New England. In constant pain, he could no longer walk and had to be carried on a litter. Sixty-eight years of chaotic comings and goings, restless transmissions, had come to an end. This ending left Henry James "in darkness . . . abandoned and afraid."[2] The elder brother was a pillar shoring up Henry's unstable emotions. "His death changes and blights everything for me," Henry wrote, staggering under the weight and finality of loss.

Given William James's fame, the search for his spirit would not remain a family affair. Indeed, the philosopher's worst fears about his intellectual legacy unfolded in the pages of American newspapers from

Hartford to Portland to Miami (Figure 18). Within a month of his death, headlines announced a secret pact between James and Hyslop, a sealed letter in a safe. If a medium could channel the text of James's letter, this would prove the reality of the spirit world. Hyslop denied any such plan. Meanwhile, the Metropolitan Psychical Society, an ASPR splinter group led by vehement debunker Joseph Rinn, announced a $10,000 prize for the contents of the apocryphal letter. This bounty provoked fifty mediums to answer Rinn's call. "The expressions [they] used are similar to those of professional mediums since the days of the Fox sisters," Rinn scoffed. Of course, they could never match James's letter, since no such letter existed—rather, Rinn's stunt proved the duplicity of mediums.[3]

Hyslop, too, rejected all of the resulting claims, concluding that the sealed-letter story was a fabrication from top to bottom. However, the tidal wave of mediumship had been unleashed. The press ran regular updates on the latest James rappings. The usual suspects, well-known Spiritualists like M. S. Ayer and the Reverend Frederick A. Wiggin, formed the crest of the wave, but beneath them rose scores of amateur mediums and chance experimenters who claimed that they had little knowledge of or interest in the works of the dead Harvard professor.

Typical of these was a young woman from Washington, DC, who claimed that James contacted her only four days after he died. "She did not know Professor James," the press reported, "and had not read any of his writings." A constant refrain with female mediums—investigators assumed, or the mediums cannily attested, that they'd never read a book, never entertained a thought about public matters. In reality

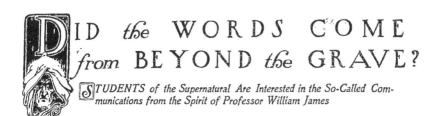

DID the WORDS COME from BEYOND the GRAVE?

STUDENTS of the Supernatural Are Interested in the So-Called Communications from the Spirit of Professor William James

FIGURE 18.   The search for William James's spirit received sensational media coverage. This syndicated story ran in the New York Herald, November 20, 1910.

William James and his ideas were known to anyone who'd seen a newspaper. While riding a train in September of 1910, the woman received a rambling message in which James explained the difficulties of communicating without a body: "The spirit must work out its more or less gradual emancipation from the labyrinth of the earth conditions." An underwhelmed Hyslop read the text and "failed to find anything which suggests the style of Professor James."[4]

Despite such flippant remarks, Hyslop did not actually believe that literary style could prove a spirit's identity. He shared the standard Spiritualist explanation for gibberish from the beyond: in their transcendent new state of consciousness, spirits no longer thought in mortal language, and struggled to translate their ideas and transmit them along unreliable channels. In the same interview where he condemned the chorus of James channelers, Hyslop waxed philosophical on the very nature of communication: "There are enormous difficulties associated with the communication of ideas normally," he reflected, "and only a laboriously-constructed process of artificial symbols ever enables us to establish intellectual relations between minds at all. What we suppose to be an easy and natural means of ascertaining each other's thoughts is an exceedingly difficult one."[5] All speech is an elaborate translation, in which meaning and intent are often misconstrued. So much more with speech across the unfathomable abyss of death. The real terror is not dissolution, but the flimsiness of our superficial solidity.

Rather than a spot-on imitation of James's prose style, Hyslop had quietly begun searching for "the little, trivial incidents"—intimate details known only to family and close friends of the public philosopher. He proposed that the scientific way to confirm spirit identity was to trace these bits of unconscious flotsam.[6] To find such clues, he consulted two mediums who had earned his personal trust, Minnie Soule of Boston (known as "Mrs. Chenoweth") and Mrs. Willis M. Cleaveland of Virginia (known as "Mrs. Smead"). Around September 5, 1910, Smead contacted Hyslop claiming that she saw James's apparition on the night of his death and had been receiving transmissions ever since. Smead seems no less opportunistic than any of the psychics duped by the Metropolitan Society contest, but Hyslop took her seriously based on her previous cooperation with the ASPR. Moreover, she lived in "in one of the southern states in the mountains, 13 miles from a railway."[7] Naturally she claimed to know nothing about James. Hyslop rushed to rural Virginia to sit at the séance table with the Smeads. For someone who believed in telepathy, he found it surprisingly hard to imagine how information might reach women by ordinary means.

Meanwhile, the spirit-James cavalcade was rapidly coming to resemble "the most farcical [of] vaudeville skits."[8] On November 14, a New York man produced a spirit photograph of James, along with a gushing, sentimental message; the reporter bemoaned "a marked change in the literary style of the late Professor of Psychology and a falling off of logical faculty as well."[9] By January James reached the West Coast, appearing in the automatic writing of Los Angeles psychologist Herbert Luzon. Hyslop publicly decried these reports as "nothing but cases of hysteria" or "fakers pure and simple."[10] He maintained that he was not investigating any James appearances. Contrary to this statement, Hyslop had already established a series of cross-correspondences between the mediums Smead and Chenoweth. He believed that clues repeated independently by both mediums could verify James's identity.

It took almost two years for Hyslop to go public with his investigation. By that time the media frenzy had subsided, but reporters happily picked up where they left off. From Hyslop's exhaustive explanation of the Smead and Chenoweth cross-correspondences in the ASPR's *Journal*, they extracted the money headline: "Pajamas from Spirit Land," the papers declared, "Pink Pajamas Talked of by Spirit." Indeed, the clue that persuaded Hyslop was a recurring reference to James's pink pajamas, the trivial detail known to no one else. "Was that the most characteristic thing about himself the philosopher could think of?" jeered the *New York Tribune*. "He might have told the world whether or not he found his theory of pragmatism true."[11] And there it was—in the crucial years when students and followers could have secured James's intellectual legacy, this drawn-out survival debate reduced the philosopher and his ideas to a laughingstock. In a 1913 incident, James's spirit reportedly ordered Hyslop to "write a paper against woman suffrage. It is my desire that you do this . . . PS: Don't let your wife see it."[12]

Jesting headlines also obscured the larger problem of how identity, writing, and translation connect the living and the dead. Hyslop believed he'd solved it with the cross-correspondence method, but this represented another retreat into the familiar, a projection of the map onto the territory. Hyslop and his fellow investigators, communing with their dead colleagues, conceived of the afterlife as a site of big science parallel to the big science of psychical research. In their view, the spirits were leading the way, making advances in scientific methodology and sending data from the furthest periphery back to the imagined center. Hyslop extolled "the detail, the large and comprehensive way in which [the spirit control] worked as by a chart."[13] With efforts to know and channel the dead leading down these solipsistic blind alleys, newspaper satirists weren't the only ones wishing that inquiring minds would leave the dearly departed alone.

Drifting in his grief from Boston to New York to London, and finally back to his retreat in Rye, Henry James ignored the tabloid headlines from America for months. Inevitably, though, his brother's ventriloquized spirit penetrated Henry's intimate circles. In 1912, his close friend Theodate Pope, one of the first female architects in America and an ASPR trustee, sent Henry a transcript of a séance in which William appeared. Henry referred to it as "the dreadful document . . . without hesitation the most abject and impudent, the hollowest, vulgarest, and basest rubbish I could possibly conceive." Clearly, he took deep personal offense at the tone-deaf Spiritualist maneuver of countering grief with a piece of spirit-writing, which he dismissed as a "tissue of trash."[14]

Henry was the wrong person to ply with the Spiritualist reanimation trick; he knew his brother's voice inside and out. For four decades they had bared their souls to each other in written exchanges, so that William's identity was his letters, his words—language was not a mere tool, but the substance of their relationship. If the conditions of spirit life reduced William James to something "utterly empty and illiterate . . . a mere babble of platitudinous phrases," then immortality was worse than the abyss.[15]

Henry consoled himself by editing the unfinished work that William left behind, organizing his brother's correspondence, and building the intellectual monuments that keep the thoughts of the dead on the tongues of the living. For the literary- and literal-minded Henry, this was the only survival that mattered, a corpus fixed as its author intended, safe from the bizarre, degrading whims of mediumship. To this end, somewhat ironically, Henry acted as a medium upon his brother's literary remains, channeling an illustrious image of William shorn of its darkest doubts and terrors, as well as of its indulgence in what Henry believed to be false Spiritualist hopes.

A realist novelist of meticulous psychological insight, Henry James stood at the precipice of modernism. The more obsessively he captured his characters' fragmentary memories, contradictory desires, and unconscious motives, the closer he came to dissolving the unitary Enlightenment self that made novels possible to begin with. Whether this tendency is related to William's psychological theories or not, the brothers were in constant communication. They both struggled throughout their lives with episodes of paralyzing despair; one could suggest, as a causal factor, the suspicion that we are nothing more than a fleeting, unstable bundle of impressions and influences. Henry especially worried over the feminine valence of sensitivity, that receiving too much of others could unmake and unman. Yet through sheer force of authorship—persuasive, dazzling authorship—both brothers tried to assert a unified self that persists. Even in this lonely masculine project, each was necessary to the other.

Many things shattered in the transition from Henry James's *The Turn of the Screw* to a text like Virginia Woolf's *Mrs Dalloway*. William James anticipated many of these things, but he denied the inevitability of despair—he asserted the nineteenth-century ideal of constant, disciplined self-making as a bulwark against the void. As modernist and postmodern poets adopted channeling as a writing technique, it became a discipline of dissolution, a poetics of confused, layered, fragmentary voices coming through from the far reaches of time and space. The poet taking dictation was the "tissue of trash" that Henry decried, a doomed explorer, a linguist translating from nonsense to nonsense, and ultimately, a specter. However, the channeling practice of poets like Jack Spicer was not easy or for show; Spicer was wholly consumed by the duty to take dictation. At some point, his determination to produce good art elided into a perilous responsibility to the dead.

Mediumistic texts make the tragicomedy of communication palpable. They dramatize the medium's struggle against projection, mere echoing, and the spirits' struggle to make themselves known with only shreds of a shared language. Though I'm uneasy about how this practice traveled from the lips of nineteenth-century women to poetry MFA programs, in any case it's what I want out of poetry: many voices trying and failing to communicate, and still trying. The idea that, no matter where we drift, there will always be someone to pick up the call on the other end. That art is not a map of an individual, but of what we mean to each other.

A young woman given the pseudonym "Ida Ritchie" received some messages from William James that model how the unschooled drama unfolds:

> October 14, 1912: "William James will not Prof. James for there are no professor here. God * * but will W James Prof Jam . . . [ran off paper] James * * Jams James William James."

> October 15, 1912: "William James Mind better Mind better the law the law . . . Mind the law as [?] of the trees. the [y] fall no matter how beautiful or how strong or large the trees . . . but we live again like the sturdy oak in life made perfect."[16]

Hyslop investigated Ritchie and found that the "alleged messages from Professor James do not present evidence of identity in any form that is scientifically recognizable."[17] No pink pajamas, that is. But Hyslop didn't really know James. James, in fact, harbored mild personal dislike towards his ASPR successor, who he saw as blunt and unempathetic. The assumption that Hyslop would be the target of James's efforts at communication, out of mere professional courtesy, is somewhat absurd.

In Ritchie's trance she mingled the initials W. J. and H. J. Supposedly unaware of either individual's work, she scrawled William—Henry—James—Henry—William across the page. Said the dead one to the one who survived: "James lives my brother lives lives. Asking brother where my pen is." Said the surviving brother of the dead one: "He is a possession, of real magnitude, and I shall find myself still living upon him to the end."[18]

CHAPTER 5

THE WILDERNESS
OF INSANITY

O n a quiet summer evening in Maine, a young couple, Mr. and
Mrs. J., were walking across a grassy field towards their beach cottage. Mrs. J. noticed the door of the cottage open; a "woman wearing
a peculiar shawl . . . and an old-fashioned dress" emerged and passed
them on the cobblestone path. No one spoke a word. Once inside, Mrs. J.
asked her husband if he knew the woman, and he replied, "Yes, that was
my grandmother"—who had been dead for many years. "My husband
and myself were both in good health at the time," Mrs. J. asserted at the
end of her written account. "I have never had any other experiences of
the kind." Similarly, Mrs. E. of Chicago explained that she was "in perfect
health, and very active in mind and body" when she foresaw a train accident in a dream. People like Mrs. J. and Mrs. E. who reported contested
experiences to the ASPR had many reasons to double- or triple-under-
score their mental soundness.[1]

For one thing, the ASPR and other groups requesting cases from the
public routinely included a "good health" clause in their solicitations.
"Have you ever . . . when in good health, and completely awake" became boilerplate for queries about apparitions, hallucinations, and coincidences. During the period from the 1870s through the 1920s, when
scientists debated the reality of such phenomena, the mental state of subjects was a crucial question for believers and debunkers alike. For either
side to prove its case, witnesses had to put their inner lives under the
magnifying glass and willingly expose themselves to insinuations of mental illness. Most subjects did not think themselves deluded, yet they were
also not ready to embrace the spirit hypothesis. They sought another

form of naturalistic explanation that supported the reality of their experiences, and proving their objectivity as observers was crucial to opening up this middle path.

These in-betweens needed a way to examine experiences without a foregone interpretation—a community in which the borders of reality and illusion, sanity and madness, could be mutually negotiated.[2] At its best, psychical research became a space where intimate questions were asked and answered outside the pathology-or-faith binary. Though other such middle spaces existed around the turn of the twentieth century, some affiliated with liberal Protestants, others with new religions, and often featuring overlapping personnel and ideas, the ASPR sought to distinguish itself by adopting the rhetoric and institutional apparatus of science. Not that it was antireligious or even areligious—many participants felt that their work supported some form of Christian theology—but, as a scientific society, it performatively disclaimed metaphysics and foregrounded empirical evidence.

However, psychical research, as an amateur science struggling for recognition, did not apply the ideal of cooperative inquiry uniformly. Participants frequently had to argue for the neutral register in which they wanted their experiences interpreted, against insinuations of nervous pathology and/or blind faith. Leaders of psychical research especially felt that they needed to name and claim authority on mental illness in order to legitimate their field; their detached clinical posture towards public reports recapitulates the suspicion cast on them by scientific peers.

ASPR officials sorted possible relationships between psychical phenomena and mental health status into four rough categories: First, many people suffered from mental illness which caused false perceptions; their reports were invalid as evidence, though useful as clinical cases. Second, some mentally ill people were receptive to genuine psychical phenomena, and their evidence could be salvaged for scientific purposes—Walter Franklin Prince attempted this in the case of a young woman he called "Doris Fischer." Prince diagnosed Doris's multiple personalities as a psychiatric condition produced by childhood trauma but also believed that this disordered state gave her mediumistic abilities.[3] Third, many normal people suffered temporary derangements such as fevers or daydreams that caused false perceptions of the supernatural, and their reports had to be culled out. Finally, some normal people experienced genuine phenomena—this was the best and most unproblematically valid evidence. Differentiating among these categories, especially through written correspondence, proved at times extremely difficult.

At other times the sorting process was straightforward, as in the case of one W. Lambert of Chicago. Lambert declared himself a skeptic of the spirit hypothesis and a proponent of scientific rationality. However, as he described levitating tables, controlling the behavior of others with his mind, and developing the power of "visible thought"—causing images to materialize in the air—it emerged that his experience of reality probably differed significantly from that of the people around him, who may have regarded him as eccentric or unwell.[4] Richard Hodgson seems to have politely let his correspondence with Lambert drop. Madness was the elephant in the room when sifting the testimony of strangers, and through the good health clause, investigators did their best to protect themselves and their informants from the contamination of unreason.

This work was constant and somewhat Sisyphean, since skeptics would always play the trump cards of foolishness or madness—those who attempted to make a science of the supernatural were, as Joseph Jastrow put it, "well-meaning but logically defective."[5] For Jastrow, the serious study of psychical phenomena itself represented a break with reality. Indeed, psychical researchers found themselves in a paradoxical position, enforcing rationality upon their informants in order to test the limits of the materialism that underpins scientific rationality. "It would be strange," James Hyslop averred, with this in mind, "if Materialism were discredited by the study of the very phenomena upon which it has hitherto relied for the proof of its claims."[6]

In this cause, psychical researchers preferred ordinary people over mediums and lifelong clairvoyants whose nervous temperaments verged on the pathological. They preferred singular events that struck sensible people like Robert Rawlinson, a stern-faced engineer who his wife described as "the last person in the world to imagine anything."[7] Nevertheless, Rawlinson admitted that he saw his dying friend's apparition one morning in his dressing chamber. "I never on any other occasion had any hallucination of the senses, and I sincerely trust I never again shall," the stolid Rawlinson, known for his work on public sanitation, declared. Especially ideal were correspondents like this, whose experiences did not convert them to Spiritualism or any other supernatural explanation.

Rawlinson's story, cited by the London SPR in *Phantasms of the Living*, exemplified British conventions of gentlemanly witnessing that William James and Richard Hodgson viewed as appropriate for the ASPR as well. However, those in the early ASPR pushing for modern scientific methods assailed the British presumption of genteel competency. Harvard logician Charles Sanders Peirce, critiquing *Phantasms* in the ASPR's *Proceedings*, declared Mr. Rawlinson "anxious" and therefore in a deranged mental state at the time of the apparition. Peirce made this diagnosis, of a man who inspected gruesome battlefield hospitals during the Crimean War, with no specific evidence except that "cultivated people"—the best witnesses in the psychical researchers' stable—were "inclined to superstitious credulity."[8] On either side of the Atlantic, Peirce implied, the well-heeled (or upwardly mobile) connoisseurs of curiosity suffered from a touch of mental rot.

The eighteenth-century psychology of the Enlightenment supposedly granted all minds equal capacity for reason, though whiteness and maleness were usually prerequisites for participating in reasoned discourse. Further, the truth value of an individual's words often hung on class- or profession-based respectability, as Peirce observed. Part of what made Spiritualism and certain strains of psychical research so radical was their acceptance of lower-class, female, and less-credentialed witnesses. Ironically, this rush to testify at the tribunal of science helped drive academic psychology away from a model of the self as rational agent and towards a self puppeteered by unconscious forces—unable to know its own motives except as refracted through the laboratory. To jettison the testimony of distinguished Spiritualists, skeptics had to saw off the epistemological branch of introspection that they, too, were sitting on and locate objectivity somewhere else, in tables of reflex reaction times and nerve conduction tests. People who trusted what they experienced, whether the landed gentry, progressive engineers, or zealous Spiritualists, were victims of a basic human error.

Though flawed perception and memory appeared universal, it was hard for scientists to see them as normal and healthy. The rational self persisted as a psychological ideal. Widespread irrationality suggested some kind of decay at work: William James observed of his age that "few of us are not in some way infirm, or even diseased," a reassurance that sickness was the new normal.[9] The specter of a hidden mental weakness that preyed indiscriminately on the highest and lowest rungs of society was widespread at the fin de siècle, manifesting in ubiquitous concerns about degeneration, decadence, exhaustion, and neurasthenia.

The first rumblings of this wave came in the late 1860s, when New York physician George Beard noticed that his patients in the "brain-working classes" suffered from a panoply of strange symptoms ranging from headaches to hallucinations (Figure 19). Beard coined the diagnosis of neurasthenia to describe these phenomena, which he blamed on the depletion of nervous energy. In medical journals and the popular press, he sounded the alarm about a growing plague of "American nervousness."[10]

Beard warned gravely that Americans were burning through their vital life force merely by partaking in "modern civilization," which he identified with "steam-power, the periodical press, the telegraph, the sciences, and the mental activity of women." At first Beard's critics sniped at this capacious theory as a sign of "insanity on the part of the author," but it quickly took hold among its intended audience: educated people in search of explanations for their nagging ailments, their sense of being somehow unwell.[11] Thanks to neurasthenia, the very people most favored in America's skewed calculus of democratic and scientific virtue were now at risk for, or already suffering from, an amorphous pathology that called into question their status as rational, responsible citizens. Despite these fears, society and science ground onward through the dust of uncertainty kicked up by their motion; as Charles Sanders Peirce himself supposedly remarked to James, "Reality is that which finally and universally will be believed."[12]

Throughout this book I have not questioned the sanity of psychical researchers, allowing their own discourse on belief, witnessing, and experience to speak for itself. I hope that, by now, you have come to view

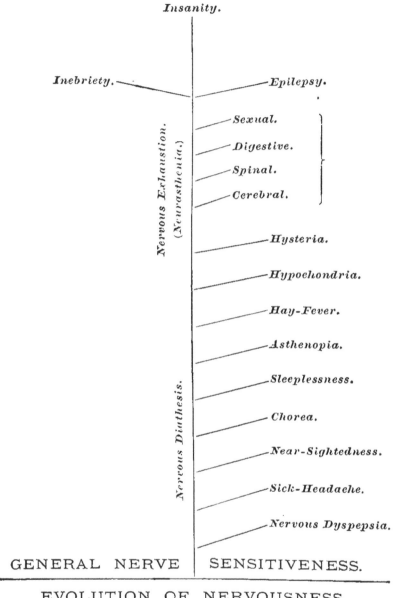

Insanity.

Inebriety. — *Epilepsy.*

Nervous Exhaustion.
(Neurasthenia.)

Sexual.
Digestive.
Spinal.
Cerebral.

Hysteria.
Hypochondria.
Hay-Fever.
Asthenopia.
Sleeplessness.
Chorea.
Near-Sightedness.
Sick-Headache.
Nervous Dyspepsia.

Nervous Diathesis.

GENERAL NERVE | SENSITIVENESS.

EVOLUTION OF NERVOUSNESS.

FIGURE 19. The progression from nervousness to neurasthenia to, potentially, insanity. George Miller Beard, *American Nervousness* (New York: Putnam 1881), frontispiece.

their accounts as real and meaningful in the context of their world. In *The Varieties of Religious Experience*, James inveighed against "medical materialists" who reduced religious ecstasies to mere mental illness. He insisted that studying "religion's existential conditions" meant refraining from judgment on its ultimate causes.[13] The preceding chapters traced how constellations of relational meaning produced psychical phenomena, and, indeed, made possible the experiencing subjects of those phenomena. In these starry relations dwells a kind of reality that pragmatism regards as sufficient—indeed, the best we can probably do. James did admit that he longed for more, for a visceral and final accounting in the stark terms of God or no God, purpose or no purpose, faith or folly. He remained candid about his own desires, and those of his readers, to push further towards an absolute reality. Yet such desire, matched at each step by the skepticism of the modern scientific mind, could lead to madness.

Gatekeepers at the Vague Boundary

That course takes us where we need to go, to the boundaries of sanity. Psychical research was constantly negotiating these boundaries—sometimes communal and democratic, sometimes clinical and authoritarian. To pursue the real into a wilderness where perceptions could deceive, it had to standardize its sources within a certain range of reliability. Thus, Beard's framework of nervous economy appealed to psychical researchers as a gradated model that allowed for the separate but interconnected functioning of mind and body. It allowed them to accept evidence from certain people with nervous disorders on the grounds that physiological troubles did not negate their ability to testify. At the same time, researchers could reject evidence that they thought was compromised by nerves. This differentiation had no fixed or clearly articulated criteria. Widespread anxiety over neurasthenia was chipping away at the very notion of mental normalcy; this state of flux gave psychical researchers freer play in probing their informants' mental states and placing them on a spectrum between purely physical and purely mental disorder.

But this free play had limits and very high stakes. By admitting that they saw things or heard voices that others did not, informants skirted dangerously close to insanity—an untreatable condition that landed victims in the asylum, often for life. Though madness was romantically associated with flights of genius, the clinical diagnosis of insanity often brought with it social death. William James demonstrated his susceptibility to this widespread stigma when his brother, Henry, suffered a mental collapse in 1910. William was careful to call it "a bad nervous breakdown" and warned his son to avoid using any term that "suggests insanity, which this is not."[14] Insanity was believed to run in families, making word choice a matter of shared interest.

For the cerebral James brothers, the idea of losing one's mind, and thus one's self and voice in society, was a terror beyond any bodily suffering. The same aversion runs through the letters of less prominent psychical researchers, who used the language of nerves to manage and contain the unspoken, destabilizing specter of madness. As Henry James's breakdown shows, very severe and persistent mental disturbances could pass politely under the cloak of nervousness. With livelihoods and social standing at stake, families, friends, and doctors gladly took up the faddish diagnosis to protect sufferers. George Beard and his medical followers constantly asserted that neurasthenia was a "physical not a mental state." He admitted that "nervousness sometimes leads to insanity," but assured "there is no necessary correlation . . . thousands and thousands are nervous who are not and never will be insane."[15] Beard's somatization of mental illness can be seen as a protective maneuver, giving patients permission to seek treatment for stigmatized symptoms. Yet his attempts to protect the mildly afflicted from fear of being regarded as or actually becoming insane reflect an underlying awareness that such boundaries were human constructions built on the mind's quicksand.

ASPR correspondents were always talking through madness, talking around it, locating their experiences in relation to the social and clinical borders of sanity. Close up, the border is not a mathematical line, but a cloud where normal and abnormal states shade into each other; modern psychiatrists describe it as necessary vagueness, freeing the practitioner to make case-by-case judgments.[16] Vagueness was necessary for psychical researchers as well; it allowed them to carve trustworthy data out of borderline accounts, while politely disqualifying others. Correspondents shared experiences that they would not share with a doctor because the

ASPR represented partnership rather than diagnosis. Even those with histories of mental affliction could sway the society's leadership through reasoned discourse and intimate disclosure.

Partnership, however, could become too close for comfort. Psychical researchers needed some markers of detached, objective authority, which they found by taking a diagnostic and classificatory stance towards subjects marked as unfit for participation. Institutionalized people, hysterical women, and teenage wards like Prince's Doris Fischer were not in a position to complain about their exclusion from the collegial search for the secrets of the soul, and psychical researchers evaluated these subjects to bring clinical rigor to their writings. This expedient use of psychiatric authority may seem a logical enough strategy, but it takes on added significance in light of what came before: the decades-long association, in medicine and popular culture, between Spiritualism, mediumship, and madness. Trading the position of the diagnosed for that of the diagnoser was necessary to entice respectable scientists into a field that took the supernormal seriously.

In 1854, with the table-tipping craze tearing through the American countryside, Illinois state senator James Shields set the pattern for fearmongering with a petition signed by 15,000 constituents, calling Spiritualism "a partial derangement of the mental faculties, produced by a diseased condition of the physical organization."[17] He demanded a government inquiry into its seemingly epidemic spread—a remarkable call for state intervention echoed for the next century by rationalist skeptics, eugenicists, progressives, and Harry Houdini, among other concerned citizens.

The connection between Spiritualism and mental pathology proved enduring. In 1920, then-ASPR secretary Walter Prince received a letter from Ora J. Parker, a county lawyer in Minnesota. Parker reported his ongoing experiments with a "lady of remarkable telepathic ability," a young schoolteacher named Myra Maxwell. However, a few months later Parker wrote to Prince in despair; Maxwell was "insane," hallucinating, and the experiments were discontinued. Did dabbling in telepathy cause a psychotic break? Parker shifted the blame away from his psychical experiments and placed it squarely on the excesses of Spiritualism: Maxwell had gone to see a lecture by the Spiritualist evangelizer Sir Oliver Lodge, which Parker believed caused her attack. Parker emphatically separated his controlled experiments from Lodge's unruly fantasies precisely because others might not see such a clear distinction.[18]

Embracing and utilizing the views of psychiatrists was supposed to ally psychical researchers with the official arbiters of sanity and break off association with characters like Oliver Lodge and James John Garth Wilkinson, a British Spiritualist who proposed that the insane were hearing real spirit voices which they simply needed proper training to interpret. Wilkinson represents the threat to the credibility of psychical research posed by those who would flip the polarities of the real, or at least assert reality's relative nature: perhaps it's the asylum keeper, rather than the inmate, who fails to perceive the truth. William James, who encountered Wilkinson during his youth, clearly had a foot in this camp. James's mental breakdown in his early twenties, discussed later in this chapter, instilled him with a stark horror of madness but at the same time opened his eyes to the value of divergent experiences of reality.

In his 1901 Gifford lecture on "the sick soul," James asserted that "morbid minds" may be the "best key to life's significance, and possibly the only openers of our eyes to the deepest levels of truth." The deepest level of truth, when James's peered through his morbid glasses, was that we inhabit an uncaring universe filled with evil and suffering—to which madness is a reasonable reaction. "The lunatic's visions of horror are all drawn from the material of daily fact," he continued bleakly. "Our civilization is founded on the shambles, and every individual existence goes out in a lonely spasm of helpless agony."[19] Those who would face grim reality could hardly emerge unscathed. From this perspective, the distorted visions of the insane and melancholic were not only reasonable, but deeply informative about the human condition. Their "peculiar form of consciousness" deserved to be heard in society, though James acknowledged that it made life for some a "prison-house."[20]

Psychical research would seem like a perfect forum for this "peculiar form of consciousness"—James's notion of the sick soul isn't far from Josiah Royce's interest in "the fantastic man, the dreamer," the odd genius whose mind is unusually receptive to liminal experiences. However, at

the turn of the twentieth century the ASPR had to reckon wi
of mad Spiritualists and the emerging problem of neurasl
of which made the sick soul's testimony a liability rather tha
their scientific authority.

George A. Thacher was one of these liabilities. He openly confessed
that he was on the wrong side of the ASPR's "good health" clause. Yet
through intimate disclosure of his personal history and reasoning process, he managed to get his extraordinary experiences published as
model testimony in the ASPR's journal. A back injury around 1885,
when he was only twenty-three, left him "physically disabled," unable to
walk or sit for long periods of time. Though his doctors diagnosed "dis-
placement of one of the lumbar vertebrae," the fact that his discomfort
had no visible cause made it easy for people to doubt its authenticity, a
familiar predicament for anyone afflicted with what we might now label
chronic pain. "I supposed there are many people who consider my disability as imaginary and probably all consider it nervous," he explained
to James Hyslop in 1907. Thacher admitted that the pain, combined with
the "severe mental strain" of writing and legal work, caused him "cruel
nervous suffering."[21] Skeptics often cited similar nervous conditions to
disqualify reports of psychical phenomena. Peirce combed *Phantasms of
the Living* identifying neurasthenics like Robert Rawlinson and throwing
out their cases. Their prolific reports were often rebuffed with red x's
from the ASPR secretary's grease pencil. One jaggedly scrawled 1897 letter received an emphatic "HOEY" in the margins from the usually sympathetic Richard Hodgson.

Certain nervous observers could make it past the scrutiny of ASPR
officials. Writers who demonstrated self-awareness of their nervous condition, who explicitly described the nature of their trouble and efforts to
manage it, were seen as furnishing their personal equation, a way of qual-
ifying and calibrating their evidence. If no one in American society was
immune to neurasthenia—indeed, Beard framed it as a natural by-prod-
uct of American exceptionalism—it seemed untenable to disqualify those
who acknowledged their susceptibility. "I have struggled to live as other
men do," Thacher wrote of his handicaps. "I believe I have succeeded in
keeping in touch in a sane fashion with normal human interests." With

this statement, he tried to square his status as a prostrated neurasthenic with being a socially and psychologically integrated individual, accomplished through the hard work of self-management. Hyslop accepted it as an honest disclosure. Despite a good deal of eccentricity, Thacher's introduction came across to its intended reader as a virtuous, self-aware, and self-critical account. It helped that he produced letters of support from "a large list of men who are among the well known and intelligent people in the United States." Hyslop, unlike Peirce, set great store by the opinions of the "cultivated." He took assurance that Thacher was on the normal side of the vague boundary.[22]

Thacher's respectable friends proved that he was well liked, but finding social acceptance was not a guarantee of scientific competency. Spiritualists formed a supportive community whose illustrious members eagerly vouched for each other's experiences. The sheer prevalence of Spiritualism meant that it encompassed prominent businessmen, writers, and politicians, much to the chagrin of militant skeptics like Harry Houdini, who harped on the dangers of putting public trust in the hands of people who harbored a secret mental pathology.[23] But unless Hyslop dispensed with human testimony altogether—which his foils in laboratory psychology happily did—he had to believe someone. He felt that if Thacher's judgment was truly compromised, one of his many references in the scientific community would have a duty to out him. The system of social validation that Peirce assailed as a genteel delusion could, Hyslop believed, function as an objective tool given the right participants.

With the delicate question of his mental fitness settled, Thacher unfolded a long, disjointed chronicle of premonitions, family coincidences, levitating mediums, and spirit manifestations. Hyslop extolled this outpouring as "a very good example of how to observe and record one's experience." Perhaps the stream-of-consciousness style appealed to him as direct and authentic when it came from someone with good references, though similar tales from anonymous strangers were routinely weeded out of the ASPR's mail heap. On the surface, Thacher's stories have no more or less to support them than others that Hyslop dismissed out of hand. It seems to be Thacher's narrative voice that communicated "his intelligence and fitness to record and discuss the problems of psychical research"; he did this so effectively that Hyslop reprinted the correspondence almost in full as a model of observational acuity.[24]

What made Thacher such a paragon of epistemic virtue? He did a modest amount of critical distancing: frequent ringing sounds that he attributed to spirits "may be hallucinations," he acknowledged, and Hyslop praised his critical detachment. But then Thacher walked back his concession. "If they are hallucinations, they impress every person who happens to be with me in the same way," a claim which he didn't substantiate with supporting testimony. A certain circularity of reasoning emerged: "If they were hallucinations I should immediately . . . ask to be shut up in an insane asylum," Thacher declared, assuming that he would be able to diagnose his own wrong perceptions. In Hyslop's view, however, the correspondent's willingness to even mention the possibility of mental illness showed a self-awareness that should "protect him against criticism."[25]

Though many letters to the ASPR came from people suffering distress, delusions, and obvious impairment of their ability to function in society, the majority came from functioning individuals like Thacher. These people developed idiosyncratic ideas and struggled with personal challenges; today's practitioners would place most of them within a normal psychological range. If they'd viewed their experiences more explicitly through the lens of Christianity, they would have found camaraderie and acceptance in many churches. But, to varying degrees, they were infected with the doubt that characterized James's sick souls; they wanted an affirmation from science that what they had seen was materially, not just spiritually, real. Science, in turn, required an affirmation of their mental integrity. It's clear that Thacher's seductive performance of rationality succeeded because the interior he disclosed was so very recognizable to Hyslop, a man of similar background and training, though his reasoning was riddled with logical inconsistencies. This clearly demonstrates the problems of class and cultural bias that Peirce pointed out. For existential reasons, psychical researchers could not dismiss all experience as hopelessly tainted by nervous disorder. They could attempt, as Hyslop did, to play asylum keeper, at risk of reproducing arbitrary social biases, or they could throw in their lot with the madmen.

Inmates Running the Asylum

Although Thacher and other ASPR participants did not want the world to perceive them as mad, they recognized that their field was highly relevant to the study and treatment of mental illness. There was no denying that asylums were full of people who claimed to experience psychical phenomena. Committed patients made a safe and desirable population for psychical investigators; nineteenth-century psychiatry had a well-established precedent for evaluating, classifying, and theorizing about its subjects while giving them little voice in the process. Throughout the 1880 and 90s, psychical researchers held up Jean-Martin Charcot and Pierre Janet, French neurologists who conducted large-scale, systematic studies of indigent female patients at Paris's Salpêtrière Hospital, as an example of how they would proceed with the "abnormal" branch of their work, if given the resources. The idea resurfaced in 1907, with Hyslop's unrealized scheme for Section A, a branch of the ASPR with its own psychiatric clinic and hospital. "The abnormal," Hyslop explained, "is sometimes the medium through which supernormal facts find their way"; constant observation and experiment on patients would finally establish an objective distinction between genuine psychical phenomena, as they struck sane or insane individuals, and those that were merely illusions of the diseased brain.[26]

Had Hyslop's vision come to pass, metal bars would have demarcated Section A's subjects from its investigators. A corresponding institutional division would separate Section A, devoted to "abnormal psychology," from Section B, devoted to "supernormal psychology" (telepathy, clairvoyance, and spirit communication in seemingly healthy subjects). How would the ASPR sort abnormal from supernormal? "At certain points the two fields tend to merge into each other," Hyslop stated vaguely, while "at others they are widely separated . . . it is important not to associate the investigations of the two fields."[27] This crucial distinction was contingent on the eventual development of methods not yet available. The asylum's iron boundaries proved an illusory certainty; they couldn't keep at bay questions that haunted psychical research. Were psychical experiences inherently pathological even when they struck the sane—an acute episode, like a heart attack, of temporary derangement? Further, could believing in supernatural phenomena actually cause madness? From the 1840s onward, skeptics and the popular press had played this social panic both ways, blaming séances for insanity while also insinuating that Spiritualism exploited people suffering from mental disease.[28]

Looking back over the nineteenth century for precedents to Hyslop's proposal, we see that most psychical investigators held the question of mental disorder at arm's length with the polite discourse of nervousness, attempting to normalize a wide range of mental states without passing judgment. A few, however, took a more proactive tack. When theologians and physicians warned that talking to spirits rotted peoples' minds, certain believers countered that their knowledge could actually cure insanity, as well as less severe psychoneuroses. This sense that spirit communion had healing qualities for participants, a sort of mediumistic talk therapy, emerged during the first heyday of Spiritualism in the 1850s.[29] While Hyslop envisioned disciplined, orderly medical treatment, the volatile logic of "spirit-cure" risked fracturing the linear spectrum of sanity into a hall of mirrors. In this space, pathology, faith, and therapy refracted off each other, blurring the lines between doctor and patient, scientist and subject.

Spiritualism drew psychological scrutiny from its inception—the strange behavior of mediums resembled that of madmen, but also born-again Christians at a tent revival, a common sight for generations touched by the Second Great Awakening of the early 1800s. Completing the pathology-faith-therapy triumvirate, Spiritualism also echoed animal magnetism, a popular healing practice that threw patients into fits and spasms controlled by a "magnetizer." None of these practices can be reduced purely to pathology, faith, or therapy—the absence of such categorical boundaries was integral to how they worked for practitioners—and thus purifying out a single meaning was often the project of critics. While Spiritualism took on the potency of an all-encompassing system for believers, critics tried to distinguish between clinical pathologies and socially acceptable religious beliefs, hobbled by the growing suspicion that certain delusions could become real if they were shared widely enough.

James John Garth Wilkinson was a homeopathic physician and fol-
lower of Emanuel Swedenborg, the eighteenth-century philosopher and
mystic. Already committed to homeopathy's democratic proving process,
and to the Swedenborgian notion of divine "influx," Wilkinson embraced
spirit communication with evangelical enthusiasm in the 1850s.[30] It represented a perfect fusion of his metaphysical and medical values. Skeptics used the similarities between mediumship and insanity to argue that
séances agitated people into madness.[31] Homeopaths, however, believed
in curing like with like—they administered substances that produced a
mild form of illness as remedies for those illnesses. For asylum inmates,
Spiritualism could be the poison that cured.

Wilkinson's 1857 pamphlet, "The Homoeopathic Principle Applied
to Insanity," was widely reprinted and quoted in the British and American
homeopathic communities. In this text, he explained the process of "in-
oculating" patients against mental illness by training them as Spiritualist
mediums. A supervised program of automatic drawing, writing, sculpture,
and music—"in short, any kind of art production which comes spontaneously" from spirit sources—would, he claimed, release the repressed
"natural emotions, with all their scars and disorders."[32] This was not mere
catharsis, however. Rather than returning patients to a life free from supernatural visitations, Wilkinson's process would teach them to sort authentic from inauthentic spirit messages. Asylum keepers who denied and
repressed patients' mediumship only worsened their conditions.

Wilkinson acknowledged that insanity was often accompanied, and
sometimes triggered, by belief in spirit voices and supernormal powers of
mind. While this state of severe excitement was pathological, he maintained
the underlying metaphysical reality of spirit communication. Curing insanity meant training patients to separate the authentic signal from the noise of
agitated delusions. Not only would these patients return to meaningful social lives—more importantly for Wilkinson, recording and cataloging their
visions would provide invaluable data about the human soul. This echoed
the systematizing efforts of the period's reform-minded psychiatrists.

Based on his own experiences, Wilkinson sketched a plan to bring
Spiritualist mediums into asylums and have them train the patients, first
one-on-one, then collectively, in spirit channeling. Patients who learned

to "govern themselves" would then teach the others and form a utopian-sounding fellowship within the institution's walls—madmen retailored as citizens worthy of democratic self-rule. The universal cure, Wilkinson promised, "will be very quick indeed." The universal cure, however, meant switching the polarities of madness and sanity, creating a new social order in which supernatural belief became normal. The asylum taken over by its mediumistic inmates became an allegory for Spiritualism's menacing power to "turn the brains of all the world," beginning with those brains prostrated beneath the treads of religious orthodoxy and secular rationality.

"This pamphlet is full of absurd nonsense," a Boston allopathic medical journal wrote of Wilkinson's asylum plan.[33] Wilkinson's homeopathic colleagues pointed out that mainstream medicine had no better alternative. No accepted treatments for severe mental illness had any meaningful success, and the public asylums of Wilkinson's London were notoriously filthy and mismanaged. By the turn of the twentieth century, overcrowded American asylums came under attack for their abysmal treatment of patients, famously exposed by journalist Nellie Bly after ten days undercover in New York's Blackwell's Island asylum.[34] This reformist moment likely inspired Hyslop in his criticisms of psychiatry and his proposed psychical alternative, which echoed Wilkinson in suggesting some supernormal influence in mental illness. British asylum doctors had dismissed Wilkinson as a mere "enthusiast" despite his medical degree; what hope did Hyslop, with a PhD in philosophy, have of gaining access to patients after psychiatrists had spent a half century professionalizing their domain?[35]

William James on the Brink

Even if given the chance, Wilkinson probably had no illusions that he could personally implement his plan for a Spiritualist asylum—he put his ideas in print as a gesture to inspire others. Unsurprisingly, he found his most sympathetic audience in the United States, wellspring of modern Spiritualism and incubator of countless heterodoxies. In contrast to critical and even mocking accounts in the British press, some Americans found Wilkinson's proposals "eminently worthy of trial." "We have ourselves successfully adopted them in our treatment of the insane," wrote

Dr. Henry C. Preston, superintendent of the Connecticut Retreat for the Insane. Preston had trained under Amariah Brigham, a founder of the *American Journal of Insanity* and the American Psychiatric Association—hardly a fringe figure.[36] Dr. William Henry Holcombe chimed in, calling Wilkinson's pamphlet "the breaking forth of a star in the midst of the darkest storm."[37] Holcombe added that "Emerson, our greatest American philosopher, has pronounced Dr. Wilkinson to be the 'Bacon of the 19th century.'" This was not quite correct—Emerson called the homeopath "Bacon's own son"—but Wilkinson's scientific and metaphysical stature meant that his ideas about mental healing would influence other radical thinkers of the period.[38]

One American philosopher who felt this influence was none other than the teenage William James, whose father, Henry Sr., was a close friend of Wilkinson and joined his eclectic London circle during a period abroad in the 1850s. Historian Krister Dylan Knapp believes that Wilkinson was "like a second father" to James and that Wilkinson's empirical spirit cure won out in the boy's mind over Henry Sr.'s doctrinal disapproval of Spiritualism. Knapp proposes that this triumph of empiricism over dogma led James to probe metaphysical questions using the scientific method instead of theology, eagerly experimenting with homeopathy, hypnotism, and mind-cure therapies.[39] Tracing all this back to Wilkinson is somewhat speculative, but it's clear that James sought an empirical consensus about what is real, a consensus that held science accountable to human experience as well as the other way around.

The emotion of fear weaves through this period's disputes about experience, faith, and madness. It was a dark foil to nineteenth-century secularism, which promised to stamp out antiquated superstition with modern scientific certainty. Enlightenment thinkers characterized fear as primitive and irrational, yet, as Andreas Sommer points out, their need to conquer it established this particular emotion as an existential threat to Enlightenment—a fear of fear itself.[40] At the same time that scientific critics attributed Spiritualism's appeal to fear of death, Spiritualists accused critics of fearing what they lacked the tools to understand, both sides equating certainty with freedom from fear. James's significantly more intimate musings on fear suggest the perils of a middle way that resists easy commitments. James swam against the current in psychology, insisting that "the true opposites of belief, psychologically considered, are doubt and inquiry, not disbelief."[41] This observation—that belief and disbelief boil down to the same unfounded certainty—was the ground of his continuing search for a third way, a *tertium quid*, built from the content of experience. Positioning the philosopher-scientist within experience meant asserting the human ability to think through and with the fear.

As much as James sought to hold open an anarchic space of possibility, to protect the haunting of our minds and our world as something vital, and even sacred, he had a lifelong acquaintance with the fear that motivated secular efforts to beat back the unknown. His father's brush with madness, when James was only two years old, left in its wake a long period of doubt and despair. Henry James Sr. dragged his young family with him back and forth across the Atlantic for years in search of respite.[42] William James's biographers point to this unstable childhood as the source of various woes, his nervousness and irresolution. It marked him with a fatalistic sense that his father's crisis would strike him too, at a time and place unknown, and that he, too, would face that desert without God, or his wits, to protect him.

"You might be in some doubt about my sanity as most people are about Hamlet's," James wrote to his brother Henry in April of 1868, after he fled to Germany seeking relief from his worsening physical illness and depression.[43] Shakespeare's mad Dane was a staple of the nineteenth-century American stage from New York's Winter Garden to rural traveling sideshows. James, a devoted theatergoer, had recently seen two productions of the play. A symbol and warning for many "brain-working" Americans, the ambivalent Hamlet represented insanity brought on by too much thinking and too little moral conviction, the neurasthenic erosion of masculine will. For a young intellectual like James who sat out the Civil War and still lived in his father's house, it was an obvious comparison.[44]

Thus, James had failed the good health clause years before his most devastating mental crisis struck. Like Thacher, he was afflicted with back pain that cascaded into a host of ailments: during his travels in 1868, he wrote home of dyspepsia, chronic gastritis, and thoughts of suicide. His condition fluctuated after his return to Boston, and he completed his MD at Harvard with vague plans to pursue scientific work. But by the winter of 1870 James was prostrated again with back pain, "philosophic pessimism and general depression of spirits."[45] His near break with sanity occurred one evening in his family home, as he entered a darkened dressing room. "There arose in my mind the image of an epileptic patient whom I had seen in the asylum, a black-haired youth with greenish skin, entirely idiotic . . . he sat there like a sort of sculptured Egyptian cat or Peruvian mummy, moving nothing but his black eyes and looking absolutely non-human."[46] The memory of this epileptic patient may have come from James's medical school clinical rounds (Figure 20); nineteenth-century Americans regarded epilepsy with special horror as a type of blighting, inborn insanity.[47] "Nothing that I possess can defend me against that fate," James realized. "It was as if something hitherto solid within my breast gave way entirely, and I became a mass of quivering fear. After this the universe was changed for me altogether."[48]

After his death, James's family destroyed his journals and correspondence that made reference to this crisis. They saved pages upon pages about his mood swings, anxiety, and other nervous woes, but the vision of the epileptic boy was too potentially damaging. This further reveals how madness, reputation, and inheritance were very much entwined, even for the enlightened Jameses. We only know of the crisis because, decades later, James incorporated it into *The Varieties of Religious Experience*, passing it off as the testimony of an anonymous Frenchman. He left a clue to the anecdote's family significance by footnoting his father's mental breakdown as "another case of fear equally sudden." Then, in a 1904 letter to his translator, he breezily confessed that "the document . . . is my own case. Acute neurasthenia attack with phobia. I naturally disguised the provenance!"[49] While working to normalize public discussion of such experiences, James felt it was "natural" (i.e., reasonable and prudent) to hide that it happened to him. This was exactly the kind of material that he hoped to gather from the ASPR's members, with affidavits from their families and friends. Despite his ever humane and sympathetic tone, he was not ready to promote acceptance by making an example of himself.

FIGURE 20. This sketch from James's medical school notebook, possibly inspired by his observation of asylum patients, prefigures the imagery of his mental breakdown in the 1870s. *Gremlin-like man*, ca. 1864–1869. MS Am 1092.2, by permission of the Houghton Library, Harvard University.

The nineteenth century was a crucible for social and psychological developments that changed what it meant to be a person moving through the world.[50] Historians speak of a crisis of the individual that accompanied the adoption of a bounded, unitary conception of self: selfhood felt fragile, subject to the contagious frenzies of urban crowds, nervous disorders, and occult magnetizers. Religious belief, dangerously proximal to primitive superstition, posed another challenge which the autonomous, private, reasoning individual had to resolve with sober analysis, not blind enthusiasm. All of these forces battered at the fortress of the self; if they overran its defenses, madness was a likely outcome.

Doctors such as George Miller Beard connected psychological crises with the refinements of civilization, opposed to an imagined past when people lacked the complexity to suffer. Medieval peasantry, modern nonwhite races, and the mentally ill occupied equivalent positions in this hierarchy. Like James's epileptic patient, they all seemed "absolutely non-human" to a particular kind of Western, male observer. James condensed his "panic-fear" into an image that blended the primitive, indigenous, and animal—a carved Egyptian cat and a Peruvian mummy, plundered antiquities which he would have studied at Harvard's Peabody Museum or in the great collections of Europe. He mapped these exotic symbols of otherness onto the concrete form of a Boston asylum inmate. Without recognizable subjectivity, yet still animated by a life force that defied pure mechanism, these Others became objects of mystery and dread.

This explains why the stakes were so high when "panic-fear" seized an educated, upper-middle-class person like William James and threatened to shred his sanity. It cut at his sense of being human, synonymous with the willful productive labor of self-making. James's long, agonizing struggle to form himself against the entropy of disintegration, to steer himself off the rails of "iron determinism," gave him empathy with others in similar straits; much of his public career was devoted to counseling audiences anxious about building and maintaining a meaningful self in the modern world. His reflective, reassuring authorial voice suggested the wisdom of a man who had held himself together at the brink of the precipice. Yet there is a labored "sunshine" in James's telling of the crisis moment, an explicit effort to sort himself with the type of people he termed "healthy-minded." Only through narrative alienation from his shattering experience could he speak with authority about experience on the whole—only through an act of will could he constitute himself as a guide for the perplexed, able to plumb the depths of others' terror or elation without losing his own way. His words carried the promise that gentle, genuine inquiry into the full range of human experiences was not only safe, but necessary.

This is all to acknowledge the historically specific nature of mental illness, the particular cultural and social forms in which it manifests. Historians have shown how insanity became a diagnosis used to silence certain voices and to secure the logic of a disenchanted universe against ongoing testimony of the supernatural. With all these nuanced considerations on the table, it remains that mental illness in its varied forms does not feel good. Mental and emotional distress are real—terror, disorientation, paralysis, hearing voices or seeing apparitions are often unpleasant regardless of whether they indicate psychopathology or a supernormal phenomenon. James spoke from his own experience of the "grisly blood-freezing heart-palpitating sensation of [evil] close upon one" when he lectured about the sick soul, which was at times his own soul.[51] Families who have felt the wave of a crisis break over a loved one also feel the fear and sadness of their loss—which they hope is temporary and which they try to recover with help from authorities on healing mind and spirit.

Given James's precarious mental health throughout his twenties, his parents, siblings, and friends worried about this scenario. At the beginning of his severe depression in 1867, William wrote to his friend Henry Bowditch, ostensibly in jest, urging the budding physiologist to "take charge of a big state lunatic asylum . . . say at Sommerville" so that James could retreat there as an inpatient.[52] Slowly, fitfully, during moribund years while he watched his former classmates rocketing ahead in their careers, he pulled himself together. By 1876, when he became Harvard's first professor of psychology, he was on course to make his mark as a public intellectual. Instead of falling into Hamlet-like paralysis, he emerged active and vigorous from an existential struggle with the nature of the self.

The Jameses, however, did not escape the stigma of a mental breakdown in the family. It was Robertson James (known as Bob), a Civil War veteran overshadowed by his famous elder siblings, who took refuge in the McLean Asylum at Sommerville in the 1880s. Never truly recovered from his war experience, Bob suffered repeated business failures, violent outbursts, artistic frustration, a divorce—he seemed congenitally unable to make his way in the world.[53] During Bob's period in the asylum, the medical staff there lent their support to an ambitious new research program promoted by his psychologist brother: the American Society for Psychical Research. McLean physician William Noyes and progressive superintendent Edward Cowles joined the ASPR as full members, receiving its publications for the asylum library. Neither actively contributed, but they were among numerous asylum doctors and neurologists who joined and participated. This suggests that mental health professionals saw psychical research as a promising new approach to the study of abnormal mental states, a position clearly held by the Philadelphia homeopath Weston Bayley, who appeared in Chapter 1 eagerly demonstrating hypnotism for his medical colleagues. Perhaps, frustrated by their therapeutic limitations, these clinicians were willing to cast a wider net than their counterparts in the laboratory, who had no distressed patients or families to answer to.

In 1892, the *New York Times* explicitly linked the ASPR's work with the quest for psychiatric cures: "The interest which the public has taken" in psychical research was driven, they asserted, by a popular belief that it had "some bearing upon the treatment of disease." The *Times* pointed a finger at James as the purveyor of this hope. "Some years ago at a meeting in Boston, Prof. James expressed the belief that a good psychical researcher turned loose in an insane asylum might discover some things that had been overlooked by the doctors."[54] Of course, discovering "some things" was not the same as curing patients. James did, however, cite the hypnotic methods of Charcot and Janet to imply that experimental manipulation of unconscious states could serve as therapy. Unsatisfied with this vague insinuation, the *Times* complained that James was "not very explicit as to the performance of the cure." Basic research in psychology and psychiatry has never been very explicit in this regard—practical applications hover at a fixed distance of about twenty years away, and attempts to speed up the process lead to outrages like Walter Freeman's ice-pick lobotomies. But what's important here is that James had buried the vision of Wilkinson's subversive asylum, where patients and doctors, believers and investigators, became indistinguishable from each other in the light of revealed truth. Instead, psychical researchers would stand firmly on the clinician's side of the bars, looking in on madness, learning from it, even trying to heal it.

Psi Goes into the Clinic and out of It

The idea for Section A of the American Institute for Scientific Research (Hyslop's front for the reconstituted ASPR) did not, then, materialize out of thin air. Investigators, physicians, and the public saw the need for clinical work at the nexus of psychical experience and psychopathology. However, Hyslop's intentions for Section A differed in important ways from the visions of James and Wilkinson. Wilkinson, of course, thought that the insane could become each other's guides to communal spiritual transcendence. James saw, in an agglomeration of the mentally ill, a chance for psychical research to achieve its own scientific ends. Collecting data on this population could lead to an objective distinction between authentic and pathological experiences, allowing the ASPR to defend against critics who argued that all psychical phenomena, even in the sane, were a form of disordered thinking. The treatment James alluded to would evolve in some unspecified way from basic research.

Hyslop took a different and rather curious angle. His proposed mental institution was a rhetorical critique of ineffective psychiatry. Its scope was dizzying: inpatient and outpatient care for psychological disturbances, organic troubles, amnesia, secondary personality, functional melancholia, neurasthenia and psychasthenia, hysteria and hystero-epilepsy, obsessions, monomanias, phobias, delusions, alcoholism, "and all functional troubles that may ultimately be made to yield to the various forms of suggestion." Hyslop politely nodded to the expertise of his psychiatric colleagues but repeatedly scolded them for their narrow focus on neurological lesions. Section A would embrace the "psychological as well as . . . physiological relations," since understanding the "phenomena of consciousness" had immediate benefits for diagnosis and therapy. "Important facts may be obtained for practical life antecedent to the autopsy," he quipped, referring to standard asylum operating procedure in which patients languished in cells until they died, whereupon a pathologist dissected their brains to search for the cause of their illness. Autopsy "never aids in the treatment of the individual patient," Hyslop observed dryly.[55]

This reformist platform allowed Hyslop to tap general dissatisfaction with the state of psychiatry and obtain letters of support from prominent experts. Pierre Janet, whose studies of hysteria and traumatic memory laid the foundations for the fin-de-siècle "discovery of the unconscious," furnished a gushing endorsement. The American Institute for Scientific Research's charter "promises to realize all my dreams," he wrote, "for developing in a complete manner the science of the human mind." He pointed to the looming crisis of middle-class neurosis, "those unhappy neuropathic subjects who live on the borders of insanity." They clearly did not belong in the hopeless cells of the asylum. "It is very difficult to find a retreat where any one will consent to consider their distress or to aid them in restoring their health." Before the psychoanalyst's couch became the accepted venue for the "psychopathologies of everyday life," Janet and Hyslop shared the assumption of many clinicians that a new kind of hospital was needed to provide inpatient care to educated, bourgeois neurotics (whose minds, Janet noted, "are frequently very useful" if treated at an early stage).[56] Indeed, Janet gave Hyslop no credit for originality—"All these things are in the air, as we say." In this atmosphere of mental health reform, many affirmed that psychical research, as an intermediary between clinical psychiatry and experimental psychology, was suited to step into the breach.

Only as a secondary consideration did Hyslop revisit James's talking points about studying abnormal states to illuminate normal psychology and the value of collecting true psychical phenomena generated by the mentally ill. To this end, he described the ASPR's hypothetical facility as a training site for the nation's asylum physicians, who would learn to record and report patient experiences. This would increase the society's already unmanageable burden of correspondence, but on paper the plan made an elegant complement to their network of "normal" informants.

In a book published just a year before he relaunched the ASPR, Hyslop laid out his views on normal, abnormal, and supernormal psychology at length, setting the stage for Section A with a critique of materialism.[57] The notion of a "borderland" had always been popular in Spiritualism and psychical research, connoting the border between life and death as well as the border between normal and pathological, orthodox and heterodox, reason and faith—inherently shifting, unstable, and subjective zones. *The Borderland of Psychical Research*, as Hyslop titled

his psychological tome, attempted to carve out and stabilize an area between abnormal and normal psychology—what Hyslop termed the "supernormal"—as the legitimate space of inquiry for psychical research.
Philosophers of science apply the term "boundary-work" for cultural and
institutional efforts to demarcate science from nonscience.[58] Since psychical research took place entirely on a border, a zone rather than a line,
Hyslop set himself the unenviable task of defining two boundaries and
justifying the area between them as an object of study. He did so with a
very intentional emphasis on the dual power of the borderland to satisfy
normal curiosity about the unknown while rescuing those in thrall to abnormal delusions. "We cannot break away from normal experience and
ignore its guidance," he insisted.[59] Psychic exploration would be tethered
to, and indeed, would serve, the needs of a normal mental order.

Given the ASPR's always meager finances, Section A was not a realistic possibility, as Hyslop understood. In his budget estimates, he requested ten thousand dollars a year for Section B, which took up the
traditional investigative duties of the ASPR, a million-dollar endowment
for the umbrella American Institute for Scientific Research, and merely
observed that "a large sum will be needed for Psychopathology" (Section
A). The strategy was to aim high and accept whatever came. However,
as Janet observed in his endorsement, "ambitious plans become ridicu-
lous when we have only small resources at our disposal." Like Wilkinson,
Hyslop printed his proposal as a clarion call rather than an action plan.
The ASPR quickly abandoned abnormal psychology and returned to the
bread-and-butter of psychical research: liminal experiences that struck
mentally "normal" individuals.

Despite Hyslop's insistence that "it is important not to associate"
abnormal and supernormal psychology, Section B was immediately
swamped with abnormal material. Without a viable Section A devoted
to psychopathology, and without cooperation from psychiatrists, psychical researchers still had no way to effectively draw the boundary and
disaggregate the effects of mental illness from genuine phenomena. As
always, correspondents to the ASPR had to furnish details about their
personal circumstances and mental health, with references to vouch for
their soundness. As always, a certain proportion of letters came from

people who were not mentally sound by the standards of their time. A red grease pencil in the hand of Hyslop, or his assistant Gertrude Tubby, neither trained in psychiatric evaluation, continued to guard the gates of objectivity.

What would it mean for a participatory, democratic science to ally itself with the insane, to question the validity of that border and drop the defensive armature of the clinician? As psychiatry built professional authority at the turn of the twentieth century, it leveraged more refined nosologies and increasing diagnostic power. Psychical research was unable to center itself on the uncertain borderland without partaking, in its intellectual fabric, of the contamination of madness. Its practices were permeable, depending on trust, relationality, and subjective self-report. This not only raised the possibility of insane subjects corrupting the evidence, it seeped into the reputation of the society, its leadership, and their scientific agenda.

At the same time, the humane imperative to relieve suffering that reverberated through Wilkinson's Spiritualist asylum, Progressive Era asylum reform movements, and the hypothetical Section A also penetrated into professional psychiatry around the turn of the twentieth century. Some psychiatrists developed a new interest in patient expression—following Wilkinson's instructions almost to the letter, asylum doctors handed out pencil and paper for inmates to record their visions. New Yorkers flocked to see the "art of the insane" at the Museum of Modern Art and avant-garde downtown galleries in the 1930s. Not just a means for emotional catharsis, drawings also worked as objective evidence more easily studied, classified, and evaluated than numinous psychical experiences. Visual art was everything that reported experiences were not: fixed in time and space, free from the snares of intersubjective communication. Thus, art therapy and projective testing borrowed a mediumistic practice but stripped away the basic rationale of mediumship—that the hand and mind could fall into rapport with forces beyond the individual.

Meanwhile, psychical research in the 1930s and 40s was transforming into parapsychology under the leadership of J. B. Rhine, adopting the principles and practices of elite laboratory and statistical sciences.[60] The psychiatric status of subjects was just another variable in ESP card-guessing tests, which assessed "objective performance alone, not the state of mind."[61] Intuition suggested that the mentally ill might be more receptive to telepathic signals, but investigators found no special sensitivity distinct from normal controls.[62] Early experiments with LSD and altered states likewise yielded no results in the Rhineian quantitative paradigm. However, insights from these experiments led researchers across the sciences to pursue more expansive notions of consciousness. Popular translations of Carl Jung, growing interest in Eastern spirituality and meditation practices, and mind-altering drugs impacted parapsychology while also making it an attractive field for young explorers on the frontiers of consciousness. They sought meaning in the content of experience, disdaining behaviorism's shallow stimulus-response logic.

In 1947, a group of psychiatrists led by Jan Ehrenwald, Jule Eisenbud, and Montague Ullman finally formed a Medical Section of the ASPR, reviving the dream of Hyslop's Section A. As research-oriented clinicians, they had the patient access and institutional authority to do the kind of work that William James and Hyslop had only imagined. They wanted to revive the Jamesian "pursuit of psi effects in their natural environment"—the hunt for "wild facts"—as a counterpoint to Rhineian parapsychology.[63] These clinicians' sympathy for James and the ASPR seemed to stem from their psychoanalytic orientation; psychoanalysis, though it rose to surprising heights of cultural prestige and clinical preeminence by the 1940s, still came from a marginal position, attacked by scientific positivists as a mystery cult.

Moreover, psychoanalysts since Freud had tiptoed around uncanny phenomena of transference and countertransference that many patients and practitioners felt were "psi" in nature. A 1948 survey of 723 American psychiatrists showed that 68 percent wanted more research into ESP.[64] Thus, the Medical Section opened a long-desired path into organized hospital-based work, with the clinic as a controlled and optimized field. Psychical researchers would wear the authoritative white coats, yet would probe rather than pathologize the contested experiences of subjects. Unfortunately for the ASPR, psychiatry itself soon changed in ways that would once again snatch the mantle of orthodox science away from psychical research.

The founders of the Medical Section held significant professional sway. In 1962, a middle-aged doctor named Montague Ullman left his successful private practice to establish a new department of psychiatry at Maimonides Hospital in Brooklyn, where he also opened the city's first community psychiatric clinic. Ullman belonged to the progressive camp that would move psychiatry away from institutionalization to community-based care. However, another motivation for the move to Maimonides was his desire to create a sleep laboratory for the study of telepathic dreaming. Since his youthful experiences in a séance circle, Ullman had hypothesized the existence of what he called a "field effect," an emotional entanglement of energies, needs, and desires that seemed conducive to psi phenomena. The physicist's definition of a field as a zone affected by the action of an invisible force was layered over the "field" of natural history, the uncontrolled space where life unfolds.

This relational psi field was completely antithetical to the sterile ESP card-guessing paradigm; indeed, J. B. Rhine struggled throughout his career to refute insinuations that his own personality, and positive relationships among lab workers and subjects, had conjured his unreproducible results. In contrast, Ullman was deeply psychoanalytic in his embrace of patient-practitioner feedback and interrogation of the practitioner's unconscious through "personal and mutual self-exploration."[65] Yet he also chose to seek legitimacy through laboratory work and had to develop systematic methods for controlling and manipulating intimate personal bonds.

The Maimonides Sleep Laboratory operated from 1962 until 1974, producing studies on telepathy, psychokinesis, and precognition. In one experiment, Ullman appropriated the projection screen at a Grateful Dead concert, instructing 2,000 fans to telepathically transmit an image to the sleeping recipient, who was hooked up to an REM monitor in Brooklyn. Mostly they tested single senders and receivers in the lab. Given the psychedelic flavor of the proceedings, perhaps they purposely chose innocuous "fine art prints" of Impressionist paintings as telepathic targets. Despite this precaution, one multisensory experiment using Van Gogh's "Hospital Corridor at St. Remy" inadvertently brought insanity to the fore. Upon waking from sleep, the healthy subject was "given a pill with a glass of water [and] led down a darkened corridor to a room where he was presented with paintings by mental patients as well as the Van Gogh art print."[66] A soundtrack of hysterical laughter played in the background. A simulation of a madman's painting of a psychiatric ward staged in an actual psychiatric ward seems like an allegory for the way psychical research had been deployed in the clinic. Clear boundaries between doctor and patient were built in to the medical setting, but Ullman's openness to a wide variety of ideas and methods, and to the field effect generated in his experiments, exposed him to insinuations that he had crossed into the ranks of the unwell or at least the unreasonable.

Like much parapsychology research, the Maimonides studies showed small degrees of statistical significance and have not been satisfactorily replicated, leading to decades of simmering disputes among debunkers and factions within the psi community. However, Ullman and his colleagues in the ASPR's Medical Section shaped clinical attitudes towards psychical phenomena in ways that are not visible in the published scientific literature. In addition to laboratory experiments, these doctors provided everyday care from a perspective that did not deny the reality of abnormal mental experiences.

The mainstream profession was moving towards a less autocratic, more humanistic approach. Carl Rogers advanced a "person-centered" psychology that diffused the analyst's mystical aura, while radicals coalescing around R. D. Laing advocated bold new forms of social inclusion for the mentally ill. In both views, acknowledging the patient's account of their experience was crucial to moving forward in a therapeutic encounter; there could be no taboos or dismissals. The Medical Section of the ASPR carried that directive to an extreme that few clinicians were prepared to handle. While traumatic recovered memories were par for the course in analysis, telepathy and psychokinesis were still explained away as complexes. They did not compute within the framework that most clinicians used to sort reality from delusion. Freudians interpreted psi phenomena symbolically, in terms of regressive magical thinking or repressed desires. Practitioners associated with the Medical Section took these experiences seriously—not as pathological symptoms, but as real events with significance in the patient's life. Subsequent generations would continue developing therapeutic approaches that valued the spiritual content of patients' supernormal accounts. If a patient did not want to be "cured" of hearing spirit voices or picking up others' thoughts, then the clinician had to help them live a full and functional life with these abilities. The Maimonides laboratory space probably had less practical impact than the clinical and informal spaces where psychiatrists and patients developed these ideas.

Ullman's group ultimately focused on intersubjective relations. Unlike Rhine, they tried to analyze the bonds they developed with their "subjects," some of whom were professional colleagues like Robert van de Castle, whose eight nights in the sleep laboratory were followed by in-depth, psychodynamic interviews each morning. These encounters plumbed depths of experience that were hard to access and articulate, altogether rig up in an experiment. Moreover, they created a kind of horizontal power structure that had not existed in psychical research of the 1880s through 1930s, which was shaped by the geographical and critical distance built into written communication. The intimate and interactive setting of the sleep laboratory led Ullman to engage deeply with participants around the phenomena themselves, rather than legalistic problems of reporting and testimony. The format of the psychodynamic interview trained participants in the disciplined self-observation that Richard Hodgson had tried valiantly to instill in his correspondents, while also empowering them to guide the experimental process.

Ullman's circle was small and limited in reach precisely because the large-scale asylum psychiatry that shaped Wilkinson's, James's, and Hyslop's respective visions for clinical deployment of psychical research had declined in prominence with the rise of community-based care. Ullman did try to identify psychic sensitives in the mentally ill populations he worked with, and ventured some empirical hypotheses about the relationship between illnesses like schizophrenia and ESP performance.[67] However, while Hyslop expected clinical psychical research to diagnose and cure the masses, the Medical Section materialized at a moment when psychiatry was questioning and overturning the power structures that had made it an authoritative ally to begin with.

For this very reason, Ullman was ambivalent about the laboratory setting at Maimonides. The chance to leverage institutional resources and legitimacy for psi investigation drew him there, but a decade of managing the hospital's clinic and his own lab prevented him from "engaging more personally in the research and from having the opportunity to experience and explore the personal dynamics of the field." Though satisfied with his statistical results, Ullman resented "having to prove something in order to get funds necessary to keep the laboratory going."[68] He came to question the underlying value structure of experimental research and concluded that its criteria for significance and validity were simply not appropriate for the kind of exploration that he cared about.

Ullman's path to disillusionment with normal science echoed that of Timothy Leary, another mid-century clinician who abandoned the knowledge-producing spaces of hospital and laboratory for more radical social interventions. However, Ullman offered a far milder medicine when he retired from Maimonides to become a cult figure on the scientific borderlands. Rather than an LSD-fueled mass spiritual awakening, he promoted the sharing of dreams in small-group settings and international coordination among groups to collate and interpret dreams. This process would produce new knowledge of a sort ungraspable by science—but it would also cultivate the phenomena it studied, an expansive field effect spreading harmony as it folded more individuals into affective communion. This vision was not so far from the harmonial chords of the Spiritualists. Their idea of impalpable but real bonds latent in all of humanity, waiting for the right note of sympathy to be struck, was transposed into a sort of group therapy. Interestingly, his workshops focused on what he called "natural affective pairings . . . e.g. male-female, doctor-nurse, parent-child," recapitulating the normative domestic sympathies of earlier psychical researchers from Mary Craig and Upton Sinclair in the 1920s to the Bryant family in 1880s Michigan.[69] Psychic forces, however utopian or countercultural their theoretical conception, seemed always to flow into the channels of existing social norms.

For decades, Ullman led group meetings in the library of the ASPR's Upper East Side brownstone. Clinicians who participated in these meetings recall that they always attracted some people who showed signs of mental illness or distress; part of the group's routine included guiding those who needed medical support into a treatment setting.[70] As the ASPR itself had always asserted, such experiences struck people in both good and bad psychological health. Wilkinson had proposed training the insane to use their mediumistic potential to demonstrate the truth of Spiritualism; a small group of clinicians and parapsychologists in the 1960s and 70s saw a similar possibility: by treating the mentally ill in a way that preserved possible psi phenomena, they could both heal and reveal.

Rather than producing definitive laboratory proof of the soul's immortality or the reality of communication beyond the known senses, Ullman lingered in the border zone that nineteenth-century psychical researchers so deeply feared. The ASPR's anxiety about contamination by credulous believers and the genuinely unwell were not resolved by the Medical Section's foray into the clinic. Proximity to unreason, the lack of a hard epistemological and ontological divide between patient and practitioner, researcher and subject, meant that parapsychology would continue to dwell in an uncanny borderland. The most radical clinicians concluded that it didn't matter who was running the asylum, that sanity was relative and based in asymmetries of power that should be questioned. However, this dizzying relativism hardly offered an authoritative public face for parapsychology during the mid-century golden age of medicine, when physicians hushed patient concerns with the mantra "doctor knows best." It went further than James ever could in embracing uncertainty.

James posited that social reality is a fluctuating consensus created by a society's members. For him, radical openness did not mean unconditional acceptance of all lived experiences as equally real; that would allow individuals, and society, to fly apart. Of course, economically secure white men have reasons to push away threats to the epistemological order that keeps them at the center of reality; all the better for the inmates if, through their "mad" resistance, they crack open an oppressive asylum or an oppressive society. Psychical research was not this radical voice of resistance from below. Culturally and socioeconomically, it spoke for the emerging middle and professional classes. Yet its epistemology was permeable, unlike that of the strident scientific materialism that opposed it.

Its reliance upon witness testimony, and the realization that all witnesses are in various ways unreliable, allowed determined participants like Mary Craig Sinclair and George Thacher to negotiate their way in from the margins. Such investigation would not yield a singular, conclusive reality binding all its denizens. Rather, the reality that emerged would inhere in the inquiry itself, in the commitment to examining experience. It is telling that this modicum of faith in the possibility of communication across difference relegated psychical research to the fringes of science.

TO KEEP ALIVE AND
HEAP UP DATA

The remains of American psychical research are so thoroughly scattered and tarnished that even its heirs apparent never claimed their patrimony. Joseph Banks Rhine, the ex-botanist who founded the Duke University Parapsychology Laboratory, wrote to the president of Harvard in 1936 to inquire about "more active utilization of the Richard Hudson Memorial Fund of your university."[1] Whether a typo or a more grievous misremembering, the "Hudson" to whom Rhine referred was the ASPR's late secretary, Richard Hodgson. Thirteen years earlier, donors established a $10,000 endowment in Hodgson's honor for studying phenomena "the origin or expression of which appear to be independent of the ordinary sensory channels."[2] At the time, James Hyslop boasted that recognition from "so conservative a university as Harvard . . . makes it impossible for any other institution in this country to disrespect or disregard the work."[3] Hyslop failed to appreciate that nothing was impossible in psychical research. The Hodgson Memorial Fund was drawn upon three times during its first twelve years of existence, but after 1925 it seemed to vanish. Hugo Münsterberg had feared it would bring embarrassment to his world-class psychology department, and others at Harvard apparently agreed.[4]

Rhine never received a reply to his letter, in which he also asserted the need for "some adequate memorial to William James." In the decades after James's death, his scientific star sank low. His rejection of what he called the psychologist's fallacy—the faith that cognition in the abstract must be like the psychologist's personal experience of cognition—alienated him from the rising "new psychology" of the period, and though his groundbreaking textbook held his place as the "father" of the discipline in the United States, the next generation of behaviorist researchers was reluctant to engage with his legacy.[5] Psychical research was actually among James's most vigorous survivals in the 1930s—literally as well as figuratively, for it was the inglorious fate of dead psychical researchers to speak on through mediums about everything from pink pajamas to reincarnation. If James, in death, was "often obscure, cryptic, or puzzling," this was not the first time his ideas had refused to cohere.[6] What would a monument to the situated and ever-shifting nature of experience look like? In 1963, Harvard erected a fifteen-story modernist tower to house what were then called the "behavioral sciences" and christened it William James Hall. One architectural historian described the building as "conceptually unrelated to its environment"; though possessing an "undeniable grace," it is flanked by "vacant terraces, dry pools, and empty gardens."[7]

Meanwhile, Rhine, William McDougall, and a "third generation" of psychical researchers in the 1930s built up the discipline of parapsychology through forceful assertion of a laboratory paradigm. They chased out spirits and metaphysics, but at the same time harnessed a backlash against behaviorism throughout the social sciences.[8] The brief institutional success of parapsychology has become a case study in the social construction of science: Rhine black-boxed the destabilizing epistemological and metaphysical quandaries that plagued James's generation of psychical researchers without resolving them. Instead, Rhine focused on boundary work and professional development, marshaling the social, political, and cultural resources that would legitimate his flagship institution, the Duke Parapsychology Laboratory.[9] Rhine's effort to exorcize the ghost of William James makes his inquiry about a memorial all the more piquant—perhaps, reflecting on his own uncertain legacy, he felt uneasy that a man of James's epochal stature could die and be forgotten. Had the president of Harvard condescended to reply, Rhine would have learned that, the previous year, the school had acquired a supposed memorial to James in the form of a Baroque bust of René Descartes—a marble philosopher whose notions of "clear and distinct thought" James roundly rejected, insisting that thought inheres in the "passing and evanescent," in "fringes and halos . . . inarticulate perceptions."[10] It seems more inconsiderate than no memorial at all.

Parapsychology was not the genetic successor of psychical research, or a scientific butterfly emerging from its gnarled nineteenth-century cocoon. It was a rather dense and well-connected point in a cloud of continuities—of interrelated practices, beliefs, theories, experiences, and institutions—that circulated across the nineteenth and early twentieth centuries. This cloud became increasingly dispersed, spiraling off to feed emerging systems across the human sciences and popular culture. Not monuments, but shadowy survivals.

We've seen how psychical research was modeled on the observational practices of established disciplines like meteorology and astronomy, emphasizing induction from huge piles of evidence—James's imperative to "keep alive and heap up data."[11] The potential for a collective unconscious made visible by mass data gathering connected dreams with the weather and with notions of a mental atmosphere. Not just psychiatry, but also anthropology became enamored with the collection and analysis of dreams; anthropologists' purposes in continuing this practice differed from the ASPR's, yet they shared a notion of archiving the unconscious to discover local and universal properties of the mind. Historian Rebecca Lemov describes how, in the 1950s and 60s, the U.S. National Research Council built a database of dreams and other psychological metrics extracted by anthropologists from populations around the globe; psychical researchers' trepidation about a mental atmosphere that transgressed boundaries of race and class had been clearly realized in the geopolitical sweep of the Cold War. Mass data collection was the only way to render strange minds knowable and thereby to regain control.[12] Notoriously, parapsychology contributed to this effort through the Defense Department's Stargate project, which employed psychic "remote viewers" to gather data from inaccessible locations—but their efforts proved inferior to the tried-and-true method of placing observers on the ground.[13]

In twentieth-century anthropology and psychology, the reporting forms of psychical research morphed into standardized questionnaires and tests that extracted experience from the field and processed it more smoothly into a knowledge product for disciplinary use. The expert-administered standardized test became a staple of psychology and other human sciences; secured a decisive role in military, corporate, and educational placement; and now has come full circle, with laypeople self-administering gamified psychological tests on social media. The desire of nonscientists to measure and sort themselves suggests that the enclosed individual posited by experimental psychology serves our needs in a Western, capitalist society where self-definition and self-improvement are both moral and economic imperatives.[14] If our data is detachable and free from its context, then we, too, must be free. This understanding of freedom was forged in the Cold War climate that also saw the decline of pragmatism, a philosophy oriented around mutually defined realities, in favor of logical positivism and rational choice theory.[15]

Psychical researchers were not free; their reports came tangled in history, burdened with lists of references whose accounts collectively produced an event. They couldn't simply deliver data to scientists, they needed the scientists to give them something back, to enter their world. This problem presented itself to the Duke Parapsychology Laboratory, which, though dedicated to the new experimental paradigm, soon began receiving bales of letters from people who had psychic experiences to report. Responsibility for these letters fell upon J. B. Rhine's wife and collaborator, Louisa Rhine, who sorted and verified anecdotes much as Hodgson had done for the ASPR in the 1880s. She continued this work for thirty-five years. Though she pursued other projects and was an important collaborator in many ways, this division of labor is telling. Her husband, invested in the masculine politics of the laboratory, recognized the low value of anecdotal reports to his disciplinary vision. Lived experience remains elusive and unstable, bound to its idiosyncratic subjects.

This book has argued that the emergence of a hierarchy of professional and amateur, science and parascience, was a gradual and incomplete one. My decision to conclude in the mid twentieth century acknowledges the changing context of American politics, society, and culture that made the specifically nineteenth-century notion of scientific citizenship which I've examined here obsolete. Correspondence between scientists and a particular public, and the horizontal arrangement of knowledge-making that it entailed, gave way to a popular science more oriented towards the dissemination and consumption of expert knowledge. The Smithsonian Institution is a symbolic pivot point: once the center of Spencer F. Baird's amateur correspondence network, in the 1920s it launched the Science Service, a news organization devoted to advancing public "appreciation" of science, as opposed to understanding or inquiry.[16] This anticipated a popular mode of celebrating the products of scientific ingenuity in medicine, commerce, and warfare, as well as submitting to its governing logics. Americans continued to collect and analyze psychical experiences, but their belief in this as a scientific practice put them in conflict with the scientific and medical establishments. No longer seeing their investigative activity as an aspect of normative citizenship, they framed their quests for truth as clashing with the interests of authorities. Importantly, though, they continued to claim a democratic epistemology, locating truth in the immediacy of firsthand experience and inviting others to witness it for themselves.

The specter of democratic epistemology still shapes today's scientific orthodoxies and heterodoxies. Subcultures of paranormal belief shade into alternative medicine, patient advocacy groups, and online communities, all areas where people attempt to develop and assert knowledge claims based on their collection and analysis of subjective experience. In the lingering fallout of the science wars of the 1990s, contesting scientific orthodoxy became a moral issue—especially in the United States—with purveyors of pseudoscience accused of damaging the nation's science literacy and leading policy astray. The recent rise of opposition to vaccinations for preventable diseases and other symptoms of ideological science denial in the U.S attest to this danger. In a moment when scientific research is exponentially more productive than ever before, we face a serious problem with generating inclusive knowledge about the world that we share.

That world is stratified and sliced by many forms of inequality and mistrust, as was the nineteenth-century world of psychical researchers. They certainly never resolved these deep-seated tensions over who defines reality and who is subjected to it. They were, however, able to engage a small constituency in a generative practice of observation, experiment, and recording. Many of these participants were satisfied that the ASPR's methods represented their experiences and that adopting a set of shared practices and criteria gave them a meaningful voice in an important national conversation. Indeed, psychical research offered them a new way of understanding the modern nation as a space through which invisible forces flowed, in which orderly relations were both given and revealed in nature's laws, and where the dead became a resource for the living. One way for science to reconnect with the lived experience of a diverse population is to simply expand this franchise, to engage the inquisitive in the kind of respectful, mutually rewarding discourse that the ASPR reserved for those favored by social circumstances. Any such effort, however, would require a nuanced historical awareness of how science has already ordered and been ordered by society and the nation—how the received category of "experience," upon which we ground private, knowing selves, is a political cut through much denser, wilder relations. This would mean remapping what experience is, not just who gets to have it.

I would look, for this new map, to the liminal spaces within psychical research's border zone, to the negotiations of subjectivity between Mary Craig Sinclair and Walter Prince, to the reincarnation of Wilkerson's Spiritualist asylum as the ASPR's Medical Section, to the theft-by-dream of James Russell Lowell's "Commemoration Ode," and to the uneasy appropriations of the Indian control and the channeling secretary. The possibility that the world of experience is radically relational at times provoked anxiety and retrenchment. At times it was misconstrued as a colonial entitlement to mine the interiors of others. But some people rose to meet it with curiosity and recognition. William James located shared experience on a deeply submerged plane, from which individuals spring "like islands in the sea, or like trees in the forest." "The maple and the pine may whisper to each other with their leaves, and Conanicut and Newport hear each other's fog-horns," he wrote in his final reflection on psychical research. "But the trees also commingle their roots in the darkness underground, and the islands also hang together through the ocean's bottom."[17] This powerful, hopeful, melancholic image has always moved me, but I am not a tree or an island. In the ASPR's archives, I saw many things trying to be trees and islands which were not. Experience, relations, and history string us in their web from moment to moment. These are the common phantoms that make possible any experience of wholeness, however fleeting.

The preceding chapters have traversed the landscape of late nineteenth and early twentieth-century American culture and society, tracking divergent models of the mind in their complexity and richness and pursuing their logics down unexpected paths. Structuring metaphors flow into each other in telling ways: the circulation of air masses becomes the circulation of ideas, which becomes a market panic or the desire for a cream puff. Such occult transmissions carried an undercurrent of menace—the subconscious, the repressed, and the silenced were their unruly agents—and we can view psychical research as an effort to contain that menace, to enclose a republic of experience for the virtuous and law-abiding scientific citizen. At the same time, the multiplicity of experience, the impossibility of pinning down the moment when we come into relation with the world that makes us, emerges from the archive of psychical research. What was a problem for James and his colleagues represents an opening for us. It places us together in uncertainty, among our phantoms, in vibrant wonder and profound disquiet.

NOTES

Introduction: At Home, with Ghosts

1. Letter from F. G. in Josiah Royce, "Report of Committee on Phantasms and Presentiments," *PASPR* 1:4 (1889): 422.

2. E. V. Smalley to Richard Hodgson, April 12, 1894, folder 1, box 3, ASPR.

3. Anna E. Seymour to Walter Franklin Prince, June 8, 1933, folder 4, box 37, ASPR.

4. Mary V. Asmann, Evansville, Illinois, to James Hyslop, Sept. 29, 1900, folder 3, box 37, ASPR.

5. R. W. Fenn to James Hyslop, July 20, 1908, folder 3, box 37, ASPR.

6. This definition of psychical experience is based on Ann Taves's discussion of self-alien religious experience in *Fits, Trances, and Visions: Experiencing Religion and Explaining Experience from Wesley to James* (Princeton, NJ: Princeton University Press, 1999), 7–9.

7. Marlene Tromp, *Altered States: Sex, Nation, Drugs, and Self-Transformation in Victorian Spiritualism* (Albany, NY: SUNY Press, 2007), 4.

8. Taves, *Fits, Trances, and Visions*, 6–7.

9. Some liberal Protestant clergy embraced this "complementarity," mobilizing universalist notions of spirituality, energy, and life force in their healing practices. Pamela E. Klassen, *Spirits of Protestantism: Medicine, Healing, and Liberal Christianity* (Berkeley and Los Angeles: University of California Press, 2011), 91–92.

10. William James to George Croom Robertson, August 29, 1886, in *The Correspondence of William James*, Vol. 6, eds. Ignas K. Skrupskelis and Elizabeth M. Berkeley, (Charlottesville: University Press of Virginia, 1992–2004), 158.

11. Herbert L. Spence to William James, April 9, 1890, box 36, folder 1, ASPR.

12. William James to Frederic W. H. Myers, January 30, 1890, in *The Correspondence of William James*, Vol. 7, 139.

13. The term *data* has taken on a much broader significance in the twenty-first century; nineteenth-century researchers used *data* for items of scientific information gathered through observation and experiment. However, this use of *data* for large-scale observation of human behavior contributed to later developments in the human sciences and the rise of "big data." For histories of big data,

see Rebecca M. Lemov, *Database of Dreams* (New Haven, CT: Yale University Press, 2015).

14. Wayne Proudfoot, *Religious Experience* (Berkeley and Los Angeles: University of California Press, 1987).

15. Robert H. Sharf, "The Rhetoric of Experience and the Study of Religion," *Journal of Consciousness Studies* 7, no. 11–12 (2000): 267–71.

16. William James, "What Psychical Research Has Accomplished," *Forum* 13 (August 1, 1892): 727.

17. Aziz Rana, *The Two Faces of American Freedom* (Cambridge, MA: Harvard University Press, 2010). For democracy and republicanism as themes in religious studies, see Nathan O. Hatch, *The Democratization of American Christianity* (New Haven, CT: Yale University Press, 1989); in histories of science, B. Zorina Khan, *The Democratization of Invention: Patents and Copyrights in American Economic Development, 1790–1920* (Cambridge: Cambridge University Press, 2005), Andrew J. Lewis, *A Democracy of Facts: Natural History in the Early Republic* (Philadelphia: University of Pennsylvania Press, 2011).

18. Deborah J. Coon, " 'One Moment in the World's Salvation': Anarchism and the Radicalization of William James," *The Journal of American History* 83, no. 1 (1996): 70–99; Russ Castronovo, *Necro Citizenship: Death, Eroticism, and the Public Sphere in the Nineteenth-Century United States* (Durham, NC: Duke University Press, 2001), xi–xii, 66–70.

19. George H. Hyslop, quoted in Arthur S. Berger, *Lives and Letters in American Parapsychology: A Biographical History, 1850–1987* (Jefferson, NC: McFarland, 1988), 70.

20. For accounts of Spiritualism's borrowing from Indian and African cultures and the uses that these groups made of Spiritualist ideas, see John Kucich, *Ghostly Communion: Cross-Cultural Spiritualism in Nineteenth-Century American Literature* (Lebanon, NH: University Press of New England, 2004); Molly McGarry, *Ghosts of Futures Past: Spiritualism and the Cultural Politics of Nineteenth-Century America* (Berkeley: University of California Press, 2008); Kathryn Troy, *The Specter of the Indian: Race, Gender, and Ghosts in American Seances, 1848–1890* (Albany, NY: SUNY Press, 2017); Britt Rusert, *Fugitive Science: Empiricism and Freedom in Early African American Culture* (New York: NYU Press, 2017).

21. Beth Robertson points out that psychical research often involved middle-class male investigators studying working-class female mediums, indirectly performing class-based social control. Beth A. Robertson, *Science of the Seance: Transnational Networks and Gendered Bodies in the Study of Psychic Phenomena, 1918–40* (Vancouver: UBC Press, 2016), 15–17.

22. Ian Hacking's research often uses such flash points to illustrate the processes of social construction at work in establishing scientific categories, for instance, *Mad Travelers: Reflections on the Reality of Transient Mental Illnesses* (Charlottesville: University of Virginia Press, 1998) and *Rewriting the Soul: Multiple Personality and the Sciences of Memory* (Princeton, NJ: Princeton University Press, 1995).

23. "Circular No. 1," *PASPR* 1:1 (July 1885): 2–3.

24. I draw upon John Lardas Modern's understanding of secularism, which he describes as a conceptual environment, materialized in and through a set of social formations and styles of discourse that did not exclude religion, but rather reconfigured it as a matter of reasonable conviction for both believers and non-believers. Modern, *Secularism in Antebellum America* (Chicago: University of Chicago Press, 2011), 1–8.

25. See R. L. Moore, *In Search of White Crows: Spiritualism, Parapsychology, and American Culture* (Oxford: Oxford University Press, 1977); Bret E. Carroll, *Spiritualism in Antebellum America* (Bloomington and Indianapolis: Indiana University Press, 1997); Anne Braude, *Radical Spirits: Spiritualism and Women's Rights in Nineteenth-Century America*, 2nd ed. (Bloomington and Indianapolis: Indiana University Press, 2001); Richard Noakes, "Natural Causes? Spiritualism, Science, and the Supernatural in Mid-Victorian Britain," in *The Victorian Supernatural*, eds. N. Bown, C. Burdett, P. Thurschwell (Cambridge: Cambridge University Press, 2004), 23–43.

26. Edwin G. Boring, *History of Experimental Psychology* (New York: D. Appleton-Century Company, 1929).

27. A cluster of recent biographies gives full credence to James's interest in psychical research. See Linda Simon, *Genuine Reality: A Life of William James* (Chicago: University of Chicago Press, 1999); Gerald E. Myers, *William James: His Life and Thought* (New Haven, CT: Yale University Press, 2001); and Robert D. Richardson, *William James: In the Maelstrom of American Modernism* (New York: Houghton Mifflin Harcourt, 2007).

28. Or, as Bruno Latour might put it, "We have never been disenchanted." Jason A. Josephson-Storm, *The Myth of Disenchantment: Magic, Modernity, and the Birth of the Human Sciences* (Chicago: University of Chicago Press, 2017). Andreas Sommer also advances this argument in *Psychical Research and the Formation of Modern Psychology*, forthcoming from Stanford University Press (my thanks to the author for sharing with me his manuscript).

29. On the relation between communication technologies and inner experience, see Jeffrey Sconce, *Haunted Media: Electronic Presence from Telegraphy to Television* (Durham, NC: Duke University Press, 2000); Pamela Thurschwell, *Literature, Technology, and Magical Thinking, 1880–1920* (Cambridge: Cambridge University Press, 2005); Roger Luckhurst, *The Invention of Telepathy 1870–1901* (Oxford: Oxford University Press, 2002); Jill Nicole Galvan, *The Sympathetic Medium: Feminine Channeling, the Occult, and Communication Technologies, 1859–1919* (Ithaca, NY: Cornell University Press, 2010); Clément Chéroux, *The Perfect Medium: Photography And the Occult* (New Haven, CT: Yale University Press, 2005).

30. On Romantic-era popular and scientific interest in invisible forces, see John Tresch, *The Romantic Machine: Utopian Science and Technology after Napoleon* (Chicago: University of Chicago Press, 2012), particularly the Introduction and chapters 2 and 5.

31. Adam Crabtree, *From Mesmer to Freud: Magnetic Sleep and the Roots of Psychological Healing* (New Haven, CT: Yale University Press, 1993). English psychical

researchers Edward Cox and William Crookes introduced and popularized "psychic force"; see Edward W. Cox, *Spiritualism Answered by Science* (New York: H. L. Hinton, 1872).

32. Taves, *Fits, Trances, and Visions*, 226; Christopher G. White, *Unsettled Minds: Psychology and the American Search for Spiritual Assurance*, 1830–1940 (Berkeley: University of California Press, 2009).

33. Discussions of medico-legal concerns related to liminal states include Ian Hacking, *Rewriting the Soul* and *Mad Travelers*; Susanna L. Blumenthal, *Law and the Modern Mind: Consciousness and Responsibility in American Legal Culture* (Cambridge, MA: Harvard University Press, 2016).

34. George Miller Beard, *The Scientific Basis of Delusions: A New Theory of Trance, and Its Bearings on Human Testimony* (New York: G.P. Putnams' Sons, 1877); *American Nervousness, Its Causes and Consequences: A Supplement to Nervous Exhaustion (Neurasthenia)* (New York: Putnam, 1881).

35. Anne Harrington, *Medicine, Mind, and the Double Brain: A Study in Nineteenth-Century Thought and Culture* (Princeton, NJ: Princeton University Press, 1987), 106–10.

36. Taves, *Fits, Trances, and Visions*, 254–58.

37. James Rodger Fleming, *Meteorology in America, 1800–1870* (Baltimore: Johns Hopkins University Press, 2000), 171.

38. James, "What Psychical Research Has Accomplished," 727.

39. This chronology is drawn from Berger, *Lives and Letters in American Parapsychology*.

40. Lucy Edmunds to James Hyslop, June 18, 1907, box 185, folder 7, ASPR. For more on filing systems as instruments in this period, see Markus Krajewski and Peter Krapp, *Paper Machines: About Cards & Catalogs, 1548–1929* (Cambridge, MA: MIT Press, 2011), 87–92.

41. William James, *Essays in Psychical Research* (Cambridge, MA: Harvard University Press, 1986), 494.

42. Edmunds to Hyslop, June 18, 1907, box 185, folder 7, ASPR.

43. Such survey data consistently comes from the Chapman University Survey of American Fears, the Pew Research Center, and Gallup. See: "Paranormal America 2017: Chapman University Survey of American Fears 2017," https://blogs.chapman.edu/wilkinson/2017/10/11/paranormal-america-2017/; Pew Research Center, "When Americans Say They Believe in God, What Do They Mean?" http://www.pewforum.org/2018/04/25/when-americans-say-they-believe-in-god-what-do-they-mean/; David W. Moore, "Three in Four Americans Believe in Paranormal," https://news.gallup.com/poll/16915/Three-Four-Americans-Believe-Paranormal.aspx.

Chapter 1: The Weather Map at the Bottom of the Mind

1. T. D. Crothers, "Mental Atmosphere: Does It Influence the Progress of Disease?" *Medical and Surgical Reporter*(1858–1898) 29, no. 6 (August 9, 1873), 98.

2. T. D. Crothers, "Spiritism, Telepathy, Hypnotism and the Case of Mrs.

Piper," in *Spiritism, Hypnotism and Telepathy as Involved in the Case of Mrs. Leonora E. Piper*, ed. Clark Bell (New York: Medico-legal Journal, 1902) 85–88.

3. Sharon A. Hill, *Scientifical Americans: The Culture of Amateur Paranormal Researchers* (Jefferson, NC: McFarland, 2017), 17–18. Following the activist tendencies of recent citizen science, some now define it as "knowledge production by and for nonscientists," but it conventionally denotes lay participation in a professionally managed project. See Gwen Ottinger, "Buckets of Resistance: Standards and the Effectiveness of Citizen Science," *Science, Technology, and Human Values* 35, no. 2 (2010): 245. Citizenship was and is entwined with scientific definitions of biological and psychological fitness; see John Carson, "The Science of Merit and the Merit of Science," in *States of Knowledge: The Co-Production of Science and the Social Order*, ed. Sheila Jasanoff (New York: Routledge, 2004), 181–206.

4. Robert V. Bruce traces how cultural nationalism has shaped the sciences in the United States, while Felix Driver and Tony Bennett follow this argument as it pertains to geography and natural history museums, respectively. Robert V. Bruce, *The Launching of Modern American Science* 1846–1876 (Ithaca, NY: Cornell University Press, 1988); Felix Driver, *Geography Militant: Cultures of Exploration and Empire* (Wiley, 2000); Tony Bennett, *Pasts Beyond Memory: Evolution, Museums, Colonialism* (London and New York: Routledge, 2004).

5. Lorraine Daston and Peter Galison, *Objectivity* (New York: Zone Books, 2007), 42–50.

6. The "prehistory" of the unconscious is addressed by Henri F. Ellenberger, *The Discovery of the Unconscious: The History and Evolution of Dynamic Psychiatry* (New York: Basic Books, 1981); John J. Cerullo, *The Secularization of the Soul: Psychical Research in Modern Britain* (Philadelphia: Institute for the Study of Human Issues, 1982); and Alex Owen, *The Place of Enchantment: British Occultism and the Culture of the Modern* (Chicago: University of Chicago Press, 2007).

7. David A. Zimmerman, *Panic!: Markets, Crises, and Crowds in American Fiction* (Chapel Hill: University of North Carolina Press, 2006); "Frank Norris, Market Panic, and the Mesmeric Sublime," *American Literature*, 75, no. 1 (2003), 61–90.

8. Walt Whitman, *Specimen Days in America* (W. Scott, 1887), 101. For the important interplay of weather observation and collective wartime experience, see M. Wynn Thomas, "Weathering the Storm: Whitman and the Civil War," *Walt Whitman Quarterly Review* 15, no. 2 (Fall 1997): 87–109.

9. Terry Castle, *The Female Thermometer: Eighteenth-Century Culture and the Invention of the Uncanny* (Oxford: Oxford University Press, 1995).

10. Joint Committee on Meteorology of the American Philosophical Society and the Franklin Institute, *Directions for Making Meteorological Observations* (Philadelphia: 1837).

11. Circular of the American Aelloscope Company of Rochester NY, 1866, bound with Cleveland Abbe, *Historical Notes on the Systems of Weather Telegraphy, and Especially Their Development in the United States* (American Philosophical Society Library, 1871).

12. T. D. Crothers, "Mental Atmosphere: Does It Influence the Progress of Disease?" *Medical and Surgical Reporter* (1858–1898) 29, no. 6 (August 9, 1873), 98.

13. Ibid.

14. Ernest Hollenbeck to Hodgson, Aug. 2, 1887, box 172, folder 3, ASPR.

15. Whitman, *Specimen Days in America*, 102.

16. Toward the end of the nineteenth century, interest in these forces shaped American psychological and social theory significantly through the work of William James, James Mark Baldwin, William McDougall, and George Herbert Mead, for which see Ruth Leys, "Mead's Voices: Imitation as Foundation, or, the Struggle against Mimesis," *Critical Inquiry* 19, no. 2 (January 1, 1993): 277–307; William James, "Great Men and Their Environment," in *The Will to Believe: And Other Essays in Popular Philosophy* (New York: Longmans, Green, and Co., 1911); J. Mark Baldwin, "Imitation: A Chapter in the Natural History of Consciousness," *Mind*, New Series, 3, no. 9 (January 1, 1894): 26–55.

17. William McDougall, *The Group Mind: A Sketch of the Principles of Collective Psychology, with Some Attempt to Apply Them to the Interpretation of National Life and Character* (New York, London: G. P. Putnam's Sons, 1928); William McDougall, *Is America Safe for Democracy? Six Lectures Given at the Lowell Institute of Boston . . .* (New York: C. Scribner's Sons, 1921). Contagion was an equally important metaphor in group psychology and was often woven together with the mental atmosphere by way of miasmatic language.

18. Mary Craig Sinclair to Mrs. [Paul Jordan] Smith, July 1927, box 36, folder 5, ASPR.

19. Foundational works on professionalization in the sciences include George H. Daniels, *The Process of Professionalization in American Science: The Emergent Period, 1820–1860* (Notre Dame, IN: History of Science Society, 1967); and Bruce, *The Launching of Modern American Science 1846–1876*.

20. Many scholars have traced the gradual and partial process of professionalization in different scientific fields. Sally Gregory Kohlstedt presents a case for the marginalization of amateur natural historians, while Marc Rothenberg argues that professional astronomers maneuvered to keep amateurs within their scientific community. Kohlstedt, "The Nineteenth-Century Amateur Tradition: The Case of the Boston Society of Natural History," in *Science and Its Public: The Changing Relationship*, 173–90 (Dordrecht: Reidel, 1976); Rothenberg, "Organization and Control: Professionals and Amateurs in American Astronomy, 1899–1918," *Social Studies of Science* 11, no. 3 (August 1, 1981): 305–25.

21. For more nuanced discussion of how American naturalists adapted ideals of Enlightenment reason to function in a pluralistic and experience-centered context, see Andrew J. Lewis, *A Democracy of Facts: Natural History in the Early Republic* (Philadelphia: University of Pennsylvania Press, 2011); and Joyce Elizabeth Chaplin, "Nature and Nation: Natural History in Context," in *Stuffing Birds, Pressing Plants, Shaping Knowledge: Natural History in North America 1730–1860*, ed. Sue Ann Prince (Philadelphia: American Philosophical Society, 2003).

22. Catherine L. Albanese, *A Republic of Mind and Spirit: A Cultural History of American Metaphysical Religion* (New Haven, CT: Yale University Press, 2007), 10–13.

23. G. Brown Goode, *An Account of the Smithsonian Institution: Its Origin, History, Objects and Achievements* (Washington, DC: The Smithsonian Institution, 1895), 6.

24. Daniel Goldstein, "'Yours for Science': The Smithsonian Institution's Correspondents and the Shape of Scientific Community in Nineteenth-Century America," *Isis* 85, no. 4 (December 1, 1994): 573–99.

25. Bruno Latour, *We Have Never Been Modern* (Cambridge, MA: Harvard University Press, 1993), 35–37.

26. John Tresch, *The Romantic Machine: Utopian Science and Technology after Napoleon* (Chicago: University of Chicago Press, 2012), 12.

27. Ibid., xiii, 30–31.

28. Ibid., 36–37; 46–47. See, for instance, the popular writing of Alexandre Bertrand, a physician and magnetic healer who promoted the unity of "imponderable matter" in the French popular press.

29. William James, "Comment and Criticism," *Science* 7, no. 156 (January 29, 1886): 89.

30. Timothy W. Kneeland, "Robert Hare: Politics, Science, and Spiritualism in the Early Republic," *The Pennsylvania Magazine of History and Biography* 132, no. 3 (July 1, 2008): 245–60.

31. Richard Noakes, "Haunted Thoughts of the Careful Experimentalist: Psychical Research and the Troubles of Experimental Physics," *Studies in History and Philosophy of Science Part C: Studies in History and Philosophy of Biological and Biomedical Sciences* 48, Part A (December 2014): 46–56.

32. Edwin Garrigues Boring, *History of Experimental Psychology* (New York: D. Appleton-Century Company, 1929), 133–46; Simon Schaffer, "Astronomers Mark Time: Discipline and the Personal Equation," *Science in Context* 2, no. 1 (1988): 115–45.

33. John Lankford, *American Astronomy: Community, Careers, and Power, 1859–1940* (Chicago: University of Chicago Press, 1997), 15; Charlotte Bigg, "Staging the Heavens: Astrophysics and Popular Astronomy in the Late Nineteenth Century," in *The Heavens on Earth: Observatories and Astronomy in Nineteenth-Century Science and Culture*, eds. David Aubin, Charlotte Bigg, and H. Otto Sibum (Durham, NC: Duke University Press, 2010).

34. Albert E. Moyer, *A Scientist's Voice in American Culture: Simon Newcomb and the Rhetoric of Scientific Method* (Berkeley: University of California Press, 1992), 86–90.

35. Rothenberg, "Organization and Control," 309–313.

36. Moyer, *A Scientist's Voice in American Culture*, xiv. For a similar approach in Paris, see Theresa Leavitt, "'I thought this might be of interest . . .' The Observatory as Public Enterprise," in *The Heavens on Earth: Observatories and Astronomy in Nineteenth-Century Science and Culture*, eds. David Aubin, Charlotte Bigg, and H. Otto Sibum (Durham, NC: Duke University Press, 2010), 286.

37. Moyer, *A Scientist's Voice in American Culture*, 174–75.

38. James, "Comment and Criticism," 89.

39. Richard Hodgson to Simon Newcomb, November 17, 188[?], Simon Newcomb Papers, box 26, Library of Congress.

40. Simon Newcomb, "Address of the President," *PASPR* 1:1 (1885): 63.

41. Simon Newcomb, "The Universe as an Organism," *Science* 17, no. 421 (1903): 121–25. Newcomb was by no means a skeptic about finding a scientific basis for faith in the divine, but he ultimately found explorations of fourth-dimensional space more rational than séances. See Christopher G. White, *Other Worlds: Spirituality and the Search for Invisible Dimensions* (Cambridge, MA: Harvard University Press, 2018), 57–59.

42. James Rodger Fleming, *Meteorology in America, 1800–1870* (Baltimore: Johns Hopkins University Press, 2000), xvii.

43. Ibid., xxi.

44. Ibid., xx.

45. "Appendix A: Directions for Making Experiments", *PASPR* 1:1 (1885): 13.

46. The essays in Peter Becker and William Clark, *Little Tools of Knowledge: Historical Essays on Academic and Bureaucratic Practices* (Ann Arbor: University of Michigan Press, 2001) elaborate on the function of charts and tables in systematizing scientific and social knowledge.

47. On the significant role of the post office in building national identity through communication infrastructure, see Winifred Gallagher, *How the Post Office Created America: A History* (New York: Penguin Press, 2016).

48. William James, "Address of the President before the Society for Psychical Research," *Science* 3, no. 77 (June 19, 1896): 883.

49. "Circular 2," *PASPR* 1:1 (1885): 5.

50. Ibid.

51. Ibid.

52. Naomi Rogers, *An Alternative Path: The Making and Remaking of Hahnemann Medical College and Hospital of Philadelphia* (New Brunswick, NJ: Rutgers University Press, 1998): 51–53.

53. Weston D. Bayley, "Dropsy (A Fragment)," *The Hahnemannian Monthly* (1901): 443, 447.

54. Samuel Hahnemann, letter in *Allgem Anzeiger der Deutschen*, No. 24 (January 25, 1839), translated in Richard Haehl, *Samuel Hahnemann: His Life and Work: Based on Recently Discovered State Papers, Documents, Letters, Etc.* (New Delhi, India: B. Jain Publishers, 2003), 102–3.

55. Ibid.

56. Ibid., 107.

57. Rogers, *An Alternative Path*, 18–19.

58. American Provers' Union, "Suggestions for the Proving of Drugs on the Healthy; Report of the Committee Appointed for That Purpose . . . " (Philadelphia: American Provers' Union, 1853), 6.

59. Ibid.

60. Weston D. Bayley, "The Saturday Night Club of Microscopists," *The Hahnemannian Monthly News and Advertiser* 32 (1897), 14.

61. See references in *The Hahnemannian Monthly News and Advertiser*: (1897) 11, 14, 25, 138, 146, 176; (1901) 3, 443, 508; (1903) 3, 23, 132, 146.

62. "Miscellaneous Notes," *The Hahnemannian Monthly News and Advertiser* (1897), 143.

63. Hodgson to Bayley, November 25, 1898, box 184, folder 1, ASPR.

64. Hodgson to Weston D. Bayley, April 7, 1899, box 184, folder 1, ASPR. All quotations in the following paragraph are from this letter.

65. Hodgson to Bayley, April 17, 1901, box 184, folder 1, ASPR.

66. Hodgson to Bayley, March 3, 1900, box 184, folder 1, ASPR.

67. Hodgson to Bayley, April 17, 1901, box 184, folder 1, ASPR.

68. Weston D. Bayley, "Tribute to Hyslop," *JASPR* 14 (1920): 433–34.

69. For a discussion of the role of married women in scientific communities, see Debra Lindsay, "Intimate Inmates: Wives, Households, and Science in Nineteenth-Century America," *Isis* 89, no. 4 (December 1, 1998): 631–52.

70. Weston D. Bayley, "The Therapeutic Result," *The Hahnemannian Monthly* 38 (1903): 23–24.

71. Bayley, "Mrs. Henry Sidgwick and the Psychology of the Piper Trance," *JASPR* 11 (1917): 421.

72. Ann Braude, *Radical Spirits: Spiritualism and Women's Rights in Nineteenth-Century America* (Boston, MA: Beacon Press, 1989), 4–5.

73. Goldstein, "'Yours for Science,'" 577–79; Elizabeth B. Keeney, *The Botanizers: Amateur Scientists in Nineteenth-Century America* (Chapel Hill: University of North Carolina Press, 1992), 79–80, 125–27, 141–45; Kohlstedt, "The Nineteenth-Century Amateur Tradition," 173–90.

74. Most historians point out a decline in the status of amateur scientific investigation in the late nineteenth century associated with professionalization in the sciences. However, as Elizabeth Keeney argues in the case of botany, amateurs continued to organize their own clubs and societies in pursuit of their scientific values (Keeney, *The Botanizers*, 125–33).

75. Today's popular narratives around do-it-yourself science, from biohackers who inject themselves with modified genes to the spectacularly reckless blood-testing startup Theranos, trumpet a revival of the prototypically American spirit of Franklin and Edison (see, for instance, Jack Hitt, *Bunch of Amateurs: A Search for the American Character* [New York: Crown, 2012]). Although there are continuities, DIY science differs significantly in motive and method from the organized amateur science of the nineteenth century. See Robert A. Stebbins on the sociology of twentieth-century amateurism: *Amateurs, Professionals, and Serious Leisure* (Montreal: McGill-Queen's Press, 1992) and "Avocational Science: The Amateur Routine in Archaeology and Astronomy," *International Journal of Comparative Sociology* 21, no. 1 (January 1, 1980): 34–48.

76. Hill, *Scientifical Americans*.

77. Ernest Hollenbeck to Hodgson, August 2, 1887, box 172, folder 3, ASPR.

78. Asprem notes the essential misunderstandings of statistics that characterized the quantitative efforts of the SPR and ASPR in the 1880s and 90s. However, rather than evaluating these efforts from the vantage point of later parapsychology, which sought legitimacy through mastery of statistical methods, it is important to examine the concepts of probability, control, and randomization developed by nonmathematicians from the qualitative and experiential foundations of their own work. Rather than a deficient grasp of statistics, their approaches reflect close observation of the many complex factors shaping human behavior. Egil Asprem, *The Problem of Disenchantment: Scientific Naturalism and Esoteric Discourse* 1900–1939 (Leiden, The Netherlands: Brill, 2014), 350–51.

79. Hollenbeck, "Davison Society for Psychical Research, Copy of Minutes, July 25, 1887," box 172, folder 3, ASPR.

80. Ibid.

81. Hollenbeck to Hodgson, August 2, 1887, box 172, folder 3, ASPR.

82. Hollenbeck to Hodgson, August 28, 1887, box 172, folder 3, ASPR.

83. Ibid.

84. See Granville Stanley Hall, "The Contents of Children's Minds on Entering School," *Princeton Review* (May 1883): 249–72; and *Aspects of Child Life and Education* (New York: D. Appleton and Company, 1921), 11.

85. Hollenbeck to Hodgson, August 28, 1887, box 172, folder 3, ASPR.

86. Hollenbeck to Hodgson, October 2, 1887, box 172, folder 3, ASPR.

87. Josiah Royce, "Report of the Committee on Phantasms and Presentiments," *PASPR* 1:4 (1886): 416.

88. On the significance of subscription literature for readers living outside of urban centers, see Lisa Lindell, "Bringing Books to a 'Book-Hungry Land': Print Culture on the Dakota Prairie," *Book History* 4 (2007): 215–38.

89. Herbert L. Spence to James, April 9, 1890, box 36, folder 1, ASPR.

90. Spence to Hodgson, April 16, 1890, box 36, folder 1, ASPR.

91. Spence to James, April 29, 1890, box 36, folder 1, ASPR.

92. William James margin note on letter from Herbert L. Spence to James, April 9, 1890, box 36, folder 1, ASPR.

93. John Edward Woodhead, Chicago, to Hodgson October 13, 1888, box 185, folder 6, ASPR.

94. Woodhead to Hodgson October 25, 1888, box 185, folder 6, ASPR.

95. Woodhead to Hodgson, November, 26, 1888, box 185, folder 6, ASPR.

96. Solomon Quint to Hyslop, March 31, 1914, box 36, folder 8, ASPR.

97. Frank T. Lloyd to Hyslop, December 24, 1907, box 37, folder 2, ASPR.

98. Flora Ticknor to James, February 23, 1900, box 37, folder 4, ASPR.

99. William McDougall, "Psychical Research as a University Study," in *The Case For And Against Psychical Belief*, ed. Carl Murchison (Worcester, MA: Clark University, 1927), 159.

100. William James, in *The Letters of William James*, ed. Henry James (New York: Atlantic Monthly Press, 1920), 229.

101. Mary Paddock Reese to Hodgson, April 18, 1898, box 36, folder 1, ASPR.

102. William Romaine Newbold to Hodgson, December 30, 1900, box 37, folder 4, ASPR.

103. Account from J. H. Manning of Telepathic Experiments, Special Agent of the Palatine Insurance Company, Ltd., of Manchester, England, 1892, box 36, folder 1, ASPR; William Wallace Mills to Hodgson, February 8, 1901, box 36, folder 1, ASPR; Margaret Riviere Pendleton et al. to Hodgson, September 25, 1891, box 172, folder 3, ASPR; Mary Paddock Reese to Hodgson, May, 13, 1894, box 36, folder 1, ASPR.

104. Prince's formal service to the ASPR began as an investigator for Hyslop in 1917; he served as principal research officer from 1920 to 1925, when he was deposed by the society's spiritualist faction and founded the Boston Society for Psychical Research, which he led until his death in 1934.

105. Mrs. Anna Berger to Prince, November 24, 1932 and January 21, 1933, box 31, folder 18, ASPR; Prince to Berger, January 16 and February 21, 1933, box 31, folder 18, ASPR.

106. Samuel Copp Worthen to Prince, April 17, 1933, box 36, folder 5, ASPR.

107. Prince to Worthen, April 26, 1933, box 36, folder 5, ASPR.

108. Worthen to Prince, June 2, 1933, box 36, folder 5, ASPR.

109. *Proceedings of the Davenport Academy of Natural Sciences* IV (1883): 188, 240; Ibid., Volume VI (1894) 333, 346.

110. G. H. Hinrichs to Hyslop, September 16, 1909, box 37, folder 3, ASPR.

111. J. R. Ashton, San Diego, California, to Hyslop, March 5, 1918, box 172, folder 3, ASPR; Hyslop to Ashton, March 16, 1918, box 172, folder 3, ASPR.

112. Seymour H. Mauskopf and Michael Rogers McVaugh, *The Elusive Science: Origins of Experimental Psychical Research* (Baltimore: Johns Hopkins University Press, 1980), 241; Arthur S. Berger, "The Early History of the ASPR: Origins to 1907," *JASPR* 79, no. 1 (1985): 39–60.

113. Fleming, *Meteorology in America*, 58–60.

114. The National Weather Bureau runs a number of programs that rely on skilled volunteers, for example, the Cooperative Observer Program (COOP) and the SKYWARN Amateur Radio Network. See also the National Research Council, Committee on Developing Mesoscale Meteorological Observational Capabilities to Meet Multiple Needs, *Observing Weather and Climate from the Ground Up: A Nationwide Network of Networks* (Washington, DC: National Research Council, 2009).

115. Eugene Taylor, "Radical Empiricism and the New Science of Consciousness," *History of the Human Sciences* 8, no. 1 (February 1, 1995): 50–52.

116. William James, *Pragmatism: A New Name for Some Old Ways of Thinking* (New York: Longman Green & Co., 1907), 65.

117. James to Thomas Davidson, December 13, 1890, in *The Correspondence of William James*, eds. Ignas K. Skrupskelis and Elizabeth M. Berkeley (Charlottesville and London: University Press of Virginia, 1992), 122.

Tedium

1. James to Henry Sidgwick, July 11, 1896, quoted in William James, *Essays in Psychical Research* (Cambridge, MA: Harvard University Press, 1986), 75–76.

2. Charles Darwin to Adolph von Morlot, October 10, 1844, in Charles Darwin, *The Correspondence of Charles Darwin*, ed. Frederick Burkhardt et al., Vol. 3, 64–66; Alistair Sponsel, *Darwin's Evolving Identity* (Chicago: University Of Chicago Press, 2018), 220–23.

3. Charles Fraser, "The Moral Influence of Steam," *The Merchants' Magazine and Commercial Review* (June, 1846), 503.

4. "Psychical Research," *Medical and Surgical Reporter* 53, no. 11 (September 12, 1885): 306.

5. Elizabeth Stuart Phelps, "The Great Psychical Opportunity," *The North American Review*, September 1885, 254. For the impact of Phelps's *Gates Ajar* series (Boston: Fields, Osgood, 1869), which sold over 200,000 copies by 1900, see John Kucich, *Ghostly Communion: Cross-Cultural Spiritualism in Nineteenth-Century American Literature* (Lebanon, NH: University Press of New England, 2004), 71–72.

6. "Circular 4" and "Circular 5," *PASPR* 1:1 (1885): 10, 47.

7. Ernest Hollenbeck, "Davison Society for Psychical Research, Copy of Minutes," July 12, 1887, box 172, folder 3, ASPR.

8. William James, "The Confidences of a Psychical Researcher," *The American Magazine*, 1909, 585.

9. "Address of the President," *PASPR* 1:1 (1885): 81.

10. James, *Essays in Psychical Research*, 374.

11. James, "The Confidences of a Psychical Researcher," *The American Magazine* 68 (1909): 589.

12. James to F.W.H. Myers, January 30, 1890, in *The Correspondence of William James*, eds. Ignas K. Skrupskelis and Elizabeth M. Berkeley (Charlottesville: University Press of Virginia), 139.

13. W. Lambert to Hodgson, February 8, 1894, box 36, folder 1, ASPR.

14. Vita D. Scudder to Hodgson, August 5, 1887, box 38, folder 5, ASPR.

15. James to Carl Stumpf, January 1, 1886, in *The Letters of William James* (New York: Atlantic Monthly Press, 1920), 248; see also James, *Essays in Psychical Research*, 11–12, 469.

16. James Wiswell Mudge to Hyslop, August 12, 1908, box 37, folder 2, ASPR.

17. Hyslop to J. R. Ashton, March 16, 1918, box 172, folder 3, ASPR.

18. Elizabeth Stuart Phelps, "The Great Psychical Opportunity," *The North American Review*, September 1885, 256.

19. E. E. Adele, Groveport, Ohio, to Hodgson, January 18, 1892, box 172, folder 3, ASPR.

20. Hollenbeck, "Davison Society for Psychical Research, Copy of Minutes," July 12, 1887, box 172, folder 3, ASPR.

Chapter 2: Machines That Dream Together

1. Declaimed by the fictional character Thomas Alva Edison in the 1886 novel *L'ève future*. Auguste Villiers de l'Isle-Adam, *L'ève future* (Paris: Bibliotheque Charpentier, 1891), 37.

2. Letter from "Mr. W." quoted in Josiah Royce, "Report of Committee on Phantasms and Presentiments," *PASPR* 1:4 (1889): 373.

3. Martin Griffin, "Reconciliation and Irony, 1865–1905: James Russell Lowell, Henry James, Paul Laurence Dunbar, and Ambrose Bierce," (PhD diss., University of California, Los Angeles, 2002), 46–47. Quotation from Lowell to James B. Thayer, January 18, 1886, in *Letters of James Russell Lowell*, Vol. II, ed. Charles Eliot Norton (New York: Harper & Brothers, 1893), 10. Bail reconstructs the emergence of this myth and presents evidence that Lowell in fact spent many months crafting the "Ode." See Hamilton Vaughan Bail, "James Russell Lowell's Ode Recited at the Commemoration of the Living and Dead Soldiers of Harvard University, July 21, 1865," *The Papers of the Bibliographical Society of America* 37 (1943).

4. Horace Elisha Scudder, *James Russell Lowell: A Biography* (Cambridge: Riverside Press, 1901), 63–65. Giving birth to the "Ode" apparently produced a miraculous overnight weight loss of ten pounds.

5. Charles Pickard Ware, ed., *1862–1912 Class Report: Class of 'Sixty-Two Harvard University, Fiftieth Anniversary* (Norwood, MA: The Plimpton Press, 1912). Bail also identifies Mr. W. as Ware (Bail, "James Russell Lowell's Ode," 177). Ware, an abolitionist, traveled to Port Royal, South Carolina, as part of the New England Freedmen's Aid Society and transcribed the songs of enslaved people there.

6. Josiah Royce, "Report of Committee on Phantasms and Presentiments," *PASPR* 1:4 (1889): 373. Royce personally attested to Mr. W.'s character, noting that he was a "well-known gentleman of a suburban community" near Boston.

7. Ibid., 375–77.

8. James Russell Lowell quoted in ibid., 374.

9. During the war, recording and sharing dreams was a significant activity for soldiers and families. Jonathan W. White, *Midnight in America: Darkness, Sleep, and Dreams during the Civil War* (Chapel Hill: The University of North Carolina Press, 2017).

10. Francis George Gosling, *Before Freud: Neurasthenia and the American Medical Community, 1870–1910* (Urbana: University of Illinois Press, 1987), 69.

11. An example of this metaphor is Oliver Wendell Holmes, *Mechanism in Thought and Morals. An Address Delivered Before the Phi Beta Kappa Society of Harvard University, June 29, 1870* (Boston: J. R. Osgood & Co., 1871); for the long history of the metaphor see Margaret Boden, *Mind As Machine: A History of Cognitive Science* (Oxford: Oxford University Press, 2008).

12. Ibraham Ali Mahomed Hafez, *The New and Complete Fortune Teller: Being a Treatise on the Art of Foretelling Future Events by Dreams, Moles, Cards, &c. &c. &c* (New York: Richard Scott, 1816), 26.

13. *The New Dream Book, Or, Interpretation of Remarkable Dreams: According to the Most Celebrated Authors and Philosophers* (Boston: Printed for Nathaniel Coverly, 1818), 5.

14. *The Dreamer's Oracle and Faithful Interpreter, Wherein Is Explained All the Phenomena of Spiritual Imagination in Dreams* (London: J. March, 1861). Cited in Maureen Perkins, "The Meaning of Dream Books," *History Workshop Journal*, no. 48 (October 1, 1999): 105.

15. Maureen Perkins, "The Meaning of Dream Books," *History Workshop Journal*, no. 48 (October 1, 1999): 104–6.

16. Ibid., 111.

17. White, *Midnight in America*, xix.

18. Natalya Lusty and Helen Groth, *Dreams and Modernity: A Cultural History* (London and New York: Routledge, 2013); Hendrika Vande Kemp, "The Dream in Periodical Literature: 1860–1910," *Journal of the History of the Behavioral Sciences*, 17 (1981), 88–113.

19. J. Allan Hobson, "The Study of Dreaming in the Nineteenth Century," *The Dreaming Brain* (New York: Basic Books, 1988), 23–51.

20. Lusty and Groth, *Dreams and Modernity*, 26.

21. Robert Macnish, *The Philosophy of Sleep* (W.R. M'Phun, 1827) 86.

22. Philip A. Emery, *The Rational Dream Book: The Science of Dreams* (Chicago: M. A. Emery and Son, 1876); James Sully, "The Laws of Dream Fancy," *Cornhill Magazine* 34, no. 203 (November 1876):536–55.

23. G. W. Pigman writes bluntly, "Freud's review of the dream literature makes his own theory appear more revolutionary than it actually is." G. W. Pigman, "The Dark Forest of Authors: Freud and Nineteenth-Century Dream Theory," *Psychoanalysis and History*, 4 (2002): 141–65. See Hobson, 42–47, for the often repeated view that pre-Freud dream theories were largely valueless. Since Henri Ellenberger's groundbreaking 1970 work on pre-Freudian theories of the unconscious, a return to the texts and debates of nineteenth-century researchers has led to a richer appreciation of their efforts to establish a scientific basis for the study of dreams. See Vande Kemp, "The Dream in Periodical Literature: 1860–1910," 88–113; Kelly Bulkeley and Hendrika Vande Kemp, "Introduction to the Special Issue on Historical Studies of Dreaming," *Historical Studies of Dreaming*, 10 (2000): 1–6.

24. Horatio Alger, Jr., *Ragged Dick, Or, Street Life in New York with the Boot-Blacks* (Boston: Loring, 1868), 221. A classic work on American success gospel is Richard Weiss, *The American Myth of Success: From Horatio Alger to Norman Vincent Peale* (Champaign, IL: University of Illinois Press, 1969); more recently, see Jeffrey Louis Decker, *Made in America: Self-Styled Success from Horatio Alger to Oprah Winfrey* (Minneapolis: University of Minnesota Press, 1997).

25. Historians have named this inventor-hero genre the "Edisonade"; see Nathaniel Langdon Williams, "Steam Men, Edisons, Connecticut Yankees: Technocracy and Imperial Identity in Nineteenth-Century American Fiction" (PhD diss., University of Kansas Department of English, 2010). Interestingly, astronomer

and ASPR president Simon Newcomb published a contribution to this genre: *His Wisdom, the Defender: A Story* (New York: Harper & Brothers, 1900).

26. Josiah Royce, "Report of the Committee on Phantasms and Presentiments," *PASPR* 1:4 (1889): 352.

27. Josiah Royce, "Report of Committee on Apparitions and Haunted Houses," *PASPR* 1:3 (1887), 229.

28. John Ferguson Nisbet, *The Insanity of Genius and the General Inequality of Human Faculty Physiologically Considered* (London: Ward & Downey, 1891). Francis Galton's ideas about hereditary genius shaped this popular and scientific discourse in combination with much older notions of melancholia. See Penelope Murray, ed., *Genius: The History of an Idea* (New York: Blackwell, 1989).

29. Nisbet, *The Insanity of Genius*, 228.

30. Sellers letter excerpted in Josiah Royce, "Report of the Committee on Phantasms and Presentiments," *PASPR* 1:4 (1889): 360.

31. B. Zorina Khan, *The Democratization of Invention: Patents and Copyrights in American Economic Development, 1790–1920* (Cambridge: Cambridge University Press, 2005), 107.

32. Royce, "Report of the Committee on Phantasms and Presentiments," *PASPR* 1:4 (1889): 360.

33. For Francis Power Cobbe's popularization of "unconscious cerebration," see Lusty and Groth, *Dreams and Modernity*, 43–47.

34. Jeff Wilson, *Mindful America: The Mutual Transformation of Buddhist Meditation and American Culture* (New York: Oxford University Press, 2014).

35. "Sellers, Coleman, Ed.D., Sci. D.," in *American Biography: A New Cyclopedia* (New York: American Historical Society, 1922), 227.

36. Domenic Vitiello, *Engineering Philadelphia: The Sellers Family and the Industrial Metropolis* (Ithaca, NY: Cornell University Press, 2013), 91–93.

37. Patent Technology Monitoring Team, "U.S. Patent Activity Calendar Years 1790 to the Present," United States Patent and Trademark Office. Accessed May 3, 2014. http://www.uspto.gov/web/offices/ac/ido/oeip/taf/h_counts. htm.

38. Stacy V. Jones, *The Patent Office* (New York: Praeger, 1971), viii, 13–14; Lisa Gitelman, *Paper Knowledge: Toward a Media History of Documents* (Durham, NC: Duke University Press, 2014).

39. *Colonial and Revolutionary Families of Pennsylvania: Genealogical and Personal Memoirs* (New York: Lewis Historical Publishing Company, 1911), 1417–18.

40. Carla Gerona, *Night Journeys: The Power of Dreams in Transatlantic Quaker Culture* (Charlottesville: University of Virginia Press, 2004), 2–4.

41. Quoted in Josiah Royce, "Report of the Committee on Phantasms and Presentiments," *PASPR* 1:4 (1889): 359.

42. The Sellers's family history is recounted in Vitiello, *Engineering Philadelphia*.

43. See the recollections of Harold Sellers Colton, Escol's grandnephew, in "Mark Twain's Literary Dilemma and Its Sequel," *The Arizona Quarterly* 17 (January 1, 1961): 229.

44. "Coleman Sellers," *American Biography*.

45. Coleman Sellers to Furness, November 3, 1884, Ms. Coll. 412, box 4, folder 202, Rare Books and Manuscripts Library, University of Pennsylvania. His early experience did not dispose him against Fox Kane; he would later attend her séances with the Seybert Commission.

46. Untitled note, Samuel Byron Brittan, *The Spiritual Telegraph* (Partridge & Brittan, 1855), 372.

47. Lawrence R. Samuel, *The American Dream: A Cultural History* (Syracuse, NY: Syracuse University Press, 2012).

48. "Blank G: Committee on Experimental Psychology, October 1887," *PASPR* 1:3 (1887): 270.

49. Josiah Royce, "Report of the Committee on Phantasms and Presentiments," *PASPR* 1:4 (1889): 351.

50. Ibid. On unconscious repetitions as identifying clues, see Carlo Ginzburg, "Morelli, Freud, and Sherlock Holmes: Clues and Scientific Method," trans. Anna Davin, *History Workshop Journal*, no. 9 (1980): 5–36.

51. This very broad summary of Foucault's arguments about the Paris Clinic and the medical gaze is situated historiographically in Caroline Hannaway and Ann Elizabeth Fowler La Berge, "Paris Medicine: Perspectives Past and Present," in *Constructing Paris Medicine*, eds. Caroline Hannaway and Ann Elizabeth Fowler La Berge (Rodopi, 1998) 1–70.

52. Coleman Sellers to Horace Howard Furness, June 28, 1887, Ms. Coll. 412, box 4, folder 217, Rare Books and Manuscripts Library, University of Pennsylvania; Sellers quoted in Josiah Royce, "Report of the Committee on Phantasms and Presentiments," *PASPR* 1:4 (1889): 351.

53. Holmes, *Mechanism in Thought and Morals*, 36–38.

54. James J. Belcher, "The Romance of Sleep," *Harper's New Monthly Magazine* (April 1867), 645.

55. Páraic Finnerty, "A Dickinson Reverie: The Worm, the Snake, Marvel, and Nineteenth-Century Dreaming," *The Emily Dickinson Journal* 16, no. 2 (2007): 94–118.; Jonathan C. Glance, "Revelation, Nonsense or Dyspepsia: Victorian Dream Theories," *Scribd*. Accessed August 25, 2014. http://www.scribd.com/doc/105245364/Glance-Jonathan-C-Revelation-Nonsense-or-Dyspepsia-Victorian-Dream-Theories.

56. Ambrose Bierce, "Visions of the Night," *The Collected Works of Ambrose Bierce . . . : In Motley: Kings of Beasts: Two Administrations; Miscellaneous* (New York and Washington: The Neale Publishing Co., 1911; orig. *San Francisco Examiner,* July 24, 1887), 123.

57. Ibid., 122.

58. Ibid.

59. Katherine Roeder, *Wide Awake in Slumberland: Fantasy, Mass Culture, and Modernism in the Art of Winsor McCay* (Jackson: University Press of Mississippi, 2013); Walter Cooper Dendy, *On the Phenomena of Dreams, and Other Transient Illusions* (Whittaker, Treacher & Co., 1832); William Alexander Hammond, *Sleep and Its Derangements* (Philadelphia: J. B. Lippincott, 1869).

60. Roeder, *Wide Awake in Slumberland*, 159.

61. Ibid., 164.

62. Winsor McCay, "How the Rarebit Fiend Happened," *The Idaho Daily Statesman*, October 15, 1907, 13.

63. Ibid.

64. Ibid.

65. Roeder, *Wide Awake in Slumberland*, 165–66.

66. McCay, "How the Rarebit Fiend Happened."

67. Ibid.

68. Tim Blackmore, "McCay's McChanical Muse: Engineering Comic-Strip Dreams," *Journal of Popular Culture* 32 (1998), 15–38.

69. William James, *The Principles of Psychology*, Authorized Ed., Unabridged (Dover Publications, 1918), 199–218.

70. Ibid., 373–74.

71. Royce, "Report of the Committee on Phantasms and Presentiments," *PASPR* 1:4 (1889): 363.

72. James, *The Principles of Psychology*, 217.

73. Royce, "Report of the Committee on Phantasms and Presentiments," *PASPR* 1:4 (1889): 363.

74. Royce, "Report of the Committee on Phantasms and Presentiments," *PASPR* 1:4 (1889). W. S. was probably Boston notable Winthrop Sargent. His wife was an associate member of the ASPR from 1886 to 1889.

75. Royce, "Report of the Committee on Phantasms and Presentiments," *PASPR* 1:4 (1889): 366.

76. Ibid., 456.

77. Ibid., 467.

78. Ian Hacking explores these uses of historical dreaming, or historical uses of dreaming, in "Dreams in Place," *Journal of Aesthetics and Art Criticism* 59 (2001): 245–60.

79. Alan Taylor, "The Early Republic's Supernatural Economy: Treasure Seeking in the American Northeast, 1780–1830," *American Quarterly* 38 (1986): 6–34.

80. Ibid., 6–34.

81. The classic study of this phenomenon is Wolfgang Schivelbusch, *The Railway Journey: The Industrialization of Time and Space in the Nineteenth Century* (Berkeley: University of California Press, 1986).

82. Roeder, *Wide Awake in Slumberland*, 177; McCay, *Dreams of the Rarebit Fiend*, 2.

83. Thomas De Quincey, *The English Mail-Coach and Joan of Arc* (Ginn & Company, 1902); see also Thomas Creevey's account in Creevey and Herbert Maxwell, *The Creevey Papers: A Selection from the Correspondence and Diaries of Thomas Creevey, M. P., Born 1768–Died 1838; Edited by Sir Herbert Maxwell* (London: Murray, 1904), 204; and Schivelbusch, *The Railway Journey*, 129–33 (which quotes Creevey and other commentators on the risks of railroad travel).

84. Josiah Royce, "Appendix to Report on Phantasms and Presentiments," *PASPR* 1:4 (1889): 478.

85. Josiah Royce, "Report of the Committee on Phantasms and Presentiments," *PASPR* 1:4 (1889): 386.

86. Pamela E. Klassen, *Spirits of Protestantism: Medicine, Healing, and Liberal Christianity* (Berkeley and Los Angeles: University of California Press, 2011).

87. Marshall Wait to Hodgson, July 1, 1897, box 37, folder 6, ASPR.

88. James Hervey Hyslop, Statement, March 12, 1909, box 37, folder 3, ASPR.

89. "A Disastrous Boiler Explosion a Pedestrian Killed and Rails Displaced by the Flying Shell," *Philadelphia Inquirer*, August 3, 1890, 1.

90. "The Fatal Boiler Again," *New York Herald*, August 10, 1883, 4.

91. Coleman Sellers, "Mechanical Engineering," *Journal of the Franklin Institute* (1885): 426.

92. Havelock Ellis, *The World of Dreams* (Boston: Houghton Mifflin, 1922), 10.

93. C. S. Peirce, "Criticism on 'Phantasms of the Living,'" *PASPR* 2:1 (1907): 150–56; Royce, "Report of Committee on Phantasms and Presentiments," *PASPR* 1:4 (1889): 350–428.

94. For nineteenth-century views on the "good death" and the challenges posed to this tradition by sudden death in accident and war, see Drew Gilpin Faust, *This Republic of Suffering: Death and the American Civil War* (New York: Vintage Books, 2009), 6–9. Jonathan White analyzes many visions of the dying from the Civil War, when families often experienced their sons' battlefield deaths remotely. White, *Midnight in America*, 101–21.

95. Mark Twain, "Mental Telegraphy: A Manuscript with a History," *Harper's New Monthly Magazine*, December 1, 1891.

96. James Hervey Hyslop to Richard Hodgson, December 12, 1894, series 35, box 37, folder 2, ASPR.

97. Twain, "Mental Telegraphy," 97.

98. Ibid., 101.

99. Orlando C. Blackmer to Ellen P. Child, February 20, 1911, box 37, folder 3, ASPR.

100. Walter Franklin Prince to Theodore Roosevelt, October 16, 1919, box 209, folder 14, ASPR.

101. John R. Eldridge to Hodgson, September 5, 1892, box 37, folder 5, ASPR. See, for instance, O. Owen, Louisville, Kentucky, to William James, April 25, 1907, box 37, folder 3, ASPR.

102. Alfred Church Lane to William James, February 4, 1894, box 36, folder 1, ASPR.

103. Twain, "Mental Telegraphy," 98.

104. Ibid., 97–98.

105. A. Draheus, Chaplain, State Prison, San Quentin, to James Hyslop, May 25, 1908, box 37, folder 2, ASPR.

106. For Twain's stormy relationship with the telephone, see John Bird, "Mark Twain on the Telephone: Love (and Hate) on the Line," *The Mark Twain Annual* 6.1 (2008): 77–89.

107. Letter from Sellers excerpted in Royce, "Report of the Committee on Phantasms and Presentiments," *PASPR* 1:4 (1889): 359.

108. Vitiello, *Engineering Philadelphia*, 91.

109. Anson Rabinbach, *The Human Motor: Energy, Fatigue, and the Origins of Modernity* (Berkeley: University of California Press, 1992), 28–32.

110. Andrew Redden, "Dream-Visions and Divine Truth in Early Modern Hispanic America," in *Dreams, Dreamers, and Visions: The Early Modern Atlantic World*, eds. Ann Marie Plane and Leslie Tuttle (Philadelphia: University of Pennsylvania Press, 2013); Gerona, *Night Journeys*; Mechal Sobel, *Teach Me Dreams: The Search for Self in the Revolutionary Era* (Princeton, NJ: Princeton University Press, 2002).

111. Ann Marie Plane, *Dreams and the Invisible World in Colonial New England: Indians, Colonists, and the Seventeenth Century* (Philadelphia: University of Pennsylvania Press, 2014), 69–70.

112. See, for instance, Ellis, *The World of Dreams*, 228. Ellis, writing in the 1920s, followed Sellers's nineteenth-century sources in attributing dream inventions to the individual brain engaged in a free play of the unconscious not possible in waking life.

113. Josiah Royce, "Report of Committee on Apparitions and Haunted Houses," *PASPR* 1:4 (1889): 229.

114. Lusty and Groth, *Dreams and Modernity*, 180.

115. Walter Benjamin, *The Work of Art in the Age of Its Technological Reproducibility, and Other Writings on Media* (Cambridge, MA: Harvard University Press, 2008), 236.

116. William James, *Pragmatism: A New Name for Some Old Ways of Thinking* (New York: Longman Green and Co., 1907), 34; Louis Menand, *The Metaphysical Club: A Story of Ideas in America* (New York: Farrar, Straus and Giroux, 2002).

Contact

1. Mrs. S. E. Herschel to Hodgson, April 1, 1892, box 3, folder 1, ASPR.

2. Robert Silverberg, *The Mound Builders: Archaeology of a Myth* (Athens, OH: Ohio University Press, 1986); Bruce G. Trigger, "Alternative Archaeologies: Nationalist, Colonialist, Imperialist," *Man*, New Series, 19, no. 3 (September 1, 1984): 355–70; Bruce G. Trigger, *A History of Archaeological Thought* (Cambridge: Cambridge University Press, 1989).

3. John Kucich, *Ghostly Communion: Cross-Cultural Spiritualism in Nineteenth-Century American Literature* (Lebanon, NH: University Press of New England,, 2004), xi–xii.

4. Molly McGarry, "Indian Guides: Haunted Subjects and the Politics of Vanishing," in *Ghosts of Futures Past* (Berkeley: University of California Press, 2008), 66–93.

5. Charles F. Pidgeon, Harry Price, and Eric John Dingwall, *Revelations of a Spirit Medium* (Kegan Paul, Trench, Trubner & Company, 1922).

6. Kathryn Troy, "'A New and Beautiful Mission': The Appearance of Black Hawk in Spiritualist Circles, 1857–1888," in *The Spiritualist Movement: Speaking with the Dead in America and around the World*, ed. Christopher M. Moreman, vol. 3 (New York: ABC-CLIO, 2013), 171–85.

7. Robert F. Berkhofer, *The White Man's Indian: Images of the American Indian from Columbus to the Present* (New York: Knopf Doubleday Publishing Group, 2011), 88–89; R. Laurence Moore, "The Spiritualist Medium: A Study of Female Professionalism in Victorian America," *American Quarterly* 27, no. 2 (May 1, 1975): 200–21.

8. Berkhofer, *The White Man's Indian*, 145–52.

9. "Talked with Ghosts: Mediums Converse with Spirits of Departed Souls," *The Daily Inter Ocean*, August 5, 1895.

10. "Spiritualists and Indians," *Chicago Daily Tribune (1872-1922)*, August 3, 1895.

11. Ibid.

12. Ibid.

13. Ibid., 151.

14. Ibid., 152.

15. Robert S. Cox, *Body and Soul: A Sympathetic History of American Spiritualism* (Charlottesville: University of Virginia Press, 2003), 174–76.

16. Thomas Jefferson, *Notes on the State of Virginia* (London: Printed for John Stockdale, 1787), 156; Cyrus Thomas, *Report on the Mound Explorations of the Bureau of Ethnology* (Washington, DC, 1894).

17. Gerald Fowke, "Popular Errors Regarding Mound Builders and Indians," *Ohio Archæological and Historical Quarterly*, 1888, 380–403.

18. Gerald Fowke to Eli Lilly, September 23, 1932, quoted in James H. Kellar, "A Historical Footnote," *Midcontinental Journal of Archaeology* 4, no. 1 (1979): 140.

19. Rutherford B. Hayes to Hodgson, June 30, 1892, box 3, folder 1, ASPR.

20. Major General Force to Hayes, June 14, 1892, box 3, folder 1, ASPR.

21. J. G. Owens to Hodgson, July 7, 1892, box 3, folder 1, ASPR.

22. Ephraim George Squier, "Tongues From Tombs; or, the Stories That Graves Tell," *Frank Leslie's Weekly*, March 20, 1869, 5.

23. Warren K. Moorehead to Hodgson, June 25, 1892, box 3, folder 1, ASPR.

Chapter 3: Drawings from the Other Side

1. Jason A. Josephson-Storm, *The Myth of Disenchantment: Magic, Modernity, and the Birth of the Human Sciences* (Chicago: University of Chicago Press, 2017).

2. This chapter is based on a previously published paper, Alicia Puglionesi, "Drawing as Instrument, Drawings as Evidence: Capturing Mental Processes with Pencil and Paper," *Medical History* 60, no. 3 (July 2016): 359–87.

3. William James, *The Principles of Psychology*, Vol. 1 (New York: Henry Holt and Co., 1890), 183–96.

4. Ibid., 193.

5. William James to Alfred Church Lane, February 13, 1894, in *The Correspondence of William James*, Vol. 7, eds. Ignas K. Skrupskelis and Elizabeth M. Berkeley (Charlottesville: University Press of Virginia, 1992), 488.

6. William H. Pickering, "Appendix: Experiments on Thought-transference," *PASPR* 1:3 (1886): 115.

7. Wilma Koutstaal, "Skirting the Abyss: A History of Experimental Explorations of Automatic Writing in Psychology," *Journal of the History of the Behavioral Sciences* 28, no. 1 (February 13, 2006): 5–27.

8. Lorraine Daston and Peter Galison, *Objectivity* (New York: Zone Books, 2007), 17, 138.

9. Kurt Danziger, *Constructing the Subject: Historical Origins of Psychological Research* (Cambridge: Cambridge University Press, 1994), 16–18.

10. Arthur Efland, *A History of Art Education: Intellectual and Social Currents in Teaching the Visual Arts* (New York: Teachers College Press, 1990) 64, 69–74.

11. Ibid., 73–74.

12. Granville Stanley Hall, *Educational Problems* (New York: D. Appleton and Company, 1911), 497.

13. Ibid.

14. Ibid.

15. Clark University Catalogue 1896, 4.

16. Hall, *Educational Problems*, 497; Herman T. Lukens, "A Study of Children's Drawings in the Early Years," *Pedagogical Seminary* 4, no. 1 (October 1, 1896): 101.

17. Ibid., 81.

18. Ibid.

19. Ibid.

20. Ibid.

21. Ibid., 79–80.

22. Ibid., 81.

23. Hall, *Educational Problems*, 498.

24. Lukens, "A Study of Children's Drawings," 86.

25. Martin Krampen, *Children's Drawings: Iconic Coding of the Environment* (New York and London: Plenum Press, 1991), 32. Barbara Wittmann, "Johnny-Head-in-the-Air in America. Aby Warburg's Experiments with Children's Drawings," in *New Perspectives in Iconology: Visual Studies and Anthropology* (Brussels: Academic and Scientific Publishers, 2011), 120–42.

26. Florence L. Goodenough, *Measurement of Intelligence by Drawings* (Chicago: World Book Company, 1926).

27. John R. Morss, *The Biologising of Childhood: Developmental Psychology and the Darwinian Myth* (New York and London: Taylor & Francis, 1990), 135–36.

28. Morss, *The Biologising of Childhood*, 53–54; Rebecca Lemov, "X-rays of Inner Worlds: The Mid-Twentieth-Century American Projective Test Movement," *Journal of the History of the Behavioral Sciences* 47, no. 3 (Summer 2011): 255–63.

29. For instance, Norman England, "Drawing Upon Your Intelligence," *The Sun* (Baltimore), October 2, 1927; Catherine MacKenzie, "Mental Tests for the Baby," *New York Times*, March 30, 1941. See also Jonathan Fineberg's introductory essays in *When We Were Young: New Perspectives on the Art of the Child* (Berkeley: University of California Press, 2006); and *Discovering Child Art: Essays on Childhood, Primitivism, and Modernism* (Princeton, NJ: Princeton University Press, 1998).

30. See, for example: Leila Zenderland, *Measuring Minds: Henry Herbert Goddard and the Origins of American Intelligence Testing* (Cambridge: Cambridge University Press, 2001); Rebecca Lemov, *World as Laboratory: Experiments with Mice, Mazes, and Men* (New York: Hill and Wang, 2005).

31. Lukens, "A Study of Children's Drawings," 92.

32. The term *thought-transference* predates *telepathy*, which was introduced in the psychical research literature in 1882 as a scientific term for the same phenomenon. Though they could have slightly different connotations for certain actors, these terms were used interchangeably by many during the 1880s and 90s. Roger Luckhurst, *The Invention of Telepathy, 1870–1901* (Oxford: Oxford University Press, 2002), 9–11, 60–61.

33. Barry H. Wiley details the most notable stage acts of the late nineteenth century in *The Thought Reader Craze: Victorian Science at the Enchanted Boundary* (Jefferson, NC: McFarland, 2012).

34. See discussion of Mark Twain's "Mental Telegraphy: A Manuscript with a History" in Chapter 2.

35. Richard J. Noakes, "Cromwell Varley FRS, Electrical Discharge and Victorian Spiritualism," *The Royal Society Journal of the History of Science* 61, no. 1 (January 22, 2007): 5–21; Sungook Hong, *Wireless: From Marconi's Black-Box to the Audion* (Cambridge, MA: MIT Press, 2001), 25.

36. "Report of the Committee on Thought-Transference," *PASPR* 1:3 (1886): 111.

37. Catherine L. Albanese, *A Republic of Mind and Spirit: A Cultural History of American Metaphysical Religion* (New Haven, CT: Yale University Press, 2007), 10–13. On the use of scientific rhetoric in conjuring, see Sofie Lachapelle, "From the Stage to the Laboratory: Magicians, Psychologists, and the Science of Illusion," *Journal of the History of the Behavioral Sciences* 44, no. 4 (Fall 2008): 320–22.

38. Blackburn quoted in Barrett, "Appendix to the Report on Thought-Transference," *PSPR* 1 (1882): 63.

39. Wiley, *The Thought-Reader Craze*, 110–12.

40. Douglas Blackburn, "Confessions of a Famous Medium," *John Bull* (December 5, 1908): 590.

41. Edmund Gurney et al., "Second Report on Thought-Transference," *PSPR* 1 (1883): 79.

42. Ibid., 80.

43. Ibid., 79.

44. Ibid., 82.

45. Ibid.

46. Ibid.

47. Ibid. See "Wood Engraving: Facsimile and Fragmentation" in Gerry Beegan, *The Mass Image: a Social History of Photomechanical Reproduction in Victorian London* (London: Palgrave Macmillan, 2008), 257–66.

48. Gerry Beegan, "The Mechanization of the Image: Facsimile, Photography, and Fragmentation in Nineteenth-Century Wood Engraving," *Journal of Design History* 8, no. 4 (1995): 257.

49. See Richard J. Noakes, "Telegraphy Is an Occult Art: Cromwell Fleetwood Varley and the Diffusion of Electricity to the Other World," *The British Journal for the History of Science* 32, no. 04 (1999): 421–59; and "The 'World of the Infinitely Little': Connecting Physical and Psychical Realities circa 1900," *Studies in History and Philosophy of Science Part A*, 39, no. 3 (September 2008): 323–34.

50. Gurney et al., "Third Report of the Committee on Thought-Transference," PSPR 1 (1883): 166–67.

51. Roy Steven Turner, *In the Eye's Mind: Vision and the Helmholtz-Hering Controversy* (Princeton, NJ: Princeton University Press, 1994), 74–75.

52. Gurney et al., "Third Report of the Committee on Thought-Transference," 164.

53. Ibid., 163–64.

54. Ibid., 164.

55. E. P. Thwing, "English Psychologists," *The Phrenological Journal of Science and Health* 77, no. 5 (November 1883): 275.

56. For the ASPR's main criticisms of the British Society see Charles S. Peirce's review of *Phantasms of the Living*, Edmund Gurney's reply, and Peirce's reply to Gurney, in *PASPR* 1:3 (1887): 150–214.

57. Gurney et al., "Second Report on Thought-Transference," 173; Simon Newcomb, "Address of the President," *PASPR* 1:2 (1886): 77.

58. Simon Newcomb, "Address of the President," *PASPR* 1:2 (1886): 75.

59. William H. Pickering, "Thought-Transference by Means of Pictures," *PASPR* 1:1 (1885): 44.

60. Circular 5, *PASPR* 1:1 (1885): 48.

61. Pickering, "Thought-Transference by Means of Pictures," 44.

62. Ibid.

63. A special issue of *History of Science*, on "Seriality and Scientific Objects in the Nineteenth Century," has guided my thinking on this image. See Nick Hopwood, Simon Schaffer, and Jim Secord, "Seriality and Scientific Objects in the Nineteenth Century," *History of Science* 48, no. 3/4 (September 2010): 251–85. For the nebular hypothesis in astronomy, see Simon Schaffer, "The Nebular Hypothesis and the Science of Progress," in *History, Humanity and Evolution: Essays for John C. Greene*, ed. James R. Moore (Cambridge: Cambridge University Press, 1989), 150–51.

64. Vida D. Scudder to Hodgson, August 5, 1887, box 38, folder 5, ASPR.

65. H. P. Bowditch, "Report of the Committee on Thought-Transference," *PASPR* 1:3 (1887): 216.

66. Vida D. Scudder to Hodgson, August [illegible], 1887, box 38, folder 5, ASPR. Hodgson declined the invitation.

67. Newcomb, "Professor Newcomb's Address," 75.

68. Charles Sedgwick Minot, "Second Report on Experimental Psychology: Upon the Diagram-Tests," *PASPR* 1:4 (1889): 312.

69. Ibid., 314.

70. Ibid., 313.

71. Ibid., 314. The idea of a community of thought or a shared unconscious appeared also in the writings of the British SPR around this time, as well as in the work of the French followers of Pierre Janet.

72. Ibid.

73. Ibid., 307.

74. William James, "Note to the Foregoing Report," *PASPR* 1:4 (1889): 317–20.

75. Granville Stanley Hall, *Aspects of Child Life and Education* (New York: D. Appleton and Company, 1921), 2.

76. James, "Note to the Foregoing Report," 319.

77. See Upton Sinclair, *Mental Radio* (New York: Albert & Charles Boni, 1930) 113–14.

78. E. P. Thwing, "English Psychologists," 275.

79. Gurney et al., "Third Report of the Committee on Thought-Transference," 164.

80. See, for example, Frederick Wicks and Washington Irving Bishop, *Second Sight Explained: A Complete Exposition of Clairvoyance . . .* (Edinburgh and Glasgow: John Menzies, 1880); Hardin J. Burlingame, *Leaves from Conjurers' Scrap Books; Or, Modern Magicians and Their Works* (Donohue, Henneberry & Company, 1891); R. D. Chater, *Latest Sleights, Illusions, Mind Reading, and New Card Effects* (Dean & Son, Ltd., 1903). Some of these systems are detailed in Wiley, *The Thought Reader Craze*, 112–13.

81. Douglas Blackburn, "My Masterpiece," *John Bull* (January 9, 1909), 39.

82. James, "Psychology and the Teaching Art," in *Talks to Teachers on Psychology, and to Students on Some of Life's Ideals*, 12–14 (New York, H. Holt and Company, 1900). For James's contributions to child study, see Alice Smuts, *Science in the Service of Children*, 1893–1935 (New Haven, CT: Yale University Press, 2008) 67–78.

83. Lemov, "X-rays of Inner Worlds," 251–78; Barbara Wittmann, "Drawing Cure: Children's Drawings as a Psychoanalytic Instrument," *Configurations* 18, no. 3 (2010): 251–72; Peter Galison, "Image of Self," in *Things That Talk: Object Lessons from Art and Sciences*, 257–96 (New York: Zone Books, 2007).

84. See Wiley, *The Thought-Reader Craze*, 157–61.

85. See Christian Baumann, "Psychic Blindness or Visual Agnosia: Early Descriptions of a Nervous Disorder," *Journal of the History of the Neurosciences* 20, no. 1 (January 2011): 58–64.

86. Sir Henry Head, *Aphasia and Kindred Disorders of Speech* (Cambridge: Cambridge University Press, 1926), 359–68. For a history of Head and one of aphasia see L. S. Jacyna, *Medicine and Modernism: A Biography of Sir Henry Head*

(London: Pickering & Chatto, 2008); and *Lost Words: Narratives of Language and the Brain*, 1825–1926 (Princeton, NJ: Princeton University Press, 2000).

87. See, for instance, Lorraine Daston and Peter Galison, *Objectivity* (New York: Zone Books, 2007); Christoph Hoffmann and Barbara Wittmann, "Introduction: Knowledge in the Making: Drawing and Writing as Research Techniques," *Science in Context* 26, Special Issue 02 (June 2013): 203–13.

Intimacy

1. James E. Benedict to Walter Prince, November 16, 1924, series 35, box 37, folder 2, ASPR.

2. John Tosh, *A Man's Place: Masculinity and the Middle-Class Home in Victorian England* (New Haven, CT: Yale University Press, 2007), 53–79; Rachel Ablow, *The Marriage of Minds: Reading Sympathy in the Victorian Marriage Plot* (Stanford, CA: Stanford University Press, 2007), 17–44.

3. O. Owen to William James, April 25, 1907, box 37, folder 3, ASPR.

4. W.B.C. to William James, n.d., box 36, folder 1, ASPR.

5. Susan Lanzoni, "Sympathy in Mind (1876–1900)," *Journal of the History of Ideas* 70, no. 2 (2009): 265–87.

6. Lanzoni, "Sympathy in Mind (1876–1900)," 276–77.

7. Ablow, *The Marriage of Minds*; Audrey Jaffe, *Scenes of Sympathy: Identity and Representation in Victorian Fiction* (Ithaca, NY: Cornell University Press, 2000); Audrey Jaffe, *The Affective Life of the Average Man: The Victorian Novel and the Stock-Market Graph* (Columbus: Ohio State University Press, 2010); Lisa M. Brocklebank, *Presentiments, Sympathies and Signs: Minds in the Age of Fiction—Reading and the Limits of Reason in Victorian Britain* (Providence, RI: Brown University, 2008); Lisa Brocklebank, "Psychic Reading," *Victorian Studies* 48, no. 2 (2006): 233–39.

8. Simon Szreter and Kate Fisher, *Sex before the Sexual Revolution: Intimate Life in England* 1918–1963 (Cambridge: Cambridge University Press, 2010), 184–87.

9. Paul Horn, " 'Two Minds with but a Single Thought': W. T. Stead, Henry James, and the Zancig Controversy," 19*: Interdisciplinary Studies in the Long Nineteenth Century* 16 (2013), http://doi.org/10.16995/ntn.658.

10. Gifford Lewis, *Somerville and Ross: The World of the Irish R. M.* (New York: Penguin Books, 1987).

11. Henry James to William James, October 1907, quoted in Pamela Thurschwell, *Literature, Technology and Magical Thinking*, 1880–1920 (Cambridge: Cambridge University Press, 2005), 90.

12. Thurschwell, *Literature, Technology, and Magical Thinking*, 86; Pamela Thurschwell, "The Erotics of Telepathy: The British SPR's Experiments in Intimacy," in *The Sixth Sense Reader*, ed. David Howes (Oxford: Berg, 2009), 183–208; Pamela Thurschwell, "The Typist's Remains: Theodora Bosanquet in Recent Fiction," *The Henry James Review* 32, no. 1 (2011): 1–11.

13. Bosanquet, "Notes on a Sitting with Mrs. Hester Dowden, Feb. 15, 1933," quoted in Thurschwell, *Literature, Technology, and Magical Thinking*, 102.

14. Gertrude Ogden Tubby and Weston D. Bayley, *James H. Hyslop - X His Book: A Cross Reference Record* (York, PA: The York Printing Company, 1929).

15. Ibid., 18 (Weston D. Bayley's Introduction).

16. Ibid.

17. Frederick Edwards to G. Tubby, January 29, 1924; Tubby to Edwards, January 31, 1924, folder 14, box 209, ASPR.

18. James Wiswell Mudge to Hyslop, August 12, 1908, series 35, box 37 (current box 101), folder 2, ASPR.

Chapter 4: Psychic Domesticity

1. Mary Craig Sinclair, *Southern Belle* (Jackson, MS: University Press of Mississippi, 1999; orig. 1957), 304.

2. Peggy Whitman Prenshaw, *Composing Selves: Southern Women and Autobiography* (Baton Rouge: Louisiana State University Press, 2011), 143–45.

3. Sinclair, *Southern Belle*, 298.

4. Mary C. Sinclair to Walter Franklin Prince, January 5, 1928, box 36, folder 5, ASPR.

5. Ibid.

6. Ibid.

7. Copy of extracts of a letter from Mary Craig Sinclair to Mrs. [Paul Jordan] Smith, July 1927, box 6, folder 5, ASPR. Craig's concern about telepathic circulation of emotions ties back into the crowd psychology of the early twentieth century and the impact of psychical models of suggestion upon American social theory, discussed in the Contact interlude. Like Mark Twain's radical notions of telepathy in Chapter 2, Craig's vision emphasized the utopian potential of such a communion of affect over its dangers.

8. Mary Craig Sinclair to Walter Prince, January 5, 1928, box 6, folder 5, ASPR.

9. Mary Craig Sinclair to Walter Prince, undated ("I may have succeeded in preserving much that will inform you . . . "), box 6, folder 5, ASPR.

10. Sinclair, *Southern Belle*, 307.

11. Anthony Arthur, *Radical Innocent: Upton Sinclair* (New York: Random House, 2006), 146.

12. Susan E. Gunter, *Alice in Jamesland: The Story of Alice Howe Gibbens James* (Lincoln: University of Nebraska Press, 2009), 91–93.

13. Seymour H. Mauskopf and Michael Rogers McVaugh, *The Elusive Science: Origins of Experimental Psychical Research* (Baltimore: Johns Hopkins University Press, 1980), 17–19.

14. Mary Craig Sinclair to Walter Prince, undated, probably between January 5 and 13, 1928, box 6, folder 5, ASPR.

15. Mary Craig Sinclair to Walter Prince, January 5, 1928, box 6, folder 5, ASPR.

16. See, for instance, Craig's chapter on "First Love" in *Southern Belle*, where she discusses the appropriate management of multiple suitors.

17. See, e.g., Pamela Thurschwell, *Literature, Technology, and Magical Thinking*, 1880–1920 (Cambridge: Cambridge University Press, 2005); Jill Nicole Galvan, *The Sympathetic Medium: Feminine Channeling, the Occult, and Communication Technologies*, 1859–1919 (Ithaca, NY: Cornell University Press, 2010).

18. Sinclair, *Southern Belle*, 141, 396.

19. Prenshaw, *Composing Selves*, 239. Prenshaw notes that this is an inference of Sinclair's biographer Leon Harris based on interviews with Craig's sister Dolly, who was sixteen at the time of these events.

20. Louis M. Berg, "Rom Romano, Mystic, Identified as Count," *Miami News*, March 26, 1926.

21. Walter Prince to Upton Sinclair, November 11, 1927, box 36, folder 5, ASPR; and Walter Franklin Prince, "Rom-Romano Experiments in New York," *JASPR* 18 (1924) 368–92.

22. Frank Norris, *The Octopus: A Story of California* (Garden City, NY: Doubleday, Page & Company, 1901), 29.

23. Ransome Sutton, "What's New in Science: Power of Mind Over Body," *Los Angeles Times*, June 11, 1933.

24. Ibid.

25. Melville Ellis to Upton Sinclair, July 28, 1927, box 36, folder 5, ASPR.

26. Ibid.

27. Ibid.

28. Ibid.

29. Mary Craig Sinclair to Melville Ellis, July 30, 1927, box 36, folder 5, ASPR.

30. Melville Ellis to [Upton] Sinclair, September 13, 1927, box 36, folder 5, ASPR.

31. For the professional status of osteopathy between the 1890s and 1920s, see Paul Starr, *The Social Transformation of American Medicine* (New York: Basic Books, 1982), 108–109, 126.

32. Walter Prince to Mary Craig Sinclair, February 2, 1928, box 36, folder 5, ASPR.

33. Walter Franklin Prince, "The Sinclair Experiments for Telepathy," in Upton Sinclair, *Mental Radio* (Springfield, IL: Charles C. Thomas, 1962); orig. *Bulletin of the Boston Society for Psychical Research* 16 (April 1932): 158.

34. Prince expresses his ambivalence about Craig's relationship with Ostoja in letters of November 11 and December 28, 1927, and April 26, 1928, box 36, folder 5, ASPR, and alludes to it in his analysis of *Mental Radio*, discussed in the next section of this chapter.

35. Mary Craig Sinclair to Mrs. [Sarah Bixby] Smith, undated (between and July 13 and July 30, 1927), box 36, folder 5, ASPR.

36. Mary Craig Sinclair to Walter Prince, April 15, 1928, box 36, folder 5, ASPR.

37. Ibid.

38. Ibid.

39. Ibid.

40. Walter Prince to Mary Craig Sinclair, April 26, 1928, box 36, folder 5, ASPR.

41. Mary Sinclair to Walter Prince, undated (between January 5 and 13, 1928), box 36, folder 5, ASPR.

42. Upton Sinclair, *Mental Radio* (New York: Albert & Charles Boni, 1930), 39.

43. Ibid., 22.

44. Ibid., 21.

45. E.g., Laura Otis, *Membranes* (Baltimore: Johns Hopkins University Press, 2000); Galvan, *Sympathetic Medium*; Roger Luckhurst, *The Invention of Telepathy, 1870–1901* (Oxford: Oxford University Press, 2002). For mesmeric fiction in the American context, see David A. Zimmerman, "Frank Norris, Market Panic, and the Mesmeric Sublime," *American Literature* 75, no. 1 (2003): 61–90.

46. Carroll Smith-Rosenberg, "The Hysterical Woman: Sex Roles and Role Conflict in Nineteenth-Century America," in *Disorderly Conduct: Visions of Gender in Victorian America* (New York: Oxford University Press, 1986), 197–216; Luckhurst, *Invention of Telepathy*, 189–90.

47. Some representative texts include Annie Ritz Militz, *Prosperity through Knowledge and Power of Mind*, 4th ed. (Los Angeles: Master Mind, 1916);Frank C. Haddock, *The Personal Atmosphere* (Meriden, CT.: Pelton, 1918); Elizabeth Towne, *Practical Methods for Self-Development* (Holyoke, MA: Towne, 1904); Thomson Jay Hudson, *The Law of Psychic Phenomena* (1893; Chicago: McClurg, 1910); R. Osgood Mason, *Telepathy and the Subliminal Mind* (New York: Henry Holt, 1899).

48. For Charcot's model of nervous economy, very much influenced by mesmerism and magnetism, see Jan Goldstein, *Console and Classify: The French Psychiatric Profession in the Nineteenth Century* (Cambridge: Cambridge University Press, 1987), 326–27.

49. As in S. Weir Mitchell's *Fat and Blood* (Philadelphia: J.B. Lippincott & Co., 1877).

50. Otis, *Membranes*, 45–50.

51. Silas Weir Mitchell, *Dr. North and His Friends* (New York: The Century Co., 1900) 95–97.

52. For background on Eddy and Christian Science, especially as they emerge from America's long fascination with mesmerism, see Robert C. Fuller, *Mesmerism and the American Cure of Souls* (Philadelphia: University of Pennsylvania Press, 1982).

53. Kristin Kobes Du Mez, *A New Gospel for Women: Katharine Bushnell and the Challenge of Christian Feminism* (New York: Oxford University Press, 2015), 47–48.

54. Cynthia Schrager, "Mark Twain and Mary Baker Eddy: Gendering the Transpersonal Subject," *American Literature* 70, no. 1 (March 1, 1998): 29–62.

55. Letter from Mary Craig Sinclair to Walter Prince, undated, box 36, folder 5, ASPR. Eddy used the term "materia medica" to denote medico-scientific materialism, rather than pharmaceutical substances. Mary Baker Eddy, *Science and Health* (Boston: Christian Scientist Publishing Company, 1875), 18–19.

56. Sinclair, *Mental Radio*, 25. Sinclair's paternalistic tone was an often criticized aspect of his rhetorical style, although he respected the aims of early-century feminists, many of whom were his friends and political allies.

57. Ibid.

58. See Annmarie Adams, *Architecture in the Family Way: Doctors, Houses, and Women*, 1870–1900 (Montreal and Kingston: McGill-Queen's Press, 1996).

59. John Durham Peters, *Speaking into the Air: A History of the Idea of Communication* (Chicago: University of Chicago Press, 2001),, 63–65.

60. John C. Gunn and Johnson H. Jordan, *Gunn's New Domestic Physician, Or, Home Book of Health: A Complete Guide for Families . . .* (Cincinnati: Moore, Wilstach & Keys & Company, 1861).

61. Ibid.

62. Peters, *Speaking into the Air*, 66–77.

63. Peters, *Speaking into the Air*, 107.

64. Sinclair, *Mental Radio*, 30–32.

65. Prince, "The Sinclair Experiments for Telepathy," 151.

66. Sinclair, *Mental Radio*, 33.

67. Alan Gauld, *The Founders of Psychical Research* (New York: Routledge & K. Paul, 1968), 13.

68. Prince, "The Sinclair Experiments for Telepathy," 154.

69. Ibid., 155.

70. Ibid., 156, and Prince, *The Enchanted Boundary: Being a Survey of Negative Reactions to Claims of Psychic Phenomena* 1820 *to* 1930 (Boston: Boston Society for Psychic Research, 1930), 6–8.

71. Ibid.

72. Thurschwell, *Magical Thinking*, 86–87, 105–10.

73. Charles Sedgwick Minot explicated these problems in his "Second Report on Experimental Psychology: Upon the Diagram-Tests," *PASPR* 1:4 (1886): 302–17.

74. Sinclair, *Mental Radio*, 15.

75. Prince, "The Sinclair Experiments for Telepathy," 183.

76. Ibid., 182.

77. Ibid., 239.

78. Ibid., 153.

79. Ibid., 203.

80. For examples and discussion of the contingencies that led to the dominance of the laboratory in twentieth-century academic psychology, see Kurt Danziger, *Constructing the Subject: Historical Origins of Psychological Research* (Cambridge: Cambridge University Press, 1994); Deborah J. Coon, "Standardizing the Subject: Experimental Psychologists, Introspection, and the Quest for a Technoscientific Ideal," *Technology and Culture* 34, no. 4 (October 1993): 757–83; and Coon, "Testing the Limits of Sense and Science: American Experimental Psychologists Combat Spiritualism, 1880–1920," *American Psychologist* 47, no. 2 (1992): 143–51.

81. For an overview of these issues in recent psychology and neuroscience, see Suparna Choudhury and Jan Slaby, eds., *Critical Neuroscience: A Handbook of*

the Social and Cultural Contexts of Neuroscience (Hoboken, NJ: Wiley, 2011); and Nikolas S. Rose and Joelle M. Abi-Rached, *Neuro: The New Brain Sciences and the Management of the Mind* (Princeton, NJ: Princeton University Press, 2013).

82. Sinclair, *Southern Belle*, 403.

83. Ibid.

Loss

1. John Jay Chapman, "William James," in *William James Remembered*, ed. Linda Simon (Lincoln: University of Nebraska Press, 1999), 50.

2. *Henry James Letters*, vol. 4 (Cambridge, MA: Harvard University Press, 1974–84), 561–62, quoted in Robert D. Richardson, *William James: In the Maelstrom of American Modernism: A Biography* (New York: Houghton Mifflin Harcourt, 2007), 521.

3. "$10,000 Offered to Quote Letter," Associated Press wire, New York, October 5, 1910.

4. "Did the Words Come from beyond the Grave," *New York Herald*, November 20, 1910.

5. "Influence of Hysteria on 'Spirit Messages,'" *Cleveland Plain Dealer*, May 28, 1911.

6. Carlo Ginzburg, "Morelli, Freud, and Sherlock Holmes: Clues and Scientific Method," trans. Anna Davin, *History Workshop Journal*, no. 9 (1980): 5–36.

7. Hyslop, "Prospectus of Experiments since the Death of Professor James," *JASPR* 6 (1912): 269.

8. "New Yirk [sic] News," *New Advocate*, Baton Rouge, June 22, 1912.

9. "A Ghost Photographed," *Philadelphia Inquirer*, November 14, 1910.

10. "Influence of Hysteria on 'Spirit Messages,'" *Cleveland Plain Dealer*, May 28, 1911.

11. "Pajamas from Spirit Land," *Charlotte Observer*, June 22, 1912.

12. "James's Spirit Warns Hyslop," *Bridgeport Evening Farmer*, Bridgeport, Conn., January 21, 1913.

13. James H. Hyslop, "A Case of Hysteria," *PASPR* 5, 1911: 634.

14. Henry James to Theodate Pope, January 12, 1912, in *Henry James, Selected Letters* (Cambridge, MA: Harvard University Press, 1987), 394.

15. Ibid.

16. James H. Hyslop, "A Case of Musical Control," *PASPR* 7, 1913: 433.

17. "Did the Words Come from beyond the Grave," *New York Herald*, November 20, 1910.

18. *Henry James Letters*, vol. 4 (Cambridge, MA: Harvard University Press, 1974–84), 561–62, quoted in Richardson, *Maelstrom*, 521.

Chapter 5: The Wilderness of Insanity

1. Quoted in Josiah Royce, "Report of the Committee on Phantasms and Presentiments" and "Appendix to the Report," *PASPR* 1 (1885): 380–81, 449.

2. In the discussions that follow, *madness* is used as a general term that

encompasses abnormal or disturbed thought and action as well as behaviors perceived as irrational. *Insanity* was used in the period under discussion to denote a pathological clinical condition affecting the brain and behavior, though of course it also appeared in informal vernacular usage.

3. Walter Franklin Prince, *The Psychic in the House* (Boston: Boston Society for Psychical Research, 1926).

4. W. Lambert to Richard Hodgson, February 8, 1894. Series 35, box 36, folder 1, ASPR. Though Spiritualists, Theosophists, and other occult practitioners cultivated similar abilities, Lambert's apparent isolation from such communities and his claims to exercise his skills in public on unsuspecting subjects would have marked him as deluded.

5. Joseph Jastrow, *Fact and Fable in Psychology* (New York: Houghton, Mifflin and Co., 1900), vii.

6. James Hervy Hyslop, "Objects of the Institute," *JASPR* 1:1 (1907): 19.

7. Quoted in Frank Podmore, Frederic William Henry Myers, and Edmund Gurney, *Phantasms of the Living* (London: Society for Psychical Research, 1886), 209.

8. Charles Sanders Peirce, "Mr. Peirce's Rejoinder," *PASPR* 1 (1885): 92.

9. William James, *The Varieties of Religious Experience: A Study in Human Nature* (New York: Modern Library, 1902), 26.

10. Beard's first medical exposition of neurasthenia came in the *Boston Medical and Surgical Journal* in 1869, with his widely cited book, *American Nervousness*, appearing in 1881.

11. George Miller Beard, *American Nervousness, Its Causes and Consequences* (New York: Putnam, 1881), x.

12. William James recorded this statement of Peirce's in his notebook circa 1864; cited in Robert D. Richardson, *William James: In the Maelstrom of American Modernism* (New York: Houghton Mifflin Harcourt, 2007), 135.

13. James, *The Varieties of Religious Experience*, 5–11.

14. Ignas K. Skrupskelis and Elizabeth M. Berkeley, eds., *The Correspondence of William James* 12 (Charlottesville: University Press of Virginia, 2004), 487. Cited in Richardson, *In the Maelstrom*, 517.

15. Beard, *American Nervousness*, 17.

16. Peter Hucklenbroich, "Disease Entities and the Borderline between Health and Disease: Where Is the Place of Gradations?" in *Vagueness in Psychiatry: International Perspectives in Philosophy and Psychiatry*, eds. Geert Keil, Lara Keuck, and Rico Hauswald (Oxford, New York: Oxford University Press, 2016), 75–93.

17. Christine Ferguson, *Determined Spirits: Eugenics, Heredity and Racial Regeneration in Anglo-American Spiritualist Writing*, 1848–1930 (New York: Oxford University Press, 2012), 58.

18. Ora J. Parker to Walter F. Prince, January 3, 1920. Series 35, box 36, folder 1, ASPR.

19. James, *The Varieties of Religious Experience*, 159–60.

20. Ibid., 133.

21. George A. Thacher to George Hervy Hyslop, August 21, 1906, in Hyslop, "A Record of Experiences by G.A.T.," *PASPR Section B* 2:3 (1907): 546.

22. George Hervy Hyslop, "A Record of Experiences by G.A.T," *PASPR Section B* 2:3 (1907): 537.

23. United States House of Representatives, Committee on the District of Columbia, "Fortune Telling: Hearings before the Subcommittee on Judiciary . . . on H.R. 8989" (Washington: Government Printing Office, 1926), 6–7.

24. George Hervy Hyslop, "A Record of Experiences by G.A.T," *PASPR Section B* 2:3 (1907): 536-7.

25. Ibid., 593, 537.

26. Hyslop, "Objects of the Institute," *JASPR* 1:1 (1907): 22.

27. Ibid., 17.

28. Ferguson, *Determined Spirits*, 59–60.

29. Daniel Herman, "Whose Knocking? Spiritualism as Entertainment and Therapy in Nineteenth-Century San Francisco." *American Nineteenth Century History* 7, no. 3 (2006): 417–42.

30. Krister Dylan Knapp, *William James: Psychical Research and the Challenge of Modernity* (Chapel Hill: University of North Carolina Press Books, 2017), 52–56.

31. "Review of Report on Spiritualism of the Committee of the London Dialectical Society," *The Journal of Mental Science*, January 1872: 579.

32. James John Garth Wilkinson, *The Homoeopathic Principle Applied to Insanity* (Otis Clapp, 1857), 12–13. All subsequent Wilkinson quotes are from this pamphlet unless otherwise noted.

33. "Bibliographical Notices," *Boston Medical and Surgical Journal* (1853): 163.

34. Nellie Bly, *Ten Days in a Mad-House* (New York: Ian L. Munro, 1887), https://ebooks.adelaide.edu.au/b/bly/nellie/ten-days-in-a-mad-house/chapter13.html.

35. "Review: 'The Homeopathic Principle Applied to Insanity,'" *The Asylum Journal of Mental Science* 4:25 (1858): 367.

36. Henry C. Preston, "Review: 'The Homeopathic Principle Applied to Insanity,'" *The North American Journal of Homeopathy* 6 (1857), 106. See Preston's biography in Thomas Lindsley Bradford, *Biographies of Homeopathic Physicians, Volume 25: Percy—Quisling* (Philadelphia: Hahnemann Medical College, 1916), 304–5.

37. William H. Holcombe, "A Proposal to Treat Lunacy by Spiritualism," *The North American Journal of Homeopathy* 6 (1857): 259.

38. Ralph Waldo Emerson, *Journals and Miscellaneous Notebooks: 1847–1848* (Cambridge, MA: Harvard University Press, 1960), 146.

39. Knapp, *William James*, 55–56.

40. Andreas Sommer, "Are You Afraid of the Dark? Notes on the Psychology of Belief in Histories of Science and the Occult," *European Journal of Psychotherapy & Counselling* 18, no. 2 (2016): 116. On the "will to disbelieve," see Thomas Nagel, "Evolutionary Naturalism and the Fear of Religion," in *The Last Word* (Oxford: Oxford University Press, 1997), 127–43.

41. William James, "The Psychology of Belief," *Mind* 14 (1889): 322.

42. On Henry James Sr.'s "vastation," see Henry James, Sr., *Society: The Redeemed Form of Man* (Boston: Houghton, Osgood, & Co., 1879), 44–45; and William James, ed., *The Literary Remains of Henry James* (New York: Houghton Mifflin, 1884), 59–64.

43. William James to Henry James, April 13, 1868, in *William and Henry James: Selected Letters*, eds. Ignas K. Skrupskelis and Elizabeth M. Berkeley (Richmond: University of Virginia Press, 1997), 32.

44. This brief summary of James's complex relationship with Hamlet is based on George Cotkin's chapter, "Hamlet to Habit," in *William James, Public Philosopher* (Baltimore: Johns Hopkins University Press, 1990), 40–72.

45. Biographers disagree about the precise date of James's panic-fear; it likely occurred in 1870, but possibly in 1872. See Richardson, *In the Maelstrom*, 543.

46. James, *The Varieties of Religious Experience*, 157–58.

47. For the history of this cultural stigma, see Jeannette Stirling, *Representing Epilepsy: Myth and Matter* (Liverpool: Liverpool University Press, 2010), 67–71.

48. James, *The Varieties of Religious Experience*, 157.

49. William James to Frank Abauzit, June 1, 1904. William James Correspondence, Series I. Houghton Library, Harvard University.

50. Charles Taylor, *Sources of the Self: The Making of the Modern Identity* (Cambridge: Cambridge University Press, 1992).

51. James, *The Varieties of Religious Experience*, 159.

52. William James to Henry P. Bowditch, January 24, 1869, in *The Letters of William James*, ed. Henry James (Boston: Atlantic Monthly Press, 1920), 149.

53. Jane Maher, *Biography of Broken Fortunes: Wilkie and Bob, Brothers of William, Henry, and Alice James* (Hamden, CT: Archon Books, 1986).

54. "Results of Psychical Research," *New York Times*, September 4, 1892. James had just renewed the sentiment in his August *Forum* essay, "What Psychical Research Has Accomplished."

55. Hyslop, "Objects of the Institute," *JASPR* 1:1 (1907): 18.

56. Pierre Janet, "Letter of Dr. Pierre Janet," *JASPR* 1 (1907): 88–92.

57. James H. Hyslop, *The Borderland of Psychical Research* (London: G. P. Putnam's Sons, 1906).

58. For a summary of this literature by one of its originators, see Thomas F. Gieryn, *Cultural Boundaries of Science: Credibility on the Line* (Chicago: University of Chicago Press, 1999).

59. Hyslop, *Borderland of Psychical Research*, 388.

60. John Beloff, "The Rhine Legacy," *Philosophical Psychology* 2, no. 2 (January 1, 1989): 231–39.

61. Ibid., 231.

62. Scott D. Rogo, "Psi and Psychosis: A Review of the Experimental Evidence," *The Journal of Parapsychology* 39, no. 2 (1975): 170.

63. Montague Ullman, "Psychical Research: A Personal Perspective," *The Psi Researcher* 22, August 1996.

64. J. B. Rhine, "Psi Phenomena and Psychiatry," *Proceedings of the Royal Society of Medicine* 43, no. 11 (November 1, 1950): 804. For a study of how the "residues of the uncanny" arising from psychoanalytic transference persist in Kleinian projective identification, see Mikita Brottman, *Phantoms of the Clinic: From Thought-Transference to Projective Identification* (New York: Karnac Books, 2011).

65. Ullman, "Psychical Research."

66. Stanley Krippner, "The Maimonides ESP-Dream Studies," *Journal of Parapsychology* 57 (1993): 43.

67. Montague Ullman, "Psi and Psychiatry: The Need for Restructuring Basic Concepts," *Parapsychology Research*, 1972. http://www.siivola.org/monte/papers_grouped/copyrighted/Parapsychology_&_Psi/Psi_%20and_Psychiatry.htm.

68. Ullman, "Psychical Research."

69. Ibid.

70. These accounts of the ASPR's activities in the 1970s and 80s come from conversations with Patrice Keane, who assisted Ullman in that period and has served as the society's executive director since 1993.

Conclusion: To Keep Alive and Heap Up Data

1. J. B. Rhine to James Bryant Conant, November 16, 1936, box 1, folder 11, Duke University Archives, William McDougall Papers 1892–1982.

2. "Harvard Recognizes Psychical Research: First American University to Take It Up," *New York Times* (January 20, 1913).

3. Ibid.

4. Among many of his public criticisms, see Hugo Münsterberg, "Communicating with the Dead," *New York Tribune* (November 3, 1907), 13.

5. See discussion of James's legacy in Arthur Still, "Introduction," *History of the Human Sciences* 8, no. 1 (February 1, 1995): 2–3; Edward Reed, "The Psychologist's Fallacy as a Persistent Framework in William James's Psychological Theorizing," *History of the Human Sciences* 8, no. 1 (February 1, 1995): 63–64.

6. "James's Spirit Warns Hyslop," *Bridgeport Evening Farmer*, January 21, 1913.

7. Bainbridge Bunting, *Harvard: An Architectural History* (Cambridge, MA: Harvard University Press, 1998), 239.

8. Egil Asprem, "A Nice Arrangement of Heterodoxies: William McDougall and the Professionalization of Psychical Research," *Journal of the History of the Behavioral Sciences* 46, no. 2 (April 12, 2010): 131. This conflict is made explicit in John Broadus Watson and William McDougall, *The Battle of Behaviorism: An Exposition and an Exposure* (New York: W. W. Norton, 1929).

9. Egil Asprem, *The Problem of Disenchantment: Scientific Naturalism and Esoteric Discourse* 1900–1939 (Leiden, The Netherlands: Brill, 2014), 375–88.

10. William James, "On Some Omissions of Introspective Psychology," *Mind* 9, no. 33 (1884): 18–19.

11. William James, "Address of the President before the Society for Psychical Research," *Science* 3, no. 77 (June 19, 1896): 885.

12. Rebecca Lemov, *Database of Dreams: The Lost Quest to Catalog Humanity* (New Haven, CT: Yale University Press, 2015).

13. Michael D. Mumford, "An Evaluation of Remote Viewing: Research and Applications" (The American Institutes for Research, September 1995).

14. Rebecca Lemov, "X-Rays of Inner Worlds: The Mid-Twentieth-Century American Projective Test Movement," *Journal of the History of the Behavioral Sciences* 47, no. 3 (Summer 2011); Merve Emre, *The Personality Brokers: The Strange History of Myers-Briggs and the Birth of Personality Testing* (New York: Doubleday, 2018).

15. John McCumber, *The Philosophy Scare: The Politics of Reason in the Early Cold War* (Chicago: University of Chicago Press, 2016), 55–66.

16. Katherine Pandora, "Popular Science in National and Transnational Perspective: Suggestions from the American Context," *Isis* 100, no. 2 (June 1, 2009): 357; Science Service Records, circa 1910–1963, SIA RU007091, Smithsonian Institution Archives.

17. William James, "The Confidences of a Psychical Researcher," *The American Magazine* (1909): 589.

BIBLIOGRAPHY

Abbreviations

ASPR   Material from the archives of the American Society for Psychical Research is indicated by folder and box numbers with the repository abbreviated as ASPR.

JASPR *Journal of the American Society for Psychical Research*

PASPR *Proceedings of the American Society for Psychical Research*

PSPR *Proceedings of the Society for Psychical Research* (UK)

Primary Sources

Abbe, Cleveland. *The Aims and Methods of Meteorological Work: Especially as Conducted by National and State Weather Services.* The Baltimore: Johns Hopkins Press, 1899.

Alger, Horatio, Jr. *Ragged Dick, Or, Street Life in New York with the Boot-Blacks.* Boston: Loring, 1868.

American Provers' Union. "Suggestions for the Proving of Drugs on the Healthy; Report of the Committee Appointed for That Purpose . . . " Philadelphia: American Provers' Union, 1853, 6.

Anonymous. "Chapter on Dreams." *Harper's New Monthly Magazine,* May 1851.

"The Art of Little Children." *Pedagogical Seminary* 3, no. 2 (October 1, 1895).

Atkinson, William Walker. *Practical Mental Influence and Mental Fascination: A Course of Lessons on Mental Vibrations, Psychic Influence, Personal Magnetism, Fascination, Psychic Self-Protection, Etc.* . . . Chicago: Advanced Thought Publishing Company, 1908.

Baldwin, J. Mark. "Imitation: A Chapter in the Natural History of Consciousness." *Mind,* New Series, 3, no. 9 (January 1, 1894): 26–55.

Barnes, Earl. "A Study on Children's Drawings." *Pedagogical Seminary* 2, no. 1 (January 1, 1892).

Bayley, Weston D. "Dropsy (A Fragment)," *The Hahnemannian Monthly* (1901): 443, 447.

———. "Hereditary Spastic Paraplegia." *Journal of Nervous and Mental Disease* 24, no. 11 (1897): 697–701.

———. "The Therapeutic Result." *The Hahnemannian Monthly* 38 (1903): 23–24.

Beals, Edward A. "Psychic Effects of the Weather." *American Meteorological Journal. A Monthly Review of Meteorology and Allied Branches of Study* 12, no. 2 (June 1895).

Beard, George Miller. *American Nervousness, Its Causes and Consequences: A Supplement to Nervous Exhaustion (Neurasthenia)*. New York: Putnam, 1881.

———. *The Scientific Basis of Delusions: A New Theory of Trance, and Its Bearings on Human Testimony*. New York: G. P. Putnams' Sons, 1877.

Belcher, James J. "The Romance of Sleep." *Harper's New Monthly Magazine*, April 1867.

Berg, Louis M. "Rom Romano, Mystic, Identified as Count." *Miami News*, March 26, 1926.

"Bibiographical Notices." *Boston Medical and Surgical Journal* (1853).

Bierce, Ambrose. "Visions of the Night." In *The Collected Works of Ambrose Bierce . . . : In Motley: Kings of Beasts: Two Administrations; Miscellaneous*. New York and Washington: The Neale Publishing Co., 1911.

Blackburn, Douglas. "Confessions of a Famous Medium," *John Bull* (December 5, 1908): 590.

———. "Ghosts and Mediums I Have Known." *Tonbridge Free Press*, February 18, 1920.

———. "My Masterpiece," *John Bull* (January 9, 1909), 39.

———. *Thought-Reading, Or, Modern Mysteries Explained: Being Chapters on Thought-Reading, Occultism, Mesmerism, &c., Forming a Key to the Psychological Puzzles of the Day*. London: Field & Tuer: Simpkin, Marshall & Co.: Hamilton, Adams & Co., 1884.

Blair, Mrs. *Dreams and Dreaming Philosophically and Scripturally Considered: Illustrated by Several Remarkable Instances, All Well Authenticated*. London: G. Groombridge, 1843.

Bly, Nellie. *Ten Days in a Mad-House*. New York: Ian L. Munro, 1887.

Bonner, John. "Dream-Reading." *Harper's New Monthly Magazine*, April 1866.

Bradford, Thomas Lindsley. *Biographies of Homeopathic Physicians, Volume 25: Percy—Quisling*. Philadelphia: Hahnemann Medical College, 1916, 304–5.

Brain, W. Russell. "Visual Object-Agnosia with Special Reference to the Gestalt Theory." *Brain* 64, no. 1 (1941): 43–62.

Bray, Charles. *On Force, Its Mental and Moral Correlates; and on That Which Is Supposed to Underlie All Phenomena: With Speculations on Spiritualism, and Other Abnormal Conditions of Mind*. London: Longmans & Company, 1866.

Brewer, Ebenezer Cobham. *A Guide to the Scientific Knowledge of Things Familiar*. New York: J. Miller, 1864.

Brittan, Samuel Byron. *The Spiritual Telegraph*. London: Partridge & Brittan, 1854.

Britten, Emma Hardinge. *Modern American Spiritualism: A Twenty Years' Record of the Communion between Earth and the World of Spirits*. New York: Author, 1870.

Bruce, H. Addington. "The Ghost Society And What Came of It." *Outlook (1893–1924)*, February 26, 1910.

Buckley, J. M. "Presentiments, Visions, and Apparitions." *Century Illustrated Magazine (1881–1906)*, July 1889.

Burlingame, Hardin J. *Leaves from Conjurers' Scrap Books; Or, Modern Magicians and Their Works.* Donohue, Henneberry & Company, 1891.

Caird, Mona. *The Morality of Marriage: And Other Essays on the Status and Destiny of Woman.* Cambridge: Cambridge University Press, 2010.

Carpenter, William Benjamin. *Principles of Mental Physiology: With Their Applications to the Training and Discipline of the Mind, and the Study of Its Morbid Conditions.* London: H. S. King & Co., 1876.

Chater, R. D. *Latest Sleights, Illusions, Mind Reading, and New Card Effects*, 1903.

Circular of the American Aelloscope Company of Rochester. Rochester, NY, 1866. Bound with Abbe, Cleveland, *Historical Notes on the Systems of Weather Telegraphy, and Especially Their Development in the United States.* American Philosophical Society Library, 1871.

Clum, Henry A. Barometer. U.S. Patent No. US28454 A, issued May 29, 1860.

———. Barometer. U.S. Patent No. US32050 A, issued April 16, 1861.

Cockerell, T.D.A. "The Borderland of Psychical Research." *The Dial; a Semi-Monthly Journal of Literary Criticism, Discussion, and Information (1880–1929)*, February 16, 1910.

Colonial and Revolutionary Families of Pennsylvania: Genealogical and Personal Memoirs. New York: Lewis Historical Publishing Company, 1911.

Coover, John Edgar. *Experiments in Psychical Research at Leland Stanford Junior University.* Stanford, CA: Stanford University, 1917.

Coues, Elliott. *Signs of the Times, from the Standpoint of a Scientist: An Address Delivered at the First Methodist Church, April 26, 1888, under the Auspices of the Western Society for Psychical Research.* Chicago: Religio-Philosophical Publishing House, 1889.

Cox, Edward W. *Spiritualism Answered by Science.* New York: H. L. Hinton, 1872.

Creevey, Thomas, and Herbert Maxwell. *The Creevey Papers: A Selection from the Correspondence & Diaries of Thomas Creevey, M.P., Born 1768—Died 1838; Edited by Sir Herbert Maxwell.* London: Murray, 1904.

Crichton-Browne, Sir James. "Occultism and Telepathic Experiments." *The Westminster Gazette*, January 29, 1908.

Crothers, Thomas Davison. "Mental Atmosphere: Does It Influence the Progress of Disease?" *Medical and Surgical Reporter (1858–1898)* 29, no. 6 (August 9, 1873): 98.

———. "Spiritism, Telepathy, Hypnotism and the Case of Mrs. Piper." In Clark Bell, ed., *Spiritism, Hypnotism and Telepathy as Involved in the Case of Mrs. Leonora E. Piper.* New York: Medico-legal Journal, 1902: 85–88.

———. *The Trance State in Inebriety: Its Medico-Legal Relations.* Hartford, CT: Case, Lockwood & Brainard Company, 1882.

Cumberland, Stuart C. *A Thought-Reader's Thoughts, Being the Impressions and*

Confessions of Stuart Cumberland . . . London: S. Low, Marston, Searle & Rivington, Limited, 1888.

Darwin, Charles. *The Correspondence of Charles Darwin,* edited by Frederick Burkhardt et al. Vol. 3. Cambridge: Cambridge University Press, 2014.

Davenport Academy of Natural Sciences. *Proceedings of the Davenport Academy of Natural Sciences.* Davenport, Iowa, Academy of Natural Sciences [etc.], 1883.

Day, George D. "What Is Thought-Transference?" *Cassell's Family Magazine,* October 1884, 621–23.

Dendy, Walter Cooper. *On the Phenomena of Dreams, and Other Transient Illusions.* Whittaker, Treacher & Co., 1832.

De Quincey, Thomas. *The English Mail-Coach and Joan of Arc.* London: Ginn & Company, 1902.

Dexter, Edwin G. "The Child and the Weather." *Journal of Genetic Psychology,* 1898, 512–22.

———. "Conduct and the Weather: An Inductive Study of the Mental Effects of Definite Meteorological Conditions." *The Psychological Review: Monograph Supplements* II, no. 6 (1899): 1–89.

———. "Drunkenness and the Weather." *Annals of the American Academy of Political and Social Science* 16 (November 1, 1900): 77–90.

———. "Ethics and the Weather." *International Journal of Ethics* 11, no. 4 (1901): 481–92.

"Did the Words Come from beyond the Grave?" *New York Herald,* November 20, 1910.

"A Disastrous Boiler Explosion a Pedestrian Killed and Rails Displaced by the Flying Shell." *Philadelphia Inquirer,* August 3, 1890, 1.

Donkin, Horatio B. "A Note on Thought-Reading." *Nineteenth Century,* 1882.

———. "Occultism and Common Sense." *Westminster Gazette,* November 27, 1907.

"Dr. Thomas Davison Crothers." *British Medical Journal* 1, no. 2993 (May 11, 1918): 550.

The Dreamer's Oracle and Faithful Interpreter, Wherein Is Explained All the Phenomena of Spiritual Imagination in Dreams. London: J. March, 1861.

Du Maurier, George. *Trilby.* New York: Harper and Brothers, 1894.

Eddy, Mary Baker. *Science and Health.* Boston: Christian Scientist Publishing Company, 1875.

Editor of the Journal of Practical Metaphysics. "Mental Atmosphere and Disease." *Health [a Monthly Devoted to the Cause and Cure of Disease],* 1899, 209–13.

Ellis, Havelock. *The World of Dreams.* Boston: Houghton Mifflin, 1922.

Emerson, Ralph Waldo. *Journals and Miscellaneous Notebooks: 1847–1848.* Cambridge, MA: Harvard University Press, 1960.

Emery, Philip A. *Rational Dream Book: The Science of Dreams, Volume 1.* Chicago: M. A. Emery and Son, 1876.

Estabrooks, G. H. "The Enigma of Telepathy." *The North American Review* 227, no. 2 (February 1, 1929): 201–11.

"The Fatal Boiler Again." *New York Herald*, August 10, 1883, 4.

Force, M. F. *Some Considerations on the Mound Builders*. Cincinnati: R. Clarke & Co., n.d.

———. "Some Considerations on the Mound Builders. A Paper Read before the Cincinnati Literary Club." *Cincinnati Daily Gazette*, June 26, 1873.

Foster, John Wells. *Prehistoric Races of the United States*. Chicago: S. C. Griggs & Co., 1873.

Fowke, Gerald. "Popular Errors Regarding Mound Builders and Indians." *Ohio Archæological and Historical Quarterly*, 1888, 380–403.

Fraser, Charles. "The Moral Influence of Steam." *Merchants' Magazine and Commercial Review* (June, 1846).

Freud, Sigmund. *On Aphasia: A Critical Study*. Translated by E. Stengle. New York: International Universities Press, 1953.

———. *The Interpretation of Dreams*. 8th ed., rev. New York: Avon, 1965.

Gale, Harlow. "Psychical Research in American Universities." *Proceedings of the Society for Psychical Research* 13 (1898): 583–88.

Galton, Francis. *Inquiries into Human Faculty and Its Development*. New York: E. P. Dutton & Co., 1907.

Garretson, James Edmund. *Nineteenth Century Sense: The Paradox of Spiritualism*. Philadelphia: J. B. Lippincott, 1887.

Gault, Robert H. "A History of the Questionnaire Method of Research in Psychology." *The Pedagogical Seminary*, 1906, 366–83.

Godwin-Austen, R. B. "A Case of Visual Disorientation." *Journal of Neurology, Neurosurgery & Psychiatry* 28, no. 5 (October 1, 1965): 453–58.

Goode, G. Brown. *An Account of the Smithsonian Institution: Its Origin, History, Objects and Achievements*. Washington, DC: The Smithsonian Institution, 1895, 6.

Goodenough, Florence L. *Measurement of Intelligence by Drawings*. Chicago: World Book Company, 1926.

Gunn, John C. and Johnson H. Jordan. *Gunn's New Domestic Physician, Or, Home Book of Health: A Complete Guide for Families . . .* Cincinnati: Moore, Wilstach & Keys & Company, 1861.

Gurney, Edmund. "Psychical Research." *Science* 4, no. 96 (December 5, 1884): 509–11.

Haddock, Frank Channing. *The Personal Atmosphere: Ten Studies in Poise and Power*. Meriden, CT: Pelton Publishing Co., 1918.

Hafez, Ibraham Ali Mahomed [pseud]. *The New and Complete Fortune Teller: Being a Treatise on the Art of Foretelling Future Events by Dreams, Moles, Cards, &c. &c. &c.* New York: Richard Scott, George Largin, 1816.

Hall, Granville Stanley. *Aspects of Child Life and Education*. New York: D. Appleton and Company, 1921.

———. "The Contents of Children's Minds on Entering School." *Princeton Review*, May 1883, 249–72.

———. *Educational Problems*. New York: D. Appleton and Company, 1911.

———. "Some Aspects of the Early Sense of Self." *The American Journal of Psychology* 9, no. 3 (April 1, 1898): 351–95.

Hammond, William Alexander. *Sleep and Its Derangements*. Philadelphia: J. B. Lippincott, 1869.

Hare, Robert. *Experimental Investigation of the Spirit Manifestations: Demonstrating the Existence of Spirits and Their Communion with Mortals, Doctrine of the Spirit World Respecting Heaven, Hell, Mortality, and God: Also, the Influence of Scripture on the Morals of Christians*. Partridge & Brittan, 1856.

———. "Objections to Mr. Redfield's Theory of Storms." *American Journal of Science*, 1842, 140–46.

———. "On Free Electricity." *The London Journal of Arts and Sciences (and Repertory of Patent Inventions) [afterword]. Newton's London Journal of Arts and Sciences*, 1847, 142–44.

Hartmann, William C. *Hartmann's Who's Who in Occultism, New Thought, Psychism and Spiritualism*. 2nd ed. Jamaica, NY: The Occult Press, 1927.

"Harvard Recognizes Psychical Research: First American University to Take It Up." *New York Times*, January 20, 1913.

Hazard, Samuel. *Hazard's Register of Pennsylvania*. W. F. Geddes, 1835.

Head, Sir Henry. *Aphasia and Kindred Disorders of Speech*. Cambridge: Cambridge University Press, 1926.

Henry, Joseph. "Meteorology." In *Congressional Serial Set*. U.S. Government Printing Office, 1859.

Hollenbeck, Ernest. "Letters." *Cement World* 7 (1913): 90.

———. "Winter-Made Jellies." *Watson's Magazine* 6 (1906): 274.

Holcombe, William H. "A Proposal to Treat Lunacy by Spiritualism." *The North American Journal of Homeopathy* 6 (1857): 259.

Holmes, Oliver Wendell. *Mechanism in Thought and Morals. An Address Delivered before the Phi Beta Kappa Society of Harvard University, June 29, 1870*. Boston: J. R. Osgood & Co., 1871.

Hovey, William Alfred. *Mind-Reading and Beyond*. Boston: Lee and Shepard; New York: C. T. Dillingham, 1885.

Hudson, Thomson Jay. *The Law of Psychic Phenomena*. Chicago: McClurg, 1910. First published 1893.

Hyslop, J. H. *The Borderland of Psychical Research*. London: G. P. Putnam's Sons, 1906.

———. "Thought-Transference and Telepathy." *The Independent . . . Devoted to the Consideration of Politics, Social and Economic Tendencies, History, Literature, and the Arts*, April 30, 1891.

"Influence of Hysteria on 'Spirit Messages.'" *Cleveland Plain Dealer*, May 28, 1911.

"The Influence of the Weather on the Mental State." *Woman's Medical Journal* 7 (1898): 243–44.

"Influence of Weather upon Mind." *Scientific American*, June 9, 1894.

"Influence of Weather upon Mind." *Phrenological Journal and Science of Health*, 97, no. 5 (May 1894): 264.

James, Henry. *Henry James, Selected Letters*. Cambridge, MA: Harvard University Press, 1987.

James, Henry, Sr. *Society: The Redeemed Form of Man.* Boston: Houghton, Osgood, & Co., 1879.

James, William. "Address of the President before the Society for Psychical Research." *Science* 3, no. 77 (June 19, 1896): 881–88.

———. "A Case of Automatic Writing." *Popular Science Monthly,* January 1904, 195–201.

———. "Comment and Criticism." *Science* 7, no. 156 (January 29, 1886): 89.

———. "The Confidences of a Psychical Researcher." *The American Magazine,* 1909, 580–89.

———. *The Correspondence of William James,* edited by Ignas K. Skrupskelis and Elizabeth M. Berkeley. 12 vols. Charlottesville: University Press of Virginia, 1992–2004.

———. *Essays in Psychical Research.* Cambridge, MA: Harvard University Press, 1986.

———. "Great Men and Their Environment." In *The Will to Believe: And Other Essays in Popular Philosophy.* New York: Longmans, Green, and Co., 1911.

———. *The Letters of William James,* edited by Henry James. New York: Atlantic Monthly Press, 1920.

———, ed. *The Literary Remains of Henry James.* New York: Houghton Mifflin, 1884.

———. "Mssrs. Lehmann and Hansen on Telepathy." *Science* IX, no. 227 (May 5, 1899): 654–55.

———. "On Some Omissions of Introspective Psychology." *Mind* 9, no. 33 (1884): 18–19.

———. "A Plea for Psychology as a 'Natural Science.'" *Philosophical Review* I, no. 2: 153–55.

———. *Pragmatism: A New Name for Some Old Ways of Thinking.* New York: Longman Green and Co., 1907.

———. *The Principles of Psychology,* Vol. 1. New York: Henry Holt and Co., 1890.

———. *The Principles of Psychology,* Vol. 2. London: MacMillan and Co., 1891.

———. *The Principles of Psychology,* Authorized Ed., Unabridged. Dover Publications, 1918.

———. "Professor Newcomb's Address before the American Society for Psychical Research." *Science* 7, no. 157 (February 5, 1886): 123.

———. "Psychical Research." *Psychological Review,* 1896, 649–52.

———. "Psychology and the Teaching Art." In *Talks to Teachers on Psychology, and to Students on Some of Life's Ideals,* 12–14. New York: H. Holt and Company, 1900.

———. "The Psychology of Belief." *Mind* 14 (1889).

———. *Some Problems Of Philosophy.* London: Longmans Green & Co., 1911.

———. *The Varieties of Religious Experience: A Study in Human Nature.* New York: Modern Library, 1902.

———. "What Psychical Research Has Accomplished." *Forum* 13 (August 1, 1892): 727.

"James's Spirit Warns Hyslop." *Bridgeport Evening Farmer*, Bridgeport, Conn., January 21, 1913.

Jastrow, Joseph. "The Case of Eusapia Palladino." *Review of Reviews* 41, no. July (1910): 74–84.

———. *Fact and Fable in Psychology*. New York: Houghton, Mifflin and Co., 1900.

———. "The Logic Of Mental Telepathy." *Scribner's Magazine*, 1895.

———. "Psychological Notes Upon Sleight-Of-Hand Experts." *Science*, New Series, 3, no. 71 (May 8, 1896): 685–89.

———. "The Unmasking of Paladino. An Actual Observation of the Complete Machinery of the Famous Italian Medium." *Collier's*, 1910, 21–22, 40–42.

Jefferson, Thomas. *Notes on the State of Virginia*. London: Printed for John Stockdale, 1787.

Joint Committee on Meteorology of the American Philosophical Society and the Franklin Institute. *Directions for Making Meteorological Observations*. Philadelphia: 1837.

Knowles, James. "Wireless Telegraphy and Brain-Waves." *The Living Age*, 1899.

Lissauer, Heinrich, and Marianne Jackson. "A Case of Visual Agnosia with a Contribution to Theory." *Cognitive Neuropsychology* 5, no. 2 (1988): 157–92.

Loomis, Elias. *A Treatise on Meteorology*. New York: Harper & Brothers, 1868.

Lowell, James Russell. *Letters of James Russell Lowell*, edited by Charles Eliot Norton. Vol. II. New York: Harper & Brothers, 1893.

———. *Poems: A Fable for Critics. The Unhappy Lot of Mr. Knott. Fragments of an Unfinished Poem. An Original Apologue. Under the Willows, and Other Poems*. New York: Houghton, Mifflin, 1890.

Lukens, Herman T. "A Study of Children's Drawings in the Early Years." *Pedagogical Seminary* 4, no. 1 (October 1, 1896).

Macnish, Robert. *The Philosophy of Sleep*. London: W. R. M'Phun, 1827.

Mason, R. Osgood. *Telepathy and the Subliminal Mind*. New York: Henry Holt, 1899.

McCay, Winsor. "How the Rarebit Fiend Happened." *Idaho Daily Statesman*, October 15, 1907.

McDougall, William. *The Group Mind: A Sketch of the Principles of Collective Psychology, with Some Attempt to Apply Them to the Interpretation of National Life and Character*. 2nd ed., rev. New York, London: G. P. Putnam's Sons, 1928.

———. *Is America Safe for Democracy? Six Lectures Given at the Lowell Institute of Boston, under the Title "Anthropology and History, or The Influence of Anthropologic Constitution on the Destinies of Nations."* New York: C. Scribner's Sons, 1921.

———. "Psychical Research as a University Study." In *the Case for and against Psychical Belief*, edited by Carl Murchison. Worcester, MA: Clark University, 1927.

"The Mental Atmosphere." *Medical and Surgical Reporter* 29, no. 8 (August 23, 1873): 138.

"Mental Influence in the Treatment of Disease." *Medical and Surgical Reporter* (1858–1898) 72, no. 23 (June 8, 1895): 819.

"Mental Science: A Statistical Study of Sleep and Dreams." *Science* 13, no. 313 (February 1, 1889): 87–88.

Militz, Annie Ritz. *Prosperity through Knowledge and Power of Mind.* 4th ed. Los Angeles: Master Mind, 1916.

Minot, Charles Sedgwick. "The Problem of Consciousness in Its Biological Aspect." *Science* 16, no. 392 (1902): 1–12.

———. "The Psychical Comedy." *The North American Review* 160, no. 459 (1895): 217–30.

———. "Sedgwick Family Papers," n.d., Massachusetts Historical Society.

———. "Tricks in Mind-Reading." *The Youth's Companion (1827–1929)*, March 8, 1888.

"Minutes." *Proceedings of the Davenport Academy of Natural Sciences* IV (1883): 222.

Mitchell, Silas Weir. *Doctor and Patient.* Philadelphia: Lippincott, 1887.

———. *Dr. North and His Friends.* New York: The Century Co., 1900.

———. *Fat and Blood.* Philadelphia: J. B. Lippincott & Co., 1877.

Morris, Charles. "Psychic Research." *Lippincott's Magazine of Popular Literature and Science*, April 1885.

Mother Shipton (Ursula Southeil). *The Dreamer's Oracle: Being a Faithful Interpretation of Two Hundred Dreams?; to Which Is Added, A New Method of Eliciting from Cards the Knowledge of Our Destiny and Future Occurrence of Events: With a Plain Explanation of All Their Determinable Combinations.* Derby: T. Richardson, 1838.

Mumford, Michael D. "An Evaluation of Remote Viewing: Research and Applications." The American Institutes for Research, September 1995.

Münsterberg, Hugo. "The Case of Beulah Miller." *The Metropolitan Magazine*, 1913.

———. "Communicating with the Dead." *New York Tribune*, November 3, 1907, 13.

Murchison, Carl. *The Case for and against Psychical Belief.* Worcester, MA: Clark University, 1927.

The New Dream Book, Or, Interpretation of Remarkable Dreams: According to the Most Celebrated Authors and Philosophers. Boston: Printed for Nathaniel Coverly, 1818.

"New Yirk [*sic*] News." *New Advocate*, Baton Rouge, June 22, 1912.

Newcomb, S. "Can Ghosts Be Investigated?" *Science* 4, no. 97 (December 12, 1884): 525–27.

———. *His Wisdom, the Defender: A Story.* New York: Harper & Brothers, 1900.

———. "Professor Newcomb's Address before the American Society for Psychical Research." *Science* 7, no. 158 (February 12, 1886): 145–46.

———. "Psychic Force." *Science* 4, no. 89 (October 17, 1884): 372–74.

———. "The Universe as an Organism." *Science* 17, no. 421 (1903): 121–25.

Newton, William Wilberforce. "Hypnotic Moralization." *Harper's New Monthly Magazine*, June 1, 1887.

Nisbet, John Ferguson. *The Insanity of Genius and the General Inequality of Human Faculty: Physiologically Considered.* London: Ward & Downey, 1891.

Nocturnal Revels; Or, Universal Interpreter of Dreams and Visions: Part I. Shewing the

Nature . . . of Various Kinds of Dreams . . . Part II. Shewing the Signification of . . . Dreams . . . To Which Are Added Quotations . . . and the Singular Dream of Mrs. Lee. London: Barker and Son, 1805.

Norris, Frank. *The Octopus: A Story of California.* Garden City, NY: Doubleday, Page & Company, 1901.

"An Obscure Phenomenon in Psychology." *Medical and Surgical Reporter (1858–1898)* 29, no. 22 (November 29, 1873): 393.

"An Obscure Phenomenon in Psychology." *Scientific American (1845–1908),* December 20, 1873.

Osborn, Henry F. "Illusions of Memory." *The North American Review,* May 1884.

Phelps, Elizabeth Stuart. *Chapters from a Life.* New York: Houghton, Mifflin and Company, 1896.

———. *The Gates Ajar.* Boston: Fields, Osgood, 1869.

———. "The Great Psychical Opportunity." *The North American Review,* September 1885.

Pidgeon, Charles F., Harry Price, and Eric John Dingwall. *Revelations of a Spirit Medium.* London: Kegan Paul, Trench, Trubner & Company, 1922.

Podmore, Frank, Frederic William Henry Myers, and Edmund Gurney. *Phantasms of the Living.* 2 Vols. London: Society for Psychical Research, 1886.

Preston, Henry J. "Review: 'The Homeopathic Principle Applied to Insanity.'" *The North American Journal of Homeopathy* 6 (1857): 106.

Prince, Walter Franklin. *Enchanted Boundary: Being a Survey of Negative Reactions to Claims of Psychic Phenomena 1820 to 1930.* Boston: Boston Society for Psychic Research, 1930.

———. *Noted Witnesses for Psychic Occurrences: Incidents and Biographical Data, with Occasional Comments.* Boston: Boston Society for Psychic Research, 1928.

———. *The Psychic in the House.* Boston: Boston Society for Psychical Research, 1926.

———. *The Psychic in the House.* Kessinger Publishing, 2006.

———. "The Sinclair Experiments for Telepathy." *Bulletin of the Boston Society for Psychic Research* 16 (April 1932): 151–235.

"Psychical Research." Medical and Surgical Reporter 53, no. 11 *(September 12, 1885):* 306.

Redfield, William C., and Robert Hare. *On Whirlwind Storms: With Replies to the Objections and Strictures of Dr. Hare.* J. S. Redfield, 1842.

"Review: 'The Homeopathic Principle Applied to Insanity.'" *The Asylum Journal of Mental Science* 4, no. 25 (1858).

"Review of Report on Spiritualism of the Committee of the London Dialectical Society." *Journal of Mental Science,* January 1872.

Sellers, Coleman. "Mechanical Engineering." *Journal of the Franklin Institute,* 1885.

"Sellers, Coleman, Ed.D., Sci. D." In *American Biography: A New Cyclopedia.* New York: American Historical Society, 1922, 227.

Sellers, George Escol. *Early Engineering Reminiscences, 1815–40.* Washington, DC: Smithsonian Institution, 1965.

Seybert Commission for Investigating Modern Spiritualism. *Preliminary Report of the Commission Appointed by the University of Pennsylvania to Investigate Modern Spiritualism, in Accordance with the Request of the Late Henry Seybert.* Philadelphia: J. B. Lippincott Company, 1887.

Sinclair, Mary Craig. *Southern Belle.* Jackson, MS: University Press of Mississippi, 1999. First published 1957 by Crown Publishers (New York).

Sinclair, Upton. *The Land Of Orange Groves And Jails: Upton Sinclair's California,* edited by Lauren Coodley. Santa Clara, CA: Santa Clara University, 2004.

———. *Mental Radio.* New York: Albert & Charles Boni, 1930.

———. *Mental Radio.* Springfield, IL: Charles C. Thomas, 1962.

Skinner, William E. *Wehman's Wizards' Manual: A Practical Treatise on Mind Reading, according to Stuart Cumberland and the Late Washington Irving Bishop . . .* London: Hamley's Magical Saloons . . . and Magical Palace, 1895.

"Spiritualists and Indians." *Chicago Daily Tribune (1872–1922),* August 3, 1895.

Squier, Ephraim George. *Observations on the Aboriginal Monuments of the Mississippi Valley: The Character of the Ancient Earth-Works, and the Structure, Contents, and Purposes of the Mounds: With Notices of the Minor Remains of Ancient Art: With Illustrations.* Bartlett & Welford, 1847.

———. "Tongues From Tombs; or, the Stories That Graves Tell." *Frank Leslie's Weekly,* March 20, 1869, 5.

Squier, Ephraim George, and Edwin Hamilton Davis. *Ancient Monuments of the Mississippi Valley: Comprising the Results of Extensive Original Surveys and Explorations.* Washington, DC: Smithsonian Institution, 1848.

Stiles, Joseph D., and Josiah Brigham. *Twelve Messages from the Spirit of John Quincy Adams.* B. Marsh, 1859.

Stoker, Bram. *Dracula.* New York: Modern Library, 1897.

Sully, James. "The Laws of Dream Fancy." *Cornhill Magazine* 34, no. 203 (November 1876): 536–55.

Sutton, Ransome. "What's New in Science: Power of Mind over Body." *Los Angeles Times,* June 11, 1933.

"Talked with Ghosts Mediums Converse with Spirits of Departed Souls." *Daily Inter Ocean,* August 5, 1895.

"$10,000 Offered to Quote Letter." Associated Press wire, New York, October 5, 1910.

Thomas, Cyrus. *Report on the Mound Explorations of the Bureau of Ethnology.* Washington, DC, 1894

Thwing, E. P. "English Psychologists." *The Phrenological Journal of Science and Health* 77, no. 5 (November 1883): 275.

Towne, Elizabeth. *Practical Methods for Self-Development.* Holyoke, MA: Towne, 1904.

Tubby, Gertrude Ogden, and Weston D. Bayley. *James H. Hyslop – X: His Book: A Cross Reference Record.* York, PA: The York Printing Company, 1929.

Twain, Mark. "Mental Telegraphy: A Manuscript with a History." *Harper's New Monthly Magazine,* December 1, 1891.

Ullman, Montague. "Psi and Psychiatry—The Need for Restructuring Basic Concepts." *Parapsychology Research*, 1972. http://www.siivola.org/monte/papers_grouped/copyrighted/Parapsychology_&_Psi/Psi_%20and_Psychiatry.htm

———. "Psychical Research: A Personal Perspective." *The Psi Researcher* 22, August 1996.

United States House of Representatives, Committee on the District of Columbia. "Fortune Telling: Hearings before the Subcommittee on Judiciary . . . on H.R. 8989." Washington, DC: Government Printing Office, 1926.

Ware, Charles Pickard, ed. 1862–1912 *Class Report: Class of 'Sixty-Two Harvard University, Fiftieth Anniversary*. Norwood, MA: The Plimpton Press, 1912.

Watson, John Broadus. *Behavior: An Introduction to Comparative Psychology*. H. Holt, 1914.

Watson, John Broadus, and William McDougall. *The Battle of Behaviorism: An Exposition and an Exposure*. New York: W. W. Norton, 1929.

Weisenburg, Theodore Herman, and Katharine E. McBride. *Aphasia: A Clinical and Psychological Study*. New York: The Commonwealth Fund, 1935.

Weltmer, Sidney Abram. *Telepathy and Thought-Transference*. Becktold Printing and Book Mfg. Company, 1902.

Welworth Magic. *Perfection One Man Mind Reading Act*. Indianapolis, IN: Welworth Company, 1930.

Western Society for Psychical Research. *Constitution and Rules*. Chicago: Western Society for Psychical Research, 1885.

Whitman, Walt. *Specimen Days in America*. W. Scott, 1887.

Wicks, Frederick, and Washington Irving Bishop. *Second Sight Explained: A Complete Exposition of Clairvoyance or Second Sight, as Exhibited by the Late Robert Houdin and Robert Heller: Showing How the Supposed Phenomena May Be Produced*. Edinburgh and Glasgow: John Menzies, 1880.

Wilkinson, James John Garth. *The Homeopathic Principle Applied to Insanity*. Otis Clapp, 1857.

Wood, Horatio C. "The Mind and the Weather." *American Medico-Surgical Bulletin*, 1894, 324–25.

Zancig, Julius, and Agnes Zancig. *Two Minds with But a Single Thought*. Paul Naumann, 1907.

Secondary Sources

Ablow, Rachel. *The Marriage of Minds: Reading Sympathy in the Victorian Marriage Plot*. Stanford, CA: Stanford University Press, 2007.

Ackerknecht, Erwin Heinz. *Medicine at the Paris Hospital, 1794–1848*. Baltimore: Johns Hopkins University Press, 1967.

Adams, Annmarie. *Architecture in the Family Way: Doctors, Houses, and Women, 1870–1900*. Montreal and Kingston: McGill-Queen's Press, 1996.

Adams, Rebecca G., and Graham Allan. *Placing Friendship in Context*. Cambridge: Cambridge University Press, 1999.

Albanese, Catherine L. *A Republic of Mind and Spirit: A Cultural History of American Metaphysical Religion.* New Haven, CT: Yale University Press, 2007.

Alder, Ken. *The Lie Detectors: The History of an American Obsession.* Lincoln: University of Nebraska Press, 2009.

Allen, Garland E. "Mechanism, Vitalism and Organicism in Late Nineteenth and Twentieth-Century Biology: The Importance of Historical Context." *Studies in History and Philosophy of Science Part C: Studies in History and Philosophy of Biological and Biomedical Sciences,* Mechanisms in Biology 36, no. 2 (June 2005): 261–83.

Alvarado, Carlos S. "Dissociation in Britain during the Late Nineteenth Century: The Society for Psychical Research, 1882–1900." *Journal of Trauma & Dissociation* 3, no. 2 (May 14, 2012): 9–33.

Anderson, Katharine. *Predicting the Weather: Victorians and the Science of Meteorology.* Chicago: University of Chicago Press, 2005.

Anderson, Rodger I. *Psychics, Sensitives and Somnambules: A Biographical Dictionary with Bibliographies.* Jefferson, NC: McFarland & Company, 2006.

Armstrong, Nancy. *Desire and Domestic Fiction: A Political History of the Novel.* Oxford: Oxford University Press, 1987.

Arthur, Anthony. *Radical Innocent: Upton Sinclair.* New York: Random House Digital, Inc., 2006.

Asprem, Egil. "A Nice Arrangement of Heterodoxies: William McDougall and the Professionalization of Psychical Research." *Journal of the History of the Behavioral Sciences* 46, no. 2 (April 12, 2010): 123–43.

———. *The Problem of Disenchantment: Scientific Naturalism and Esoteric Discourse 1900–1939.* Leiden, The Netherlands: Brill, 2014.

Aubin, David, Charlotte Bigg, and H. Otto Sibum. *The Heavens on Earth: Observatories and Astronomy in Nineteenth-Century Science and Culture.* Durham, NC: Duke University Press, 2010.

Bailey, Solon I. *Biographical Memoir of Edward Charles Pickering, 1846–1919, Fifth Memoir* Vol. 15 of *National Academy of Sciences, Biographical Memoirs.* Literary Licensing, LLC, 2011.

Bail, Hamilton Vaughan. "James Russell Lowell's Ode Recited at the Commemoration of the Living and Dead Soldiers of Harvard University, July 21, 1865." *The Papers of the Bibliographical Society of America* 37 (January 1, 1943).

Baird, Alex. *The Life of Richard Hodgson.* London: Psychic Press, 1949.

Baker, David B. *Thick Description and Fine Texture: Studies in the History of Psychology.* Ohio: University of Akron Press, 2003.

Bank, Rosemarie K. "Staging the 'Native': Making History in American Theatre Culture, 1828–1838." *Theatre Journal* 45, no. 4 (December 1, 1993): 461–86.

Bannet, Eve Tavor. *Empire of Letters: Letter Manuals and Transatlantic Correspondence, 1680–1820.* Cambridge: Cambridge University Press, 2006.

Barnes, Barry. *Natural Order: Historical Studies of Scientific Culture.* Thousand Oaks, CA: Sage Publications, 1979.

Barnhart, Terry A. *Ephraim George Squier and the Development of American Anthropology*. Lincoln: University of Nebraska Press, 2005.

Barrow, Logie. *Independent Spirits: Spiritualism and English Plebeians, 1850–1910*. New York: Routledge & Kegan Paul, 1986.

Bartky, Ian R. *Selling the True Time: Nineteenth-Century Timekeeping in America*. Stanford, CA: Stanford University Press, 2000.

Basham, Diana. *The Trial of Woman: Feminism and the Occult Sciences in Victorian Literature and Society*. London: Macmillan, 1992.

Baumann, Christian. "Psychic Blindness or Visual Agnosia: Early Descriptions of a Nervous Disorder." *Journal of the History of the Neurosciences* 20, no. 1 (January 2011): 58–64.

Becker, Peter, and William Clark. *Little Tools of Knowledge: Historical Essays on Academic and Bureaucratic Practices*. Ann Arbor: University of Michigan Press, 2001.

Beegan, Gerry. *The Mass Image: A Social History of Photomechanical Reproduction in Victorian London*. London: Palgrave Macmillan, 2008.

———. "The Mechanization of the Image: Facsimile, Photography, and Fragmentation in Nineteenth-Century Wood Engraving." *Journal of Design History* 8, no. 4 (1995): 257–74.

———. "The Studio: Photomechanical Reproduction and the Changing Status of Design." *Design Issues* 23, no. 4 (September 2007): 46.

Beer, Janet, and Bridget Bennett. "Crossing Over: Spiritualism and the Atlantic Divide." In *Special Relationships: Anglo-American Antagonisms and Affinities, 1854–1936*, 89–109. Manchester, UK: Manchester University Press, 2002.

Behrens, Peter J. "The Metaphysical Club at the Johns Hopkins University (1879–1885)." *History of Psychology* 8, no. 4 (November 2005): 331–46.

Bell, Joshua A., and Alison K. Brown, eds. *Recreating First Contact: Expeditions, Anthropology, and Popular Culture*. Washington, DC: Smithsonian Institution Scholarly Press 2013.

Bellin, Joshua David. *Medicine Bundle: Indian Sacred Performance and American Literature, 1824–1932*. Philadelphia: University of Pennsylvania Press, 2008.

Beloff, John. *Parapsychology: A Concise History*. New York: St. Martin's Press, 1993.

———. "The Rhine Legacy." *Philosophical Psychology* 2, no. 2 (January 1, 1989): 231–39.

Belshe, Francis Bland. *A History of Art Education in the Public Schools of the United States*. University Microfilms, 1967.

Ben-Atar, Doron S. *Trade Secrets: Intellectual Piracy and the Origins of American Industrial Power*. New Haven, CT: Yale University Press, 2008.

Bender, Courtney. *The New Metaphysicals: Spirituality and the American Religious Imagination*. Chicago: University of Chicago Press, 2010.

Bender, Courtney, and Pamela E. Klassen, eds. *After Pluralism: Reimagining Religious Engagement*. New York: Columbia University Press, 2012.

Benjamin, Walter. *The Work of Art in the Age of Its Technological Reproducibility, and Other Writings on Media*. Cambridge, MA: Harvard University Press, 2008.

Bennett, Bridget. "Sacred Theatres: Shakers, Spiritualists, Theatricality, and the

Indian in the 1830s and 1840s." *TDR: The Drama Review* 49, no. 3 (Fall 2005): 114–34.

———. *Transatlantic Spiritualism and Nineteenth-Century American Literature*. London: Macmillan, 2007.

Bennett, Tony. *Pasts beyond Memory: Evolution, Museums, Colonialism*. London and New York: Routledge, 2004.

Berger, Arthur S. *Lives and Letters in American Parapsychology: A Biographical History, 1850–1987*. Jefferson, NC: McFarland, 1988.

Berger, Arthur S. "The Early History of the ASPR: Origins to 1907." *Journal of the American Society for Psychical Research* 79, no. 1 (1985): 39–60.

Bergland, Renée L. *The National Uncanny: Indian Ghosts and American Subjects*. Lebanon, NH: University Press of New England, 2000.

Berman, Marshall. *All That Is Solid Melts into Air: The Experience of Modernity*. New York: Verso, 1983.

Bernard, Catherine A. "Dickens and Victorian Dream Theory." In *Victorian Science and Victorian Values: Literary Perspectives*, 197–216. New York: New York Academy of Sciences, 1981.

———. "Dickens and Victorian Dream Theory." *Annals of the New York Academy of Sciences* 360, no. 1 (April 1, 1981): 197–216.

Biehl, João, and Amy Moran-Thomas. "Symptom: Subjectivities, Social Ills, Technologies." *Annual Review of Anthropology* 38, no. 1 (2009): 267–88.

Bigg, Charlotte. "Staging the Heavens: Astrophysics and Popular Astronomy in the Late Nineteenth Century." In *The Heavens on Earth: Observatories and Astronomy in Nineteenth-Century Science and Culture*, edited by David Aubin, Charlotte Bigg, and H. Otto Sibum, 302–324. Durham, NC: Duke University Press, 2010.

Bird, John. "Mark Twain on the Telephone: Love (and Hate) on the Line." *The Mark Twain Annual* 6, no. 1 (2008): 77–89.

Bjork, Daniel W. *The Compromised Scientist: William James in the Development of American Psychology*. New York: Columbia University Press, 1983.

Blackmore, Tim. "McCay's McChanical Muse: Engineering Comic-Strip Dreams." *Journal of Popular Culture* 32, no. 1 (Summer 1998): 15–38.

Blanco, Maria del Pilar, and Esther Peeren, eds. *Popular Ghosts: The Haunted Spaces of Everyday Culture*. New York: Continuum International Publishing Group, 2010.

Blum, Deborah. *Ghost Hunters: William James and the Search for Scientific Proof of Life after Death*. New York: Penguin, 2007.

Blumenthal, Susanna L. *Law and the Modern Mind: Consciousness and Responsibility in American Legal Culture*. Cambridge, MA: Harvard University Press, 2016.

Boakes, Robert. *From Darwin to Behaviourism: Psychology and the Minds of Animals*. Cambridge: Cambridge University Press Archive, 1984.

Boden, Margaret. *Mind As Machine: A History of Cognitive Science*. Oxford: Oxford University Press, 2008.

Bordogna, Francesca. *William James at the Boundaries: Philosophy, Science, and the Geography of Knowledge*. Chicago: University of Chicago Press, 2008.

Boring, Edwin Garrigues. *History of Experimental Psychology*. New York: D. Appleton-Century Company, 1929.

Bourdieu, Pierre. *Outline of a Theory of Practice*. Cambridge: Cambridge University Press, 1977.

Bown, Nicola, Carolyn Burdett, and Pamela Thurschwell. *The Victorian Supernatural*. Cambridge: Cambridge University Press, 2004.

Brandon, Ruth. *The Spiritualists: The Passion for the Occult in the Nineteenth and Twentieth Centuries*. London: Weidenfeld and Nicolson, 1983.

Brantlinger, Patrick. "Imperial Gothic: Atavism and the Occult in the British Adventure Novel, 1880–1914." In *Rule of Darkness: British Literature and Imperialism, 1830–1914*, 227–55. Ithaca, NY: Cornell University Press, 2013.

Braude, Ann. *Radical Spirits: Spiritualism and Women's Rights in Nineteenth-Century America*. 2nd ed. Bloomington and Indianapolis: Indiana University Press, 2001.

Brent, Joseph. *Charles Sanders Peirce: A Life*. Bloomington: Indiana University Press, 1998.

Brewer, William F., and Bruce L. Lambert. "The Theory-Ladenness of Observation and the Theory-Ladenness of the Rest of the Scientific Process." *Philosophy of Science* 68, no. 3 (September 2001): S176–86.

Bro, Harmon H. *A Seer Out of Season: The Life of Edgar Cayce*. London: Macmillan, 1996.

Brocklebank, Lisa M. *Presentiments, Sympathies and Signs: Minds in the Age of Fiction—Reading and the Limits of Reason in Victorian Britain*. Providence, RI: Brown University, 2008.

———. "Psychic Reading." *Victorian Studies* 48, no. 2 (2006): 233–39.

Brodhead, Richard H. *Cultures of Letters: Scenes of Reading and Writing in Nineteenth-Century America*. Chicago: University of Chicago Press, 1993.

Bronfen, Elisabeth. *The Knotted Subject: Hysteria and Its Discontents*. Princeton, NJ: Princeton University Press, 1998.

Brottman, Mikita. *Phantoms of the Clinic: From Thought-Transference to Projective Identification*. New York: Karnac Books, 2011.

Bruce, Robert V. *The Launching of Modern American Science 1846–1876*. Ithaca, NY: Cornell University Press, 1988.

Bukatman, Scott. *The Poetics of Slumberland: Animated Spirits and the Animating Spirit*. Berkeley: University of California Press, 2012.

Bulkeley, Kelly. *Visions of the Night: Dreams, Religion, and Psychology*. New York: SUNY Press, 1999.

Bulkeley, Kelly, and Hendrika Vande Kemp. "Introduction to the Special Issue on Historical Studies of Dreaming." *Dreaming, Historical Studies of Dreaming* 10, no. 1 (March 2000): 1–6.

Bunting, Bainbridge. *Harvard: An Architectural History*. Cambridge, MA: Harvard University Press, 1998.

Bynum, W. F., Roy Porter, and Michael Shepherd. *The Anatomy of Madness: Essays in the History of Psychiatry*. London: Taylor & Francis, 2005.

Canales, Jimena. "Exit the Frog, Enter the Human: Physiology and Experimental

Psychology in Nineteenth-Century Astronomy." *British Journal for the History of Science* 34, no. 2 (June 1, 2001): 173–97.

———. *A Tenth of a Second: A History.* Chicago: University of Chicago Press, 2010.

Caplan, Eric. *Mind Games: American Culture and the Birth of Psychotherapy.* Berkeley: University of California Press, 1998.

Capshew, James H. "Psychologists on Site: A Reconnaissance of the Historiography of the Laboratory." *American Psychologist* 47, no. 2 (February 1992): 132–42.

———. *Psychologists on the March: Science, Practice, and Professional Identity in America,* 1929–1969. Cambridge: Cambridge University Press, 1999.

Carroll, Bret E. *Spiritualism in Antebellum America.* Bloomington and Indianapolis: Indiana University Press, 1997.

Carson, John. "Minding Matter/Mattering Mind: Knowledge and the Subject in Nineteenth-Century Psychology." *Studies in History and Philosophy of Science Part C: Studies in History and Philosophy of Biological and Biomedical Sciences* 30, no. 3 (September 1999): 345–76.

———. "The Science of Merit and the Merit of Science." In *States of Knowledge: The Co-Production of Science and the Social Order,* edited by Sheila Jasanoff, 181–206. New York: Routledge, 2004.

Carter, Edward Carlos. *Surveying the Record: North American Scientific Exploration to 1930.* Philadelphia: American Philosophical Society, 1999.

Castle, Terry. "The Female Thermometer." *Representations,* no. 17 (January 1, 1987): 1–27.

———. *The Female Thermometer: Eighteenth-Century Culture and the Invention of the Uncanny.* Oxford: Oxford University Press, 1995.

Castronovo, Russ. "The Antislavery Unconscious: Mesmerism, Vodun, and 'Equality.' " *Mississippi Quarterly* 53, no. 1 (Winter/2000 1999): 41–56.

———. *Necro Citizenship: Death, Eroticism, and the Public Sphere in the Nineteenth-Century United States.* Durham, NC: Duke University Press, 2001.

Caterine, Darryl V. "The Haunted Grid: Nature, Electricity, and Indian Spirits in the American Metaphysical Tradition." *Journal of the American Academy of Religion* 82, no. 2 (June 1, 2014): 371–97.

———. *Haunted Ground: Journeys through a Paranormal America.* Santa Barbara, CA: Praeger, 2011.

Cerullo, John J. *The Secularization of the Soul: Psychical Research in Modern Britain.* Philadelphia: Institute for the Study of Human Issues, 1982.

Chaplin, Joyce Elizabeth. "Nature and Nation: Natural History in Context." In *Stuffing Birds, Pressing Plants, Shaping Knowledge: Natural History in North America 1730–1860,* edited by Sue Ann Prince. Philadelphia: American Philosophical Society, 2003.

Chapman, John Jay. "William James." In *William James Remembered,* edited by Linda Simon. Lincoln: University of Nebraska Press, 1999.

Chéroux, Clément. *The Perfect Medium: Photography And the Occult.* New Haven, CT: Yale University Press, 2005.

Choudhury, Suparna and Jan Slaby, eds., *Critical Neuroscience: A Handbook of the Social and Cultural Contexts of Neuroscience*. Hoboken, NJ: Wiley, 2011.

Coen, Deborah R. "The Common World: Histories of Science and Domestic Intimacy." *Modern Intellectual History* 11, no. 02 (August 2014): 417–38.

———. "A Lens of Many Facets: Science through a Family's Eyes." *Isis* 97, no. 3 (September 1, 2006): 395–419.

———. *Vienna in the Age of Uncertainty*. Chicago: University of Chicago Press, 2007.

Collins, Harry, and Robert Evans. *Rethinking Expertise*. Chicago: University of Chicago Press, 2007.

Collis, Maurice. *Somerville and Ross: A Biography*. London: Faber, 1968.

Colton, Harold S. "Mark Twain's Literary Dilemma and Its Sequel." *Arizona Quarterly* 17 (January 1, 1961): 229.

Cook, James W. *The Arts of Deception: Playing with Fraud in the Age of Barnum*. Cambridge, MA: Harvard University Press, 2001.

Coon, Deborah J. "'One Moment in the World's Salvation': Anarchism and the Radicalization of William James." *Journal of American History* 83, no. 1 (1996): 70–99.

———. "Standardizing the Subject: Experimental Psychologists, Introspection, and the Quest for a Technoscientific Ideal." *Technology and Culture* 34, no. 4 (October 1993): 757–83.

———. "Testing the Limits of Sense and Science: American Experimental Psychologists Combat Spiritualism, 1880–1920." *American Psychologist* 47, no. 2 (1992): 143–51.

Coontz, Stephanie. "Historical Perspectives on Family Studies." *Journal of Marriage and Family* 62, no. 2 (May 1, 2000): 283–97.

———. *Marriage, a History: How Love Conquered Marriage*. New York: Penguin, 2005.

———. *The Social Origins of Private Life: A History of American Families, 1600–1900*. New York: Verso, 1988.

Cotkin, George. "Hamlet to Habit." In *William James, Public Philosopher*, 40–72. Baltimore: Johns Hopkins University Press, 1990.

Cox, John D. *Storm Watchers: The Turbulent History of Weather Prediction from Franklin's Kite to El Niño*. Hoboken, NJ: Wiley, 2002.

Cox, Robert S. *Body and Soul: A Sympathetic History of American Spiritualism*. Charlottesville: University of Virginia Press, 2003.

Crabtree, Adam. *Animal Magnetism, Early Hypnotism, and Psychical Research, 1766–1925: An Annotated Bibliography*. Millwood, NY: Kraus International Publications, 1988.

———. "'Automatism' and the Emergence of Dynamic Psychiatry." *Journal of the History of the Behavioral Sciences* 39, no. 1 (January 21, 2003): 51–70.

———. *From Mesmer to Freud: Magnetic Sleep and the Roots of Psychological Healing*. New Haven, CT: Yale University Press, 1993.

Csiszar, Alex. "Seriality and the Search for Order: Scientific Print and Its

Problems During the Late Nineteenth Century." *History of Science* 48, no. 3/4 (September 2010): 399–434.

Curti, Merle. "The American Exploration of Dreams and Dreamers." *Journal of the History of Ideas* 27, no. 3 (July 1, 1966): 391–416.

Daniels, George H. *Nineteenth-Century American Science: A Reappraisal*. Chicago: Northwestern University Press, 1972.

———. *The Process of Professionalization in American Science: The Emergent Period, 1820–1860*. Notre Dame, IN: History of Science Society, 1967.

Danziger, Kurt. *Constructing the Subject: Historical Origins of Psychological Research*. Cambridge: Cambridge University Press, 1994.

———. *Naming the Mind: How Psychology Found Its Language*. Thousand Oaks, CA: Sage, 1997.

Daston, Lorraine. *Biographies of Scientific Objects*. Chicago: University of Chicago Press, 2000.

Daston, Lorraine, and Peter Galison. *Objectivity*. New York: Zone Books, 2007.

Daston, Lorraine, and Elizabeth Lunbeck. *Histories of Scientific Observation*. Chicago: University of Chicago Press, 2011.

Davidoff, Leonore. *The Family Story: Blood, Contract, and Intimacy, 1830–1960*. London: Longman, 1999.

Decker, Jeffrey Louis. *Made in America: Self-Styled Success from Horatio Alger to Oprah Winfrey*. Minneapolis: University of Minnesota Press, 1997.

Deloria, Philip Joseph. *Playing Indian*. New Haven, CT: Yale University Press, 1998.

Didi-Huberman, Georges. *Invention of Hysteria: Charcot and the Photographic Iconography of the Salpêtrière*. Cambridge, MA: MIT Press, 2004.

Dimock, George. "Anna and the Wolf-Man: Rewriting Freud's Case History." *Representations*, no. 50 (April 1, 1995): 53–75.

Dobyns, Kenneth W. *A History of the Early Patent Offices: The Patent Office Pony*. Fredericksburg, VA: Sergeant Kirkland's, 1997.

Driver, Felix. *Geography Militant: Cultures of Exploration and Empire*. Hoboken, NJ: Wiley, 2000.

Dror, Otniel Yizhak. "The Scientific Image of Emotion: Experience and Technologies of Inscription." *Configurations* 7, no. 3 (1999): 355–401.

Du Mez, Kristin Kobes. *A New Gospel for Women: Katharine Bushnell and the Challenge of Christian Feminism*. New York: Oxford University Press, 2015.

During, Simon. *Modern Enchantments: The Cultural Power of Secular Magic*. Cambridge, MA: Harvard University Press, 2009.

Eco, Umberto, and Thomas Albert Sebeok. *The Sign of Three: Dupin, Holmes, Peirce*. Bloomington: Indiana University Press, 1988.

Efland, Arthur. *A History of Art Education: Intellectual and Social Currents in Teaching the Visual Arts*. New York: Teachers College Press, 1990.

Ellenberger, Henri F. *The Discovery of the Unconscious: The History and Evolution of Dynamic Psychiatry*. New York: Basic Books, 1981.

Emre, Merve. *The Personality Brokers: The Strange History of Myers-Briggs and the Birth of Personality Testing*. New York: Doubleday, 2018.

Epperson, Gordon. *The Mind of Edmund Gurney*. Cranbury, NJ: Fairleigh Dickinson University Press, 1997.

Erickson, Paul, and Judy L. Klein. *How Reason Almost Lost Its Mind*. Chicago: University of Chicago Press, 2014.

Ewing, Heather P. *The Lost World of James Smithson: Science, Revolution, and the Birth of the Smithsonian*. New York: Bloomsbury, 2007.

Farah, Martha J. *Visual Agnosia*. Cambridge, MA: MIT Press, 2004.

Faust, Drew Gilpin. *This Republic of Suffering: Death and the American Civil War*. New York: Vintage Books, 2009.

Feinstein, Howard M. *Becoming William James*. Ithaca, NY: Cornell University Press, 1999.

Ferguson, Christine. *Determined Spirits: Eugenics, Heredity and Racial Regeneration in Anglo-American Spiritualist Writing, 1848–1930*. New York: Oxford University Press, 2012.

Fiedler, Leslie. *Love and Death in the American Novel*. Chicago: Dalkey Archive Press, 2003. First published 1960 (New York: Stein and Day).

Fineberg, Jonathan. *Discovering Child Art: Essays on Childhood, Primitivism, and Modernism*. Princeton, NJ: Princeton University Press, 1998.

———. *The Innocent Eye: Children's Art and the Modern Artist*. Princeton, NJ: Princeton University Press, 1997.

Fineberg, Jonathan David, Phillips Collection, and Krannert Art Museum. *When We Were Young: New Perspectives on the Art of the Child*. Berkeley: University of California Press, in association with the Phillips Collection Center for the Study of Modern Art and Illinois at the Phillips, a program of the University of Illinois at Urbana-Champaign, 2006.

Finnerty, Páraic. "A Dickinson Reverie: The Worm, the Snake, Marvel, and Nineteenth-Century Dreaming." *The Emily Dickinson Journal* 16, no. 2 (2007): 94–118.

Finucane, Ronald C. *Appearances of the Dead: A Cultural History of Ghosts*. London: Junction Books, 1982.

Fisher Fishkin, Shelley. *Lighting Out for the Territory: Reflections on Mark Twain and American Culture*. New York: Oxford University Press, 1996.

Fleming, James Rodger. *Meteorology in America, 1800–1870*. Baltimore: Johns Hopkins University Press, 2000.

Fleming, James Rodger, Vladimir Janković, and Deborah R. Coen. *Intimate Universality: Local And Global Themes in the History of Weather And Climate*. Sagamore Beach, MA: Science History Publications/USA, 2006.

Foucault, Michel. *The Birth of the Clinic: An Archaeology of Medical Perception*. Translated by Alan Sheridan. London: Tavistock Publications Ltd., 1973.

Foy, Jessica H., and Thomas J. Schlereth. *American Home Life, 1880–1930: A Social History of Spaces and Services*. Knoxville, TN: University of Tennessee Press, 1994.

Frazier, Kendrick. *Encounters with the Paranormal: Science, Knowledge, and Belief*. Amherst, NY: Prometheus Books, 1998.

———. *Science under Siege: Defending Science, Exposing Pseudoscience*. Amherst, NY: Prometheus Books, 2009.

Fuller, Robert C. *Mesmerism and the American Cure of Souls*. Philadelphia: University of Pennsylvania Press, 1982.

Galison, Peter. "Blacked-out Spaces: Freud, Censorship and the Re-Territorialization of Mind." *British Journal for the History of Science* 45, no. 2 (June 1, 2012): 235–66.

Galison, Peter. "Image of Self." In *Things That Talk: Object Lessons from Art and Science*, 257–96. New York: Zone Books, 2007.

Gallagher, Winifred. *How the Post Office Created America: A History*. New York: Penguin Press, 2016.

Galvan, Jill Nicole. *The Sympathetic Medium: Feminine Channeling, the Occult, and Communication Technologies, 1859–1919*. Ithaca, NY: Cornell University Press, 2010.

Gauld, Alan. *The Founders of Psychical Research*. New York: Routledge & K. Paul, 1968.

Gerona, Carla. *Night Journeys: The Power of Dreams in Transatlantic Quaker Culture*. Charlottesville: University of Virginia Press, 2004.

Gieryn, Thomas F. *Cultural Boundaries of Science: Credibility on the Line*. Chicago: University of Chicago Press, 1999.

Ginzburg, Carlo. *Clues, Myths, and the Historical Method*. Baltimore: Johns Hopkins University Press, 1992.

———. "Morelli, Freud, and Sherlock Holmes: Clues and Scientific Method." Translated by Anna Davin. *History Workshop Journal*, no. 9 (1980): 5–36.

Gitelman, Lisa. *Paper Knowledge: Toward a Media History of Documents*. Durham, NC: Duke University Press, 2014.

———. *Scripts, Grooves, and Writing Machines: Representing Technology in the Edison Era*. Stanford, CA: Stanford University Press, 1999.

Glance, Jonathan C. "Revelation, Nonsense or Dyspepsia: Victorian Dream Theories." *Scribd*. Accessed August 25, 2014. http://www.scribd.com/doc/105245364/Glance-Jonathan-C-Revelation-Nonsense-or-Dyspepsia-Victorian-Dream-Theories.

Goetz, Christopher G., Michel Bonduelle, and Toby Gelfand. *Charcot: Constructing Neurology*. Oxford: Oxford University Press, 1995.

Goldstein, Daniel. "'Yours for Science': The Smithsonian Institution's Correspondents and the Shape of Scientific Community in Nineteenth-Century America." *Isis* 85, no. 4 (December 1, 1994): 573–99.

Goldstein, Jan. *Console and Classify: The French Psychiatric Profession in the Nineteenth Century*. Cambridge: Cambridge University Press, 1987.

Golinski, Jan. *British Weather and the Climate of Enlightenment*. Chicago: University of Chicago Press, 2010.

———. *Making Natural Knowledge*. Cambridge: Cambridge University Press, 1998.

Gooday, Graeme. "Placing or Replacing the Laboratory in the History of Science?" *Isis* 99, no. 4 (December 1, 2008): 783–95.

Gosling, Francis George. *Before Freud: Neurasthenia and the American Medical Community*, 1870–1910. Urbana: University of Illinois Press, 1987.

Gottschalk, Stephen. *Rolling Away the Stone: Mary Baker Eddy's Challenge to Materialism.* Bloomington: Indiana University Press, 2006.

Gray, Stephen. *Douglas Blackburn.* Boston: Twayne Publishers, 1984.

Greenwood, M., and M. Smith. "William McDougall. 1871–1938." *Obituary Notices of Fellows of the Royal Society* 3, no. 8 (January 1, 1940): 39–62.

Griffin, Martin. "Reconciliation and Irony, 1865–1905: James Russell Lowell, Henry James, Paul Laurence Dunbar, and Ambrose Bierce." PhD diss., University of California, Los Angeles, 2002.

Grimes, Hilary. *The Late Victorian Gothic: Mental Science, the Uncanny, and Scenes of Writing.* Farnham, UK: Ashgate Publishing, Ltd., 2011.

Guiterrez, Cathy. *Plato's Ghost: Spiritualism in the American Renaissance.* Oxford: Oxford University Press, 2009.

Gundlach, Horst. "Vocational Aptitude Tests (psychotechnics)." In *Instruments of Science: An Historical Encyclopedia*, 648–50. New York and London: Taylor & Francis, 1998.

Gunter, Susan E. *Alice in Jamesland: The Story of Alice Howe Gibbens James.* Lincoln: University of Nebraska Press, 2009.

Gyimesi, Júlia. "The Problem of Demarcation: Psychoanalysis and the Occult." *American Imago* 66, no. 4 (2009): 457–70.

Hacking, Ian. "Dreams in Place." *Journal of Aesthetics and Art Criticism*, 59 (2001), 245–60.

———. *The Emergence of Probability: A Philosophical Study of Early Ideas about Probability, Induction and Statistical Inference.* Cambridge: Cambridge University Press, 1984.

———. *Mad Travelers: Reflections on the Reality of Transient Mental Illnesses.* Charlottesville: University of Virginia Press, 1998.

———. *Representing and Intervening: Introductory Topics in the Philosophy of Natural Science.* Cambridge: Cambridge University Press, 1983.

———. *Rewriting the Soul: Multiple Personality and the Sciences of Memory.* Princeton, NJ: Princeton University Press, 1995.

———. *The Social Construction of What?.* Cambridge, MA: Harvard University Press, 1999.

———. *The Taming of Chance.* Cambridge: Cambridge University Press, 1990.

———. "Telepathy: Origins of Randomization in Experimental Design." *Isis* 79, no. 3 (September 1, 1988): 427–51.

Haehl, Richard. *Samuel Hahnemann: His Life and Work: Based on Recently Discovered State Papers, Documents, Letters, Etc.* New Delhi, India: B. Jain Publishers, 2003.

Hale, Matthew. *Human Science and Social Order: Hugo Munsterberg and the Origins of Applied Psychology.* Philadelphia: Temple University Press, 1980.

Hall, Trevor H. *The Strange Case of Edmund Gurney.* London: Duckworth, 1980.

Halttunen, Karen. *Confidence Men and Painted Women: A Study of Middle-Class Culture in America, 1830–1870*. New Haven, CT: Yale University Press, 1982.

Hamilton, T. *Immortal Longings: FWH Myers and the Victorian Search for Life after Death*. Exeter, UK: Imprint Academic, 2009.

Hammerton, A. James. *Cruelty and Companionship: Conflict in Nineteenth Century Married Life*. London and New York: Routledge, 1992.

Hannaway, Caroline, and Ann Elizabeth Fowler La Berge. "Paris Medicine: Perspectives Past and Present." In *Constructing Paris Medicine*. New York: Rodopi, 1998.

Harrington, Anne. *Medicine, Mind, and the Double Brain: A Study in Nineteenth- Century Thought and Culture*. Princeton, NJ: Princeton University Press, 1987.

Harvey, Sean P. *Native Tongues: Colonialism and Race from Encounter to the Reservation*. Cambridge, MA: Harvard University Press, 2015.

Haskell, Thomas L. *The Authority of Experts: Studies in History and Theory*. Bloomington: Indiana University Press, 1984.

Hatch, Nathan O. *The Democratization of American Christianity*. New Haven, CT: Yale University Press, 1989.

Hayward, Rhodri. "Policing Dreams: History and the Moral Uses of the Unconscious." *History Workshop Journal*, no. 49 (April 1, 2000): 142–60.

———. *Resisting History: Religious Transcendence and the Invention of the Unconscious*. Manchester, UK: Manchester University Press, 2007.

Hazelgrove, Jennifer. "Spiritualism after the Great War." *Twentieth Century British History* 10, no. 4 (January 1, 1999): 404–30.

———. *Spiritualism and British Society between the Wars*. Manchester, UK: Manchester University Press, 2000.

Hazen, Craig James. *The Village Enlightenment in America: Popular Religion and Science in the Nineteenth Century*. Urbana: University of Illinois Press, 2000.

Herman, Daniel. "Whose Knocking? Spiritualism as Entertainment and Therapy in Nineteenth?Century San Francisco." *American Nineteenth Century History* 7, no. 3 (2006): 417–42.

Hess, David J. *Science In The New Age: The Paranormal, Its Defenders and Debunkers*. Madison: University of Wisconsin Press, 1993.

Hill, Annette. *Paranormal Media: Audiences, Spirits and Magic in Popular Culture*. New York: Taylor & Francis, 2010.

Hill, Sharon A. *Scientifical Americans: The Culture of Amateur Paranormal Researchers*. Jefferson, NC: McFarland, 2017.

Hines, Terence. *Pseudoscience and the Paranormal*. Amherst, NY: Prometheus Books, 2003.

Hitt, Jack. *Bunch of Amateurs: A Search for the American Character*. New York: Crown, 2012.

Hobson, J. Allan. "The Study of Dreaming in the Nineteenth Century." In *The Dreaming Brain*, 23–51. New York: Basic Books, 1988.

Hoffmann, Christoph. "Processes on Paper: Writing Procedures as Non-Material

Research Devices." *Science in Context* 26, Special Issue 02 (June 2013): 279–303.

Hoffmann, Christoph, and Barbara Wittmann. "Introduction: Knowledge in the Making: Drawing and Writing as Research Techniques." *Science in Context* 26, Special Issue 02 (June 2013): 203–13.

Hong, Sungook. *Wireless: From Marconi's Black-Box to the Audion.* Cambridge, MA: MIT Press, 2001.

Hopwood, Nick, Simon Schaffer, and Jim Secord. "Seriality and Scientific Objects in the Nineteenth Century." *History of Science* 48, no. ? (September 2010): 251–85.

Horn, Paul. "'Two Minds with But a Single Thought': W. T. Stead, Henry James, and the Zancig Controversy." *19: Interdisciplinary Studies in the Long Nineteenth Century* 0, no. 16 (April 23, 2013).

Hucklenbroich, Peter. "Disease Entities and the Borderline between Health and Disease: Where is the Place of Gradations?" In *Vagueness in Psychiatry: International Perspectives in Philosophy and Psychiatry,* edited by Geert Keil, Lara Keuck, and Rico Hauswald, 75–93. Oxford and New York: Oxford University Press, 2016.

Jacyna, L. S. *Lost Words: Narratives of Language and the Brain, 1825–1926.* Princeton, NJ: Princeton University Press, 2000.

———. "Starting Anew: Henry Head's Contribution to Aphasia Studies." *Journal of Neurolinguistics,* 18, no. 4 (July 2005): 327–36.

———. *Medicine and Modernism: A Biography of Sir Henry Head.* London: Pickering & Chatto, 2008.

Jacyna, L. S., and Stephen T. Casper. *The Neurological Patient in History.* Rochester, NY: University of Rochester Press, 2012.

Jaffe, Audrey. *The Affective Life of the Average Man: The Victorian Novel and the Stock-Market Graph.* Columbus: Ohio State University Press, 2010.

———. *Scenes of Sympathy: Identity and Representation in Victorian Fiction.* Ithaca, NY: Cornell University Press, 2000.

Jamieson, Lynn. *Intimacy: Personal Relationships in Modern Societies.* Hoboken, NJ: Wiley, 1998.

Jasanoff, Sheila, ed. *States of Knowledge: The Co-Production of Science and the Social Order.* New York: Routledge, 2004.

Jenkins, Philip. *Dream Catchers: How Mainstream America Discovered Native Spirituality.* Oxford: Oxford University Press, 2004.

Jolley, Richard P. *Children and Pictures: Drawing and Understanding.* Hoboken, NJ: Wiley, 2010.

Jones, Stacy V. *The Patent Office.* New York: Praeger, 1971.

Jordanova, L. J. *The Look of the Past: Visual and Material Evidence in Historical Practice.* Cambridge: Cambridge University Press, 2012.

Josephson-Storm, Jason A. *The Myth of Disenchantment: Magic, Modernity, and the Birth of the Human Sciences.* Chicago: University of Chicago Press, 2017.

Junior, Alexandre Sech, Saulo de Freitas Araujo, and Alexander Moreira-Almeida.

"William James and Psychical Research: Towards a Radical Science of Mind." *History of Psychiatry* 24, no. 1 (March 1, 2013): 62–78.

Kaufmann, Doris. "Dreams and Self-Consciousness: Mapping the Mind in the Late Eighteenth and Early Nineteenth Centuries." In *Biographies of Scientific Objects*, 67–85. Chicago: University of Chicago Press, 2000.

Keeney, Elizabeth B. *The Botanizers: Amateur Scientists in Nineteenth-Century America.* Chapel Hill: University of North Carolina Press, 1992.

Keep, Christopher. "Blinded by the Type: Gender and Information Technology at the Turn of the Century." *Nineteenth-Century Contexts* 23, no. 1 (2001): 149–73.

Kemp, Hendrika Vande. "The Dream in Periodical Literature: 1860–1910." *Journal of the History of the Behavioral Sciences* 17, no. 1 (January 1, 1981): 88–113.

Kerr, Howard. *Mediums, and Spirit-Rappers, and Roaring Radicals: Spiritualism in American Literature*, 1850–1900. Urbana: University of Illinois Press, 1972.

Kerr, Howard, and Charles L. Crow. *The Occult in America: New Historical Perspectives.* Urbana: University of Illinois Press, 1983.

Khan, B. Zorina. *The Democratization of Invention: Patents and Copyrights in American Economic Development*, 1790–1920. Cambridge: Cambridge University Press, 2005.

Kidd, Ian James. "Was Sir William Crookes Epistemically Virtuous?" *Studies in History and Philosophy of Science Part C: Studies in History and Philosophy of Biological and Biomedical Sciences* 48, Part A (2014), 1–8.

Kirschner, Ann. " 'Tending to Edify, Astonish, and Instruct': Published Narratives of Spiritual Dreams and Visions in the Early Republic." *Early American Studies: An Interdisciplinary Journal* 1, no. 1 (2003): 198–229.

Kittler, Friedrich A. *Discourse Networks*, 1800/1900. Stanford, CA: Stanford University Press, 1992.

———. *Gramophone, Film, Typewriter.* Stanford, CA: Stanford University Press, 1999.

Klassen, Pamela E. "Radio Mind: Protestant Experimentalists on the Frontiers of Healing." *Journal of the American Academy of Religion* 75, no. 3 (2007): 651–83.

———. *Spirits of Protestantism: Medicine, Healing, and Liberal Christianity.* Berkeley and Los Angeles: University of California Press, 2011.

Knapp, Krister Dylan. *William James: Psychical Research and the Challenge of Modernity.* Chapel Hill: University of North Carolina Press Books, 2017.

Kneeland, Timothy W. "Robert Hare: Politics, Science, and Spiritualism in the Early Republic." *The Pennsylvania Magazine of History and Biography* 132, no. 3 (July 1, 2008): 245–60.

Knoper, Randall. "Mediumship, 'Mental Telegraphy,' and Masculinity." In *Acting Naturally Mark Twain in the Culture of Performance*, 119–40. Berkeley: University of California Press, 1995.

Kohlstedt, Sally Gregory. "From Learned Society to Public Museum: The Boston Society of Natural History." In *The Organization of Knowledge in Modern America*, 1860–1920, 386–406. Baltimore: Johns Hopkins University Press, 1979.

———. "The Nineteenth-Century Amateur Tradition: The Case of the Boston

Society of Natural History." In *Science and Its Public: The Changing Relationship*, 173–90. Dordrecht: Reidel, 1976.

Koutstaal, Wilma. "Skirting the Abyss: A History of Experimental Explorations of Automatic Writing in Psychology." *Journal of the History of the Behavioral Sciences* 28, no. 1 (February 13, 2006): 5–27.

Krajewski, Markus, and Peter Krapp. *Paper Machines: About Cards and Catalogs, 1548–1929.* Cambridge, MA: MIT Press, 2011.

Krampen, Martin. *Children's Drawings: Iconic Coding of the Environment.* New York and London: Plenum Press, 1991.

Krass, Peter. *Ignorance, Confidence, and Filthy Rich Friends: The Business Adventures of Mark Twain, Chronic Speculator and Entrepreneur.* Hoboken, NJ: Wiley, 2007.

Krippner, Stanley. "The Maimonides ESP-Dream Studies." *Journal of Parapsychology* 57, no. 1 (March 1, 1993): 39–54.

Kroker, Kenton. *The Sleep of Others and the Transformations of Sleep Research.* Toronto: University of Toronto Press, 2007.

Kucich, John. *Ghostly Communion: Cross-Cultural Spiritualism in Nineteenth-Century American Literature.* Lebanon, NH: University Press of New England, 2004.

Kuklick, Henrika. "Personal Equations: Reflections on the History of Fieldwork, with Special Reference to Sociocultural Anthropology." *Isis* 102, no. 1 (March 1, 2011): 1–33.

Lachapelle, Sofie. "Attempting Science: The Creation and Early Development of the Institut Métapsychique International in Paris, 1919–1931." *Journal of the History of the Behavioral Sciences* 41, no. 1 (January 5, 2005): 1–24.

———. "From the Stage to the Laboratory: Magicians, Psychologists, and the Science of Illusion." *Journal of the History of the Behavioral Sciences* 44, no. 4 (Fall 2008): 319–34.

———. *Investigating the Supernatural: From Spiritism and Occultism to Psychical Research and Metapsychics in France, 1853–1931.* Baltimore: Johns Hopkins University Press, 2011.

Lankford, John. "Amateurs and Astrophysics: A Neglected Aspect in the Development of a Scientific Specialty." *Social Studies of Science* 11, no. 3 (August 1, 1981): 275–303.

———. *American Astronomy: Community, Careers, and Power, 1859–1940.* Chicago: University of Chicago Press, 1997.

Lankford, John, and Ricky L. Slavings. "The Industrialization of American Astronomy, 1880–1940." *Physics Today* 49, no. 1 (January 1996): 34–40.

Lanzoni, Susan. "Sympathy in Mind (1876–1900)." *Journal of the History of Ideas* 70, no. 2 (2009): 265–87.

Latour, Bruno. *We Have Never Been Modern.* Cambridge, MA: Harvard University Press, 1993.

———. "Why Has Critique Run Out of Steam? From Matters of Fact to Matters of Concern." *Critical Inquiry* 30, no. 2 (January 2004): 225–48.

Lears, T. J. Jackson. *No Place of Grace: Antimodernism and the Transformation of American Culture, 1880–1920.* Chicago: University of Chicago Press, 1994.

Leary, David E. "Telling Likely Stories: The Rhetoric of the New Psychology, 1880–1920." *Journal of the History of the Behavioral Sciences* 23, no. 4 (1987): 315–31.

———. "William James, the Psychologist's Dilemma and the Historiography of Psychology: Cautionary Tales." *History of the Human Sciences* 8, no. 1 (February 1, 1995): 91–105.

Leavitt, Theresa. " 'I thought this might be of interest . . . ' The Observatory as Public Enterprise." In *The Heavens on Earth: Observatories and Astronomy in Nineteenth-Century Science and Culture,* edited by David Aubin, Charlotte Bigg, and H. Otto Sibum, 285–302. Durham, NC: Duke University Press, 2010.

Lemov, Rebecca M. *Database of Dreams: The Lost Quest to Catalog Humanity.* New Haven, CT: Yale University Press, 2015.

———. *World as Laboratory: Experiments with Mice, Mazes, and Men.* New York: Hill and Wang, 2005.

———. "X-Rays of Inner Worlds: The Mid-Twentieth-Century American Projective Test Movement." *Journal of the History of the Behavioral Sciences* 47, no. 3 (Summer 2011): 251–78.

Lewis, Andrew J. *A Democracy of Facts: Natural History in the Early Republic.* Philadelphia: University of Pennsylvania Press, 2011.

Lewis, Gifford. *Somerville and Ross: The World of the Irish R. M.* New York: Penguin Books, 1987.

Lightman, Bernard. *Victorian Popularizers of Science: Designing Nature for New Audiences.* Chicago: University of Chicago Press, 2009.

Lightman, Bernard V., ed. *Victorian Science in Context.* Chicago: University of Chicago Press, 1997.

Lindell, Lisa. "Bringing Books to a 'Book-Hungry Land': Print Culture on the Dakota Prairie." *Book History* 4 (2007): 215–38.

Lindsay, Debra. "Intimate Inmates: Wives, Households, and Science in Nineteenth-Century America." *Isis* 89, no. 4 (December 1, 1998): 631–52.

Livingstone, David N., ed. *Geographies of Nineteenth-Century Science.* Chicago: The University of Chicago Press, 2011.

London, Bette Lynn. *Writing Double: Women's Literary Partnerships.* Ithaca, NY: Cornell University Press, 1999.

Lucier, Paul. "The Professional and the Scientist in Nineteenth-Century America." *Isis* 100, no. 4 (December 1, 2009): 699–732.

Luckhurst, Roger. *The Invention of Telepathy, 1870–1901.* Oxford: Oxford University Press, 2002.

Luhrmann, T. M. *When God Talks Back: Understanding the American Evangelical Relationship with God.* New York: Random House Digital, Inc., 2012.

Lunbeck, E. *The Psychiatric Persuasion: Knowledge, Gender, and Power in Modern America.* Princeton, NJ: Princeton University Press, 1995.

Lusty, Natalya, and Helen Groth. *Dreams and Modernity: A Cultural History.* London and New York: Routledge, 2013.

Maher, Jane. *Biography of Broken Fortunes: Wilkie and Bob, Brothers of William, Henry, and Alice James*. Hamden, CT: Archon Books, 1986.

Mattson, Kevin. *Upton Sinclair and the Other American Century*. Hoboken, NJ: Wiley, 2006.

Mauskopf, Seymour H. *The Reception of Unconventional Science*. Boulder, CO: Westview Press/American Association for the Advancement of Science, 1979.

Mauskopf, Seymour H., and Michael Rogers McVaugh. *The Elusive Science: Origins of Experimental Psychical Research*. Baltimore: Johns Hopkins University Press, 1980.

McClenon, James. *Deviant Science: The Case of Parapsychology*. Philadelphia: University of Pennsylvania Press, 1984.

McCumber, John. *The Philosophy Scare: The Politics of Reason in the Early Cold War*. Chicago: University of Chicago Press, 2016.

McGarry, Molly. *Ghosts of Futures Past: Spiritualism and the Cultural Politics of Nineteenth-Century America*. Berkeley: University of California Press, 2008.

McLoughlin, William G. *Revivals, Awakenings, and Reform*. Chicago: University of Chicago Press, 1980.

McVaugh, Michael, and Seymour H. Mauskopf. "J. B. Rhine's Extra-Sensory Perception and Its Background in Psychical Research." *Isis* 67, no. 2 (June 1, 1976): 161–89.

Medick, Hans, and David Warren Sabean. *Interest and Emotion: Essays on the Study of Family and Kinship*. Cambridge: Cambridge University Press, 1988.

Menand, Louis. *The Metaphysical Club: A Story of Ideas in America*. New York: Farrar, Straus and Giroux, 2002.

Menke, Richard. *Telegraphic Realism: Victorian Fiction and Other Information Systems*. Stanford, CA: Stanford University Press, 2008.

Meyer, Donald. *The Positive Thinkers*. New York: Random House, 1965.

Meyer, William B. *Americans and Their Weather*. Oxford: Oxford University Press, 2000.

Micale, Mark S. *Approaching Hysteria: Disease and Its Interpretations*. Princeton, NJ: Princeton University Press, 1995.

Mielke, Laura L. *Moving Encounters: Sympathy and the Indian Question in Antebellum Literature*. Amherst: University of Massachusetts Press, 2008.

Mindell, David A. *Between Human and Machine: Feedback, Control, and Computing Before Cybernetics*. Baltimore: Johns Hopkins University Press, 2004.

Mintz, Steven. *Domestic Revolutions: A Social History Of American Family Life*. New York: Simon and Schuster, 1989.

Modern, John Lardas. *Secularism in Antebellum America*. Chicago: University of Chicago Press, 2011.

Moore, R. Laurence. *In Search of White Crows: Spiritualism, Parapsychology, and American Culture*. Oxford: Oxford University Press, 1977.

———. "The Spiritualist Medium: A Study of Female Professionalism in Victorian America." *American Quarterly* 27, no. 2 (May 1, 1975): 200–221.

Morawski, Jill G. "Reflexivity and the Psychologist." *History of the Human Sciences* 18, no. 4 (November 1, 2005): 77–105.

Morse, Edward S. "Biographical Memoir of Charles Sedgwick Minot, 1852–1914." *National Academy of Sciences*, 1920.

Morss, John R. *The Biologising of Childhood: Developmental Psychology and the Darwinian Myth*. New York and London: Taylor & Francis, 1990.

Morus, Iwan Rhys. *Bodies/Machines*. Oxford, UK: Berg, 2002.

Moyer, Albert E. *A Scientist's Voice in American Culture: Simon Newcomb and the Rhetoric of Scientific Method*. Berkeley: University of California Press, 1992.

Murison, Justine S. *The Politics of Anxiety in Nineteenth-Century American Literature*. Cambridge: Cambridge University Press, 2011.

Murray, Penelope, ed. *Genius: The History of an Idea*. New York: Blackwell, 1989.

Myers, Gerald E. *William James: His Life and Thought*. New Haven, CT: Yale University Press, 2001.

Nadis, Fred. *Wonder Shows: Performing Science, Magic, and Religion in America*. New Brunswick, NJ: Rutgers University Press, 2005.

Nagel, Thomas. "Evolutionary Naturalism and the Fear of Religion." In *The Last Word*, 127–43. Oxford: Oxford University Press, 1997.

Nash, David. "Reassessing the 'Crisis of Faith' in the Victorian Age: Eclecticism and the Spirit of Moral Inquiry." *Journal of Victorian Culture* 16, no. 1 (2011): 65–82.

National Research Council, Committee on Developing Mesoscale Meteorological Observational Capabilities to Meet Multiple Needs. *Observing Weather and Climate from the Ground Up: A Nationwide Network of Networks*. Washington, DC: National Research Council, 2009.

Nebeker, Frederik. *Calculating the Weather: Meteorology in the 20th Century*. San Diego, CA: Academic Press, 1995.

Noakes, Richard. "Haunted Thoughts of the Careful Experimentalist: Psychical Research and the Troubles of Experimental Physics." *Studies in History and Philosophy of Science Part C: Studies in History and Philosophy of Biological and Biomedical Sciences* 48, Part A (December 2014): 46–56.

———. "Natural Causes? Spiritualism, Science, and the Supernatural in Mid-Victorian Britain." In *The Victorian Supernatural*, edited by N. Bown, C. Burdett, P. Thurschwell, 23–43. Cambridge: Cambridge University Press, 2004.

———. "The 'World of the Infinitely Little': Connecting Physical and Psychical Realities circa 1900." *Studies in History and Philosophy of Science Part A*, , 39, no. 3 (September 2008): 323–34.

Noakes, Richard J. "Cromwell Varley FRS, Electrical Discharge and Victorian Spiritualism." *The Royal Society Journal of the History of Science* 61, no. 1 (January 22, 2007): 5–21.

———. "Telegraphy Is an Occult Art: Cromwell Fleetwood Varley and the Diffusion of Electricity to the Other World." *The British Journal for the History of Science* 32, no. 04 (1999): 421–59.

Noble, David F. *America By Design*. New York: Alfred A. Knopf, 1977.

———. *The Religion of Technology: The Divinity of Man and the Spirit of Invention*. New York: Knopf Doubleday Publishing Group, 2013.

O'Connor, Ralph. *The Earth on Show: Fossils and the Poetics of Popular Science*, 1802–1856. Chicago: University of Chicago Press, 2008.

Oleson, Alexandra, and John Voss. *The Organization of Knowledge in Modern America*, 1860–1920. Baltimore: Johns Hopkins University Press, 1979.

Oppenheim, Janet. *The Other World: Spiritualism and Psychical Research in England*, 1850–1914. Cambridge: Cambridge University Press, 1988.

Otis, Laura. *Membranes*. Baltimore: Johns Hopkins University Press, 2000.

———. "The Metaphoric Circuit: Organic and Technological Communication in the Nineteenth Century." *Journal of the History of Ideas* 63, no. 1 (January 1, 2002): 105–28.

———. *Networking: Communicating with Bodies and Machines in the Nineteenth Century*. Ann Arbor: University of Michigan Press, 2001.

Ottinger, Gwen. "Buckets of Resistance: Standards and the Effectiveness of Citizen Science." *Science, Technology, & Human Values* 35, no. 2 (2010): 244–70.

Owen, Alex. *The Darkened Room: Women, Power, and Spiritualism in Late Victorian England*. Chicago: University of Chicago Press, 2004.

———. *The Place of Enchantment: British Occultism and the Culture of the Modern*. Chicago: University of Chicago Press, 2007.

Paine, Albert Bigelow. *Mark Twain, a Biography: The Personal and Literary Life of Samuel Langhorne Clemens*. New York: Harper & Brothers, 1912.

Pandora, Katherine. "Knowledge Held in Common: Tales of Luther Burbank and Science in the American Vernacular." *Isis* 92, no. 3 (September 1, 2001): 484–516.

———. "Popular Science in National and Transnational Perspective: Suggestions from the American Context." *Isis* 100, no. 2 (June 1, 2009): 346–58.

Parker, Gail. "Mary Baker Eddy and Sentimental Womanhood." *New England Quarterly* 43, no. 1 (March 1, 1970): 3–18.

Parker, Gail Thain. *Mind Cure in New England: From the Civil War to World War I*. Lebanon, NH: University Press of New England, 2002.

Patent Technology Monitoring Team. "U.S. Patent Activity Calendar Years 1790 to the Present." United States Patent and Trademark Office. Accessed May 3, 2014. http://www.uspto.gov/web/offices/ac/ido/oeip/taf/h_counts.htm.

Pauwels, Luc, ed. *Visual Cultures of Science: Rethinking Representational Practices in Knowledge Building and Science Communication*. Lebanon, NH: University Press of New England, 2006.

Pena, Carolyn Thomas. *The Body Electric: How Strange Machines Built the Modern American*. New York: New York University Press, 2005.

Perkins, Maureen. "The Meaning of Dream Books." *History Workshop Journal*, no. 48 (October 1, 1999): 102–13.

———. *The Reform of Time: Magic and Modernity*. London: Pluto Press, 2001.

Peters, John Durham. *Speaking into the Air: A History of the Idea of Communication*. Chicago: University of Chicago Press, 2001.

Pettit, Michael. "Joseph Jastrow, the Psychology of Deception, and the Racial Economy of Observation." *Journal of the History of the Behavioral Sciences* 43, no. 2 (Spring 2007): 159–75.

Pick, Daniel, and Lyndal Roper. *Dreams and History: The Interpretation of Dreams from Ancient Greece to Modern Psychoanalysis.* New York: Routledge, 2004.

Pigman, G. W. "The Dark Forest of Authors: Freud and Nineteenth-Century Dream Theory." *Psychoanalysis and History* 4 (2002): 141–65.

Plane, Ann Marie. *Dreams and the Invisible World in Colonial New England: Indians, Colonists, and the Seventeenth Century.* Philadelphia: University of Pennsylvania Press, 2013.

Plane, Ann Marie, and Leslie Tuttle. "Dreams and Dreaming in the Early Modern World." *Renaissance Quarterly* 67, no. 3 (September 1, 2014): 917–31.

———. *Dreams, Dreamers, and Visions: The Early Modern Atlantic World.* Philadelphia: University of Pennsylvania Press, 2013.

Poovey, Mary. *A History of the Modern Fact: Problems of Knowledge in the Sciences of Wealth and Society.* Chicago: University of Chicago Press, 1998.

Prenshaw, Peggy Whitman. *Composing Selves: Southern Women and Autobiography.* Baton Rouge: Louisiana State University Press, 2011.

Price, Katy. "Testimonies of Precognition and Encounters with Psychiatry in Letters to J. B. Priestley." *Studies in History and Philosophy of Science Part C: Studies in History and Philosophy of Biological and Biomedical Sciences* 48, Part A (December 2014): 103–11.

Price, Leah, and Pamela Thurschwell. *Literary Secretaries/Secretarial Culture.* Farnham, UK: Ashgate Publishing, Ltd., 2005.

Prince, Sue Ann. *Stuffing Birds, Pressing Plants, Shaping Knowledge: Natural History in North America* 1730–1860. Philadelphia: American Philosophical Society, 2003.

Proudfoot, Wayne. *Religious Experience.* Berkeley and Los Angeles: University of California Press, 1987.

Proudfoot, Wayne, ed. *William James and a Science of Religions: Reexperiencing The Varieties of Religious Experience.* New York: Columbia University Press, 2004.

Puglionesi, Alicia. "Drawing as Instrument, Drawings as Evidence: Capturing Mental Processes with Pencil and Paper." *Medical History* 60, no. 3 (July 2016): 359–87.

Rabinbach, Anson. *The Human Motor: Energy, Fatigue, and the Origins of Modernity.* Berkeley: University of California Press, 1992.

Rana, Aziz. *The Two Faces of American Freedom.* Cambridge, MA: Harvard University Press, 2010.

Redden, Andrew. "Dream-Visions and Divine Truth in Early Modern Hispanic America." In *Dreams, Dreamers, and Visions: The Early Modern Atlantic World*, edited by Ann Marie Plane and Leslie Tuttle. Philadelphia: University of Pennsylvania Press, 2013.

Reed, Edward. "The Psychologist's Fallacy as a Persistent Framework in William James's Psychological Theorizing." *History of the Human Sciences* 8, no. 1 (February 1, 1995): 61–72.

Reingold, Nathan. "Definitions and Speculations: The Professionalization of Science in America in the Nineteenth Century." In *The Organization of Knowledge in Modern America, 1860–1920*, 33–69. Baltimore: Johns Hopkins University Press, 1979.

Rhine, J. B. "Psi Phenomena and Psychiatry." *Proceedings of the Royal Society of Medicine* 43, no. 11 (November 1, 1950).

Richardson, Robert D. *William James: In the Maelstrom of American Modernism: A Biography*. New York: Houghton Mifflin Harcourt, 2007.

Risser, Anthony H.. "Katharine McBride, 1935, and 'Aphasia.'" In *The Oxford Handbook of History of Clinical Neuropsychology*, ed. William B. Barr and Linas A. Bieliauskas. New York: Oxford University Press, 2016, https://www.oxfordhandbooks.com/view/10.1093/oxfordhb/9780199765683.001.0001/oxfordhb-9780199765683-e-51.

Robertson, Beth A. *Science of the Seance: Transnational Networks and Gendered Bodies in the Study of Psychic Phenomena, 1918–40*. Vancouver: UBC Press, 2016.

Roeder, Katherine. *Wide Awake in Slumberland: Fantasy, Mass Culture, and Modernism in the Art of Winsor McCay*. Jackson: University Press of Mississippi, 2013.

Rogers, Naomi. *An Alternative Path: The Making and Remaking of Hahnemann Medical College and Hospital of Philadelphia*. New Brunswick, NJ: Rutgers University Press, 1998.

Rogo, Scott D. "Psi and Psychosis: A Review of the Experimental Evidence." *Journal of Parapsychology* 39, no. 2 (1975): 170.

Rose, Nikolas S. *The Psychological Complex: Psychology, Politics and Society in England, 1869–1939*. New York: Routledge & Kegan Paul, 1985.

Rose, Nikolas S., and Joelle M. Abi-Rached. *Neuro: The New Brain Sciences and the Management of the Mind*. Princeton, NJ: Princeton University Press, 2013.

Ross, Dorothy. *G. Stanley Hall: The Psychologist As Prophet*. Chicago: University of Chicago Press, 1972.

Rothenberg, Marc. "Organization and Control: Professionals and Amateurs in American Astronomy, 1899–1918." *Social Studies of Science* 11, no. 3 (August 1, 1981): 305–25.

Ruetenik, Tadd. "Last Call for William James: On Pragmatism, Piper, and the Value of Psychical Research." *The Pluralist* 7, no. 1 (2012): 72–93.

Rusert, Britt. *Fugitive Science: Empiricism and Freedom in Early African American Culture*. New York: NYU Press, 2017.

Ryan, Vanessa L. *Thinking without Thinking in the Victorian Novel*. Baltimore: Johns Hopkins University Press, 2012.

Saler, Michael. "Modernity and Enchantment: A Historiographic Review." *American Historical Review* 111, no. 3 (June 2006): 692–716.

Samuel, Lawrence R. *The American Dream: A Cultural History*. Syracuse, NY: Syracuse University Press, 2012.

———. *Supernatural America: A Cultural History*. Santa Barbara, CA: Praeger/ABC-CLIO, 2011.

Schaffer, Simon. "Astronomers Mark Time: Discipline and the Personal Equation." *Science in Context* 2, no. 01 (1988): 115–45.

———. "The Nebular Hypothesis and the Science of Progress." In *History*,

Humanity and Evolution: Essays for John C. Greene, edited by James R. Moore, 150–51. Cambridge: Cambridge University Press, 1989.

Schivelbusch, Wolfgang. *Disenchanted Night: The Industrialization of Light in the Nineteenth Century*. Berkeley: University of California Press, 1988.

———. *The Railway Journey: The Industrialization of Time and Space in the Nineteenth Century*. Berkeley: University of California Press, 1986.

Schmidt, Leigh Eric. *Hearing Things: Religion, Illusion, and the American Enlightenment*. Cambridge, MA: Harvard University Press, 2000.

Schoepflin, Rennie B. *Christian Science on Trial: Religious Healing in America*. Baltimore: Johns Hopkins University Press, 2002.

Schrager, Cynthia D. "Mark Twain and Mary Baker Eddy: Gendering the Transpersonal Subject." *American Literature* 70, no. 1 (March 1, 1998): 29–62.

Sconce, Jeffrey. *Haunted Media: Electronic Presence from Telegraphy to Television*. Durham, NC: Duke University Press, 2000.

Scott, Joan Wallach. *Gender and the Politics of History*. New York: Columbia University Press, 2018.

———. *Sex and Secularism*. Princeton, NJ: Princeton University Press, 2017.

Scudder, Horace Elisha. *James Russell Lowell: A Biography*. Cambridge: Riverside Press, 1901.

Seltzer, Mark. *Bodies and Machines (Routledge Revivals)*. New York: Routledge, 2014.

———. "The Postal Unconscious." *The Henry James Review* 21, no. 3 (2000): 197–206.

Shannon, Edward A. "Something Black in the American Psyche: Formal Innovation and Freudian Imagery in the Comics of Winsor McCay and Robert Crumb." *Canadian Review of American Studies* 40, no. 2 (July 2010): 187.

Shapin, Steven, and Simon Schaffer. *Leviathan and the Air-Pump: Hobbes, Boyle, and the Experimental Life*. Princeton, NJ: Princeton University Press, 1985.

Sharf, Robert H. "The Rhetoric of Experience and the Study of Religion." *Journal of Consciousness Studies* 7, no. 11-12 (2000): 11-12.

Shermer, Michael. *The Borderlands of Science: Where Sense Meets Nonsense*. Oxford: Oxford University Press, 2001.

———. *Why People Believe Weird Things: Pseudoscience, Superstition, and Other Confusions of Our Time*. New York: Henry Holt and Company, 2002.

Shortt, S.E.D. "Physicians and Psychics: The Anglo-American Medical Response to Spiritualism, 1870–1890." *Journal of the History of Medicine and Allied Sciences* 39, no. 3 (July 1, 1984): 339–55.

Silverberg, Robert. *The Mound Builders: Archaeology of a Myth*. Athens, OH: Ohio University Press, 1986.

Simon, Linda. *Genuine Reality: A Life of William James*. Chicago: University of Chicago Press, 1999.

Smith, Crosbie, Jon Agar, and Gerald Schmidt. *Making Space for Science: Territorial Themes in the Shaping of Knowledge*. New York: St. Martin's Press, 1998.

Smith, Pamela H. *The Body of the Artisan: Art and Experience in the Scientific Revolution*. Chicago: University of Chicago Press, 2004.

Smith, Roger. *Being Human: Historical Knowledge and the Creation of Human Nature.* Manchester: Manchester University Press, 2007.

———. *Between Mind and Nature: A History of Psychology.* London: Reaktion Books, 2013.

———. *Inhibition: History and Meaning in the Sciences of Mind and Brain.* Berkeley: University of California Press, 1992.

Smith-Rosenberg, Carroll. *Disorderly Conduct: Visions of Gender in Victorian America.* Oxford: Oxford University Press, 1986.

Smuts, Alice. *Science in the Service of Children,* 1893–1935. New Haven, CT: Yale University Press, 2008.

Sobel, Mechal. *Teach Me Dreams: The Search for Self in the Revolutionary Era.* Princeton, NJ: Princeton University Press, 2002.

Sommer, Andreas. "Are You Afraid of the Dark? Notes on the Psychology of Belief in Histories of Science and the Occult." *European Journal of Psychotherapy & Counselling* 18, no. 2 (2016): 105–122.

———. "Professional Heresy: Edmund Gurney (1847–88) and the Study of Hallucinations and Hypnotism." *Medical History* 55, no. 3 (July 2011): 383–88.

———. "Psychical Research and the Origins of American Psychology Hugo Münsterberg, William James and Eusapia Palladino." *History of the Human Sciences* 25, no. 2 (April 1, 2012): 23–44.

———. "Psychical Research in the History and Philosophy of Science. An Introduction and Review." *Studies in History and Philosophy of Science Part C: Studies in History and Philosophy of Biological and Biomedical Sciences* 48, Part A (December 2014): 38–45.

Sponsel, Alistair. *Darwin's Evolving Identity.* Chicago: University of Chicago Press, 2018.

Star, Susan Leigh, and James R. Griesemer. "Institutional Ecology, 'Translations' and Boundary Objects: Amateurs and Professionals in Berkeley's Museum of Vertebrate Zoology, 1907–39." *Social Studies of Science* 19, no. 3 (August 1, 1989): 387–420.

Starr, Paul. *The Social Transformation of American Medicine.* New York: Basic Books, 1982.

Stebbins, Robert A. *Amateurs, Professionals, and Serious Leisure.* Montreal: McGill-Queen's Press, 1992.

———. "Avocational Science: The Amateur Routine in Archaeology and Astronomy." *International Journal of Comparative Sociology* 21, no. 1 (January 1, 1980): 34–48.

Stiles, Anne. *Popular Fiction and Brain Science in the Late Nineteenth Century.* Cambridge: Cambridge University Press, 2011.

Still, Arthur. "Introduction." *History of the Human Sciences* 8, no. 1 (February 1, 1995): 1–7.

Still, Arthur, and Windy Dryden. "The Social Psychology of 'Pseudoscience': A Brief History." *Journal for the Theory of Social Behaviour* 34, no. 3 (September 2004): 265–90.

Stirling, Jeannette. *Representing Epilepsy: Myth and Matter.* Liverpool: Liverpool University Press, 2010.

Strathern, Marilyn. *After Nature: English Kinship in the Late Twentieth Century.* Cambridge: Cambridge University Press, 1992.

———. *Kinship, Law and the Unexpected: Relatives Are Always a Surprise.* Cambridge, MA: Cambridge University Press, 2005.

Szreter, Simon, and Kate Fisher. *Sex before the Sexual Revolution: Intimate Life in England* 1918–1963. Cambridge: Cambridge University Press, 2010.

Taves, Ann. *Fits, Trances, and Visions: Experiencing Religion and Explaining Experience from Wesley to James.* Princeton, NJ: Princeton University Press, 1999.

Taylor, Alan. "The Early Republic's Supernatural Economy: Treasure Seeking in the American Northeast, 1780–1830." *American Quarterly* 38, no. 1 (1986): 6–34.

Taylor, Charles. *Sources of the Self: The Making of the Modern Identity.* Cambridge: Cambridge University Press, 1992.

Taylor, Eugene. "On the First Use of 'Psychoanalysis' at the Massachusetts General Hospital, 1903 to 1905." *Journal of the History of Medicine and Allied Sciences* 43, no. 4 (October 1, 1988): 447–71.

———. "Radical Empiricism and the New Science of Consciousness." *History of the Human Sciences* 8, no. 1 (February 1, 1995): 47–60.

———. *Shadow Culture: Psychology and Spirituality in America.* Washington, DC: Counterpoint Press, 1999.

———. *William James on Consciousness beyond the Margin.* Princeton, NJ: Princeton University Press, 1996.

Thomas, M. Wynn. "Weathering the Storm: Whitman and the Civil War." *Walt Whitman Quarterly Review* 15, no. 2 (Fall 1997): 87–109.

Thurschwell, Pamela. "The Erotics of Telepathy: The British SPR's Experiments in Intimacy." In *The Sixth Sense Reader*, edited by David Howes, 183–208. Oxford: Berg, 2009.

———. *Literature, Technology, and Magical Thinking, 1880–1920.* Cambridge: Cambridge University Press, 2005.

———. "The Typist's Remains: Theodora Bosanquet in Recent Fiction." *The Henry James Review* 32, no. 1 (2011): 1–11.

Tosh, John. *A Man's Place: Masculinity and the Middle-Class Home in Victorian England.* New Haven, CT: Yale University Press, 2007.

Trachtenberg, Alan. *The Incorporation of America: Culture and Society in the Gilded Age.* New York: Hill and Wang, 2007.

Treitel, Corinna. *A Science for the Soul: Occultism and the Genesis of the German Modern.* Baltimore: Johns Hopkins University Press, 2004.

Tresch, John. *The Romantic Machine: Utopian Science and Technology after Napoleon.* Chicago: University of Chicago Press, 2012.

Trigger, Bruce G. "Alternative Archaeologies: Nationalist, Colonialist, Imperialist." *Man*, New Series, 19, no. 3 (September 1, 1984): 355–70.

———. "Anglo?American Archaeology." *World Archaeology* 13, no. 2 (October 1, 1981): 138–55.

———. *A History of Archaeological Thought.* Cambridge: Cambridge University Press, 1989.

Tromp, Marlene. *Altered States: Sex, Nation, Drugs, and Self-Transformation in Victorian Spiritualism.* Albany, NY: SUNY Press, 2007.

Troy, Kathryn. "'A New and Beautiful Mission': The Appearance of Black Hawk in Spiritualist Circles, 1857–1888." In *The Spiritualist Movement: Speaking with the Dead in America and around the World,* edited by Christopher M. Moreman, 3:171–85. New York: ABC-CLIO, 2013.

———. *The Specter of the Indian: Race, Gender, and Ghosts in American Seances, 1848–1890.* Albany, NY: SUNY Press, 2017.

Turner, Roy Steven. *In the Eye's Mind: Vision and the Helmholtz-Hering Controversy.* Princeton, NJ: Princeton University Press, 1994.

———. "Vision Studies in Germany: Helmholtz versus Hering." *Osiris* 8 (January 1, 1993): 80–103.

van Schlun, Betsy. *Science and the Imagination: Mesmerism, Media, and the Mind in Nineteenth-Century English and American Literature.* Berlin: Galda & Wilch, 2007.

Vande Kemp, Hendrika. *The Dream in Periodical Literature: 1860–1910: From "Oneirocriticon" to "Die Traumdeutung" Via the Questionnaire.* PhD diss., Department of Psychology. University of Massachusetts, Amherst, 1977.

———. "The Dream in Periodical Literature: 1860–1910." *Journal of the History of the Behavioral Sciences,* 17 (1981), 88–113.

———. "Psycho-Spiritual Dreams in the Nineteenth Century: II. Metaphysics and Immortality." *Journal of Psychology and Theology* 22, no. 2 (1994): 109–19.

Vaz-Hooper, Onita. "Dream Technology: The Mechanization of the De Quinceyan Imagination." *Nineteenth-Century Contexts* 36, no. 2 (March 15, 2014): 165–77.

Vidal, Fernando. *Piaget before Piaget.* Cambridge, MA: Harvard University Press, 1994.

———. *The Sciences of the Soul: The Early Modern Origins of Psychology.* Chicago: University of Chicago Press, 2011.

Villiers de l'Isle-Adam, Auguste. *L'ève future.* Paris: Bibliotheque Charpentier, 1891.

Vitiello, Domenic. *Engineering Philadelphia: The Sellers Family and the Industrial Metropolis.* Ithaca, NY: Cornell University Press, 2013.

Wallis, Roy. *On the Margins of Science: The Social Construction of Rejected Knowledge.* Keele, UK: University of Keele, 1979.

Ward, Steven C. *Modernizing the Mind: Psychological Knowledge and the Remaking of Society.* Westport, CT: Greenwood Publishing Group, 2002.

Warner, John Harley. *Against the Spirit of System: The French Impulse in Nineteenth-Century American Medicine.* Baltimore: Johns Hopkins University Press, 2003.

Weiss, Richard. *The American Myth of Success: From Horatio Alger to Norman Vincent Peale.* Champaign, IL: University of Illinois Press, 1969.

White, Christopher G. *Other Worlds: Spirituality and the Search for Invisible Dimensions.* Cambridge, MA: Harvard University Press, 2018.

————. *Unsettled Minds: Psychology and the American Search for Spiritual Assurance,* 1830–1940. Berkeley: University of California Press, 2009.

White, Jonathan W. *Midnight in America: Darkness, Sleep, and Dreams during the Civil War.* Chapel Hill: The University of North Carolina Press, 2017.

White, Sheldon H. "G. Stanley Hall: From Philosophy to Developmental Psychology." *Developmental Psychology* 28, no. 1 (1992): 25–34.

Wiley, Barry H. *The Thought Reader Craze: Victorian Science at the Enchanted Boundary.* Jefferson, NC: McFarland, 2012.

Willburn, Sarah A., and Tatiana Kontou. *The Ashgate Research Companion to Nineteenth-Century Spiritualism and the Occult.* Surrey, England; Burlington, VT: Ashgate, 2012.

Williams, J. P. *The Making of Victorian Psychical Research: An Intellectual Elite's Approach to the Spiritual World.* Unpublished dissertation, Cambridge University, 1984.

————. "Psychical Research and Psychiatry in Late Victorian Britain: Trance as Ecstasy or Trance as Insanity." In *The Anatomy of Madness,* 1:233–54. London and New York: Routledge, 2004.

Williams, Nathaniel Langdon. *Steam Men, Edisons, Connecticut Yankees: Technocracy and Imperial Identity in Nineteenth-Century American Fiction.* PhD diss., University of Kansas Department of English, 2010.

Willis, Martin. *Mesmerists, Monsters, and Machines: Science Fiction and the Cultures of Science in the Nineteenth Century.* Kent, OH: Kent State University Press, 2006.

Wilson, Jeff. *Mindful America: The Mutual Transformation of Buddhist Meditation and American Culture.* New York: Oxford University Press, 2014.

Wilson, Leigh. "Dead Letters: Gender, Literary History and the Cross-Correspondences." *Critical Survey* 19, no. 1 (2007): 17–28.

Winiarski, Douglas L. "Souls Filled with Ravishing Transport: Heavenly Visions and the Radical Awakening in New England." *The William and Mary Quarterly,* Third Series, 61, no. 1 (January 1, 2004): 3–46.

Winter, Alison. *Memory: Fragments of a Modern History.* Chicago: University of Chicago Press, 2012.

————. *Mesmerized: Powers of Mind in Victorian Britain.* Chicago: University of Chicago Press, 2000.

Wittmann, Barbara. "Drawing Cure: Children's Drawings as a Psychoanalytic Instrument." *Configurations* 18, no. 3 (2010): 251–72.

————. "Johnny-Head-in-the-Air in America. Aby Warburg's Experiments with Children's Drawings." In *New Perspectives in Iconology: Visual Studies and Anthropology,* 120–42. Brussels: Academic and Scientific Publishers, 2011.

————. "A Neolithic Childhood: Children's Drawings as Prehistoric Sources." *Res* 63/64 (2013): 125–42.

————. "Outlining Species: Drawing as a Research Technique in Contemporary Biology." *Science in Context* 26, no. Special Issue 02 (June 2013): 363–91.

Wolffram, Heather. "Parapsychology on the Couch: The Psychology of Occult Belief in Germany, c. 1870–1939." *Journal of the History of the Behavioral Sciences* 42, no. 3 (June 30, 2006): 237–60.

———. *The Stepchildren of Science: Psychical Research and Parapsychology in Germany, c.* 1870–1939. New York: Rodopi, 2009.

Woodward, Susan L., and Jerry N. McDonald. *Indian Mounds of the Middle Ohio Valley: A Guide to Mounds and Earthworks of the Adena, Hopewell, Cole, and Fort Ancient People.* Granville, OH: McDonald & Woodward Publishing Company, 2002.

Wynne, B. "Physics and Psychics: Science, Symbolic Action, and Social Control in Late Victorian England." In Barry Barnes and Steven Shapin, eds., *Natural Order: Historical Studies of Scientific Culture,* 167–86. Beverly Hills, CA: Sage Publications, 1979.

Yeager, Jennifer A. "Opportunities and Limitations: Female Spiritual Practice in Nineteenth-Century America." *ATQ* 7, no. 3 (September 1993): 217.

Yearley, Steven. *Making Sense of Science: Understanding the Social Study of Science.* Thousand Oaks, CA: Sage, 2005.

Young, Robert Maxwell. *Mind, Brain, and Adaptation in the Nineteenth Century: Cerebral Localization and Its Biological Context from Gall to Ferrier.* Oxford: Oxford University Press, 1970.

Zenderland, Leila. "Education, Evangelism, and the Origins of Clinical Psychology: The Child-Study Legacy." *Journal of the History of the Behavioral Sciences* 24, no. 2 (1988): 152–65.

———. *Measuring Minds: Henry Herbert Goddard and the Origins of American Intelligence Testing.* Cambridge: Cambridge University Press, 2001.

Zimmerman, David A. "Frank Norris, Market Panic, and the Mesmeric Sublime." *American Literature* 75, no. 1 (2003): 61–90.

———. *Panic!: Markets, Crises, and Crowds in American Fiction.* Chapel Hill: University of North Carolina Press, 2006

INDEX

accidents, 91–92, 97–99

amateurs: in archaeology, 108; in astronomy, 36; in child psychology, 124, 127; in meteorology, 37–41, 61; in natural history, 32–33, 88; in psychical research, 5–6, 49–50, 57–61, 71, 171–72, 188–89

American Society for Psychical Research (ASPR): founding, 5, 12; leadership of, 18–22; observational networks, 43–44, 49–54; use of drawing tests, 139–45; Medical Section, 229–34

anecdotal evidence, 47, 56–57, 79; of dreams, 96–104; in the Duke Parapsychology Laboratory, 239

animal magnetism, 34, 215

archaeology, 111–13

astronomy, 36–37, 141

automatism, 15, 84, 120, 143, 146, 152

Baconianism, 31–33, 49, 63, 130

barometers, 29–31, 35, 39–40, 53

Bayley, Weston D., 44–49

Beard, George Miller, 15, 205–7, 222

Bierce, Ambrose, 90

Blackburn, Douglas, 131–38, 146–47

borderlands, 3, 24, 226–28, 234

Bosanquet, Theodora, 155

Boston Society for Psychical Research, 20, 163, 184

British Society for Psychical Research (BSPR), 12, 18, 131–38, 146

Census of Hallucinations, 64

child study, 122–27

Christian Science, 160, 177

citizen science, 27–28, 37, 188

Civil War, 75, 108

Crothers, Thomas Davidson, 26–27, 30

crowds. *See* psychology: of crowds

Darwin, Charles, 66–67, 124

Davison Society for Psychical Research, 50–54

SPIRITUAL PHENOMENA

TANYA MARIE LUHRMANN and ANN TAVES, Series Editors

Spiritual Phenomena features investigations of events, experiences, and objects, both unusual and everyday, that people characterize as spiritual, paranormal, magical, occult, and/or supernatural. Working from the presupposition that the status of such phenomena is contested, it seeks to understand how such determinations are made in a variety of historical and cultural contexts. Books in this series explore how such phenomena are identified, experienced, and understood; the role that spontaneity and cultivation play in the process; and the similarities and differences in the way phenomena are appraised and categorized across time and cultures. The editors encourage work that is ethnographic, historical, or psychological, and, in particular, work that uses more than one method to understand these complex phenomena, ranging from qualitative approaches to quantitative surveys and laboratory-based experiments.

———————

Yoram Bilu, *With Us More Than Ever: Making the Absent Rebbe Present in Messianic Chabad*

David J. Halperin, *Intimate Alien: The Hidden Story of the UFO*

J. Bradley Wigger, *Invisible Companions: Encounters with Imaginary Friends, Gods, Ancestors, and Angels*

Kelly Bulkeley, *Lucrecia the Dreamer: Prophecy, Cognitive Science, and the Spanish Inquisition*

Printed in the USA
CPSIA information can be obtained
at www.ICGtesting.com
JSHW022152181223
53972JS00005B/17